God Knows My Heart

God Knows My Heart

CHRISTINE WICKER

ST. MARTIN'S PRESS
NEW YORK

Excerpt from *The Dallas Morning News* reprinted with
permission.

Excerpt from *In the Beginning* by Karen Armstrong quoted
with permission of Random House, Inc. Copyright 1996 by
Karen Armstrong. Published by Alfred A. Knopf, 1996.

Excerpt from *Sources of Strength* by Jimmy Carter quoted with
permission of Random House, Inc. Copyright 1997 by Jimmy
Carter. Published by Times Books, 1997.

Book design by Ellen R. Sasahara

Library of Congress Cataloging-in-Publication Data

Wicker, Christine.
    God knows my heart: finding a faith that fits/Christine
Wicker.
        p. cm.
    ISBN 0-312-19272-X
    1. Wicker, Christine.   2. Christian biography—United
States.   I. Title.
    BR1725.W444   A3   1999
    277.3'0825'092—dc21
    [B]
                                                    98-48159
                                                       CIP

First Edition: March 1999

10 9 8 7 6 5 4 3 2 1

To Philip

Acknowledgments

MANY PEOPLE HELPED make this book possible. Foremost among them was my agent, Janet Manus, who supported my ideas even during those times when I didn't. Jeremy Katz planted the seed that became this book. Jennifer Weis helped harvest it. Thanks to all the members of my family who were patient during so many months when I didn't give them the time they deserve. Sharon Grigsby, Olivia Casey, and Sue Smith read the first draft and gave me courage to keep going. Sophia Dembling, Dee Lyons, and Darla Walker listened to my ideas during long hours that probably weren't as interesting to them as they were to me. Thanks also to Buddy Kenneweg, who always gives me more credit that I deserve.

And thanks to my uncle Johnny Lee, who didn't live to see this book published but who believed in me before I could even talk.

Introduction

❧❦❧

WHEN I WAS a Bible-touting teenager in the Southern Baptist Church, preachers often talked about how you could tell the people who really knew Jesus by the smiles on their faces. Sad-sack Christians weren't real Christians, they said. Besieged by the terrors of teenage life, I didn't always feel like smiling, which troubled me quite a bit. One day I asked my mother about my apparent lack of faith. She answered breezily, "Oh, I don't smile all the time either, but I figure the Lord knows my heart, and it's all right."

My mother had just uttered some of the most theologically profound words I would ever hear. But I didn't know it. I thought her answer so misguided that I didn't even reply. How could faith be so easy and private a matter? Depend on God? Of course, but first the preachers tell us what He is thinking, and we accept it. If we're really zealous, we look in the Bible, somebody tells us how to interpret the verses, and we accept their version. If we don't, it's called make-it-up-as-you-go religion. And that's sinful. You go to hell for that. My childhood religion had tattooed that on my brain.

But it's a funny thing about my mother's words. In the years since, I've forgotten almost everything the preachers were preaching that year, and I remember my mother's answer almost every day. If I had followed her counsel, I would have saved myself a lot of pain. What she meant is that God could be trusted to understand me, and that I could be trusted to seek Him and rely upon my own experience.

SECTION 1

Falling away from the God of my childhood was a long drop and hard landing

Chapter 1

Inside the Bedrock of Faith

❦❦❦

NOT LONG AGO, a former preacher called me a recovering fundamentalist. "You'll never really get away from it," he said. "It's a way of thinking and being that you don't just walk away from." The analogy was so apt that I responded with a startled laugh. He went on to say that the guilt, the sexual inhibitions, the grandiose ideas, the black-and-white thinking of fundamentalism is like a drug that shores up people's self-confidence. You may think you have left it behind, he said, but it hangs on. Somewhere far back in your self, it waits to emerge.

I stopped automatically tacking Jesus' name onto my prayers twenty-five years ago. Boyfriends who sat with me and my open Bible beneath streetlights while I pled for their souls have grown children now. I cannot even remember the last time I raised my face toward a handsome young preacher and felt my breath grow ragged in response to the power of his words. I no longer read my Bible, bless my food, or tell people they won't go to heaven unless they believe as I do. When avid soul winners ask if I've been saved by the blood of Jesus, I push their concern gently, and sometimes not so gently, aside. Asked what I believe, I might say, "Everything." I might say, "Nothing."

But time, experience, and even disbelief are not enough to erase the memory of what I once had. Sometimes I still long for those heady days when everything that God required could be known and was. In some buried part of my soul, I still miss that sweet safety, that sense of being chosen, of having an in with God that would withstand anything in life. I am sometimes still rueful that I can't go back. I may sit cross-legged with the Buddhists, hug trees with the Wiccans, or enthuse with the New Agers. But hand me a book of C. S. Lewis, put me in a pew before a Bible-thumper who knows his stuff, and I can feel a yearning every bit as piercing as the ex-smoker's sigh when that first thread of blue smoke wafts over from the table across the room.

Being a fundamentalist is living in the Garden of Eden. God walks with you, He talks with you, He sends signs of His presence all the time. The rest of the world lives by luck or coincidence or effort, but you live by grace. The rest of the world wonders how the story is going to end, but you know. God's your buddy. He chose you. He'd die for you. In fact, you think He already has. A lot of other people are in the garden with you, and they agree on exactly what's real and what isn't. They tell one another how special they are, how misunderstood by the world they are, how brave, how right, how righteous they are.

To the rest of the world, the garden looks like a box, but to you, it's the only safe place. Even when you go out in the world, the garden stays in your head. No matter where you go or what you see, you feel separate. Saved. God is going to take care of you. In this life or in the next. It is a lovely way to live. In return, you must have faith, no matter what your brain or your senses or your experience say. If you can make the trade, it is worth it.

I grew up in churches where the rules were very clear. You listened to the preacher, and he told you what the Bible said. Nothing he said strained your brain too much. He explained all contradictions by saying that we can't understand the ways of God. If you got confused or started to waver, he gave you a simple remedy: Remember that you must have faith and that your own understanding won't get you to heaven. Remember that you are a worthless sinner and only God's grace keeps the horrors at bay. To outsiders, the preacher's advice may sound restrictive. He'll play on that perception. He'll emphasize what a sacrifice you are making and how hard it is to stay in the garden. In fact, the better he creates that sense of separation, the stronger the church is likely to be, and the more money the congregation is likely to cough up.

The one big prohibition in the garden is "Don't eat of the Tree of Knowledge." If you do, you'll be cast out into a world of chaos, a place where truth slips away as soon as you grasp it, a place where God does not rule, a place where His will is not heeded. That is exactly what I did. And everything the preachers said about the world outside the garden was true. Except one thing.

They were wrong about God. God was still there, ever at hand, always available. I just wasn't in the mood to look for Him, and so I didn't know it. And one other thing the preachers of my childhood were wrong about: When I did look for Him, I found Him without having to go back to the little box that all the world's God limiters told me He lived in.

My drift away from the faith of my childhood began in college, as such movements often do. I'd grown up hearing preachers warn against losing your children to the false wisdom of the university. So I knew the danger.

I was a girl for whom *Reader's Digest* was highbrow reading. The only people I knew who had traveled abroad were guys who had been drafted. The university I attended was a state school. I lived at home. I was as protected as anyone could be, but even so, the world came rushing at me, and I was overwhelmed. My professors were disdainful of Christian ways. What passed for gospel in my family was treated as nonsense if I was foolish enough to voice it in class. As a replacement for the old-time religion, my teachers funneled outrageous, exciting new ideas into my head. They seemed to delight in tearing down my idols.

Their know-it-all arrogance made me furious. And so I resisted them and all the other worldly blandishments. I spent many afternoons praying and singing at the Baptist Student Union. When my sorority held a Halloween party, the talk of the Greek crowd was the frat boy who dressed up as a huge breast. My sisters were shocked but happily titillated by such daring. I was outraged. I complained and it wasn't long before I resigned from the sorority. My reasoning was that I'd be better off spending what little time I had on campus working for Christ at the Baptist Student Union.

But life at the university wasn't all that was drawing me away. The church was doing its part. One Sunday our congregation was delighted by the honor of having a former Miss Texas visit with her testimony. Feminism was gaining steam in those days, and I was just beginning to think that how a woman looked might not be her greatest glory. The leaders of my church, all male, weren't there yet. Grinning and fidgeting, they squired the beautiful beauty queen from room to room and finally to the front of the church so that we all could marvel over how lucky God was to have such radiance in His house. When they came to my Sunday school class, I looked around the room at the plain round faces of my fellow churchwomen and I thought, "Compared to her, we look like bowls of oatmeal."

I knew that despite all the preachers said about valuing godliness and virtue, they felt just like everybody else. Beauty and fame and riches meant as much to them as they did to people in the outside world, only they would never tell the truth. At the Baptist camps, boys and girls couldn't even go swimming together for fear their lust might be excited. But Miss Texas, who had stripped off and paraded down the runway in a bathing suit before all of America, was given great honor. All she had to do was stand up and declare herself one of us. Wasn't God lucky?

Perhaps it's the curse of youth to be so clear-sighted. Miss Texas and the gaggle of dizzy-looking preachers around her made me want to gag. Was I jealous? Of course. I was living in a box labeled "religion" because it was supposed to be constructed out of different values. If it wasn't, what did it have to recommend it? A bowl of oatmeal needs all the help she can get. If the church had none to give, I needed to be looking elsewhere.

My disillusionment was helped along by my new Sunday school teachers, a young married couple who had recently become Christians, which meant their zeal was especially keen. When the husband pulled his chair out of the circle to give his wisdom, his wife stayed in the background, hands folded in her lap, sweet smile in place. Our leader decided to teach the writings of Paul, and when he came to the part about how women were to keep silent in the church, an amazing thing happened—something I'd never seen before. A girl in the class objected. She said she didn't think she was made to be subordinate to men. I was shocked but emboldened, and soon I chimed in. Before long my teacher called my mother to say he feared for my salvation.

Chapter 2

Why I Can't Fit In

I'D BE AS happy as the next guy if I could turn my spiritual life over to some great authority and be done with it. But I can't. The times we live in are part of the reason. My own personality is another part. To that observation, the religious authorities of my childhood would likely reply that God is unchanging and I am trying to cut Him to fit my own sinful desires. Perhaps.

Like many other nontraditional God seekers, I find myself in a tug-of-war. I am on one side. People who claim to know exactly what I must believe in order to have God are on the other. God is the rope we fight over. If we could just relax and stop pulling in opposite directions, I think we might realize that we're grasping the same rope, just different sections. But we're unlikely to do that because traditional religion is based on beliefs. And beliefs aren't very important to religion-rejecting God seekers like me. The reason they aren't important has to do with the realities of the present age.

My mother and I had our conversation in the early seventies. In those days and in the days to follow, authority of all kinds was attacked—not out of willfulness or arrogance, as the preachers liked to say, but because in an era of dizzying change, "received truth" was proving itself a shaky base on which to build a life. People who had learned that they must ask hard questions of their doctors, their government, and themselves were finding it more and more difficult to turn off their brains, open their mouths, and swallow whatever the preachers were serving up each Sunday.

It isn't sinfulness that's the problem. If it were merely that ancient plague, we could use ancient interpretations of God as the remedy. The problem is the twentieth century. It has shaped us in ways that no one foresaw and that we can barely begin to perceive ourselves.

Much of the religious rhetoric around us fails to connect because it is totally at odds with the very fabric of what we know. Let me give you examples that are on the modern Western mind almost constantly. Is God powerful or is He impotent? Is God benevolent or is He indifferent? Or perhaps even evil? We don't conjure such questions from our own willfulness. History presents them. And history presents some compelling answers.

Old Testament scholar and ordained minister Walter Brueggemann sums up the shaky state of twentieth-century theological certitude succinctly: "The great certitude is that God is sovereign. Well, all you have to say is 'Holocaust' and the whole question of the sovereignty of God is on the table and nobody knows what to say about it." Something is wrong with man or God or both when a confirmed Christian civilization that is steaming along toward perfection in all sorts of ways suddenly skids down such a bloody road to hell as that one. It has caused us to question ourselves and our faith and the goodness of both ourselves and God. It could not be otherwise.

If our moral uncertainties were confined to only these big-picture matters, we might be able to put away such questions. Unfortunately, the collapse of moral certainty has gone much further. I'm not talking about divorce or pornography or abortion. In some ways, those are merely the sideshows. The main event is much more central to our identity.

In the fifties, before everything started coming apart, it was easy to know the good people from the bad, the industrious from the lazy, the healthy from the sick. It was easy to believe that people were responsible for themselves and what they did and how they reacted to life. If people did wrong or failed to succeed, it was most probably their own fault. They could take themselves in hand if they really wanted to, we thought smugly. On those occasions when we found ourselves among the losers, we couldn't be quite so smug, but we still could and did feel shamed over our lack of initiative. Either way, the world seemed to be a place where it was easy to find the responsible party when something went wrong.

Then psychology started messing with our neat equations about life. The therapists told us that maybe our mothers were to blame or our teachers or our rotten love lives. Pretty soon we didn't have bad, lazy students; we had children with developmental difficulties or attention deficit disorder or dyslexia. We didn't have depraved killers; we had mentally ill adults who had been abused until they lost all sense of right and wrong. Such reasoning gave some of us just the out we needed, and we proceeded to justify anything we felt like doing. In response, certain religious people went into full revolt against psychology, believing it had given us nothing but excuses. To them, the answer was easy: Just go back to the old values.

They have a point, but once again modern realities are exerting inexorable force against their certainty—and ours. Hard science kicked in where psychology left off. As scientists found chemicals in the brain that determine everything from shyness to aggression, they began to realize that the very elements of our character could be altered with a pill or an injection. So much that we could once condemn so easily was turning out to be truly nobody's fault, and—more to the religious point—nothing that mere preaching could change. The battle over nurture versus nature began tilting drastically toward nature. Studies of twins separated all their lives showed similarities of temperament and preferences and even lifestyles that were so close they were eerie. What does all this mean for our concept of God? Well, it means that Protestant self-determination, the bedrock of America's ideas about man's place with God, was turning shaky.

And that's only the moral side of our disillusionment. Knowledge itself is a problem. It is coming at us faster than we can possibly cope. It was Francis Bacon who said that knowledge is power. But as someone noted not long ago, *The New York Times* contains more new knowledge in one day's edition than the average person in Bacon's day confronted during an entire lifetime. Knowledge is still powerful, but today it is likely to be a powerful sea of confusion.

So much knowledge is coming so fast that it is constantly contradicting itself. Any course we set out on, no matter how well studied and approved, is likely to be proven the wrong one just as soon as we've devoted a goodly portion of our lives to it. This seems to be true in every sphere. It's true in personal ways—diet, exercise, health, relationships between the sexes. It's true in larger arenas—history, science, and yes, religion. It was so easy once to believe that we, whatever our faith, had the one true God. But when your neighbor is a Buddhist, your best friend is a Hindu, your father is Jewish, and your mother is Christian, faith becomes a much more complicated matter.

Even those of us who have managed to keep our own family and love lives pure of outside taint are caught in experiences that increasingly seem to echo the Buddhist idea that we are all one and that our failure to know that is simply illusion. The communications revolution won't let us be. We might be able to forget history, to put unpleasant "aberrations" such as the Holocaust into a category of "them," not "us," but every day that trick becomes harder to accomplish—if only because we are so bombarded with the world's sad stories. A man is macheted in Africa and a man in Lubbock flinches.

Even the Bible is being pummeled by new knowledge. The revelations in newly discovered manuscripts have only trickled down to some congregations, but for the past twenty years, scholars who study the Bible have been backpedaling on many of the Book's most treasured tenets. Theological students know it. Lots of preachers know it. Some of the more radical among them even preach it. But most of them are keeping quiet or mounting furious defenses that make only glancing reference to what's really at issue. Nobody knows what would happen to the old-time religion if so much new knowledge were allowed to run away with it.

One result of all this is that people have quite reasonably moved away from pinning their fate to beliefs. Those who think God and beliefs are inextricably intertwined find this to be a dismal development. I see it differently. I think the disillusionments of our age have smashed some of the barriers between us and God. It is possible that we've been freed to explore new ways of being with God and that the new God seekers are part of that freedom. That might be disputed. But what is quite clear to everyone is that the world of religion is in a state of tumult that isn't likely to calm anytime soon.

Chapter 3

Leaving My First Faith

✌️✌️✌️

A

s I ENTERED my twenties, every force was massed. The life
of the mind said fundamentalism is nonsense. The life of the
spirit said fundamentalism is false. And then there was the
message coming from my body.

Sex before marriage was unthinkable in my church, which meant
a long wait for me since marriage wasn't going to take place until I'd
at least finished college. Preachers bolstered their admonitions by
telling us that men wanted only one thing, and once they got it,
they'd leave women. "Why buy the cow when the milk is free?" they
asked.

Temptation came often. Two or three days a week my boyfriend
would cook lunch at his house. What would happen after lunch was
a sinful kind of magic that exceeded anything I'd ever imagined. Nobody prepared me for the power and weakness of sex. It went beyond
words and beyond resistance. Bible reading, praying, hymn singing—
nothing could touch it.

My boyfriend was made just as dopey by what we were doing as
I was. He wasn't about to leave me, no matter what I did or didn't do.
I knew it and the fact that preachers didn't know it told me that they
were clueless about two of the most important things in life: human
nature and sex. I could see that all around me people were having sex,
living together, and then getting married. At the same time, people
who had saved themselves for marriage, gone to church, and followed all the right rules were divorcing in droves. Put those two
things together and the conclusion was inescapable to me: Those
preacher boys were operating with a cardboard cutout version of reality, and it didn't match what I was seeing.

Although religion didn't help me resist temptation, it did load on the guilt. I was frantic with remorse but only before and after the event. Nothing could compete. I was twenty years old. Sex followed me around all day. Always determined to say no, I mostly didn't. A rational, mature, less guilty person would have used birth control. But I wasn't that kind of person. I was a good girl who wasn't going to sin again. Planning would have been an admission that I wasn't merely a good girl making a mistake, but a bad girl planning to do it again.

The way I saw the world and God and myself didn't match my behavior. The disparity between who I was and who I thought I ought to be was so great that I couldn't hold both ideas in my mind. My unwillingness or inability to obey the Lord's clear commandment meant that I was somebody I couldn't even bear to think much about. I willed myself to be better, but will was not enough. I saw myself as some terrible aberration—when, in fact, what I was doing is exactly what humans are born to do. I was so intent on living the perfect life that when I turned out to be merely human, I had no resources for dealing with it.

I felt completely cut off. Everything the preachers taught me left me unable to deal with the reality of my life. And if I were to tell the truth about that reality, I'd be cast out. My transgressions separated me from the "good people." I couldn't tell them what was happening to me because they didn't do what I was doing (or if they did, they wouldn't tell it), and they'd certainly try to make me stop, which I didn't intend to do. In the end, their prohibitions weren't enough to live by. I won't say those rules were wrong, only that for me, they weren't effective. And they left me few resources with which to deal with life.

Everything weighed against faith. With it, I had to accept a narrow, handed-down wisdom from people who told me I was a filthy sinner with a brain that wasn't worth using. Without it, I could explore a huge world filled with new ideas. With faith, I had to deny a large part of what I saw in the world around me. Without it, I could question and explore as much reality as I wanted. With it, my sex life contained three options: I could be a guilty, filthy fornicator, I could be a woman who married wrong and too early, or I could be cut off from the most riveting experience of my young life. Without God, on the other hand, all is permitted, as Dostoyevsky put it.

The specifics of why I left faith are merely the details. At the core, I left not for sexual freedom or the right to think, but because I chose to live life based on my own experience rather than someone else's. When the preachers' version of reality didn't match mine, they told me to take their experience as my guide for what God wanted. But I couldn't do that. Now I realize that no one can do that and live authentically, whether inside or outside the church. But I didn't know that then.

I had given Jesus everything for most of my life, but when the tests came, everything I believed crumbled. Where was God? Probably up there with Miss Texas making sure her thighs didn't jiggle as she did her runway walk. Whose fault was my fall? Mine, of course. More guilt. But I was used to that. Guilt was an old friend. I just shouldered a little more, and then one day I dropped the load by the side of the road. Good-bye, guilt. Good-bye, God. Hello, world.

Chapter 4

The World Outside

IN THE YEARS after I left the church, I suffered a good bit but I also had a good bit of fun. It wouldn't be quite honest to say that I didn't. Those were intoxicating times, especially for women. We were the first generation to break the daughter-wife-mother mold. Later I would desperately want to fit into that mold, but when I was young, I couldn't imagine ever wanting such a thing.

I wasn't especially ambitious in my career, but I loved the heady feeling that I could invent myself. I could smoke dope. I could drink alcohol. I could have romances with anybody, anytime I wanted. I loved being the wild girl, playing the temptress, feeling worldly. I was

actually none of those things. I was a middle-class woman with traditional standards who was stepping out and thinking myself quite
daring.

I started dating a man who did "erotic art." I took a job in downtown Dallas and thought myself sophisticated and urbane. It's embarrassing to remember a lot of it, but parts of it sure were grand.
Even now, at a point in life when my blood has cooled so much that
the costs of transgressions stand out more clearly than memories of
the pleasure, I still can't quite wish that I had missed it all.

I was a sinner, that's for sure. But oh, what freedom. I thought I
could be anybody I wanted to be. Looking back, I think that was my
biggest mistake. It took hard miles down some rough roads before I
figured out that the only thing anybody can ever be is herself. If I'd
known that when I was a young Baptist, I wouldn't have had to leave
the church. I'd have been able to decipher all the clumsy instructions
that the preachers were giving. I might have been able to make the
transition from a childlike faith to a grown-up faith without ever
leaving the fold.

If I'd been able to hear my own voice, I might have been able to
hear God's. But I was too busy listening for cues on how I ought to
be. The preachers would have said that once I left the church I was
giving in to my own selfish, sinful nature, that I was doing just exactly
what I wanted to. But that isn't quite right. Just as I had once tried
so hard to please them, I was now trying to please another audience.
Once again I was trying to fit in to an image. I went right from
Snow White to Cosmo Girl without even a pause for thinking about
who I might be myself.

It didn't take too many years for my new lifestyle to feel as arid
as the old one. So I did what I knew how to do. I picked a new mold
to fit myself in to. I moved to a small town in Texas, became a teacher,
and married the second man I met. He was a Ph.D. student at the
local Baptist university, majoring in religion and philosophy. He was
from an even smaller town, a lifelong Baptist who was ordained to
preach at fourteen. It was the first time that I felt the pull of the old
ways. But it wouldn't be the last.

The university had turned my husband into a kind of Baptist I'd
never seen. He didn't believe the Bible was literally true, and he
thought a central part of Jesus' message had to do with helping the

poor—something the preachers I knew didn't talk much about. He said Jesus was killed for opposing the very powers that the Church now cozied up to. He said fighting racism would have been one of Jesus' crusades. He said Jesus wouldn't have been a Republican. He wouldn't even have been a Democrat. He would have been a radical, my husband said. I'd never heard such talk in my life. It was almost as exciting as art with the erotic artist. At least at first.

He said the preachers who preached the Bible as literally true and without error were preaching words they knew were a lie. Their duplicity put my husband into a rage that never seemed to die. It was Jesus, Jesus, Jesus, day and night, Jesus being betrayed all over again. The boy was on fire. And pretty soon I was a bucket of water.

It sometimes seemed that we talked of nothing else. All the passion my husband brought to pounding the pulpit when he was a kid he now brought to refuting the traditional, culture-affirming Christianity we once believed in. Everything set him off. If there was ever a voice crying in the wilderness, he was it.

Meanwhile the Baptists he loved so much were turning even more fundamentalist than they had been when the two of us were good sheep in the flock. "Get another denomination," I began saying to him, more and more wearily. "Forget the Baptists. Or you'll end up just like Jesus did." But he wouldn't. Maybe he couldn't.

We might have fared better if we had done more than just talk about how wrong everybody else was. But what would we have done? Gone to church with the Methodists? Joined up with the Catholics? We were small-town Texas enough to think that our way, the Baptist way, was pretty much the only way that counted. All or nothing. We were still the black-and-white kids our fundamentalist parents had raised us to be. Only now, we had all the faults and few of the virtues.

Pursuing God on our own wasn't a possibility. Nobody did that. As far as I knew it couldn't be done. And I wasn't interested in God, anyway. I'd tried God, thank you very much. I didn't need His meddling, nagging, shaming, weakening ways. I blamed Him for the fix I was in, and I wouldn't go near a church if I could help it.

I thought I'd escaped the fundamentalist way of thinking forever. But I was only kidding myself. I'd dropped the trappings, but habits of the heart I'd learned sitting in the pews had burrowed deep into my soul. Those lessons still ruled my life. Only now I didn't know it. The voices of my childhood told me the way of holiness was a narrow path: "Squash your own desires. Control your own thoughts. Deny your own self." Nothing about my life fit the Christian profile. But I was still following the same grim rules that had failed me before.

When I met him, my husband-to-be was a smart, talented guy who wanted desperately to finish his studies but didn't have the money to do it. What he needed was a patient, kind, self-sacrificing woman to help him. And that's just exactly what I decided to be. I'd done wrong. Now I'd sacrifice my way to redemption.

What a disaster that was. The weekend after we married, I knew I'd made a terrible mistake. It wasn't him; it was me. I loved my husband, but I wasn't who I claimed to be. I wouldn't admit, even to myself, that I didn't have the goodness that I'd promised to have. But neither could I summon it. I didn't want to rescue anybody. I didn't have the stuff. So I tried harder. I thought that will alone could force me into being who I wasn't. I was wrong. A little honesty would have set things right, but I didn't have that in me either.

I'd put myself in a good tight box. My husband had been divorced once before. His chances of teaching at any kind of Baptist university with two divorces on his record were nil. He had already quit his job. He was enrolled in school. We were set. The way I saw it, I'd picked up my cross and I'd better carry it.

I carried it so poorly that I don't even want to share the details. I'll just say that I was most wretched, and I behaved most wretchedly. Within three years, I'd found a boyfriend with the willpower and enough disdain for morality to pull me out of a marriage I wasn't honoring. A coward to the end, I crawled out a window the night I left my husband. I didn't have the nerve to open the door because I knew he would hear me, and I wouldn't be able to escape. I left a note saying I would be back in a few days. I thought it was true when I wrote it. But I never went back.

Chapter 5

Opening a Closed Heart

MARRIAGE HAD BEEN my try at redemption. So following my usual approach—the Ping-Pong method of life planning—I now clung to a man who was most decidedly not available to be redeemed. He was a drinker, a chaser, and a curser of such magnitude that he stood out even in Dallas. Twenty years later, stories of his exploits are still being grimaced over by people who barely knew him. I'd caught myself a legend, all right.

In a rare moment of peace, I once asked him what he thought God wanted from us. He said that when he died God would have only one question for him: "Did you have a good time?" And if he hadn't, God was going to be real disappointed.

The next years were wilder and worse than anything I ever could have imagined. When they ended, I was just happy to be alive. I didn't have religion anymore, but the guilt had come back full force. It's amazing how that part of a religious upbringing can survive after all the benefits have long faded. Guilt was always with me and now heavier than ever. In my midthirties, I knew nothing about the blessings of faith and religion, but I could write volumes about the wages of sin.

You don't have to call it sin if you don't agree with that term. I wouldn't have then, and I'm not sure the term is very useful even now. You could call my problem low self-esteem. You could call it bad choices. I call it losing track of my own best self. But whatever you call it, the end result was the same: My life was dreadful. I was lonely and wanted to marry. But I was too closed off and selfish to form a good relationship with a man. I'd hung around with folks whose values were even worse than mine for such a long time that I'd lost touch with the better parts of me. I behaved in ways that I hated, but I couldn't seem to act differently.

I'd gone to enough therapy to have a handle on my problems. I could tell anybody what was wrong with me and what I ought to do. But I couldn't do it. I had a fulfilling job, a loving family, loyal friends, enough money, and sometimes I even had plenty of dates. But life was not good. I couldn't help but remember the apostle Paul's lament: "I do the things I would not do and leave undone the things I would do."

You might think that at this point I would have headed for the nearest Southern Baptist church and signed up again. But I didn't. That might have made all sorts of sense to someone else, but I had already been down that path. I'd sat through a thousand sermons. I'd followed all sorts of advice. I'd smiled and nodded and sang those tuneless hymns. I'd memorized Scripture and given money. I'd made pledges of money and time and prayer and purity. And when the testing times came, it all fell apart. My fault, of course, but I didn't want to go through the same disillusionment again. This time, if there was to be a "this time" with God, I'd trust myself and I'd try to trust Him without intermediaries.

One of the biggest steps in my return began one fall visit home for my mother's birthday. My sister had a handsome new boyfriend that year, and my parents seemed happily adjusted. All their happiness made my loneliness even more apparent. I was standing in the middle of a department store, life swirling brightly around me, when a sense of despair flooded over me that was so acute I can recall it even now.

I knew my problem. My heart was closed. I was dating a man who outclassed my usual escorts in every way. Philip was funny and kind and well educated. He was handsome, stable, and sincere. He didn't cling, and he didn't play games. But I wasn't interested. As I told him many times, he wasn't my type. I'd never spoken truer words. For one thing, he thought far more of me than I thought of myself. I liked a man who kept me involved in struggle all the time. "No pain, no gain" might have been the slogan of my love life, except none of the pain had gained me anything.

That night in the department store, I prayed that my heart would be opened. I prayed from the depths of my being. I didn't have much faith but I had plenty of yearning. In truth, I didn't have my current boyfriend in mind. That seemed too unlikely. I planned to tell him that all bets were off as soon as I got home. Well, not immediately. First I needed him to drive me home from the airport. If he wanted to take me to dinner, I'd put my announcement off a little longer. I was a real prize, as you can see. The whole focus of my life was figuring out how to get the world—usually that meant men—to do the things that would make me feel special. Sometimes that meant adoration, sometimes it meant presents, sometimes it meant doing the things I wanted. I don't want to sell myself short. I gave a lot back. Too much. But the point is that I was never satisfied because it isn't possible for a person so focused on herself to be satisfied. But that's a religious lesson, and I was a long way from learning it.

On the plane back, a ponytailed earring wearer caught my eye as he swaggered down the aisle. He smiled. I looked away. Definitely potential there. I felt that old tingle. But this time, I examined it instead of just feeling it. Was that attraction? No, that was fear. Mr. Ponytail was trouble and I was intrigued by the opportunity of taking trouble on.

When I got off the plane, my ride home was waiting. He had a single rose in his hand. As I walked closer, I saw that his thumb was bleeding.

"What happened to you?" I asked.

"I stabbed myself picking off the thorns," he said.

I took the rose and kissed him. What else could I do? As I leaned over, I caught sight of Mr. Ponytail watching. He shrugged and turned away.

In the next few hours, everything I thought and felt about my date changed. It was as though I was seeing him for the first time. I don't know what happened exactly. I can't explain it, but it seemed as if a spell that had bound my life for years suddenly fell away.

Four months later, I married that man, and in the years since, he has done just as he promised. He has made me happier than I ever imagined being. Was my prayer the reason for this good fortune? Was it the rose? The realization on the plane? I don't know. I have generally kept my mouth shut about what happened. I haven't been sure anyone will believe my story. I haven't been sure I believe it myself. But I know two things with some certainty: My prayer was just the kind of total surrender my childhood religion specified was necessary before God would step in, and the change in my life felt like a miracle, was a miracle, to me.

SECTION 2

*My comeback
to grace*

Chapter 6

New Life

Y OU'RE PROBABLY THINKING, "Isn't that sweet? Isn't that so Southern? She found a husband, and it convinced her that there must be a God." I had been looking a long time, such a long time that I couldn't remember what happiness felt like. But nabbing a husband in itself wasn't enough to spur me into new faith. For one thing, the God of my childhood would never have picked this particular man. He's perfect for me. But God as I once perceived Him didn't care much about what was or wasn't perfect for me. He was too busy punching me into a shape that suited what I imagined to be His preferences.

When I write that marrying Philip seemed like a miracle, I'm referring to the sudden change of heart that caused me to marry him and the fact that the wisdom of that action was so beyond my normal ability. If that had been the end of it, I would have claimed the prize, said thanks, and gone right back to being who I had always been. Like an atheist in a foxhole, I was calling out to God with all my might because I was so out of luck and hope that He seemed my only chance. As soon as the shelling stopped, I planned to be on my way. Instead, life opened up as though I'd stepped through a door in the scenery.

The religious experience of my new life was that I felt totally accepted. My husband never criticized me, never tried to change me. He was fair and kind and thoughtful. When I pointed out one or another of my many faults, he pointed out that they weren't really so bad. He understood how hard I was trying and gave me full credit for it, so much credit that my faults were pardoned without any mention of them. For the first time in my life, I had found a safe place.

This was grace. I didn't know it at first. At first I thought it was some kind of trick. Early in our relationship I explained that we would never be able to get along. Philip is a precise, early-rising, neat, organized, disciplined person. I am an imprecise, forgetful, late-rising, messy, disorganized, and frequently undisciplined person. People like me are always being frowned upon by people like him, who generally fancy themselves superior to people of my kind. I agree with them. But by the time we met, I had given up impressing such superior folks and decided simply to stay away from them whenever I could.

"I am a person who sits around doing nothing for long periods of time. I don't do dishes as soon as the meal is finished. I don't always make my bed. I leave papers on the counter. I leave clothes on the floor," I told him. "That's how I am. I'm not going to change. I don't want to be nagged. I don't want to be teased. I don't want to get wry looks. I don't want to hear sighs or chuckles or pointed observations. I don't intend to feel that I am in any way deficient or inferior. I won't stand for it."

It was a passionate speech. I was worked up and pretty much out of breath by the time I finished. I expected him to quibble.

Instead he said, "Okay."

I waited for him to continue. But he didn't.

"That's it? Okay?" I shook my head at his innocence. "You can't do it. You can't imagine what it is to live with someone like me."

"We'll have the maid come more often," he said.

I didn't believe he could keep his end of such a bad bargain. But he did. When I smeared hair dye on glossy white cabinets, he said, "Accidents happen. We can probably get it off." When I apologized for having rushed to work leaving long blond strands of hair all over the bathroom after I washed and blew my hair dry, he remarked mildly that it was sort of like sharing the bath with a collie.

His responses were so flawlessly accepting that I accused him of practicing them in the shower. He couldn't keep it up, I thought. But week after week, month after month, year after year, he did.

No one made fun of me. No one bossed me around. No one criticized my ideas, my looks, my actions, my intentions, my housekeeping. But it was more than the lack of negatives. When my new husband said he loved me, he never added a "because." He never said "because you're smart," or kind or good or funny or pretty. Attributes were as absent as negatives. I had no idea why he loved me.

And so I had no standards to meet, no reasons to mold myself into a shape someone else liked. Every day I was simply, merely myself. It was an experience so new and so wonderful that it filled me with gratitude and delight that surpassed anything I had ever known. Once, in a giddy ecstasy of abundance, I said to him, "If you want us to have a happy marriage, you have to remember just three words." Then gazing about the room, I opened my arms palms out and intoned as solemn as a queen, "Me. Me. Me." Could a person possibly be more obnoxious than that? He laughed.

It was a religious experience. Nothing in the church had taught me that life could deliver religious experiences, but I knew this was one. I knew it deeper than doctrine can reach. I knew it by the way my life began to change. I knew it because I had such an overwhelming sense of gratitude. My life was so suffused with blessing and lightness that I had to thank someone. It was too much to keep inside, too hard to explain to another human. To them I seemed to be bragging or blithering. And so in the night when I walked the dog, I passed in and out of the shadows cast by the trees and I thanked the sky, my lucky stars, the universe, and finally, because He might be listening, God. How could such an unexpected and wonderful life have come from anyone but God?

I'd heard the preachers talk about grace. Sometimes they called it forgiveness. They said it washed away your sins as though they had never been. They said we were saved from our sins by grace through faith. But what did that mean? I didn't have any frame of reference to know. I couldn't ever remember a detailed, specific sermon on what grace was like. We had all sorts of examples of sin. Sin, I knew. Grace was just a nice word. As best I could tell, it boiled down to the idea that human beings weren't worth killing, but God was gracious enough to overlook our sad state.

That was grand of Him, of course. But somehow it never lifted my spirits much. I had encountered that kind of grace from plenty of humans. If I groveled enough, my faults would be tolerated, watched, and toted up so that I could repent properly. Lots of folks say that's a fine grace. It's more than any of us have a right to expect. But if that was all God had to give, I generally preferred the company of sinners.

Everything in experience and religion told me that people had to earn whatever they got. What the church called grace came with a price tag like everything else. My husband's acceptance was completely different. Here's an example. One evening around Christmas, we were set to go to a fancy dinner. Philip told me we needed to leave at six-thirty. He told me several times. He reminded me not to forget. The day of the dinner, I called him to ask again what time we were to leave. He told me again. Still I forgot.

At six-fifteen, I came steaming up to the house, thinking I had forty-five minutes to get ready. By six-forty, dressed and happy as a child, I went to the phone and started making calls. "Let's go," he said. "We need to leave."

I was amazed. "Don't I have twenty minutes?" I asked. My father, who was visiting, watched all this. Later, he marveled at my husband's attitude. "How does he do it?" he asked.

I was awed myself. So I asked Philip why he hadn't been angry. "What good would it have done?" he asked. "You would have gotten upset and felt terrible and the whole evening would have been ruined."

This was grace so complete that it didn't ask for recognition. It was grace so sufficient that it didn't require repentance. I didn't have to defend myself. I didn't have to explain. My goodwill and benign intention were wordlessly accepted.

I was rarely ready for this new grace. If I had had to sum up my philosophy, it might have been: Life's bad now and going to get worse. If someone had told me the universe was strumming with music, I'm sure I would have imagined a dirge. I thought that guilt was acceptable, that my faults were damnable, that I rarely came up to the mark, and that anxiously trying to make myself fit other people's expectations was my real reason for being on this earth. Religion as I had learned it in the church had reinforced such ideas. But the religion I was learning in life was freeing me from them.

Chapter 7

New Ideas About God

M Y HUSBAND HADN'T the slightest interest in leading me toward more knowledge of God. He doesn't think in such terms and would never set himself to that type of task. Such grandiosity is completely contrary to his nature. God isn't even a subject he contemplates much, as far as I know. The only time I can recall going to church with him was for a funeral, and he complained about the preacher's message all the way home.

In this new "religious" life, no one would mention God or the Bible. No sermons would be heard. No lectures, no admonitions, no good advice as to what I needed to do would be delivered. That's all to the best because I had already heard plenty of those, and none of them had reached me in the places where I needed to be touched.

The idea that God speaks to those who have ears to hear Him is an old religious idea. I had always taken it to mean that people with the right kind of hearing are penetrated by the preacher's words in a powerful way. But I wasn't listening to preachers and wouldn't be for years. Any kind of religious language made me roll my eyes.

The messages I was about to hear were coming from ordinary experience. They were faint in the beginning, easily shouted down by my usual glum interpretations. At first—even in the midst of grace— I went on in my ordinary way, bulling along, shoving through existence, certain that the key to a happy life was having my desires satisfied and my ego elevated as often as possible.

But life's rules had changed. I had stumbled into a kind of regard unlike anything known to me. Every day I learned a little more about it. Here's an example that so mystified me I've remembered it ever since: The day after that trip to visit my family in Kentucky, Philip and I agreed to go to a movie, and he was to pick me up at five-thirty.

I was ready. But he didn't arrive. I waited. Fifteen minutes passed. Then thirty. By now the movie had started. I waited fifteen minutes more and called his house. When he answered, I could tell that he was perfectly calm, not defensive, not apologetic, just feeling free and easy. I thought angrily that he could forget about having a relationship with me. I did not intend to be left waiting. I would not tolerate being treated in such a fashion. I began to berate him. There was silence at the other end of the phone. Then he spoke.

"You forgot to set your watch back. It's five-fifteen," he said. That was embarrassing enough, but then he said, "Don't be afraid. I'm not going to dump you."

My first impulse was to snap back, "I'm not afraid. I'm angry." His words infuriated me. That he had seen through my bluster didn't endear him to me; it threatened me into anger. I *was* afraid, but I didn't know it. The world as I perceived it was such a dangerous place that fear was the last thing I could allow myself to feel.

"Okay," I said, grumpy and suddenly foolish. "I'm ready." When he arrived, he said nothing about our conversation. It was as though it had never happened. He didn't linger over how I had misjudged him. He didn't ask me to explain or apologize or make it up to him. He had seen to the heart of me, and it had not put him off. He had heard my true self underneath the anger of my words. I didn't appreciate it. But slowly over time, this new kind of love seeped into my soul, and like warm water it began to dissolve the corrosion that kept me frozen.

I didn't connect this love with God. Not at first. But it was miraculous to me, and as the years went by, I began to think that if a person could love me with such openness, then maybe God could, too. If there is a God, and if He does love people, I began to ask, what would His love be like? Would it be less than the love my husband shows to me? It was a big leap. I toyed with the idea for a long time, trying it out.

Philip's love had seen through my bravado. His care for me had penetrated to the heart of my reasons for acting the way I did even when I didn't deserve such response. Would God do less? If I was afraid of Him, untrusting, unable to summon the faith to believe in His existence, would He send me to hell? The church of my childhood assured me that He would. But I began to wonder whether that was really Godlike. If so, my husband was better than God. Ah, blasphemy. But what honest person could think otherwise?

I disappointed God every day. I disappointed my husband every day. One sullied up and demanded that I pay for being myself, knowing full well that I couldn't help being myself even if I tried. The other laughed and loved me anyway. One understood me perfectly because He made me and knows everything. The other didn't understand me at all and didn't pretend to. Which was the giver of transforming grace? Well, even I am not so far gone as to think that my husband is better than God. So, I took one more step away from the teachings of my childhood and toward a God who seemed more and more mysterious.

Chapter 8

Grace Extended

ANOTHER EARLY LESSON in this new life I had prayed so fervently for was that grace can reach beyond what other people think. I learned that for the first time when the editors killed one of my stories before it ran. This had never happened to me. I thought the story was pretty good. I had put a lot of work and lot of myself into it. And they killed it. All the shame that waits in the wings of my life came rushing out. I wanted to hide what I had written, to bury the evidence. Philip asked to read it. I let him.

When he finished, he said, "It's good. I like it. They're wrong."

"They're not wrong," I said. "It's bad. They know what they're talking about. It's an embarrassment."

"No. It's good," he insisted. We continued in that vein for some time until finally he said, "I guess I'm going to have to get a picket sign that says 'Free Christine Wicker's Story' and stand in front of the *News* until they publish it."

He didn't care what the world thought. I was fine. The story was fine, and if every editor at the newspaper disagreed, they were wrong, and we didn't need to think any more about it. I was so accustomed to believing whatever bad thing anyone said about me that I could hardly believe he wasn't going to fall right in line with my critics. I was ashamed to be me, but he was not ashamed to be with me. This was grace for sure. I marveled at it.

And eventually, I wondered, "Could it be that God was equally unmoved by 'other people's' opinions?" I was so pinioned by the beliefs of my childhood. They so restricted access to God that I cringed at the very idea of trying to reach Him in ways the Church had condemned. To even attempt such a thing was shameful. Heresy. Foolishness. Selfishness. Weakness. Pride. That's what they thought. That's what I thought. But is that what God thinks? I didn't know and still don't. But I began to wonder. Do they know? Or do they just know how to protect established thinking?

I might not have believed this new grace so strongly if it had only made me feel good. But it also changed me. That was another lesson from the religion of my childhood. The grace of God changes you. My frenzy over whether I was smiling all the time when I was a teenager wasn't as odd as it might seem to others. The smile was the evidence that God had transformed Christians so that they were unlike other people. His grace changed people. If I didn't have the evidence, I probably didn't have God either.

So rattling around in the back of my head, even after all those years out of the church, was the idea that grace, if it was really grace, changed people. The church hadn't changed me much despite all my efforts. Professor Marcus Borg, who also grew up in a fundamentalist church, has a theory about why. Life in such churches often translates to "a life of profound selfishness," he writes. Even when we are obeying all the rules, we have to keep checking up on ourselves, checking how well we are fitting in with God and our fellow Christians. "Selfishness seldom has to do with reaching for the biggest piece of cake on the plate; rather, it is preoccupation with our selves," writes Borg in *Meeting Jesus Again for the First Time.*

Over the course of my life, lots of people had worked to change me—my boyfriends, my relatives, my employers, my teachers, and most ardently of all, myself. The multitude of efforts had made me feel guilty, worthless, remorseful, ashamed, and angry. But I didn't change. If anything, the more criticized I felt, the worse I acted. Not deliberately. Just inevitably. The criticisms weakened and spooked me even more.

My husband didn't try to change me. He didn't set standards or make demands. He encouraged me, left my faults alone, tried to make my life easier. His attitude changed the very air around me. He freed me from the polarities that I had spent my life bouncing between. Good and bad. Saved and damned. Saints and sinners. He freed me from having to pay so much attention to my bad old self.

Without all the ups and downs, all the drama and the fights and the frantic need to prove myself, I was able to live my life. The whole scope of who I could be expanded. I didn't have to compulsively pay attention to myself because I didn't have to be compulsively worried that I was doing something wrong.

My experience didn't fit a formula. This new peace and freedom felt like a connection with God. If it was that and not just something I was conjuring from my own need, it was still unsanctioned by any religious authority I knew. I could match these feelings with religious language. Jesus saying, "Come to me, all you who are weary and burdened, and I will give you rest. Take my yoke upon you and learn from me, for I am gentle and humble of heart and you will find rest for your souls. For my yoke is easy and my burden is light." But I wasn't looking toward God. I wasn't praying in Jesus' name. I wasn't even sure I believed in God.

Chapter 9

Unconditional Regard and God

S EVEN YEARS INTO my marriage, a bona fide religious authority, just the kind of guy who could speak to my old fundamentalist roots and my new secular understandings, stepped
up with a theological framework for what the experience of my second marriage had already taught me.

Psychologist Neil Clark Warren has a master's in divinity from
Princeton Theological Seminary. He's a well-respected author in even
the most conservative religious circles. He can quote the Bible at
length. He goes to church, prays every day, describes himself as a
right-of-center Christian who believes literally in the central doc-
trines of Christianity, such as the idea that Jesus died for our sins and
then rose from the dead. Many of the workshops he does around the
country are conducted in Baptist churches. He is not a person I would
have gone to for advice, and certainly not a man whom I would have
expected to understand my new spirituality.

In his book *Finding Contentment,* he described exactly what happened to me: I encountered the kind of unconditional love that allows people to become who they are meant to be. Dr. Warren
believes God is the best source for such love. He thinks the purpose
of the Church is to help us connect with God's unconditional love,
which empowers and frees us. The power of that love is so great that
religious people call its effect on us a rebirth.

Dr. Warren believes people who accept us as we are and encourage us to be ourselves are sources of Godlike love. When you find
those people, spend as much time as you can with them, he recom-
mends, because as they encourage you to be authentically yourself,
you will naturally move closer to God. Dr. Warren even thinks some
people may have such healthy, loving mothers that they get enough

unconditional love as children. Those lucky people never stop being authentic and don't have to go to God for a rebirth. But there aren't many of them.

The upshot of all this is that without any declaration or drama or belief system, I had embarked on the kind of religious journey that I once was so committed to leaving. Dr. Warren's notion that being authentically yourself is the way to connect with God was as counter to the religion I understood as anything could be. But I liked it, and Dr. Warren wasn't preaching. He was merely inviting people to try his way and see if it worked in their lives. I had already been trying it without even being able to articulate what was going on, and it did work.

I had begun a journey back to God along my own path—one that I didn't even know would lead to God. Sometime later I would meet Dr. Ray Dykes, an Oklahoma City pastor who left a thriving church to start a "personal pastor" program that would help people connect with, refine, and live by their own theology. He would have an analogy for exactly what was happening to me. He says "the bricks" of true faith are made up of clay and straw. The clay is the experience of our lives. The straw is what other people tell us about their beliefs and experiences.

"I'll tell you all about my faith, but you can't have it," he says. "It's mine. You have to build your own." His theology is merely straw blowing by your life, he says. The task of people who want their own relationship with God is to catch what applies to their experience and let the rest go. Without intending to, I was doing exactly what he recommended. But for me, a third component has been necessary. Every step of the way, as I put together my experience and other people's thoughts, I have to shake off the old ideas about who I am and who God is.

People who didn't get as big a dose of religion when they were children as I did may not need that last step as much as I do. But I suspect that even people who think of traditional religion as sheer idiocy are infected enough by other people's ideas about God to need some shaking off in order to be free and move forward. I don't want to shake all of it off. A lot of what I'm discovering is not new to me; maybe none of it is. For instance, Protestants have a great term for what I want to achieve. They call it soul freedom, and they mean that

God will speak to you in the way that communicates best and you have the right to follow your own soul's direction. Most religious people put a cap on freedom, however. You can only stray so far from group consensus. But I say, let's keep soul freedom and take the cap off.

So here are the three steps I began taking long before I put them into words: Experience, listen for what confirms your experience, and shake off what is holding you back. If we wanted to put it into physical terms, it would be: Experience with your body, take in with your head, and test in your heart.

Experience was the first step for me and the hardest to trust. Experience requires the most courage and the most concentrated attention. If I want to go forward spiritually, I must rely on myself. I have to question my reactions and pay attention to how I feel, what I think, and what happens to me. And I can't stop. If I want to continue going forward, I need to accept that there never will be a time when I can go back to taking other people's word for the state of my spirit.

Whenever I start paying attention to my experience and trying to figure it out, I start hearing messages from other people that confirm my own findings. I don't know why that happens. Some people would say the universe is giving you what you need or God is providing. I'm not comfortable with that kind of cosmic interpretation. Instead, I liken it to learning a new vocabulary word. You learn a word that you never heard before. You can't recall a single time that you ever saw that word or heard anybody use it. But once you learn it, it pops up everywhere.

One of the confirmations comes from Henri Nouwen, who agreed with Warren's idea of God as love. He said God is the one who calls us his beloved children. We discipline ourselves to seek Him because when we are with Him we feel that love. It sustains us through life's difficulties and it transforms us.

Nouwen was a Catholic priest whose books were so profound and important that he was sought out by famous people all over the world. In the last years of his life, he chose to live in a community where mentally retarded people share housing with people of normal intelligence. He said that he learned from them about giving and receiving love and about what it means to be with God. One of the reasons their love was so powerful, he said, was that they didn't know anything about his writings or his deep thoughts or his fame. Every day they related to him just as he was, and they loved him only for what he was, not what he seemed to be.

Chapter 10

Love's Power

MY EXPERIENCE SEEMS to be leading toward the idea that God is love. I hoped to end up somewhere less trite. I have all sorts of trouble with that notion. Not only is it the religious equivalent of a round yellow smiley face, but it's a statement that stops all conversation. Somebody says, "God is love." What do you say back? "No, he isn't"?

And what does it mean to say God is love? To my hard-shelled thinking, the idea that God is love has always seemed a pretty wishy-washy statement. Where's the power in that?

It's like Miss America contestants assuring us that all they want is world peace. Right. Good idea. And so what? If all they really wanted was world peace, wouldn't they be somewhere else doing something more closely related to obtaining peace? And if God were love, wouldn't the world be different? If God is love and He just sits around wringing his hands and hoping everybody will love one another, He's not going to be of much use on this old evil earth.

Or is He? Rabbi Keith Stern has a take on that question. His father spent some time in Nazi concentration camps, so the question of evil and God's power has particular import to the rabbi and his family. More recently, the rabbi's autistic brother accidentally drowned. One horror came from humans, the other horror came from natural events, and in neither case did God intervene. So I asked the rabbi where God was when such terrible things happened to innocent and helpless people. If God is so loving and has any power at all, it seems that He would have done something more than just watch. His answer was that God had done something; it just wasn't what I expected. The story of his brother's death illustrates.

The afternoon of Stephen Stern's death was a perfect Cape Cod day, clear, hot, but with a cool breeze. The Stern family always spends a month of the summer on Cape Cod. In 1995 they gathered near the cape at Pilgrim Lake to celebrate the rabbi's forty-first birthday.

A highlight of the visit for good swimmers was a quarter-mile plunge across the lake. That day, a high-school buddy of the rabbi and the rabbi's uncle, two excellent swimmers, got up from the beach and sauntered forward for their swim. Stephen also rose. "I'm going with you," he said.

When the rabbi heard his brother's words, anxiety crackled through his veins as hot and swift as fire eating dynamite fuses.

"Where are you going?" he asked.

Stephen was a big, quiet man with the soul and disposition of a six-year-old. Usually a question was enough to stop him.

"If my brother was about to take a bite of a sandwich and I asked him, 'What are you doing?' he'd put the sandwich down," said Rabbi Stern.

But this time, Stephen hardly paused. He looked his older brother straight in the eye, something he'd only done on two or three occasions in his entire life. And he said, "It's all right. I'm going to swim." The rabbi fell back. His brother had just made the most self-assertive statement of his life.

"I couldn't make him stop," he said. "I had to respect his will as a man to do what he wanted to do."

The two faster swimmers were met midlake by others coming back across. One of them, Stephen's cousin Ezra, saw Stephen's head slowly moving toward them. Too slowly, he thought. He swam out to his cousin and put his hand on his arm to ask if he was all right.

"Let go of my arm," Stephen said. "I'm all right."

Ezra moved back. Stephen sank from sight so quickly that his cousin believed he was fooling around.

"But Stephen never fooled around. He didn't know how," said Rabbi Stern.

When Stephen didn't resurface, Ezra began diving. He couldn't see anything in the murky lake. It was as though Stephen had never been there. Another swimmer joined the search. On the beach, lifeguards ran toward the water, rescue floats careening crazily behind them.

Parents hustled children out of the water. Sirens shrilled. Fire trucks, ambulances, and police cars flung sand as they plowed the beach. A search helicopter whomp, whomp, whomped through the sky like a big heart beating over the calm lake. Three hours passed before the body was found.

God didn't have anything to do with Stephen's death, the rabbi said. But God was on that beach. He didn't send a message of foreboding. He didn't pick this perfect day because Stephen's God-allotted time was up. Even so, God was there, the rabbi said.

"My God wept with me," he said. "My God comforted me during the time of my grief because I know God's love for me is constant. My God is a God of endless blessing."

When Stephen's tarp-swaddled body was carried onto land, an identification was needed. As Rabbi Stern was about to enter the ambulance, a paramedic reached out to help him up.

"That hand," said the rabbi, "was the only thing that kept me from floating away. I'll never forget it. That was the hand of God."

As a Jew, the rabbi doesn't have a physical concept of God in the way that Christians do. "I don't know of any way to experience God's presence except through other people," said Rabbi Stern. "They may know they are instruments of God and they may not. God is never absent from a truly good act."

He is also never present in a truly evil one, said the rabbi. God was not part of what happened in the Nazi concentration camps, and if people had let God live through them, those camps would never have happened, he believes.

In the days after Stephen's death, Rabbi Stern took a flood of calls from friends and congregants who had heard about his loss and wanted to comfort him. He cried for hours those first days. His wife suggested that he let someone take names of callers so that he could telephone them later when he was calmer. But the rabbi took every call. Everyone who called was the love of God, he said. "I needed it all."

More than a thousand people came to the funeral. The bus driver who delivered Stephen to his job every day as a mail room worker was there. People whose mail he delivered were there. People came who knew him only from his weekly Saturday visits to town when he went to the library, bought an ice cream, and walked the same route at exactly the same time every week. A big, gentle man who couldn't reach out to anyone had somehow touched people everywhere he went. Was that God, too?

Rabbi Stern repeatedly revisited those last moments with his brother. Although his mother never reproached him for his failure to stop Stephen, the rabbi questioned his own behavior. He didn't believe that was God speaking to him when he felt those forebodings as Stephen left to swim. But I wondered. If it was God, couldn't the Lord have spoken a bit louder?

Rabbi Stern's answer to that question comes not from any attempt to second-guess God but from his own reasoning. "That was the best day of my brother's life," he said. "It was a perfect day when he was surrounded by people who loved him. And he was expressing his freedom as a man."

The family put a bench on the beach of the lake to commemorate Stephen's life. For a year, the rabbi grieved so much that no day passed unshadowed by his feeling of loss. And then in June, almost a year after the July accident, the rabbi's oldest son was to be bar mitzvahed. Everyone who was on the beach that day gathered in the synagogue. The rabbi read a poem to the oldest of his five children. The last verse of it said:

> *A blessing on your head*
> *My beloved firstborn*
> *The narrow bridge who spans the abyss*
> *Who leads me to life.*

As the rabbi looked at all the love and life that surrounded him, his grief finally gave way.

"The beauty and abundance of life simply overwhelmed it," he said.

God, again.

The rabbi's story so impressed me that for a while I lived with it in mind. It was a new twist, religiously speaking. It even inspired me to do a few good deeds myself. I kept thinking about the power of the idea that we are God's hands. I couldn't get out of my mind the notion that God has all this goodness to release into the world if only we will let it pass through us. That way of thinking made me feel powerful and hopeful.

I had often heard that it was our duty to "bring people to Christ"; we were supposed to tell them about Jesus and press them to take him into their heart. We were also supposed to live as Jesus would, whatever that means. I've heard a million interpretations of that—all the way from how Jesus was no sissy but rather a robust, masculine kind of guy who chased money changers out of the temple to Jesus was a meek and mild type who loved little children.

It was for sure that the rabbi wasn't pushing Jesus. But he did have a concrete plan for how one might be Godlike. It was straightforward and without ambiguity. You don't have to accept any idea but that God is love, and you can define that however you like. You don't wait for revelation or rebirth or belief. You don't whine around or worry about whether God is holding up His end or transforming you. You just do good things, and when you do, you are God's hands.

The rabbi didn't definitively answer the question of whether God is love. He didn't answer the question of what that means. He did something better. He showed how to activate the idea, how to bring it into reality even if you don't believe it. And once again experience led me to a religious realization. You could sidestep belief under the rabbi's plan and not only find God, but be part of His work.

Chapter 11

Back to Prayer

NOTHING IN ADULT life, neither the sorrows nor the successes, caused me to go rushing back to the church. I didn't pray much even after my marriage. I sure didn't read the Bible. Nevertheless, my shell was beginning to crack. I wasn't sure I believed in God, but the astonishing change after my prayer in the department store made me wonder if prayer might have power. I couldn't see any evidence that it had power to affect physical events or the actions of other people, but I was beginning to wonder if it couldn't affect the person who was praying.

When I decided to try contacting God again, I didn't have a lot of time. So I gave Him what I had: the fifteen minutes it took me to drive to work. That was enough.

I started praying because I wanted to change my own behavior. In my new married-lady life, any confessions I might have had were pretty mundane. No great sins of the flesh here, but merely the small indiscretions and failures of an ordinary life, just the kinds of things that can rob a perfectly happy life of the joy it could have. Here's a petty example but one that bedeviled me: I was spending too much time saying bad things about other people.

I am a newspaper reporter. News is pretty close to gossip. My colleagues and I make our living honing our sense of what makes a hot story. On off-hours nothing gives quite the evil thrill of a good gossip fest.

Afterward, I'd feel guilty. Despite its fascination, speaking ill of others also left me feeling dragged down. It gave an ugly cast to my days, left me feeling slimy and pessimistic. I was often afraid someone would repeat my words. I dreaded having to face up to my own meanness of spirit. I tried to stop. I declared to several of my friends that I would stop. But I couldn't do it.

Gossip was robbing me of my peace of mind and good self-opinion. But that wasn't my only ill. I also felt stressed, rushed, out of control. I was competitive to the point that I couldn't enjoy anybody's successes—other people's or my own. Every time someone else had a good story or won an award, my own stock slipped a little, at least in my own eyes. When I had a good story, I knew it was only a higher perch from which to fall.

I was also afraid, afraid of making mistakes, afraid of losing my new life, afraid of death and illness and humiliation. In short, I was a normal, moderately successful American woman living in the late part of the twentieth century. No big problems; lots of angst.

One morning as I drove to work thinking about how likely I was to be caught again being someone I didn't like, it occurred to me that I might try modeling myself after someone. I didn't have any heroes. I was already trying to be like my friends who have better tempera-ments and characters than I have, but as usual I was making a mess of it. Somehow striving for goodness had never gotten me very far. Then it occurred to me that I might simply pray God would live through me for that day. The fundamentalists I'd been raised with and a lot of other people believe God can dwell in us and change us. If that was true, perhaps I could summon Him.

I'd actually gotten the idea of summoning God from the Hare Krishnas. They told me years ago that their chants were the names of God, and whenever His names were spoken, He was present. Al-though they knew that they often annoyed people by creating a ruckus on the streets, they felt they were doing everyone a favor by bringing God into their midst. If Hindu names of God could sum-mon Him, maybe Christian ones could, too.

The thought of asking God to live through me scared me. I was afraid that it might work, and I'd become a nut. I hadn't been in my wonderful marriage very long, and if I became like the Jesus of my childhood religion, I might become convinced that God meant more than my husband. Everything I'd wanted might be cast away. I might become compelled to quit my job as a reporter, which admittedly wasn't a very holy calling. I might give away everything I had and become a street person. I might become even more meek than I already was, and I felt pretty much like a doormat as it was. For weeks, I mulled my prayer idea over.

Then one day I talked with Elizabeth Espersen, a former nun and director of a Dallas interfaith site called Thanks-Giving Square. I knew she had done some praying herself, so I asked what she thought about my idea. She was reassuring. She told me that being like Jesus probably wouldn't change me so much that I'd become someone I didn't want to be. She was certain I wouldn't have to give all my money away or leave my husband.

My concern may sound foolish to you. But I got a big dose of God's grandness when I was young enough to believe anything was possible, and even though about half the time I don't believe He exists, when I do believe, I'm wary.

With Elizabeth's assurance, however, I started praying on the way to work. I'd usually remember my resolution at about the second stoplight, just as I was turning onto the entrance ramp of the highway that led downtown. I rarely had the concentration to keep praying for long. By the time I exited, I was usually thinking about whatever story I was reporting on that day. That's all I did. I hardly gave God another thought for the rest of the day.

I don't want to sound too flippant. My prayer was short but fervent. I didn't futz around. I didn't drone or pontificate. I didn't try to con God or ask for a bunch of stuff. I wanted God to live through me. I really wanted it. I'd tried goodness by will alone and it had not worked. I felt enough despair about that to know it would take a transformation for me to improve.

I don't remember how long it took. But my life began to smooth out. As I walked to the car each night, I began to notice that I didn't have as much to reproach myself for. I didn't feel so trapped in my own weaknesses. Within a year, one of my friends complained that I didn't have anything bad to say about anybody anymore. She wasn't exactly right, but I'd definitely cut down. Eventually I started giving away more of my money, but I didn't give all of it. The most unexpected thing that happened was that instead of becoming more timid, I became more assured. I began to feel that I was all right. It was as though I was becoming more solid, more real to myself. Even some of the terrors that had plagued me all my life began to recede.

I could go on, but I don't want to make too much of this. It is enough to say that that one little prayer every day seemed to make a difference. And the difference was good in every way. I don't know how it happened. My Buddhist friend Marty Berkman says that I was simply concentrating my own self in such a way that I began to change. That might be. I can't say what was really going on.

None of my Christian ideas led me to believe that one piddling little prayer on the way to work would be enough to make such a change. Much of the time, even that prayer ended with the notation "If you're there." The idea that such unbelief and such tepid commitment can make a difference seemed ridiculous. The Christian life is one of sacrifice and long prayers that bore you, but you have to say them anyway because that's what God wants. Right? Being bored is part of the test to show that you really, really, really love God and have faith. I had not been bored. I had not even had much faith.

SECTION 3

I learn that reality is not what it seems and I enter an underground society based on that very notion

Chapter 12

Reality Shifts

FIRST MY MARRIAGE taught me about grace. Then it taught me that reality is not what it seems. Grace opened the possibility that life might contain more benevolence than I imagined. Now I was ready to realize the second big lesson in my move toward faith: Reality is not what it seems. My first inkling of reality's "other nature" came when I married a man unlike any of the men I had dated. I would have never looked for the qualities in my husband that make me so happy. I knew they were good qualities; I just didn't know they were what I needed.

Once, after I'd finished telling a therapist tales of my rocky love life, he remarked, "I don't think you know what it is to really love a man." I thought he was crazy. If a person who had done so much in the service of love didn't know what love was, who did?

But after entering my second marriage, I realized he was right. What I'd taken for love was merely thrashing around, multimedia dramas that kept me stirred up. From the outside looking in, my new life was completely boring. There wasn't enough excitement to make good gossip. I should have been bored. But I was happy.

Before my marriage, I'd hear a love song on the radio and I'd yearn for such intensity. Now I hear a love song and I think, That's the silliest thing I've ever heard. They think they're talking about love, and everybody else thinks they're talking about love, but that's not love at all.

In Western culture, romantic love is everything, especially for women. Without love, you're nothing. I knew that. So when I began to realize that what the culture was telling me about the nature of love was such a colossal lie, the center of existence as I knew it went wobbly. My realization might not sound like religion to you. I certainly didn't connect the two, but my discovery about love led me to ask myself what else in this life might be a similar illusion. I remembered the preachers saying that "the things of the world" weren't what they seemed. I thought they meant that the sinful pleasures we wanted so much were going to turn into ashes. They did mean that. But maybe they also meant something more subtle. Maybe they meant that what makes people truly happy aren't the things we usually think of.

I've described my marriage in the glowing terms of its reality to me. But the essence of it doesn't yield itself up for the scrutiny of others. Like the truths of religion, it can't be captured in words or pictures or even stories. They can hint at its core. But to know the reality of my marriage, you must be in it. And only the two of us are.

I asked myself, "If something this big and this good has been so completely hidden that it eluded someone searching as desperately as I was, what other treasures might life hold that I was too blind to see?" If I've found out that reality isn't as it seems, who else knows it? Not the people in charge of television. Not the pop songwriters. Not the book writers. If they know it, they're staying real quiet about it. The fundamentalists know it, but their version of reality doesn't ring true to me either.

I am not a New Ager. I do not believe the universe supplies what we need, when we need it. But, nevertheless, the answer soon presented itself.

I'd met Marty Berkman years earlier at a party. Someone mentioned that he was a Buddhist, and I tried to hide my amazement. They could have called him a two-headed calf and I wouldn't have been any more shocked. Why somebody who was raised a perfectly good Christian—or in Marty's case, a perfectly good Jew—would decide to become a Buddhist was completely beyond what my narrow mind could grasp.

The next time we met was in a more formal situation. I was a columnist for the Sunday magazine of *The Dallas Morning News* and I wanted to do a story on a Peruvian baby who Marty and his soon-to-be wife, Janis, adopted. Marty had been wary of my intentions when I came to the house for the interview, but when the story came out, he was pleased. He framed the story and put it in the baby's room, and he kept up with me after that. We occasionally had lunch.

One day, he said he had some Buddhist ideas that would help stressed-out people become more flexible in our thinking and more resilient to the stresses of the day. He wasn't interested in making anybody a Buddhist, but he wanted to try out his ideas, and he couldn't find anyone who would commit to the time it would take. I volunteered.

For the next couple of months, we met every Tuesday for about two hours. I'd done a little meditating, but Marty had a definite program set up. We would talk about how things were going, we would do some Tibetan exercises, and then we would sit cross-legged on the floor until he rang a little bell.

Meditating isn't easy if you concentrate on doing it right. Marty instructed me to keep my mind blank or to focus on something such as my breathing or a vision of flowers. I'd try. But my mind would run like a caged squirrel. When the session ended, I would be tight and frustrated, ready to take on the guilt. Other times, I would slow my mind, keep it blank for a minute or two, and promptly fall asleep. As my head sank toward the floor, I'd jerk awake, defensive and ashamed.

Guilt and shame. Add fear, and you've got a list of my most reliable companions. There I was, an adult member of the baby boomer generation, renowned for its guiltless and shameless lifestyle. I was doing nothing more daring than sitting cross-legged in a room, and I could still find myself lacking. A Lutheran friend has a theological name for what ails me: perfectibility. Did I get that from the church, too? Maybe. There's even a Bible verse for it that often runs through my head. "Be ye perfect even as my father in heaven is perfect." Jesus said it. I learned it in Sunday school.

But Marty didn't seem to know that verse. He saw the purpose of our time together in an entirely different way. I believe that you have to struggle and work for everything you get. But Marty began to teach me that I couldn't get what he wanted me to have by striving.

The Buddhists understand better than some Christians—at least better than the Christian I had been—that some of life's deepest truths don't lend themselves to words. In fact, trying to express them merely misleads people. Experience that leads to an understanding deeper than words is a better path, they might say. And so Marty advised me to sit.

The peace I had worked so hard to wrest from God and myself

began to move closer when I stopped trying. Sitting, as the Buddhists refer to meditation, was the key. Just sitting. Not studying. Not praying. Not yearning or pondering or repenting. Just sitting. If I sat long enough and my mind was blank, I felt a profound sense of safety, not only in my mind but in my body, too. So again, I learned that what I thought life required—struggle and striving—wasn't what it called for at all.

When I moved into the peaceful state, I felt whole and strong and real. I felt happy. And so I had to wonder. It looked as though I had been wrong about love and striving. Maybe I had also been wrong about happiness. If happiness and peace and security, this wonderful feeling of being more alive than I ever had been, all came from just sitting, then why was everyone running around trying to amuse themselves into contentment? I had all those thoughts when I was able to calm my mind and let it go to whatever wordless place it went to, but I often wasn't able to do that.

When my mind would run away or I would fall asleep, Marty would just shrug. "That's all right," he'd say. "Whatever comes up is all right." The important thing was to sit. I was supposed to meditate every day and sometimes I did. But when I didn't, Marty still responded in the same calm way. "That's all right. Do what you can. It's important." I watched his face carefully. Was he telling the truth or just humoring me, condescending in hopes that I would improve? If so, I never caught him at it. And the guilt that had dogged me so long moved a few steps back.

Although he wasn't trying to convert me to Buddhism, Marty often talked about how much of what we think is reality is really an illusion. For instance, we think that we are solitary individuals, unconnected to one another, but Buddhists believe we are, in reality, all part of one whole. We think that we will be happy once we have all we want, but happiness and having don't go together in the way we think they do.

In fact, Marty said that if I wanted to stop suffering, I would have to give up desire. That's a very Buddhist idea. It makes no sense at all in a Western context. I, like everyone I know, live to work toward my dreams. That's considered a virtue in the West. To give up desire sounds like being dead to most Westerners. But Buddhists believe it is the way to freedom. As long as we clutch our things, our emotions, even our perceptions, we will be buffeted about by life.

One Buddhist story tells of the billionaire who had so much money he could do anything he wanted, buy anything he desired. As I remember it, the story goes something like this: One morning the billionaire woke up feeling pretty good. But as the butler served his coffee, it sloshed from the cup, which annoyed him. Darkly pondering the ineptitude of other humans, he picked up the morning paper and saw that the stock market had risen. That perked him up. As he dressed, he noticed that his belt was a bit tighter than the day before, and he looked with disgust at his spreading body. At lunch, a pretty girl flirted with him and he was elated. That evening the play he went to lagged, and he was bored.

The end of the story is a question: Is this man free?

Both my husband and my friend were teaching me lessons that didn't fit in to religion as I knew it. But their lessons were imbuing my life with something so wonderful that I couldn't let it go. To use a religious expression I learned as a child, "It was like coming from darkness into light." What was going on here? Could God be working through one man who didn't have much interest in Him and another who didn't even believe in His existence? I didn't think so. And yet my life was falling into place.

Chapter 13

Doing What I Need to Do

DESPITE MY RECENT spiritual victories, I was far more focused on earthly gains, especially when it came to work. Status, more money, a chance to show that I am a really deep-thinking and observant writer were what I understood best and valued. I couldn't see that changing. I was looking for truth, but mainly the kind that would further my reputation.

The Sunday magazine I worked for was phasing out. Casting around for something else to do, I decided that a gardening column would be the ticket. I wasn't much of a gardener, but I wanted to be. I could see myself becoming a sort of urban E. B. White, wise, gently funny, and in tune with life's slow rhythms.

Once again, I turned to my friend Elizabeth Espersen for advice. Before asking what she thought, I outlined the various roles I was suited for and the ideas that people had given. None of them seemed to light her up. "Have you ever thought of doing not what you could do but what you need to do?" she asked. No. I planned my life according to what my career required, not according to what I personally needed. The idea of giving myself such latitude was so foreign that I disregarded it immediately. I was willing to suffer in the service of ambition or other people's needs, but to do what would benefit me personally because I liked doing it or it helped me grow as a human being or it satisfied my needs was not a possibility.

Once all my effort went into finding and keeping love. After about ten years of failing, I switched my allegiance to work. Religious people would say I had made a God out of love and now I was making a God out of work. I didn't think in such terms.

For a decade, I worked nights and weekends. Most of my thoughts and all of my energy went toward work. I was often unhappy but I paid no attention. I learned early that unhappiness is no reason to quit. Pain was not a signal for me to stop as it is for most sentient beings; it was a signal to push harder. I would set myself to some task and keep hacking away at it until it was done. Then I would take on another. The amount of misery it caused versus the amount of joy it gave wasn't even a factor in the equation. Perfectibility was the aim. I'd lost God but I hadn't lost the idea of sacrificing myself.

The gardening column could have been some escape from that life. Spending time outdoors would have put me in touch with the peace of nature and that might have eventually set me right. But probably not. Even as I talked with Elizabeth, I was setting such high goals for the column that I would have inevitably fallen short and spent my life in the usual miserable way.

Luckily, the managing editor of the newspaper had a different plan. He wanted me to work on a new section on religion. Oh, no, I thought, I know all about religion and I don't want any. I especially didn't want to spend my life making nice with a bunch of misguided church folk. Of course not, he responded. We wouldn't waste your talent on such an unworthy task. We want you to "reinvent" religion reporting. He was a spinner of big dreams. I was a chaser of big dreams. It was a fit. I didn't know what he meant, and he probably didn't either, but we didn't let that stand in our way.

The job wasn't a prestigious move within the profession. The newsroom has its share of religious people and church members, but as a rule it is a fairly profane place. Being on the "God squad" didn't increase my stock with most of my colleagues. Some of them were so dubious about my new assignment that they asked me what management had against me. One old friend took to calling me the church lady. People who had been cheerfully cursing at me and with me for years would now glance my way and look guilty. A few even apologized. I laughed.

They were joking, I think. If they weren't, what good would it have done to make a point about it? Proving my wickedness might have set them at ease but it would have made me feel impossibly silly. One of the newsroom's most profane and cynical investigative reporters was advised to keep his desk near mine because his editors had noticed that I was having a good influence on him. I doubt that.

My favorite story of our time together was the day he noticed that his loud cursing was causing me to cover the mouthpiece of the phone during an interview. "Christine," he said solemnly when I hung up, "you've got to learn how to deal with me. When I'm too loud, just do what the last person who sat next to me did. It won't hurt my feelings. Just yell, 'Would you shut the fuck up?' "

"That's a good idea but I can't do that," I replied sweetly. "I'm talking to ministers, and they're not accustomed to hearing that kind of language."

"No problem," he said cheerfully. "When you're talking to a minister just say, 'For God's sake, shut the fuck up.' "

Outside the newsroom, I had the opposite problem. Christians, especially born-again believers, often wanted some evidence of my holiness before they felt comfortable talking. The boldest soul winners would ask right out "Do you know Jesus?" or alternatively "Are you saved?" But most people were less pushy. They asked, "Where do you go to church?"

They wanted to know where I stood. That's fair. But where I stood would have just confused them. It certainly confused me. I wasn't for 'em or against 'em. Saying "I don't go to church," always came out like a slap. It didn't matter how gently it was said. "I don't" was a judgment. It also meant I wouldn't understand them and possibly wouldn't want to. The best answer seemed to be, "I grew up Baptist." It was true. It showed that I had some knowledge, but it wasn't so cozy that they felt safer than they ought to in the presence of a reporter.

Sometimes the assumptions went the other way. I'm obviously middle class, sympathetic, soft-spoken, and sometimes that led religious people to assume that I must be right thinking. I didn't bridle at that notion for the same reason I remained silent when reporters saw me as holy. No matter what I said, I'd be misrepresenting myself.

People in the community referred to me as "the religious reporter." It seemed to put too fine a point on the matter to correct them with, "That's religion reporter, not religious reporter." Wide-eyed Christians sometimes lowered their voices to ask, "How can you do stories on all those other religions? Isn't it hard to write about them?" I knew what they meant. They were asking how I could write fairly about such nonsense and devil's work. I usually dodged that one. "I'm a reporter," I often replied with a shrug. "That's what we do."

Such an answer brought to mind the snake who bit the frog after it had carried him across the lake. Asked by the dying frog why he had done such an ungrateful thing, the snake shrugged and said, "I'm a snake." I wondered whether the questioner had the same image in mind. But I never asked. Once again, there seemed no reason to put too fine a point on it.

Early in my religion-reporting career, someone wrote a letter to the editor complaining that stories in the religion section showed clearly that we were tools of Satan. When the letter was printed, my husband read it early that morning and came into the bedroom waving it gleefully. The idea that he was married to an instrument of such awesome wickedness seemed to delight him enormously. A colleague thought that so funny that she used it in a speech. Unfortunately she chose a Southern, churchgoing crowd. She was the only person who laughed.

Image isn't the religion beat's only problem. Reportorial skepticism is severely limited in religion reporting, and skepticism is at the core of a reporter's soul. Without it, what are we? (I can answer that, but it's ugly.) Other reporters sometimes disdain religion reporting as little more than public relations for a nonexistent entity and the misguided folk who follow that mythical being. In some circles, religion reporting, with all its off-limits subjects and unquestionable assumptions, isn't considered reporting at all.

A favorite journalism story tells of the reporter who was sent to do an Easter story. When he returned, he referred to "the alleged resurrection." Sometimes the story ends with the reporter being fired, sometimes it ends with him being transferred, and sometimes it just ends with the storyteller's knowing laugh and the punch line "They never sent him out on a religion story again." The intrepid reporter is always male, for some reason. I've nodded and smiled as that story has been told about so many different reporters that about halfway through it I begin to wish desperately the bold reporter would come up with something more ingenious at the end. But he never does.

When dealing with the church's money or its scandals or its good works, religion reporting can be tough, but it doesn't usually strike at the heart of the matter; it doesn't force people to prove up their claims about God. It is constrained in other ways as well. Professionals might be held to public accounting when they violate their own codes of ethics. But the press doesn't hold religious people to their self-professed values in any but the most egregious failings. If a pastor is sleeping with the congregation, it's a story. But if a Christian businessman owns slum housing or a Muslim socialite eats pork, it probably won't make the papers. No one investigates powerful religious laypeople in order to contrast their faith's expectations with their behavior.

Other reporters may look askance at religion reporters, but their doubts are nothing compared to the feelings of the religious people being reported on. Many have no use for the values journalists hold high. The skepticism reporters treasure as among their greatest virtues is a prideful, sinful indulgence to some of the faithful. The reporter comes rudely tramping on holy ground, full of pride, ready to scoff, often unable to understand even the simplest of faith's motivations.

Ten years ago, reporters were likely to put a sarcastic spin on religion stories, as though sneering at them would somehow compensate for not having attacked their premises. We don't do that much anymore, partly because equal-opportunity sneering wasn't being practiced. The Amish, for instance, got reverential treatment if for no other reason than that they are picturesque and quaint. The Jews couldn't be sneered at if you didn't want to be charged with anti-Semitism. And the fundamentalist Christians, real touchy about being made fun of, began to organize and protest.

Earlier in my reporting career, when someone would credit God with something, I'd write a little and then put my pen down. It wasn't so much that I didn't believe them as that I didn't know how to convey what they had to say in a way that didn't seem to make fun of them. Reports of God's works don't fit into a newspaper easily. In print, I would allow my sources to say "God did it," but if they waxed too long, I cut them off. I was doing them a favor, in my opinion.

So I took the religion-reporting job with trepidation. But in truth it wasn't the work that scared me. I thought I could do the work. I didn't know enough about it to formulate my usual vision—which is to say, one I couldn't reach. Lots of religion experts tried to scare me. Knowing that I was new to the beat and didn't have any special training, they complained about having to deal with someone so unprepared. It couldn't have been the stupidity of my questions that offended them because the complainers rarely let me speak before telling me that I wasn't competent to ask. One informed me that he had talked to religion reporters before, and they didn't know enough to get the subject right. "You have five thousand years of history to catch up on before you can understand where we're coming from," he said.

He had a point, of course. But reporters are always wading into their own ignorance. Anyone who can't do that can't be a reporter. I asked that particular man to give me an example of how he had been misunderstood. When he gave it, I said, "It wasn't that the reporter didn't understand you. What you said is simple to understand. He just didn't have the same goals for the article as you had. That's a problem bigger than education."

My fears were all personal. What scared me about the religion beat wasn't the facts. It was the folks. Dallas has lots of fundamentalist Christians. In my work, I'd dealt with child abusers and sex addicts. I could interview murderers and dopeheads and insane homeless people without a second thought. But I wasn't sure that I could deal with those fundamentalists. I knew I wouldn't want to.

I feared that if I moved too close to my roots, the anger I'd once felt might come back. But more than that, the church people might spirit away the little bit of God I'd found. Once I had been completely convinced that theirs was the only way. Now I was convinced that I had to make it up as I went or I would be without faith forever. If they convinced me again that they held the only God franchise, I'd be out in the cold, or to put it the way they do, I would be lost. It's a credit to the strength of their hold that they could inspire such caution after so many years. What did that mean about the truth of their version? I didn't know, and I didn't want to find out.

But, of course, that was the very reason I needed to take the job. Elizabeth's idea that I should do something I needed to do was becoming reality. The last place I would have looked for God was in the church. The only way I would ever get inside a church was if my job took me there. I was alone in my search for God. If I found any part of Him, I planned to hide out with it for as long as it lasted. My new ideas about the Deity could not stand the scorn of organized religion. But to look for God without consulting those in the God business would have been a waste. Organized religion had lots to tell me if I could listen in the right way. Perhaps my mother understood that.

By the time I started on the religion beat, my mother had long ago stopped going to church herself. She made no pretense of holiness. But when she heard about my new job, she sent me a note saying that she was happy. To her, being a religion reporter was a high calling. She reminded me that when I was a baby my grandmother carried me to the Baptist church for a special ceremony. The church was perhaps a half mile away and my grandmother, who couldn't drive, must have walked there with me in her arms.

My grandmother treasured two memories of my babyhood. One

was the stocking cap she made to cover my bald head. The other was that morning when she dedicated me to the Lord. Not everyone wanted her to do it, she told me many times, but she carried me herself.

I don't remember the stocking cap or the dedication. What I remember is the two of us together on evenings when my relatives were out on the town. I lived with my grandmother in those days, and we had no television. I wanted to sit on her lap, but she couldn't hold me. "I'm not able," she would say when I tried to climb up on her knees.

So we sat apart. Sirens screamed across the city as the night's revelry heated up. She was old. I was young. We were powerless in a world of many dangers. My grandmother called out to the sole force she could reach. Every time a siren's squall cut through the Oklahoma wind, my grandmother moaned the only mantra, the strongest magic she knew, "Lord help us. Lord help us."

She pled. I listened. The nights were dark and long.

Chapter 14

Religion As News

T O   M Y   S U R P R I S E, the balancing act of journalism—skepticism paired with professional open-mindedness—was a boon in my own God seeking. If I had continued as a civilian, my own ideas would have tripped me again and again. But as a reporter, I had the opportunity, actually the mandate, to take everyone seriously. To convey the realities of other people's faith, I had to push aside my own ideas time and time again. I had to listen up even when I wanted to close down.

It is popular to believe that journalistic objectivity is a myth. Some people recommend that reporters relinquish the pretense and admit their bias in every story, but I don't agree. While no one can make herself a complete tabula rasa, good journalists can maintain a professional open-mindedness that is unlike their ordinary consciousness. It's like a shield that you erect between your ordinary self and your professional self. Your ordinary self might have its own loud certainties, but you stifle them. You work to concentrate on only one task: getting it right.

Sometimes I'm so in tune with the faith people are telling me about that we're right in sync. I can feel their yearning. I can believe what they believe. I can feel the hope, the wonder, the mystery. The next day, I can look at the same person and be in such a different place that I'll think, "What the hell are you talking about?" But being in tune is not essential. In fact, it sometimes gets in the way. You can see a lot from the outside looking in.

In most of journalism, what the reporter believes or doesn't believe is pertinent in determining how credible the story is. But in covering religion it's not what the reporter accepts but what the subject of the story accepts that makes the story. If we restricted ourselves to only what's credible, we would be confined to skating across the surface of a subject that has limitless depth—for the subjects, if not for every reader.

The evening I was sent to a Pentecostal service at Calvary Temple is an example of a time when I wasn't even remotely one with my sources. On the other hand, the service might have seemed as odd as a circus sideshow to some reporters. To me, it was all quite familiar.

Our family has been split between the Baptists and the Pentecostals for as far back as I can remember. My grandmother was a Baptist and her sister, Aunt Elizabeth, was a Pentecostal. Later my mother was a Baptist and her sisters were Pentecostals. Pentecostals believe that being baptized "in Jesus' name" rather than in the name of the Trinity—the Father, the Son, and the Holy Ghost—as the Baptists are baptized is of critical, salvation-determining importance. Pentecostals also think speaking in tongues, which they sometimes call receiving the Holy Ghost, is of great importance. Baptists generally frown on such activities to the point that they will cut off a church that follows what are called charismatic practices.

Pentecostals often hold the opinion that Baptists aren't truly Christians. Baptists would never make a similar claim against the Pentecostals, at least not publicly, but privately many will call their more boisterous, charismatic cousins a bunch of nuts. Christian nuts, maybe, but nuts nonetheless. In our family, the split runs deep.

Aunt Elizabeth, whom I remember as rather a cold fish, was beloved by my grandmother and revered for the good fortune that life had visited upon her. My grandmother had married twice and both husbands died. She was left with seven children. The oldest boy was deaf. The strain of it all caused her to have at least one nervous breakdown during which she wore a black coat and carried a satchel all summer long. She and her children were about as poor as people can be and still survive.

Aunt Elizabeth, on the other hand, was married to a good, steady man with a job at the gas company. She lived in a white frame house with a well-kept yard bound by a chain-link fence. As I remember, I was rarely invited inside, which caused me some grief because Aunt Elizabeth kept oranges in her basement, and I loved oranges better than anything. I often peered through the fence at that severe, pristine house, so holy and so closed to me.

Even after Uncle John died, his pension kept Aunt Elizabeth in what looked to us like prosperity. In my memory, Grandma was always trying to mold herself into a shape that would gain Aunt Elizabeth's approval. Mostly, she failed. It was true that Grandma's holiness didn't match Aunt Elizabeth's. If you pushed her far enough my grandmother might shake her fist in your face and give you a cussing that would pinpoint your failings in so precise and vivid a fashion that you'd long remember her judgment.

But she had a lock on a couple of virtues that Aunt Elizabeth had trouble mastering. Grandma didn't have a speck of pride. She didn't think of herself as any big stuff, she didn't claim any holiness, and in a long lifetime of being treated badly by all kinds of folks, religious and not, my grandmother never held a grudge or nursed a vengeful thought, as far as I know. I didn't inherit her virtues, but her legacy to me has been that I still define her type of godliness as a high form, and the one I would most like to have.

The story I best remember about Aunt Elizabeth has to do with the time she gave my grandmother what she called a love offering. She had been to some church service or other and was inspired to give her poorer sister a nice sum of money. My grandmother, who lived at the level of poverty that despairs of ever having enough control in the world to actually earn money, dreamed daily of having someone give her something free. When the government began serving free lunches to senior citizens in the sixties, she thought that was about the most marvelous, miraculous thing that had ever occurred. To say about any item whatsoever "it's free" was to give that thing irresistible cachet. Free money, of course, was incredibly rare and wonderful. So when Aunt Elizabeth called with the love offering, Grandma walked right over to her house to pick it up.

Aunt Elizabeth was as good as her promise. She put the check right into my grandma's hands. But between the time she let go of the check and the time Grandma was able to get to the bank, Aunt Elizabeth must have heard another message from the Lord. She canceled the check. My grandmother's disappointment was a terrible thing to witness.

My mother's sisters often tried to pull us toward Pentecostalism during the early days after their own conversions. Sometimes their efforts came pretty close to success. One summer when I visited, they took me to services day and night. I was pretty taken with the jazzy music and the colorful preaching. The emotionalism of it all had a powerful appeal, but being a bit of a watcher I delayed moving over to their side.

When my folks arrived, I invited them to attend services with me. My dad, who was not so moved by music with a good beat as I was, stood with his arms folded while the service heated up and the women began to shout in glossolalia. He didn't say a negative word. He just stood there, and somehow nothing seemed the same. I looked on the scene with his cool eyes, and the chance of my conversion suddenly became remote. So when it fell to me to cover a Pentecostal service as a reporter, I knew that I was likely to stand with folded arms, at least mentally.

I did. I didn't feel even a tittle of the emotion that the people at Calvary Temple felt. I was as much an outsider looking in as I had been when I stood at Aunt Elizabeth's fence looking toward her house and thinking about those oranges in her basement. This time the fruit was of a more spiritual nature. It was just as inaccessible to me, but I may have been alone in that. The rest of the congregation seemed to be sucking the juice right out. Here is some of what I wrote.

Many in the congregation talked of "waiting for the Spirit" and tried to describe how it felt when the Spirit arrived. Some called it a fire or a burning. Others described it as a flowing of water or wind.

For two hours, the people testified and sang. Drums throbbed a crazy heartbeat. The saxophone yearned. Chimes twinkled through the room.

"Tell the Lord tonight. Tell him, church," a minister exhorted.

Women moaned. A man's sobs sounded as sharp and broken as yelps. When the music died, a hundred whispered prayers rustled through the silence. A woman's voice floated over the congregation, speaking glossolalia in tones so sorrowful that in the stark, brightly lighted hall an ancient grief seemed loosed.

Faces were tilted toward heaven as the people sang. Arms waved like a sea of toothpicks.

On this night, being slain in the Spirit was the predominant sign of the Holy Spirit's presence. Preacher Marcus Lamb told people not to worry about getting hurt. The Christian men serving as catchers would be behind them.

Lie on the floor as long as you like, he said. Don't hurry. Some people would feel warm. Some people would feel weak, he said. To others, those moments flat on their backs would be "like a Holy Ghost anesthesia" working while God healed deep hurts.

"Don't anybody pray until I give you the signal," he said.

Children and old women, middle-aged men and young mothers stood with their eyes closed, their hands up like bandits surrendering to the law. When the signal came, the prayer team moved.

The Reverend Maryann Meltabarger, a dark-haired woman with a shock of white hair over her forehead, bent to hear the people's mumbled pain. Her slender, red-nailed fingers caressed their faces as she crooned a prayer. A touch on the forehead and they were down.

Sometimes they folded. Sometimes they fell stiff-kneed, toppled like trees.

A little curly-haired woman in pink sweats and matching shoes stood with crumpled face. Two ministers prayed over her. Her sobs increased, her hands trembled, but she didn't fall. As each minister moved on, she opened sad blue eyes to watch them go.

Associate pastor and prayer team member John Delgado was moving fast. A short man with wavy salt-and-pepper hair, he listened, prayed, and bestowed the Spirit with quick force. When he reached up to give John Aldridge's chest a sharp tap, the forty-seven-year-old Vietnam vet jumped as if he'd been shocked. Then the big man fell.

Mr. Aldridge was once a drug addict and an alcoholic, in and out of mental hospitals, subjected to shock treatments a half-dozen times.

The Lord first appeared to him in a hospital. Initially, he kept quiet about it.

"When you're in the nuthouse, you don't let people know you just saw Jesus," he said.

Mr. Aldridge was in a Tom Thumb grocery store parking lot sometime later waiting for his wife when, he recalls, the Spirit descended upon him, causing him to speak in tongues.

For seven years, he has ministered to people in the kind of crises he no longer experiences. This is Mr. Aldridge's second night at the revival, and he is likely to attend again.

"The minute I came here, the Spirit of the Lord came upon me," he said. "It was a spirit of joy and gladness. It was a very carefree feeling. I knew a lot of people were going to be saved."

I didn't understand this, but I wasn't about to scoff at whatever it was that had changed John Aldridge's life. I didn't understand this, but I didn't understand quantum physics either. That doesn't mean they aren't real.

Chapter 15

Grappling with the Church Folk

I WAS LIED to more in the first year of religion reporting than in all of the previous decade of reporting. Or to be more precise, I caught more people lying. I once mentioned that fact during a speech, and afterward a woman defended believers by saying, "We don't lie more than other people, we just don't lie as well as other people. So we get caught more often."

There weren't many such instances, only three or four. But in each case, ministers told me things that I was pretty sure were deliberate, outright lies. They weren't trying to cover up wrongdoing. They were merely lying to get an advantage that would put them and their work in a better light. I was so shocked that I complained about it to a minister who had befriended me.

He laughed at my innocence. "Of course they lie to you. The way they see it, their cause is holy and so it deserves protection. Your cause isn't holy and so the same rules don't apply." A veteran of many church wars, he was greatly amused that I would think religious people were more bound by the truth than other people.

When making speeches about being a religion reporter, I often tell audiences that religion is the toughest beat at the newspaper because reporters never get to talk to the source. We always have to take someone's word for what God has done. Most of the "miracles" can't be documented. Most of those messages can't be recorded. So what's to report?

For me, the results are the story. Whether an article of faith is true doesn't much matter. What matters is how believing changes people's lives. Human beings are story makers. They constantly weave their lives and the lives of those around them into patterns of meaning. Journalism usually reports the "hard facts" of their lives and takes its own reports as the reality. It's a truism that every story has two sides. Journalists focus on getting to both sides of the "real" story, and they define that in terms of "facts." But every story has a hundred sides, a thousand different "facts," and a million shifting interpretations of what those mean.

The kind of truth that shapes the lives of religious people can't be quantified, can't be proved or disproved, and its pursuit often leads into the realm of the fantastic, even the absurd, often the unbelievable. An East Texas sculptor has a vision that inspires him to put his statue of Jesus on a flatbed and truck it from town to town. A college-educated, sane, normal woman tells of the day when she was five and Jesus appeared in her bedroom. A soft-spoken middle-class Bible school teacher becomes so convinced abortion is wrong that she buys little pink plastic fetuses to hand out during a lesson for preschoolers.

This hazy, hard-to-pin-down God business motivates people in the most profound, life-changing, sometimes violent, sometimes self-sacrificial ways. A small-town Kansas white girl goes to live in a black inner-city neighborhood. A fiery Northern Irish preacher exhorts his Protestant flock to resist any move toward peace with the Papist Catholics. A multimillionaire cable television executive decides he wants significance instead of success and so devotes his life to helping build the Christian church, which he characterizes as the biggest lever for change in the world. Living a life of faith and reporting on lives of faith is a most winsome, mystical, magical experience.

I wanted to write "religion" stories, not "church" news, I told my editors. Pressed to clarify the difference, I adopted a definition given to me by a devoutly Christian colleague: "Church news is about them. Religion news is about us." I was convinced that the larger audience was interested not in church politics or even the many good works of the church, but in manifestations of God.

It was as though I'd entered an underground society, a huge population that was so little known in the popular culture that the interviews made me feel like an anthropologist. After a decade of skating the surface of people's lives, I was now dropping into the uttermost depths of what moved them most passionately.

Even the language they used was foreign. It was English. But that only made the job trickier, because the words that expressed their most profound feelings had been so debased they sounded trite. If you did nothing more than quote them, religious people sounded banal at best and often like nutcases. I was always being forced to dig around what they said, to pry out some new statement that would unlock the depths that those pat phrases expressed for them.

I recalled what a former priest and now popular professor had once told me when I asked why he never used religious language. "Because," he said, "religious language is like an old coin. It's been handled so much that the sharpness has worn off." I saw that every day.

I heard priests who had lost a huge civil suit because they hadn't protected boys from a child-abusing priest say that they were going to pray, and I heard the journalists groan. How inadequate. How irrelevant. Well, yes, maybe. Prayer is not enough in the face of wrongdoing. But for the priests it is going to the source. It is powerful action. If it isn't, then they've based their lives on nothing at all. What the secular world saw as evasion, the priests could very well have seen as the most important part of any action, as the root of the omissions that had allowed this to happen. And in that, they could be right. Or, as my journalist friends thought, calling for prayer could be just an excuse to do nothing and sound pious while not doing it.

I also saw religious people in great despair over death or failure try to communicate by turning to Bible stories, and I watched people in the larger culture glaze over, totally lost as to the relevance of such ancient fables. Alan Watts suggests that the Bible's stories have been so heavily interpreted that their meaning is lost. He says they need to be put away for a century or two until their meanings have been forgotten. Then people can take them out and listen with "clean" ears. It's almost impossible for a journalist working in the simple, constrained style of the newspaper to convey the magic that those worn, fought-over, often-interpreted, fantastical stories still have on some people.

But sometimes, I got lucky. The Sunday I visited the Central Dallas Church of Christ was one such time. Here is what I wrote.

> Five gold ornaments spike each of the woman's ears. Several more adorn her nose. She looks too old for this punk fashion, too tough to cry. And yet she is sobbing so hard her body jerks. She is a short woman and the preacher is a tall

man, so her face, pressed hard against his shirt, comes just about as high as his armpit.

The congregation sings, and still the blond woman cries. They sing some more. The song master's hand beats the time as his glasses slide down his nose.

Here in this windowless room with the ugly, stained carpet, where the singing quavers and the floor quivers with even the lightest footstep, here is sanctuary.

No one calls this meeting place at 409 North Haskell Avenue a sanctuary. It hasn't the grandeur for that. Even the name of this place, Central Dallas Church of Christ, is simple.

Nothing is holy here either, except those gathered, and they would never make such a claim. There are also the Bibles, of course. They are holy, as it says on the cover in gold letters.

"If you don't have a Bible, we've got plenty of them," announces preacher Carey Dowl, who wears loafers without socks and blue jeans gone a bit pale at the knees. Once he was a bit of a showboat, a fancy preacher who had his eye on advancement. But he says his self-serving ways brought him low, real low.

"If it wasn't for the resurrection of Jesus Christ, I wouldn't be here today," he preaches, waving a big Bible, so well-thumbed that the pages are crinkled. "I'd be out there on the streets and nothing you have would be safe because I'd be trying to steal it."

The song master was once a homeless crack–cocaine addict. Now, from the looks of him, he's as solid as a German burgher. His black chin–beard is slightly frosted with gray and juts out bravely as his head goes back to belt out these a cappella hymns. The Church of Christ allows no instruments, which is just as well since this one couldn't afford them.

The worshipers number about fifty, including children. Most are African American, with some Hispanics and some whites. Dinner, donated by suburban churches, is served free every Sunday. Few who come to eat at twelve-thirty stay to pray at the one-thirty service. One who did and was saved has testified today.

"I'm selfish about Jesus," said George Clayton, a father of

five who said he tried to blow his brains out on a Saturday night some months ago but was too doped up to do it right. "If you see me on the street now, I'm going to be talking about Jesus Christ."

Mr. Dowl, whom everyone calls Carey, and his wife, Sophia, have worked in this mission supported by the Park Cities Church of Christ for almost three years. From the poverty of the setting and the sparsity of the congregation, it might seem that they've made no great progress.

But Carey and Sophia measure differently—not in the incremental progress of those things seen but in the eternal triumph of those things unseen. "I don't care how people look or how they smell," Carey said. "I care what's inside of them."

The singing ends, and this time, the blond woman is ready to speak. Her face is doughy and splotched from the crying; her voice is clotted.

"I was saved in this church three months ago, but I haven't been coming," she starts tentatively. "The devil's been after me. He got me twice," she says, her voice fading so low it almost can't be heard.

She gives the details. It is clear even from this short telling that her life is a tangled, knotted mess of problems. Helping her won't be a short-term project. Any rational person would back away fast, shake her hand, and say "God bless."

Mr. Dowl encircles her rounded shoulders with one long arm and draws her close. He looks sadly into the faces before him.

"I stand here guilty.

"Folks, we got to get closer. This is a good woman. We've got to surround her."

It is a little congregation on a rough side of town. But there is something special here. Something holy.

Chapter 16

What's True, What's False, and What's Religion

❧❧❧

A S MY REPORTING continued, I learned to pause before discarding what looked like nonsense. And as I did, my ideas about reality began to change even more. The intellectual, logical, reasonable A-leads-to-B-leads-to-C thinking that seemed so reliable began to wobble just a little. I'll give you one example.

I have always had disdain for those cloyingly sweet semireligious phrases that people use to soothe themselves when all seems lost. For instance, when something terrible happens and everyone is moaning with good reason, some cheery soul always pops up with the assurance that "everything works out for the best in the end." I hate that sentiment. How can anybody think something so totally untrue? Did everything work out for the best in the Holocaust? Did everything work out for the best for millions of Africans who've starved to death? Does everything work out for the best for the children who are burned, clubbed, stabbed, and crushed to death by parents every day? No and no and I can give you a hundred examples of no.

So one day, I was talking to the chaplain at the local children's hospital. I asked him about that statement. What does he say to people who use such transparently false reasoning? He replied that he says nothing to counter their claim or to redirect them into more reasonable channels. In fact, he doesn't think the statement is nonsense at all. "What they're expressing is hope," he said. "And hope is always a good thing."

The utter gravity with which he defended that trite phrase caused me to realize that I was totally wrongheaded. I'd taken that sentiment at face value and misunderstood it completely. I had dismissed it as silly and saccharine because I understood only the most surface meaning of what people were expressing.

That realization gave me the strangest feeling. It was as though my universe trembled just the tiniest bit, just enough to signal once again that I wasn't as smart as I thought I was. What other profundities had I tossed off with such unchallenged and misguided arrogance?

I wanted to know what the devout believed, why they believed it, and how it affected their lives. For instance, whenever someone would say that God talked to them, I would ask, "What did He sound like? How did you know it was Him?" Those felt like impertinent questions, wiseass challenges. But I put them out with complete seriousness, and, somewhat to my surprise, nobody balked at answering.

When religious people said strange things, such as "God finds me parking places," I didn't have to gently and kindly move to the next topic as though they were idiots who would only embarrass themselves if allowed to continue. Such people were neither as fragile nor as defensive as they are often thought to be. Most of them knew they were being strange, and some were pretty puzzled themselves. Far from defensive, some were eager to examine the matter.

On a two-week trip to Jerusalem, I challenged one of my Christian traveling companions so often that she took up the game and said we would put her faith to a test. Ann Garner had forgotten her bathing suit, she told me as we stood checking into the lobby of a nice hotel. Ann's back was aching, and she desperately wanted to soak it in the hot springs. Because she was serving Him and her request was pure, God would provide a bathing suit she could afford, she told me. Israel is an expensive place, but she said she would find something for well under fifty dollars. "See that store across the lobby?" Ann asked. "I'm going to go in there, and there will be a suit I can afford."

"Have you already looked in that store?" I asked her suspiciously. No, she said. We would go there together. I had to check on my bags, I said, but "I will come back and when I do, we'll put this to the test."

I walked perhaps twenty feet toward the elevators when Ann whooped and yelled my name. She was laughing and obviously triumphant. "I have my suit!" she shouted.

An Irish tourist had overheard me say that I'd be back to put something to the test. She had asked Ann what I meant. Hearing that my traveling companion needed a suit, the woman volunteered her own.

"It doesn't count as a miracle if you go around begging people to let you wear their bathing suits," I said scornfully.

"I didn't beg. I didn't say a word about wearing her suit. I just answered her question," Ann said. "I told you God would provide."

I sighed. Then I laughed. It didn't make a believer of me, but . . . it was a bathing suit. What could I say? I could say that God ought to be spending His time doing better things. I put that to Ann, who blithely assured me, "He does other things, too."

But, in truth, it wasn't the bathing suit that really impressed me. Who could say what that meant? To Ann, it meant that God heard her prayers. It was one of a long string of answered prayers that bolstered her faith. For her it was a petite miracle, a minor instance when God intervened. Later she explained her elaborate, complicated system of intricate beliefs. Forces have to come together in a certain way for God to answer a prayer, she told me. But we ought to continue to ask for what we need when we are earnestly trying to serve Him, she said, because we never know when the circumstances are right for us to get the answer we want.

But for me, the appearance of the bathing suit was an oddity, a coincidence, a novelty act. I've repeated the story to a number of other people. Most laugh. None has been convinced by it, as far as I know. I doubt that miracles, petite or grand, push many observers over into faith—unless they are the actual recipients of the miracle—because the miracle itself is a personal event that matches the faith that produced it. I didn't have the faith before the bathing suit, and I didn't have it after the bathing suit. Ann, on the other hand, did have it before and after. And she would have kept the faith whether the suit had appeared or not.

That, in fact, is the lesson of the bathing suit that stayed with me most poignantly. As she talked about going into the store, I asked her, "If there is a suit in there, you're going to thank God for answering your prayer. But if there isn't are you going to blame Him?"

"No," she said. "I won't blame Him."

"So that's a great deal for God, isn't it?" I said. "He gets the credit either way."

Such faith gave God an easy out. He never had to prove up anything. With her lackadaisical, God-excusing attitude, we would never know whether He was good at answering her prayers because she didn't keep account of how many times He failed her. At the time, I thought that quite a devastating observation. It seemed to put her and God and faith in the proper sort of quicksand.

But now I'm not so sure. In my quick egotism, I may have altogether missed the meaning of what my patient friend was trying to show me.

Perhaps keeping a running tally on God is not the way to comprehend what He's doing. Could it be that my friend didn't hold God to account for the same reason my husband didn't hold me to account for my failings? Could it be that she had some relationship with God that caused her to believe His performance on one or two or a hundred thousand occasions was a poor measure of His love for her? And if she did, what was that relationship like?

As a religion reporter, I shifted my focus. I stopped being so fixated on "the facts as I saw them" and began to focus on what they meant in people's lives. Partly I did that for my own benefit. I wanted to know what worked and what didn't. I wanted to find God myself, and so I listened with special purpose to people who said they had found Him.

I began to realize that what affects people is not what "really happens" but how they perceive what happens. People who are deeply spiritual see life's reality in a radically different way from people who aren't. Out of that comes some great stories and some great results. If you focus only on whether their beliefs are literally and provably true, you miss the power and the essence of really amazing stories.

We hear spiritual people talk about what God has done, and we immediately begin to see them as childlike. Our condescending attitude causes us to cut them off, to dismiss them as strange and unlike normal people. We nod and smile and move on without ever asking them what they mean. We assume that we know.

After years of trying not to, I still do it. Just the other day, I was talking to a ninety-two-year-old woman. She lives alone on a tiny income, forgotten by most of the world. Days and days go by without a single person calling or coming to see her. Her husband and both her children are dead. She can no longer attend church and many of the people who remember her from church are dead. She said, "The

Lord has been so good to me. I just don't know how people who don't know Him survive."

"Isn't that true," I murmured soothingly. And soon I hung up. All my life I have heard old people talk about the good Lord. It's easy to dismiss her reality. But what is she talking about? Maybe she is only repeating what a pious woman should. Perhaps she is merely imagining some presence, conjuring up an imaginary comforter. She will never be able to prove anything. But here's the point I have reluctantly begun to understand. She can't prove God, but she doesn't have to because her life bears her out.

Here's a woman who has lost everyone she loved. She is lonely beyond comprehension. And yet, she once comforted a younger man by saying that life just gets better as you get older. What does that woman know that the rest of us don't? Whatever it is, words can't contain it or capture it. And even so, it is real enough to her that it holds her up in life's hardest days. It empowers her. I don't know all the ways it does that, but I do know one. It changes how she sees reality. And her change in perception makes all the difference. Even if God doesn't exist, He has done a mighty work in her life.

We secularists generally dismiss that change in perception as an illusion, a way of hiding from the truth. But we make a big mistake. When I was in graduate school, one of the most important things I learned came out of a research course. The professor said that whenever you are trying to determine whether a conclusion or a course of action is correct, the first order of business is to question the premise. If there is a mistake, it's most likely to be found at the starting point.

The mistake secularists make when talking about God is in the premise. We believe that we know what is real. So when spiritual people give us their stories, we say that they aren't in touch with reality. We think of reality as a static condition. We speak of it as the "hard" reality. But, in fact, there is no such thing. Every reporter, whose job is to deal with such realities, knows the truth of that and must fight against the "softness" of reality in every story.

As a reporter, I listened to the stories of religious people without passing any judgment on the truth of their claims about God. When someone would claim that her truth was the only truth and everyone else's was false, I would say nothing. Pressed to take a side, I'd tell the truth. "I'm not close enough to God to know what He does or doesn't do."

But one thing was perfectly clear: Even if God doesn't exist, He is an enormously potent reframer of reality. When my religion reporting began, I couldn't bring myself to give God any stronger affirmation than that. He might not be real, but believing in Him is enormously useful. If that sounds too cold-bloodedly pragmatic, forgive me. Ours is a pragmatic age.

One year I interviewed a woman who had lost four of her five children in a car accident that also killed her father. She told an amazing story of God intervening in her life to show care and love. That story helped her survive. I wrote it straight without questioning whether God really did the things she said He did. Some people thought the story was giving a free ride to religion's most outlandish side, but others understood the point perfectly. The unendurable had occurred, and she was still on her feet. Those were journalistic truths. How she did it was the religion story, and to my mind that was far more interesting and enlightening than any inconclusive probing of God's existence ever could be.

SECTION 4

The hardest lesson of my new religious life: Don't judge

Chapter 17

Just the Kind of Church I Dreaded

S AY YOU RE TWENTY-SIX years old, tall, good-looking, athletic. You're playing a little softball with the church team one day when a ball comes your way. You go for it. A guy in your Bible study goes for it, too. Your heads butt.

He gets a little cut on his forehead.

Your skull is crushed.

Doctors think you'll die, suffer brain damage, or end up blind.

If you're most guys, you'll have some fleeting doubt about this having been completely in accordance with God's gracious plan for your young life.

Won't you?

"Not at all," says King Harrell, still good-looking and athletic seven years after the accident. He has a few faint scars on his forehead, and he can no longer smell or taste. God used the accident to get his attention, Mr. Harrell says, and now God also uses the aftereffects.

"When I go through a department store and someone says, 'Here, smell this perfume,' I tell them why I can't, and I can just share Christ with them right there. It's kind of God's way of using something bad for His glory."

I met King Harrell on one of my earliest projects as a religion reporter. I hadn't been on the beat long before the managing editor asked me to do a series about a megachurch led by a pastor who is among the Southern Baptists' most conservative leaders. It was as though he had figured out what I most feared and assigned it. "Take all the time you need. Really get into it," he said.

This seventeen-thousand-member church is known all over town for the high-profile way it does business. Like many big, fast growing, baby boomer churches, it employs sophisticated marketing techniques to bring in the members. Everything is lavishly done. The building's central atrium and fountain cause it to resemble a shopping mall. The Christmas pageant is famous for the hundreds of elaborately costumed cast members. Young people travel all over the world in its mission trips.

The combination of conservative Bible-based teaching, glitzy productions, and full-service programs for children bring so many people in each Sunday that the church hires traffic cops to handle the crush. Since I did the story, the church has raised more than $35 million to build a newer, bigger, even more lavish church. The amount is said to be the biggest ever raised by a church building fund. The fund-raising company that helped was so astonished that they took out an ad touting their own achievement.

I spent months working on the series. I attended Sunday morning and Sunday night. I went to Wednesday-night prayer meetings. I sat through Bible classes and luncheons. I followed believers around the city. I spent hours talking to them on the phone.

All my old churchy feelings came flooding back. I stood belting out hymns filled with images once so familiar that I hardly thought about them, and now so strange: the blood that washes away sins, the Creator who sent His son to die, the God who walks and talks. Listening with a reporter's distance, it seemed so ancient and odd to see people crunching wafers they called Christ's body, drinking grape juice they called his blood.

But I also listened without distance, and sometimes it swept me away again. Memories came washing out of gullies I'd forgotten existed. And it wasn't all bad. I turned my face toward those cocksure male preachers filled with their loud certainties, and I remembered how safe that can make a woman feel. The closed-in sweetness of such good fellowship, the nodding, hand-shaking, dressed-up simplicity of being in such a well-intentioned, secure place lulled and calmed me.

I didn't agree with a lot of what I heard. On the Fourth of July, when the military officers among the congregation came marching to the front to be honored for their service to the country, I was shocked to see a church melding symbols of war and symbols of God so deliberately. When the preacher admonished his congregation to listen to those leaders who had their ears close to the heart of God, he seemed to be implying that he placed himself among them. I marveled that any man would raise himself so high.

But I liked the people I met. They were high-spirited, high-energy, warm-hearted, trying-to-be-good people. Every time I was with them I went away feeling more high spirited, high energy, and warm hearted myself. I was a bit surprised to find that I so enjoyed these church people. But I shouldn't have been surprised. When I had last been among them, I was so focused on their answers that I didn't realize the value of their questions. They were asking the same questions I was. Who is God? What are we here for? Where do we go next? These questions rule their lives and mine. Our differences were in the answers we found, and in our certainties. They were certain that they had found the Way, the Only Way. I was certain of nothing.

But one of the things I found out pretty early in my research was that many of their answers weren't as uniform as one might think. The church looked monolithic but, people being what they are, they listened, nodded, and often believed what they pleased. For instance, in a church filled with smart, well-educated, adept career women, the preachers called for men to lead and women to follow. Women were almost never seen behind the pulpit or even sitting on the dais among the men. If a family was called forward to speak to the church, the wife stood a few steps back with the children.

The women in the congregation supported those policies. But, privately, many didn't embrace them. Several told me they believed the church would change that stance as time went on. Others said they disagreed but didn't think it was worth making an issue of. After one young Bible-waving preacher went on for some time about how firmly he was in charge of his wife, I mentioned his comments to two other young ministers. They laughed and exchanged a look. "He can say that all he wants," one of them said, "but I know his wife. He's not pushing her around."

The one area where I was certain the church did speak in one voice was the very area where I doubted them most. That was in the need to proselytize. If anybody in that church had the slightest doubt that they and Christians like them were the only folks God was going to save, I never heard them speak. Everybody seemed to agree that it was the job of a Christian to comb the highways and byways looking for sinners who could be drawn into the fold. God leaves Christians on earth so they can bring others to Christ, the senior pastor told his congregation. "When you get to heaven, someone is going to ask who you brought with you," he said one Sunday. As departing church members walked toward the street, banners reminded them of their seven-day-a-week job: "You are now entering the mission field."

"Even you as children can tell your friends," said Joanie Buster, the executive pastor's wife, to her class of kindergarten and first-grade new Christians.

Deacon Mike Fechner and his wife, Laura, left tracts at restaurants with the server's tip. Deacon Paul Cheek, who believes God sets up "divine appointments" every day, always carried a softcover booklet in his back pocket titled "How Do You Know You're a Christian?"

Susanne Forbes Dicker brought 150 visitors to the church every year. She told three to five people a day about Jesus. Asked her occupation, she answered, "I'm a top producer for God and a broker-Realtor."

I shudder at the thought of behaving as these people do. It's as good a reason for refusing to sign up with their Jesus as any I know. But I also know very well where they are coming from. Sometimes it is guilt that drives the proselytizers. I remember the preachers of my childhood warning that people were going to spend eternity in hell if we didn't get out there and tell them about Jesus. "Their blood is on your hands," they thundered at us. That's the dark side.

But there's a light side, too. Some Christians, and King Harrell is obviously one of them, feel God has given them a gift so wonderful that everybody ought to have it. The experience they call a relationship with Christ so transforms them that they struggle endlessly to share what they have with people who don't believe in it and don't want it. It's easy for nonbelievers to say nothing real has happened to these people. It's easy to shrug off their stories.

But the people in that church have something wonderful. As I had once in a similar setting, many were sincerely looking for God and sincerely trying to serve Him. How could I say they weren't doing what the Almighty was telling them? The only thing I'm real clear about is that I'm not in close enough contact with Him to say what He wants people to do. Maybe some of those people are being drugged by religion, as my former-pastor friend suggested—but drugs can heal.

Every Sunday, not far from Susanne, sat another woman whom I'll call Sally. Somebody pushed her toward going to the church, and her life has been immeasurably better since, she told me.

Sally is a lovely, stylish woman in her midthirties. She has been married once and divorced. She has also had four abortions. For her they were nothing more than the logical way to get rid of a problem. Then one Sunday, depression caused her to go to the church. The preaching against abortion she heard there caused her to go to counseling for women who have aborted babies. The peace and healing she found in Christian promises of forgiveness have transformed her life, she told me one day as we sat in her apartment with Christian music playing in the background.

She said she feels clean. She said she has hope for a better future. She said that the self-loathing that caused her to let men treat her as though she was nothing more than a piece of jewelry on their arm has abated. That's a pretty good gift.

I had no counter to testimonies such as hers and King Harrell's, and as I had feared, it wasn't long before they started to work on me. Wouldn't it be nice to come to this big, pretty church and sing some nice hymns and make some sweet, well-intentioned friends? Weren't they right about the power of God? Hadn't I seen it in my own life? Why was I so stubborn and prideful? Just as my former-pastor friend predicted, the old ways were drawing me back.

What was to keep me from going? The intellectual freedom that had meant so much to me in college had taken me only so far. Adulthood had shown me the fallacy of thinking that intellectualization would provide life's most important answers. The judgments I had leveled at my fellow church members had lost the edge that youth gives. I was safely and happily married. My life outside the church was as tame and blameless as the lives of most of the people inside the church. What did I have to lose?

One afternoon I went for a walk with a friend who is the widow of a Baptist minister. She no longer goes to church or believes much of what the church teaches. But she knew exactly what I was feeling. Why wouldn't I fall in line, sit in the pews happily, and then go out to convert my friends? I asked rhetorically. I believed they really had something. So why did I ruffle like an angry turkey when one of them asked "Do you know Jesus?" I could barely answer that question in a civil manner, much less ask it of someone else. The longer I stayed among the megachurch folks the more raw I felt about being myself.

But I had gone to the right person for counsel. When I told her that I sometimes told the Baptists I was a backslider, she ruffled herself. *Backslider* is a term Baptists use for Christians who fall away from the faith. I said it jokingly as a way of putting the questions aside. But my friend would have none of it. "You're not backslidden, and it's not true to say so." Pandering to other people's ideas to such an extent was harmful to one's sense of self, she said. It was also cowardly, and she wasn't going to let me get by with behavior she considered so unworthy of me.

Old habits, however, were pulling hard. Other people were seeking God in a certain way and setting standards for how God seekers ought to behave. I didn't know anything about seeking God in my own way, and I did know a lot about molding myself to others' expectations. In truth, I am not a rebel. I like blending into the crowd. I hate breaking rules so much that when I get into the nine-item checkout line at the grocery, I have to restrain myself from compulsively counting and recounting my groceries. I like reassuring myself that I'm doing everything right. So, I asked her, shouldn't I accept their ideas, sink gratefully into defined holiness, and run around town pushing these acceptable ideas on other people as a good Christian ought to?

My friend didn't answer my question. Instead she shunted me toward another path. "Lots of people are willing to tell others how to be saved," she said. "Not so many are willing to live it." If she had offered excuses for me, I would have rejected them as an easy way out—and everybody knows God doesn't allow anyone to take the easy way. The Baptists had activated my perfectionism and my stubborn willingness to ignore myself in favor of other people's truths. But her observation set me right again. It wasn't a cop-out. Living is

harder than telling. I knew that. Nagging myself over my unwillingness to say things I didn't feel right about was putting my efforts in
the wrong direction. My task is to learn to live authentically, and ig-
noring my own feelings wasn't the way to do that.

Occasionally one of the megachurch's many preachers would
mention that I ought to join the church myself. Despite my uneasiness, I never even considered it. What they have is good for them, and
sometimes I heard things that were good for me, too, but without a
reporter's cloak of objectivity, I'd never fit in there. I'd have to squelch
more of myself than I can. And more to the spiritual point, I would
have to squelch more of myself than I think God wants me to. They
think that following the teachings of the preacher and believing that
one interpretation or another of the Bible is the last word on all spiritual matters is the way to God. I don't. For me, such thinking led to
a dead end. So I am taking a different road. Maybe we will end up in
the same place. Maybe not.

Chapter 18

Mad at God

I HAD SO much anger toward God that getting close to Him inevitably started an argument. He was mismanaging the world
completely. He was letting humans suffer horribly. His Book was
full of lies. His people were full of bad advice. Every time I thought
about Him honestly, I got mad all over again. The rules I had grown
up with—fearing God, obeying God, and accepting what the
preacher said about God—were so much easier than this new quest.
The rules kept questions at bay, forced anger underground. Now it
was in the open.

Luckily, religion was my job. Some days I was so full of churchy talk that I wanted to gag. But the next day, I had to face it all again. And because I couldn't escape, I learned.

During a Yom Kippur service one year, I listened to the rabbi tell the story of Abraham and his son Isaac. The story says that God told Abraham to take his beloved son, Isaac, to the top of the mountain and sacrifice him as an offering. As they gather wood, the son innocently asks his father why they aren't bringing along an animal to sacrifice. Abraham answers that God will provide. The story ends with Abraham about to bring the knife down on the boy when God's voice stops him. They see a ram caught in nearby bushes. God directs them to sacrifice the animal He has provided instead of the human child.

I have always hated this story. God is cruel and capricious in it. As is so often the case in the Bible, He values nothing but His own vanity. He doesn't care who gets hurt, just as long as He gets his due. I feel the same way about the story of poor Job. God wanted to prove something to his enemy, Satan, and so he sacrificed a pitiful little man who was dumb enough to love Him. I don't even approve of everything Jesus did. He was sometimes quite the smart aleck. Where did he come off talking to his mother that way?

I heard these stories so early in life that I can't remember when I didn't know them. My opinion has never changed, and I have never heard anyone voice what everyone must know is the truth about them. We all sat there nodding while the preachers told the Abraham story as though God was perfectly right and wonderful for sparing Isaac. Then we all stood up and sang a hymn of praise and went home. Never has anyone stood up and said, "That's an awful story."

But this time, I was in for a surprise. Not everybody treats the Bible like the churchgoers of my childhood did. After the rabbi finished making his points about the story, he threw the discussion open for the congregation. And they tore that old tale apart.

One objected that God had been cruel to jeopardize Isaac in such a way and declared that the boy was probably marked the rest of his life by knowing that his own father would kill him. Another questioned how God, who professed to love Abraham so much, could play such a dirty trick on him. They analyzed and criticized. Others in the congregation defended God, but nobody acted as though thinking

He was a dirty double-dealer made you a dreadful sinner. At the end of the service, the rabbi didn't resolve the issue neatly by making some authoritative pro-God pronouncement, as I imagined he would. He just reflected on the need for people to puzzle over the story. I'd never heard such discussion.

The Jews took God on as if He were some kind of uncle who didn't always get it right. I would learn later that Israel, the name given to Jacob, another biblical patriarch, after his wrestling match with God, means "one who fights with God." The Jews in the service were living up to the name—at least verbally. I was shocked, but also delighted. Their arguments were the most authentic grappling with God that I'd ever heard. Paradoxically, they brought Him closer and made the stories seem more relevant than any of the head nodding and amening I was accustomed to.

So emboldened, I argued with God, too. I began to reject whatever I wanted to—or perhaps it would be more accurate to say that I stopped hiding from what I really thought. When I didn't believe something, I grappled with it and with the God I thought was putting it forth. I accused Him of not existing when I felt like it. I didn't make a career out of shouting at the heavens, but when you cover the religion beat you have plenty of time to think about God, and I never had to think about Him much before I hit on something I didn't like. If He was offended by my effrontery, He never let me know.

It did sometimes seem that messages were coming back. They came in the form of understandings—often ones I didn't particularly like. My new ability to argue with God opened me up. While my daring allowed me to be a bit bolder about exploring things that I didn't believe, it also allowed me to move toward things I did believe. All my life I had lived at one extreme or the other. Hot or cold. Love or hate. If I couldn't take a position, I stayed neutral, out of the fray altogether. Now I was exploring a new way of being. I was learning to go my own direction. That meant testing the ground with each step. Sometimes it was hard enough to stand on. Sometimes I sank in the mud.

One of my big arguments with God was over the feeling that I had to be like the megachurch people to have a relationship with Him. It made me furious to be so plagued by the thought that they were right and I was wrong. I blamed God for that. Watching them in action convinced me that they had something to do with God. So if they did, why didn't He let them know that everyone couldn't be carbon copies of themselves?

I knew that the megachurch people wouldn't hesitate to judge my way of finding God as wrong. And so it seemed reasonable for me to be able to judge their way. But I couldn't. One of the reasons is that, to my surprise, they had helped feed my nascent desire to have God. A conservative, some would say fundamentalist, church was the last place I would have expected to encounter the kind of God who would have anything to say to me. But I'm pretty sure He was there. He was telling other people very different things. But He also had a big message for me and it was a hard one: Don't judge. I knew for sure the megachurch folks weren't getting that message. For them, it was part of Christianity itself to believe that they were saved and nobody else was. But for me, it wasn't.

I already knew Jesus had said you shouldn't judge lest you be judged likewise, which makes not judging sound like a kind of insurance policy. I always thought that was about the whole of the matter. I agreed with Jesus on that and tried not to judge any more than I had to. What that meant to me was that I shouldn't get too puffed up about myself when faced with other people's mistakes or wrongdoing. I didn't have too much trouble with that, except in one area.

I was quite likely to judge people harshly if they believed things about God that I thought were stupid. I also judged people who preached a lot of God and didn't behave as perfectly as I thought they should. That was a particularly cowardly kind of judgment because I was protected from being held to account by my refusal to declare anything. Church people, on the other hand, might not be much but at least they were brave enough to pick a side.

Still, I never felt too guilty about condemning my fellows in such ways. Then I went to the megachurch. There I realized I'd been wrong—not because it hurt them, but because it hurt me. It cut me off from what I need, which is more information about God.

I now think that judging carries a higher penalty than being judged by God at some future date. I think judging shuts your mind down and being judged likewise means that other people will shut their minds down to you. And that matters. It matters because we're in this together. Each of us is looking for God, and none of us is very good at finding Him. I think Jesus said don't judge because there's hardly a surer way to cut the pipeline between you and God than to judge and reject other people's religious experiences. Now, some people are going to read that and immediately think that attitudes like mine would allow heresy to break out all over. But I'm not convinced that any human knows God well enough to know what is or isn't the proper representation of Him—and anyone who says they do ought to be most suspect.

In the last three years, I've found that when I can bring myself to loosen up in the face of a faith that repels me, I almost always see some new part of God. It's hard to do the loosening up. The desire to judge others must be hardwired into the human psyche. Survival at its most basic level can depend on the ability to judge who is dangerous and who is safe, who lies and who tells the truth, who loves and who only pretends to.

But the whole point of the spiritual life is to go beyond life at its most basic level. Judging and rejecting other people's testimonies and versions of God keeps us earthbound like no other habit we have. It restricts us to only our own little peephole. I'm not saying that an exclusionary faith can't be a strong one. But why shut out any possible manifestation of God? It's hard enough to figure Him out with every available resource. What hope do we have if we restrict ourselves?

The first reward from my new resolve was substantial. In judging the megachurch and its people, I was judging my own childhood experience of faith. And that judgment cut me off from my past. Without a past, what do we stand on? When I opened up, I began to see the gifts my childhood faith had given me.

As an example, Baptists learn a lot of Bible verses, and I can still call up a good number of them. That beautiful old King James poetry rings in my head. I'm glad to have the words and I'm glad to have the wisdom of the verses. I've had something of a grudge against the Bible for a long time now, but those verses are still hidden in my heart, just as the Bible said they would be. And they come rising up at the strangest times.

Baptists believe that once Jesus saves you, you're always saved. Some of them would like to take that back when one of their members strays as far as I have. But I learned that promise too young to forget it, and experience has borne it out. God does seem to have stuck with me far better than I've stuck with Him.

Perhaps the most important thing my fundamentalist childhood gave me was a sense of how strong a relationship with God can be. It gave me a continuing credulity about the possibility that the supernatural might be at work in the lives of humans. It laid the groundwork for the search I'm on now, for the certainty that I can have a covenant with God that applies to me, even if it suits no one else.

And so following my don't-judge rule, I have to hold myself in tension. I don't agree with a lot of people's ideas. In fact, if I talk with anybody long enough, I'll probably find some way that I disagree. It's possible that I don't think of God in the way any other person on earth does. Maybe He hasn't shown Himself to me in exactly the way He has shown Himself to anybody else. But maybe He has shown them something equally as compelling or even more compelling. Maybe they know more of God than I do. Maybe I'll never get to the place where they are. But knowing God is not a competitive sport.

I have to respect that they, too, have access to God. That's so hard. I want to be God's favorite child. But I'm only one of the loved ones. In that statement is the tension again. They are loved. But so am I. So I have the authority to reject for myself what they think He is telling them. In fact, I must reject it if it isn't what God seems to be telling me.

Does there ever come a time when the rule of nonjudgment breaks down? Of course. If others think it's okay to kill children because God needs a sacrifice, I can judge that. In the case of their condemnation of homosexuals, I can say that I think it contradicts Christ's strong message of compassion, and that I won't believe they're right until God Himself tells me. But arguing those points probably doesn't change anybody's mind.

Chapter 19

The Don't-Judge Rule Gets a Hard Test

❧❦❧

T HE EVENING I attended a service led by the Reverend Ian Paisley was a test of my new ideas about how far tolerance ought to go. That was the week Diana, Princess of Wales, was buried, and Paisley lived up to his reputation as the fiery, bigoted leader of Northern Ireland's most militantly anti-Catholic political party.

I'd just come from London, where I covered the princess's funeral. For hours I waited in Kensington Gardens amid millions of somber, sometimes sobbing people. I watched London fall into an eerie quiet on the Friday before her burial. Grim-faced people with flowers in their hands had streamed silently toward the gardens where millions of bouquets were left as a tribute. I stood in the streets late that night as the lighted hearse rolled past and then again the next morning as it proceeded toward Westminster Abbey for the funeral. The whole world was in mourning, it seemed. But not Reverend Paisley, he wasn't in mourning. He just saw Diana's death as a chance to make a point about how right he was.

That Sunday evening after Diana was buried, he reminded his congregation that he was the only person invited to the wedding of Prince Charles and Lady Diana who didn't attend. His reason? A representative of the Catholic Church had also been invited, and Reverend Paisley didn't like it. The divorce and the early death of Diana were no surprise to him, the black-coated preacher told his flock of elderly parishioners that evening. "Nothing blessed by Rome can come to a good end," he said.

Martyrs' Memorial Free Presbyterian Church, which Reverend Paisley leads, is an austere building. Three huge iron doors seal the sanctuary before each service. Inscribed with Bible verses and Martin

Luther's thesis, the doors have no handles on the outside. So if you arrive late, you can't get in. That's a nice metaphor for the religion preached there. But it also has a practical aspect. The IRA boys with bombs and automatic weapons can't count on a full sanctuary with open doors.

The high pulpit is flanked by a gray brick wall. Mounted in dark letters are the words, "We preach Christ crucified." The ladies wearing hats and their Sunday best gave the gathering a genteel, old-world feel. During their preacher's more hate-filled utterances some nodded slightly. The benches are hard, and the vast walls are unrelieved gray. It looks as much like a prison as any place I've ever been. As a reporter, I was thrilled to hear one of the world's most notorious warmongers on his home turf. The hoary old man in the high-necked black suit was the kind of character who populates a feature writer's dreams.

But underneath my reporter's glee were the old stirrings of the fundamentalist child I once was. He would seem an oddity offered up to my readers, but to me, Reverend Paisley was nothing new at all. He sounded so much like some of the men who instructed the religion of my youth that I felt as though I were in the sixties again. I can easily remember a time when lots of Baptists didn't consider Catholics Christians at all. What the Catholics called religion we called dark business. When John F. Kennedy won the presidency, many thought a pagan had taken over the White House.

The Reverend Paisley preached hell. And he preached it hard. He preached the blood of Jesus shed for wretched sinners. He preached against the prideful and those led astray by Satan's wiles. In the bare, cold room, he preached his way as the only way.

But this time, I wasn't buying it. "I hate this. I hate this. I hate this," I thought, looking around at the grim smugness of it all. And as for the preacher's words, "You're wrong," I thought. "You're wrong, and I don't have to believe a thing you say." I rejected it all with a push so fierce it surprised even me. And that was good. Half a world away from where my fight with that version of God began, I finally won the battle. As Ray Dykes would put it, I fired that sucker. It was as though my soul was finally freed. Recovering fundamentalist? Nope. I was over it. Recovered.

As I left, the people smiled and shook my hand. They gave me leaflets and told me I was welcome to be there. I had a meeting to attend at a nearby Catholic church. So I asked directions. You might have expected they would frown at the news that I was headed into the very vipers' nest they so despised. But no. They smiled and pointed and gave directions, made me repeat them back, did everything but get into their cars to take me there.

What did their pastor's hatefulness mean in contrast with their own graciousness? I can't tell you. But I knew what it reminded me of. When I was ten years old, we moved to a little town outside Charleston, South Carolina. Civil rights marches and protests raged all over the South. People were talking about integration of the schools, and white people were scared.

We lived in a little cottage behind a big old Southern mansion. They called our two-bedroom house Katy's Dollhouse because it was built as a playhouse for the rich little girl who once lived in the mansion. When we lived there the big house was occupied by a middle-aged woman and her mother. I remember the mother as a sweet old lady of grand manners who invited my mother and me up to the porch one day. We sat there listening to the honeyed accents of her worn voice. The birds sang in the background, the Spanish moss swayed from the trees. Life couldn't have been more lovely.

Then she began talking about the South's trouble and the honey in her voice hardened. "They want to let some filthy, black thing sit right there in the classroom with white children," she said. Filthy, black, thing. She hit the vowels in each of those words harder than usual, drew them out for special emphasis, dropped them slow and hard like pebbles plunking into a bucket. I'd heard people called niggers before but I'd never heard anybody speak with the kind of deep disgust and loathing that I heard in that sweet old lady's voice.

She felt herself to be greatly superior to others of God's children, and any threat to that notion caused a startling ugliness to contort her usually kind face. She would protect that illusion at any cost. Reverend Paisley and his followers have the same cause. She based hers on skin color. They base theirs on heritage and religion. But at the core, it's the same bigotry.

One of the people I met in Northern Ireland was a Protestant named Peter Hannon. He wrote a book called *Whose Side Is God On?*—a particularly apt question in Northern Ireland, where Christian labels define the combatants. But it's also important for us all as we grapple with right and wrong. Peter answered the question by deciding that perhaps God isn't on anyone's side. Perhaps God doesn't see things the way we do, and He's not interested in who wins and who loses. Perhaps, Peter wrote, God is more interested in dealing with each of us where we are and helping us grow as much as we can.

So I'm adopting that attitude. For me, Reverend Paisley's way of finding God is as wrong as anything could ever be. His insistence that I agree with him or go to hell is nothing more than his narrow interpretation. But maybe God speaks through that message to Mr. Paisley and to all the people in that congregation. Maybe lots of good comes out of it. If I'm humble enough about my own understanding, I can make that difficult turn. What it requires, however, is double humility. I must humbly reject Reverend Paisley's answer for myself, and with equal humility recognize that it might be exactly what God is offering Reverend Paisley.

What about the bad that comes out of it? Well, I won't blame God for that. I'll say that's merely Reverend Paisley and his followers trying to struggle their way to truth, just as I am. If they are wrong in some ways, I'm willing to wager that I'm wrong in others. It's not likely that any human ever gets it completely right when it comes to God.

If I had my choice I might never listen to a fundamentalist preacher again. Resisting the push and pull they set up in me is exhausting. But my job dictates otherwise, which is lucky for me. I suspect them in all sorts of ways. I think they have their own agenda. I think some of them puff themselves up into thinking they know more than they do. I think many claim a level of authority that is close to blasphemy. But maybe my arguments with God are blasphemy. Who but God can say? And to be fair, I also know fundamentalists who have what looks like a good, strong faith. They are a hard test, but if I stick with them, they are also almost invariably the source of some reward.

Not long ago, I had the chance to listen to a real soul winner. This guy heads one of the biggest and most powerful churches in America, and it was easy to see why. He pounded and thundered and shook his finger. He put it to them straight, and he put it to them often.

I was not in the mood to hear him out. It was the evening of a long day. I was cranky and tired and not feeling charitable. I sat in the back with my arms folded across my chest thinking, "You don't fool me for one minute, you old puffed-up windbag. You're up there striking poses, admiring your own show. You've got thousands of people on a roll and that's gone to your head just like it would anybody else's. Maybe God is speaking to you but from the looks of you, you'll be hard-pressed to hear Him above the roar of your own ego." The longer he went on, the more scornful I became. "You're not God's favorite little child any more than any of the rest of us. You're just uppity enough to run around acting like you are," I thought.

But I'm trying to get away from my own prejudices. So I unfolded my arms and unpursed my mouth and told myself to remember that I'm not God's favorite child either. This preacher was pushing my button by saying that I had to be like him to have any part of God. "I can have God if I want to," my mind was shouting back at him.

And about that time, the oddest thing happened. In the middle of a sermon that was totally foreign to what I believe, this world-class hell-fire-and-damnation preacher suddenly spoke right to me. At least it felt that way.

He said that a lot of Baptists were discussing whether or not God only elected to save certain people and had preordained that others would not be among the saved no matter what they did. Then, he said that he had the final, definitive answer to that question. He knew without a doubt which ones would be saved. His heavy old head was thrust forward, that finger was extended, and he roared out, "I'll tell you who. Whosoever will. That's who is going to be saved."

"Whosoever will." I was so sure that old preacher didn't mean that to apply to me that I laughed out loud. He'd just finished setting down all the rules that everyone has to follow. He said that the whole Bible, every word, must be believed literally as total truth and fact, and then he unwound it all with that one phrase, "Whosoever will." Whosoever will may come. That's all. That's out of the Bible as a matter of fact. No strings attached. Reach out for God and He will reach back. I couldn't have put my own thoughts better if I'd had all night. I thought, "Thank you, Jesus. I believe I will."

Chapter 20

The Don't-Judge Rule Goes Wobbly

O F COURSE, MY attempts not to judge don't always work
out so neatly. I try to keep my tendency to scoff under
tight control. I've recast it as a religious objective even.
But sometimes good intentions aren't enough to counter a voice in
my head that says more and more loudly, "This is baloney." I've heard
that voice on the most sacred occasions of orthodox religion, and I've
heard it when listening to the most revered of New Age gurus. I don't
know if that means I'm completely open-minded in my scoffing or
just equally closed to everyone's truth. I fight it, but sometimes I lose.
The evening I heard Betty Eadie speak was one of those times when
the strength of my judgments set up such a clamor that I went away
without having gained anything for myself. Here's a little bit of what
I wrote on that occasion.

Sometimes Betty Eadie sounded like a foot soldier for the
Republican Party. "I heard a rumor that it takes a village to
raise children. I hope that rumor isn't widely accepted, because
you know what? It takes a mother and a father, a family to
raise a child," the author of *Embraced by the Light* told a crowd
of about four hundred people.

Sometimes she sounded like an end-times Christian fundamentalist. "I saw the mountains as they melted down just as
hot chocolate would melt down."

Sometimes she sounded like a prophet sent by a New Age
women's magazine. "You have created every single moment of
your life. . . . We need to become who we truly are inside. . . .
God our Father wants us to have what our hearts desire."

Calling the audience's attention to her own flowing movements as a way to increase healing, Mrs. Eadie told them to avoid abrupt motions. "I was shown that movement, body movement is healing."

Regardless of content, her source of authority was always divine.

"This is not just a philosophy that I made up," the fifty-four-year-old former hypnotherapist said. Repeatedly she assured listeners, "I was shown this in my experience."

"My experience" refers to the four hours twenty-three years ago when, Mrs. Eadie says, she hemorrhaged after a hysterectomy and was clinically dead. During those four hours, she says, she hugged Jesus, talked with him, and was shuttled around various universes.

Near-death accounts, such as Mrs. Eadie's, are now so common that the experiences even have their own abbreviated label: NDE, short for "near-death experiences." Author Harold Bloom dubs people who say they've returned from death the shamans of our times. Mrs. Eadie is among those who dress the part. In Dallas, she wore a fringed doeskin dress complemented by a tiny matching pouch that hung from a shoulder strap. Half Sioux, she was raised on a reservation and credits her Native American heritage with giving her extra insight.

A mother of eight and grandmother of eleven, Mrs. Eadie writes and speaks in a sincere, artless way that delighted many in her mostly female audience. Many nodded as she called upon women to take over the spiritual leadership of their families. "God gave the woman an extra dose of spirituality because she is the one who carries life."

During the question-and-answer period, one woman rose to say she agreed that God is love, but she couldn't understand how Mrs. Eadie could say there is no hell. If nobody is held accountable for their sins, she asked, why did Jesus have to die?

Mrs. Eadie replied that her near-death experience didn't include hell. "I know [God] will not shock you out of your current belief systems but will use whatever you currently believe. So if you currently believe you have to go to hell to be punished and that he is a God to throw you into hell . . . if you believe that, then it will happen to you," she said, adding that she was speaking only of near-death experiences.

A man asked about near-death experiences that don't include Jesus. He was especially curious about one account, in which a man's spirit was greeted by Elvis. The author responded by saying God graciously gives us what we expect. "If you die and you do not believe in Him, He is gracious and such a loving God that He will allow you the experience that will make you the most comfortable. . . . If the most comforting person to you is Elvis, you can experience Elvis."

Far from being surprised at her revelations, several audience members felt confirmed in their own insights. Pressed for an example, one man mentioned coincidences. "You just have the feeling that there's got to be something behind them." He also mentioned prayers for parking places. They often get answered, he said, "but you've got to remember to ask in the right spirit."

What might that be? I wondered. Given that God is letting people suffer and die all over the earth, what spirit would it take for Him to intercede so that you didn't have to walk a few extra steps? But I didn't ask. Pushing people on spiritual matters rarely gets you anywhere.

I found that out on both sides of the equation. One evening, I listened to a Bible church preacher talk about how he believed Jesus was the only path to salvation but he didn't believe that people who had never heard of him would go to hell. God's grace would cover them, the preacher told me. Usually I just nod and write down what people say. But this was a social occasion, and so I replied with my own thought. Well then, I said, if I were a heathen chief I'd kill all the missionaries before they could tell anyone in my village about Jesus because the minute they start talking God's unconditional grace becomes quite conditional and some folks are going to hell. The preacher just looked at me blankly. I felt myself quite clever, but in a kind of nasty way. And it didn't do a bit of good.

Perhaps God was whispering in Mrs. Eadie's ear all the time. The people sitting around me believed in her totally. But the mixture of political commentary with spiritual truths made me doubt. Hillary Clinton's book, *It Takes a Village,* had just been released and every Republican around was saying, "It takes a family." Something about Mrs. Eadie's presentation also caused me to be skeptical. Maybe it was the way she bounced from topic to topic as though trying to cover every political hot button of the moment. Maybe it was that she seemed contrived, too pat and at the same time too eager for approval. The accounts of God's voice I believe are usually rather mundane. I find it easier to believe people when they aren't trying to make money and don't belong to any organization that makes such messages a badge of special status.

So where does my nonjudgment rule fit with my impression of Mrs. Eadie? She obviously had messages that many in her audience connected with. That I thought she was full of nonsense doesn't mean she was. My reaction reminds me of a conversation I once had with a local preacher about another preacher whose doctrine he disagreed with. After he finished telling me how wrongheaded he thought his rival was, I asked, "Well, if he's got it so wrong how do you square that with the idea that he's a Christian? Do you think he and God are in touch at all?"

The preacher answered with a laugh. "I think God uses him. And I think that if God can use him, maybe He can use me, too." So, I guess that's my attitude. I didn't think much of Mrs. Eadie's presentation, but that doesn't mean God isn't using her. I often don't think much of my presentations either. And maybe God is using me, too, in spite of how I come across or even how negatively others might perceive me.

In the end, however, my don't-judge rule is really quite practical and self-serving. On those occasions when my tendency to judge runs totally away with me, I get nothing for myself. I come away feeling unpleasantly self-satisfied, knowing nothing more than I did when I arrived, and feeling very much the prig.

To keep this chapter from having such a cast, I'll end with two examples that bolster me in my fight to keep undue judgments at bay. I was once interviewing the author of *The Celestine Prophecy.* That book is as far from fundamentalist Christianity as one can get, and some Christians were pretty upset about it. I'd heard that Southern

Christians were outspoken and nasty in attacking the book. So I asked James Redfield for some response. His answer was mild. People have different interpretations of God, he said. He wouldn't want to shut the fundamentalists up even when they were attacking him because they serve a good purpose. Their adherence to traditional ways of looking at things keeps us from moving forward faster than we should, he said.

His openness allowed him to slip completely free of being threatened by the mean things being said about him. It also gave me a clue about how different interpretations might benefit us all.

The second example has to do with a coworker who is an orthodox Christian. He and I disagree on religion about as much as two people can. One night we were debating how the Bible ought to be taken. And he said with some exasperation, "I don't know how anyone could say they are searching for God and then say they don't go by the Bible. The Bible is God's own words. We have them right here. Why would anybody who says they are seeking God ignore His own words?"

Now, until that moment it was as though we were speaking different languages. Although we were trying hard to communicate, I couldn't understand what a person could possibly get from his version of God. And I imagine he was thinking the same of me. I was reminded of the summation that journalist and wife of an Episcopal priest, Katie Sherrod, once gave of the primary dispute in religion today. "On one side are the people who want experience to inform Scripture. On the other side are the people who want Scripture to inform experience." That's about it. My coworker was on the second side and I was on the first. It didn't look as though we would ever meet.

Then the stalemate cracked. When he said with his voice rising, his hands outstretched for emphasis, "The Bible is God's own words. We have them right here. Why would anybody who says they are seeking God ignore His own words?" it was as though a shaft of light had suddenly come through the darkness. I saw that my friend with his literal, awesome Bible was able to touch the beauty and mystery of God in a way that I could barely conceive.

I'd been looking at our difference in a totally wrongheaded fashion. Maybe our divergence wasn't merely a difference in understandings that would be cleared up by knowing more about God. Maybe it wasn't that one of us was right and one of us was wrong. Our differences weren't perceptions; they were gifts.

He had a gift for penetrating deep into the majesty. No wonder he was frustrated and passionate in protecting that version of God. It would be a terrible thing to lose, and it looked to him as though the whole of modern culture were against him. We will never agree on an enormous number of core issues. There's no reason to try for that. But if I can obey my don't-judge rule fastidiously enough, I might just get a glimpse of what he sees.

SECTION 5

*I begin to hear
that God is abundant
and the value of my
don't-judge rule
becomes clear*

Chapter 21

The God Around Us

ꞌꞌꞌ

O NE CHRISTMAS A 216-store grocery chain in England broadcast carols and a sermon by the archbishop of Canterbury. As shoppers rushed through the stores, grabbing and pushing, the Most Reverend George Carey's voice came over loudspeakers with a one-minute message. According to the Associated Press story, the store's bar code scanners bleeped remorselessly through the service, "even as the archbishop was heard to say: 'God's love for all of us is not shut up in a separate box marked, "Religion." It's not confined to what goes on in church. It's for all of us, all the time, in every aspect of life.'"

No wonder nobody is going to church in England. Saying God is everywhere and available to all of us is like giving away your trump card. You can't build an institution with that kind of thinking. But can you build a faith?

Experience seemed to be teaching me that you can. Once I began to pay attention it seemed that life was administering one religious lesson after another about grace, about reality, and about God. It was hard to trust mere experience, but once I did, it delivered. I was beginning to live not according to what someone told me was true, but to what I believed myself. I was beginning to base my life not on speculation that someone else proclaimed to be truth, but on my experience. I was going forward with some wariness, but I was going forward.

Each step of the way, I was testing experience. How do I know experience is valid? I pay attention. I notice what effect the experience has on me. I ask myself if I am becoming more who I want to be. Do I feel more peace, more happiness, more ease in the world?

I used the test with everyday events and when confronted with religious mandates. For example, I had been puzzling over the role of prayer. At about that time, I read a book that recommended praying for others without adding the "Thy will be done" ending that is common. Try to move God, the book said. You can change His mind with the passion and the frequency of your prayers.

So I tried it. When I wanted something for someone else, I prayed about it and then I prayed about it again. Throughout the day, I returned to that longing and begged God to provide what I thought this person needed. I amplified on my reasons. I stroked my desire. I imagined the fulfillment of my prayer. It was awful.

I was basically pestering God constantly. I had become a whining, carping, helpless little nag. I won't say that this idea would work out so badly for everyone, but for me it was terrible. I don't like bending anyone to my will, much less God. Fixing myself so stubbornly on what I wanted—even when it was something I wanted for someone else—wasn't good for me. It was so bad for me that even remembering it makes me shudder. So I stopped. There was a time when I would have forced myself to keep doing what was repugnant to me, but no more. I know some people say that such begging is exactly what God wants from me, but I am convinced it is not.

Oddly enough, testing experience in this way often throws me back to the answer my former boyfriend gave when I asked why he thought people were put on earth. He said when he died God was going to ask him only one question: "Did you have a good time?" I thought his answer was typically hedonistic and absurd, but now I wonder. If during the worst days of my life I had asked myself whether I was having a good time and I had taken my feelings seriously, I would have backed away from a lot of mistakes. I would have kept my footing instead of being swept away by what I was supposed to be enjoying. In fact, if I had asked myself whether I was really having a good time with that boyfriend, I would have wrenched myself away long before I did and been a better person for it.

Most people don't believe there is a connection between doing good and being happy. But I am more and more convinced of it. Somerset Maugham thought so, too. In one of his short stories, he wrote that doing good "is the purest form of happiness there is." Is having a good time and being happy the same thing?

It makes me uncomfortable to think that my reprobate boyfriend's facile answer might have been just the message I needed to hear. It's enough of a stretch to believe that my nonreligious but admirable husband might deliver God's love. But to believe that a man who helped make my life hell could also be God's messenger boy is too much. That not only contradicts all the theology I know, it irks me as well.

Could it be that God isn't merely available to us all but is plucking at our sleeves even as we run from Him? Sister Aloyius is one of those people who thinks so.

Sister Aloyius is a white-haired, sweet-faced Catholic nun who once ran a primary school in Derry, Northern Ireland, and now spends much of her time painting religious icons. I was in Northern Ireland doing a story on peacemakers. I went to meet the sister because of a story about how she faced down the boys sent by the IRA.

The nun had incurred the terrorists' wrath first by sitting on a bus they planned to bomb and refusing to leave it, thus foiling their plans. Then she went out in the street one day to give comfort to British Army officers wounded in an attack. At another time she refused to let children leave school for a protest march. She also broke all the rules by dropping an older friend off at a Protestant church every Sunday. The sister didn't go into the church, but she certainly gave aid, comfort, and car rides to the "enemy." In a province where religion is often just a label for a tribal identity, Sister Aloyius took Jesus' attitudes seriously enough to defy members of her own community. That can be a dangerous way to live in Northern Ireland.

One day, the IRA sent some of the boys to warn her that she had better watch herself. Unfortunately for them, the floor of Sister Aloyius's office was being repaired, and so instead of being able to surround her, the men had to walk in single file on a narrow board laid over the construction.

"I was so afraid that my mouth was dry," she said on the day we met in her studio over tea and biscuits. But a lifetime of telling the truth fearlessly came to her aid. "I said the first thing that came to my mind."

"What are you doing wearing those caps in the house?" she snapped at the men. "Take them off right now." Startled, they did as she told them. "And have you said your prayers this morning?" she demanded, frowning her most severe schoolmarm frown. "I bet not one of you has.

"Kneel down. Right here."

A young man at the back of the room edged out the door. "You come back here," she commanded. He did.

"Now, each one of you kneel down. Say your prayers right now."

The men did exactly as the tough old sister bid them do, and she's still laughing about it. "I bet they went out of there saying, 'Now, each of us has to swear that we won't tell what happened.in there.' "

Sister's story about the IRA boys is one of Northern Ireland's legends. But she also had something for me. "God is everywhere around us," she said. "The angels are so close that we can't pick up a piece a paper without brushing a dozen wings." To demonstrate, she swished a paper through the air and then nodded in several directions, "Excuse me. Excuse me." Then she laughed—a little bit at herself, but mostly with delight at the reality she lives within.

She likened getting in touch with God to tuning in radio waves. We don't see radio waves. We don't hear them. We could easily say that they don't exist. "But all we have to do is turn the radio dial just the slightest bit and they come flooding in."

Chapter 22

Stretching the Idea of a Limited God

HUMANIST CHARLOTTE PERKINS Gilman, a feminist author who lived in the late nineteenth and early twentieth centuries, said priests came up with the whole idea of a rationed God as a way of strengthening their own position. They made God into a big mystery and they made questioning religion into a mortal sin so they would have a lock on the God business and do very well. I can't say whether Gilman is right, but she certainly seems to be right about how things turned out. I recently heard a woman who grew up Pentecostal describe her childhood faith as "living in a totalitarian state."

But lately even Christianity is loosening its claims to exclusivity, and sometimes priests are leading the way. The Right Reverend Frank Griswold had just been elected as the new presiding bishop of the Episcopal Church when he made the following extraordinary claim about what true Christianity means. "Left to our own devices, we are critical, fearful, and protective of our own take on truth. Cracked open by the spirit and the transforming power of Jesus Christ, we are able to welcome the paradox, complexity, ambiguity, and outright contradictions, which is where real life is lived and the grace and peace of God are truly to be found." Imagine that. Christianity as a way of opening up to the world instead of closing down.

I am trying to be radically open and I must admit, it's pretty scary. To think that God might be motivating the whole spectrum of those who claim to be in touch with Him poses so many disconcerting ideas that I am becoming much more sympathetic to fundamentalists who want so desperately to shut down religious innovation. I don't blame them a bit. One day, sitting with a former tennis pro who became a Hare Krishna leader, I was close to derisive.

"Who do you think is going to listen to you?" I asked him. "What you're talking about is so foreign to this culture that I wonder how you think you're going to affect anybody." We were talking about dressing little statues that represent Hindu deities and setting offerings of food in front of them. The man was an American convert. He knew how strange all that was. And still he did it. I couldn't follow his reasoning.

He answered calmly. "I think what we're talking about will affect you." It was a bold claim. I didn't think he had a chance. But he was right. Once when I questioned him about his belief that people should not eat meat, I said, "Humans have always eaten meat. We're carnivores. Eating meat is a human thing to do."

He replied that certainly it is a human thing to do in the sense that humans are animals. But the aim of his faith is to help humans rise above their animal natures. The violence of killing other animals might be understandable, excusable, and common, but his goal was to become the kind of human who didn't harm other living things. I still eat meat, but his reasons for not eating it so impressed me that I think of them at least once a week.

At the temple, as Krishnas came in before dawn to chant and dance their morning devotions, I heard the same stories that religious people everywhere tell. "This faith changed my life." "This religion helped me cope with the death of my child." "These practices fill my days with happiness and peace." I saw people pursuing a modest, otherworldly lifestyle in the midst of a city that reveres nothing more than money and success. I saw them serving others in a selfless way.

One Hare Krishna woman told me about her conflicts with the guy who ran the kitchen operation. Food is so important to the Krishnas that they often call their belief a kitchen religion. So she couldn't avoid this guy, but she couldn't seem to get along with him either. "People think that our faith makes us all alike," she said, "but it's just the opposite. Following Krishna brings out more of who we are. Our differences don't go away. Sometimes they become more pronounced."

I thought that was the oddest reaction to religion I'd ever heard. Being Christian in my early life had been all about not being your old sinful self. But later, when my own spiritual life began to be important again, I found that she had described my experience exactly. The more I prayed to be like Jesus, the more secure and individual I became.

The more I learned about people whose beliefs were radically different from the Christian ones I'd grown up with, the more convinced I became that their ideas were as rewarding and valid as those in traditional Christianity. The stories they told me were just as convincing. Their behavior showed just as much change.

I have a friend who is a devout and conservative Christian. We often talked over the back fence about why she believed as she does. I asked her how she knew she was right, and she would reply that she knew because of the change in her life. It wasn't long before I started replying, "I believe you. But I don't believe you have the only way because tomorrow I'm almost sure to meet people who believe something totally unlike what you believe, and they will offer me the same proof. Their lives changed, too. And not through Jesus."

Some of my Christian friends would respond that those people might well change, they might well be good, but they aren't saved. I would reply, if I had the nerve, that all I can do is look at people's lives and see whether the tracks of God's passage show up. That's all any of us can do.

But doing that would be the most faith-shaking thing someone who thinks they have the only right version of God could do. The idea that people of radically different persuasions might also have a handle on God threatens many Christians. I think it shakes their own faith to admit they might not have total purchase on God. But seeing evidence of God in other beliefs affects me differently. If these bewildering people are showing the same signs of God, maybe there really is something out there.

When I began turning back toward religious ideas, I didn't trust anything—not the church, not the Bible, not God. My bad experience with faith had caused me to think that anything Christian was tainted. But seeing evidence of a life-changing faith in other religions broke through to me. If they had God, I reasoned, maybe the Christians had God, too.

At the Buddhist retreat, I saw the same glow in people's faces that I saw at the megachurch, and an even greater dedication. I was only there six days, but some people stay for months, years, even decades in a place with no television, no radios, no telephones in the rooms. People don't eat meat or drink alcohol. They make nothing more than pocket money for their labors. Their entire lives are dedicated to meditation, learning, and work. My Brazilian teacher at the retreat told how her life changed through meditation. She talked of self-knowledge that freed her, of glimpses into a transcendent reality that gave her direction.

Sometimes I just listened, but sometimes what people of different faiths told me gave me new avenues for my own explorations. A rabbi explained his faith as one that lives and gets its power through the continuing imagination of God's people. I'd never thought people might have such a partnership with God, but the idea opens up a faith of endless dimensions.

The idea that God is abundant is so radically different from what I once believed that it took years for me to comprehend what I was experiencing. And, since I discovered it on my own and I'm nobody special, I thought of it as something that only I knew.

I explored the experience. I doubted it. I reaffirmed it. The traditional Christian who still lives in me kept saying I was just justifying my own vain wishes. I was creating the kind of loophole I wanted. I was making God over in my own image. So I kept quiet about it.

Then I picked up a book and found someone else who had the very same realization. Once again, I could see a familiar pattern. If I were open to the world and God in it, my experience would soon confirm what I thought was the truth. Later, I would stumble over someone of authority who would bolster my finding. Clay and straw, as Dykes would say.

This time, John Dominic Crossan was my authority, a professor of biblical studies at DePaul University in Chicago. He bolsters his own ideas and his own scholarship with a source that I would have never thought to turn to: the Bible.

His book, *Jesus: A Revolutionary Biography,* tries to interpret Jesus' life and teachings in the light of what they would have meant in terms of his own Mediterranean Jewish peasant culture. In one chapter, Crossan deals with the fact that Jesus never settled down in any one place to teach and do miracles.

That would have been the logical thing for a man of his times to do, writes the professor. "What Jesus should have done, as any Mediterranean family knew, was settle down at his home in Nazareth and establish there a healing cult. He would be its *patron,* the family would be its *brokers,* and as his reputation went out along the peasant grapevine, the sick would come as *clients* to be healed. That would have made sense to everyone, would have been good for everyone— for Jesus, for his family, and for little Nazareth itself. But instead Jesus kept to the road, brought healing to those who needed it, and had, as it were, to start off anew every day."

Why did he do it? Because, the professor says, "For Jesus, the Kingdom of God is a community of radical or unbrokered equality in which individuals are in direct contact with one another and with God, unmediated by any established brokers or fixed locations." In other words, if Jesus' life is any indication, God is a traveling act. You might catch His performances anywhere. And when you do, you are free to make of them what you will. Nobody stands between you and Him.

But don't believe me or Professor Crossan. Look to your own life. As the Buddhists say, "Here is a proposition that might be true. Test it in your own experience." That's what I did. Every story I reported, every believer I met seemed to give me something to take away for myself. I found myself being moved in ways I could have never imagined. Inch by inch, my mind, or maybe I should say my spirit, opened.

Chapter 23

Does God Feast with Witches?

THE BUDDHISTS, THE Hare Krishnas, and the Jews all reinforced my idea that God is so abundant anyone can reach Him in a multitude of ways. But it's not too surprising that these ancient wisdoms would communicate spiritually. What about the witches? Could I give them equal time? That's a harder one. And not long afterward, I faced an even tougher test of my new ideas. A group of Taiwanese attracted worldwide attention when they settled in a suburb of Dallas and announced that God was going to arrive on March 31. Everyone—or almost everyone—was calling them a cult of crazy people. Would I?

But first, the witches. A lot of religious people can accept other religious traditions, as long as the traditions are old and a goodly number of other people believe them. That's respectable. But what about a faith that throws together traditions to make up its own belief system? Where do we draw the line? It's a question that I ask all the time in covering religion. In journalism, the line shifted. Some new religions were too far out or too small to merit coverage.

But I had bound my personal search for spirituality to a rule that said I would try to look with an open mind at other people's faith, no matter what it was. For myself, I had tossed out tradition and other people's opinions as a guide to spirituality. I had become convinced that no matter what people said, the real reason they believed a certain faith was that it had "resonance" for them. It changed their lives; it made them feel a certain way. As one religious scholar put it, people don't live by some reality outside themselves; they live by what feels right. Even people who rely on traditional religion do so because it evokes something in them. I am the same.

The pagan religions, to which Wiccans or witches belong, rely on "sages" who have a considerable latitude. They worship entities that most of us grew up thinking of as examples of ancient nonsense. I was often confused when dealing with Hare Krishnas and Buddhists, but I was totally at sea dealing with these folks. Here's a retelling of the story I wrote about them.

My question was posed as they sat in a circle on the floor of a sheet-draped room in a suburban apartment where a high priestess and a priest of Wicca lived. The light was dim and remains of the pagans' feast—ham salad and pimento cheese sandwiches, couscous, cold cuts, soft drinks, and wine—were at their feet. I was feeling a little odd about eating food surrounded by so many bare feet. But the pagans were feeling mellow as they lounged in their long white robes.

"Tell me if this is true," I asked from the edge of the circle. "You pick what you like from other religions and throw the pieces together. You might be absolutely wrong, and you know that. But this religion seems true to you, so you believe it. Is that right?"

The question was a variation on one of traditional religion's most devastating insults: the idea that people with new ideas about God have a make-it-up-as-they-go faith. I've heard many versions of that question. It's a power play. It's an attack. And it usually deflates the person it is directed against. It would have cowed me.

I fear the derision of that question. It means you're self-absorbed, indulgent of your own puny thinking, undisciplined. It means that all the forces of intelligence and godliness are massed against you. It's enough to shut most folks up.

But the pagans were delighted. They cheered and laughed and yelled, "That's it. You've got it. That's what we do."

The dozen people celebrating the beginning of spring in a Hurst, Texas, apartment were part of a revival of ancient religions that started in the fifties and has continued with a postmodern twist. Along with thousands of other Americans, they practice a brand of faith some-times called nature or earth religions because of its reverence for the natural world. It is also called neo-paganism or paganism, which comes from the Latin word meaning "country people." Today, *pagan* is often used to mean that someone has no religion. That is a charge the neo-pagans would vehemently deny.

The largest of these nature worship groups is Wicca, whose ad-herents are commonly known as witches. But neo-pagans also often worship gods from ancient Roman, Greek, Norse, Celtic, Sumerian, African, or Egyptian traditions. Female deities are a primary attrac-tion for many neo-pagans. In a given ceremony, they may throw in a little Native American tradition, dance a few Sufi dances, bring out a Wiccan cauldron, call upon some dragons, summon forth a few fairies, or, after declaiming loudly to gods with names few Americans can pronounce, evoke a Catholic saint. Like a lot of the New Age cer-emonies, these are easy to pillory. In fact, it takes some restraint not to. I had vowed to resist cheap shots, and as usual I was helped along by the fact that as odd as the religion seemed, I liked the people. I also got some help from a scholar who knows a lot about religion and takes this one quite seriously.

In fact, she says it fits right in with where we are as a society. "It's a very postmodern eclecticism," says Mary Jo Neitz, a sociologist with the University of Missouri in Columbia, who has studied the pagan movement, particularly Wiccans, for nine years. "They are making it up as they go along, but they aren't making it up from scratch." She notes that pagans draw from cultures all over the world. "It's very consistent with what we see happening in the arts and in music."

Some Christians have no problem using pagan forms and rituals and they find them valuable. The Reverend Martha Murphy Hall, a Christian ordained in the nondenominational Ministry of Service Church, says, "My own Jesus is tremendously tolerant. Sinners, Ro-mans, Samaritans. He included them all in his fold. So I don't exclude anyone."

During my research, I went to a celebration at a city park where twenty people with garlands on their heads danced around a Maypole singing first a Native American chant and then a hallelujah chorus. Most of the group was Christian but the May Queen was pagan. The twenty-year-old college student said her faith was passed on to her by her mother. "She really just wanted to take her pasta salad and go to the Methodist church, but there was no place for her," said Leigh Ann Brown. "She was too strong. She gave me her strength."

Many pagans said they were once ardent Christians. Some once dreamed of being nuns, missionaries, or preachers. It was the idea of original sin that drove Jennifer Holliman, formerly a Methodist, away from her childhood faith.

"I felt like my head always had to be down [in shame]. In Christianity, you aren't worth much because you're human," said Ms. Holliman, who was about to graduate with high honors from Texas Woman's University. She now worships mostly Norse deities. "Something about them just seemed to call to me," she said.

Harry McMaster traces his disillusionment with Christianity to his childhood when his mother divorced and was treated badly by the church. He, like many pagans, said that he didn't so much choose paganism as it chose him. "It's more like something you realize you've always believed," said Mr. McMaster, who is a Wiccan priest.

There you go again. That feeling thing. I'd like to throw out Harry's feelings, but who is to say that mine are more valid? Until we hear from God in a way that we all can agree is God, we're left guessing. Despite their rejection of Christianity, most of the pagans are less hostile to the faith they left than that faith usually is toward them. I couldn't help but wonder how a tiny group of people making it up as they go along can be so tolerant and unafraid of others while a powerful group such as the Christians with all their traditions and wealth and societal power can be so often hostile and afraid of others.

Many pagans, in fact, have quite friendly feelings toward Christianity. Marie Wilhite's nine-year-old daughter goes to a Baptist church, as Ms. Wilhite did when she was a child. "I want her to learn those teachings," she said. Ms. Wilhite, who owns a shop called Scorpio Herbs, also would like to hire a Christian to work in the store. "If you get a good solid Christian, they aren't likely to feel the energies, and they'll be more likely to stay grounded," she said, meaning they would tend to business.

Pagans talk a lot about magic but, when pressed, they often define it as a form of prayer. Some do have stories of having bent the material world with their will. Shawn, who didn't want his last name used, defined himself as a chaos magician. He said he can control fire with his will.

"A candle flame," he said. "I can cause it to move with my mind."

"Oh, piffle," said Gloria Galasso, rolling out scones that would be part of an upcoming Beltane or May Day ceremony. "That's what you perceive."

"That's right," he said, not at all abashed. "That's what I perceive."

The Wiccan concept of magic is often no more drastic than Pentecostals' belief in supernatural intervention, said Dr. Neitz, who wrote a book on Pentecostals. "For a while, I thought the Christians believed in magic even more than the witches did," she said. For instance, both often believe in "universal parking place magic." "May the universe manifest a parking place. All the religions I know do that," she said.

"There are people who do practice negative magic," said a Wiccan who asked not to be named. "We'd prefer that they not call themselves witches."

Dr. Neitz turns down invitations to present her research at seminars on the occult by saying, "I don't study the occult. I study religion." The pagan movements are real religion, unlike Churches of Satan, which are often just a reaction to Christianity, she said.

"Witchcraft is a religion because it has a story and it has an ethical platform. Satanism is a kind of adolescent rebellion," she said, although she does recognize that some Satanists might do real evil. "I don't know much about that," she said. The ethics of witchcraft involve the notion that anyone who does bad will be repaid three times. Good will also be rewarded.

Although pagan beliefs vary widely, they usually have these three elements:

> • They contain no concept of original sin. "Christians believe they fell from paradise," said Ms. Galasso, who practices Thelema, a three-thousand-member religion founded in 1904 by English poet and mystic Aleister Crowley. "We believe this is paradise."
>
> "When people ask me about Satanism, I always tell them that we don't even have a devil," said High Priestess Carrie McMaster.

• They believe that God is in everything and everyone. "God is in the trees, in the rocks, in the computer," said Ms. Galasso.

"God is in us," said Ms. McMaster.

• They believe in many gods that represent the one Deity, who is male and female. "God is too big for us to perceive," said Ms. Wilhite. "The gods and goddesses are little manageable pieces that we can understand."

Many pagans agree with the Wiccan rede, "An it harm none, do what thou wilt." (*An* is the archaic form of the word "if.") The Charge of the Goddess is also often quoted, which says in part, "All acts of love and pleasure are My rituals."

Wicca is often a difficult religion because it has no traditional ceremonies, said Ms. Dzmura. "We have to make all our rituals as we go. It's hard." But to its adherents, paganism is worth the effort. It connects them to the earth and to a sense of the holy in a way that other religions don't, they said. For them, it works.

"I don't care if your god is five thousand years old or something you just made up last Tuesday," said Ms. Galasso. "If it gets you through the dark of the night, if it's there for you when you celebrate, if it's there when you need comfort from the death of your mother or your best friend, then it's a true religion, whatever it is. My religion is there for me just as much as a Baptist's is there for him."

Chapter 24

Finding God Among a Most Far-out Flock

THE TAIWANESE WHO were waiting for God threatened me far more than the witches. The strength of their faith was unlike anything I had ever seen. Members of God's Salvation Church, also known as Chen Tao, sold their homes, quit their jobs, and came to Garland, Texas, on tourist visas because they believed God was going to meet them there. They said flying saucers were coming to rescue people from a Great Tribulation that would include nuclear bombs. They said God spoke through their leader's ring. They said the stars and moon were going to fall out of the sky. They said the sun was going to disappear. They said God was going to appear in the front yard of their leader's house, walk through walls, speak every language, shake everyone's hand, and answer all questions. All this would occur right after God appeared on television, they said.

This was a hard story not to make jokes about. For starters, God's Salvation Church had relocated to Garland, Texas, because the Taiwanese said the word *Garland* sounded like "God-land." Obviously this was a revelation in which the inability of Chinese speakers to handle certain consonants figured prominently. They wore white cowboy hats, sneakers, and all-white outfits. Their leader favored a pointed hat because he said it concentrated energy. In their backyard was a concrete pad that they said represented flying saucers God would soon send. When God arrived, they said animals would begin to talk.

Much of their theology was kindly. They assured people that God wasn't coming to judge people or punish them in any way. In their mock spaceship was a disassembled barbecue grill in a box still bound with metal packing bands. God told them to put the grill in the ship as a way of reassuring animals that people would no longer kill and eat them, they said.

When their neighbors were offended because they often rode their bicycles in packs with a van following behind, they put notes on the neighbors' doors explaining. They wrote that they didn't mean to cause any alarm. They were simply getting in shape for the journey they were soon to make with God.

At their press conferences, they answered questions so patiently and with such goodwill and sincerity that even reporters treated them gently. Their hope and anticipation of God's coming was so strong that it was painful to watch. One physician told me, his face shining, "God is coming in only two weeks. I wish it could be sooner."

Their theology has some scary parts. Nuclear wars will kill most of the people on earth, they say. They believe that many Asian people have been taken over by devils and are no longer human.

When I contacted some of the country's academic experts on new religions, they confirmed my suspicions: This might sound nutty to unbelievers, but to anyone familiar with the broad sweep of history, it's pretty mainstream stuff. Oh, great, I thought. Just as I'm trying to move back into some sort of faith, I get a front row seat to how crazy religion causes people to act.

All their prophecies failed.

Of course. We knew they would. As I went about reporting on the Taiwanese, I heard many Christians say how nuts they thought the members of God's Salvation Church were. Most of these Christians were getting ready to celebrate Easter, an event that occurred after God had a baby with a virgin. This child grew up and died because God wanted a human blood sacrifice. Then God's Son rose from the dead. Is that more believable than the idea that God is coming in flying saucers to rescue people? I don't think so. In fact, if you want to talk plausible, the Taiwanese may have a slight edge. We know that spacecraft can fly between planets. We know that this planet has life, and so it isn't so absurd to believe there might be life elsewhere. We don't, however, know of any virgins having babies two thousand years ago or any people who've come back from the dead. Those are miracles, you say? Well, sure, but they are a lot more far-fetched than what the Taiwanese cooked up.

The rest of the world may have been laughing at Chen Tao craziness. I was not. If they are crazy, I asked myself, how crazy am I? I never believed God was coming on March 31 as they did. I don't hear his voice coming out of rings, and I don't believe the contrails left by jet planes have great meaning. So bully for me. But I am starting to believe some pretty weird stuff. I sometimes feel a definite sense of God's presence. I believe He listens to me and I think He might respond. I believe evidence of His hand can be seen if you know how to look for it.

And even on the days when I don't believe any of that, I still believe that reality is not what it seems. I don't mean that aliens are coming, but the versions of reality I'm beginning to develop are just about as crazy in their own way. I believe good has a force greater than we know. I think the money and fame and acclaim, the security and possessions that we think we need are nice things to have but not the essentials of life at all. I think the primary task of a happy life is to see through the illusions that trap us. And the farther along I go, the more I believe that doing bad things separates us from the forces of life that give us the peace and security we need most.

The Taiwanese have more faith than most religious people, but they share enough understandings with other religious people to make the rest of us nervous. They believe that reality is not what it seems. They believe God will intervene in human existence because He loves what He has created. Once you begin believing those sorts of things, you can end up anywhere. It's just a matter of degree. The idea that becoming more spiritual might move me closer to a state where I could find myself standing in a suburban front yard waiting for God to touch down is a pretty frightening idea.

But the story of the Taiwanese who waited for God threatens me on an even more basic level because it reaffirms—just in case I was slipping in this area—that faith doesn't affect reality at all. The strength of the Chen Tao followers' faith couldn't have been stronger. They were absolutely convinced. But believing doesn't make it so. It's all very well for me to say that religious faith changes how you see things, but sometimes the way it changes you is completely wacky and not at all functional. History is full of people who didn't know that. They thought they had the truth and some of them died for it. But what if they were wrong? What if the missionaries and martyrs who gave their lives because they wanted to tell the lost about Jesus were wasting their lives? The only difference between a religious nut and a religious genius is often just the number of people who follow them, a professor of religious studies named Lonnie Kliever told me.

Dr. Kliever pointed out that flying saucers aren't such a crazy notion if you accept the idea that God's going to come and get us. Scientists and other well-educated people have been attracted to new religions that feature flying saucers since 1948, when the first saucer was allegedly sighted. Flying saucers are just a space-age version of the sweet chariots swinging low, he said.

The idea that people have been taken over by devils was put into a religious perspective by Catherine Wessinger of Loyola University. "They're just trying to figure out the problem of evil," she said. "They're trying to find a reason for why people take advantage of one another and do things that are strictly in their own interest."

Why are the Taiwanese so extreme? Well, they're converts, said other professors. And they are the first generation in a new religion, which always tends to be radical. Only in the second and third generations do people calm down and start being more rational and acceptable to outsiders.

So what separates the crazy folks from normal religious people? Apparently not too much. Mind control isn't a factor, the scholars told me, but temperament might be. People who join new religious movements tend to be the same people who take up extreme dietary fads or follow the latest extremist psychological regimen. Or it might be that the crazies are more tuned in to God than the rest of us.

Media from all over the world gathered on March 24, the date God was supposed to show up on television. When He didn't commandeer the airwaves as expected, the Chen Tao leader, Master Chen, told the media that they could consider all his prophecies nonsense. But it was quite obvious that his followers did not think that the visions they had based their lives on were nonsense. Instead of seeming unhappy at God's failure to appear, they seemed quite content, laughing and chattering as they filed away to their homes.

The reason is that they now believed God had sent a new sign. He didn't show up on television but, right before the scheduled program, all the Taiwanese were sitting together in Mr. Chen's backyard, praying and waiting. It was a clear, still night, and suddenly the wind picked up. A great gust blew clouds across the sky. For the journalists, it was nothing. For the Taiwanese, it was a sign from God. It meant he had come down, but not in Garland.

They announced to reporters that God had already landed on earth. More details would follow. On March 31, the day God was supposed to stand in Mr. Chen's front yard answering questions, speaking in different languages and walking through walls, the Taiwanese again faced the media. And once again, God didn't make the scene. At least not in the eyes of the media.

Before speaking a word, the Taiwanese began to kowtow to the people who had gathered to watch them. When they finished, Mr. Chen told the group that God was not only among them, He was in them. They were all God, he said, and they must all revere and respect and love one another. The Taiwanese performed like hundreds of other religious groups before them. First they made a prophecy. Then they rearranged it to suit reality. The early Christians who thought Jesus was coming back in their lifetimes did the same thing.

Such flexibility is essential in the development of many faiths, Dr. Kliever told me. First people take their faith quite literally and try to project their religious beliefs on the world in a specific, rigid way; then when that doesn't work out, they move to a more symbolic stage that serves them and the world better. The Taiwanese are unlikely to lose their faith. In fact, failure will probably strengthen it. The last I heard of them, they were on their way to the Great Lakes to wait for another promised appearance of God.

It took me some weeks to get over the idea that Mr. Chen had been right, i.e., that everything he had to say was nonsense. But by the time the Taiwanese and I came together, I was getting pretty good at looking under the obvious meaning of religious events. I was learning how to interpret life in ways that moved me forward spiritually, even when life was at its most absurd. So I kept puzzling over the Taiwanese. Could I pull something out of this for myself? The truth is, I couldn't bear to have all that faith mean nothing. If those gentle, sincere, incredibly God-focused folks were just fools, maybe those of us with less faith and less daring were equally misguided. I was taking this personally, as you can see.

The Taiwanese were obviously wrong. God didn't show up. We

know that. Maybe that means there isn't a God. Certainly it would seem to mean that God wasn't talking to them, no matter what they thought. But the more I turned that rock over, the more I thought that maybe, like an audience watching a magician's tricks, we were looking at the wrong event if we wanted to know how God works.

People just naturally want God to show up and rescue us. Can you blame us? Some of us want it more and some less. But we all want it. So maybe when some people get a little inkling of His presence, they get all excited and start thinking that He's finally going to co-operate with our fantasies. And then when He doesn't, we jump to an equally wrong conclusion, which is that He didn't do anything.

Now I'm not saying that He moved those clouds. I don't know whether He did that or not, but I do know that something moved the Chen Tao believers in an entirely positive direction. They seemed all set up for humiliation and failure. Every ten minutes or so some journalist asked whether they planned to kill themselves if God didn't appear. And sure enough the humiliation the outside world expected did happen.

But the Taiwanese weren't humiliated. They were elated because they had made an incredibly important leap in their own faith. They went from looking for God outside themselves and other people to seeing Him in everyone around them. They began to think of God not only as deus ex machina but as the inwardly dwelling, trans-forming spirit available to all. That's a stunningly powerful change. They were not quite ready to give up their rescue fantasy, as we can see by their move to the Great Lakes. But they were heading that way.

So what about how silly they looked, you may be thinking? What about all the money and status and the jobs they lost in coming to "God-land"? Why didn't God protect them from that? Well, maybe He couldn't. Maybe that path to faith was the only one open to them. Maybe because of their personalities, maybe because the mil-lennium is approaching and stirring religious imaginations to a fevered pitch, maybe because they come from a beleaguered, ignored, scorned little country like Taiwan . . . I don't know all the reasons why people take such strange ways to faith. But what I am relatively sure of now is that the Taiwanese could very well be on a path to re-warding and important faith. I don't think too many people are going to take that path. I'm sure not. But I'm at peace again with the idea that we can take faith where we find it, and we can allow others to take it in the ways they find it.

And so, on to the next step.

Chapter 25

Is God Abundant Enough to Be in a Godless Religion?

A BOUT A YEAR after my lessons with Marty ended, I went to a week-long Buddhist retreat at his urging. It might seem an odd move for a woman in such hot pursuit of God. Buddhism is a godless path that eschews faith almost entirely. But, in fact, a little Buddhist-path walking was exactly what I needed to push me forward.

I espoused the idea that God could be defined by personal experience, even if that included doubt. I asserted that faith could be separated from belief. But I was still spending a great deal of my energy arguing those points with myself.

Buddhism was precisely and completely the reassurance I needed to move forward. Although Buddhism now has plenty of tradition, authority, and ritual, Buddha didn't rest his teachings on any of them. As for God's existence, Buddha apparently didn't concern himself much with the question.

Huston Smith, in his wonderful book *The Religions of Man,* writes that Buddha flatly refused to discuss metaphysics. To illustrate, the author tells the story of a time when one of Buddha's disciples complained, "Whether the world is eternal or not eternal, whether the world is finite or not, whether the soul is the same as the body or whether the soul is one thing and the body another, whether a Buddha exists after death or does not exist after death—these things, the

Lord does not explain to me. And that he does not explain them to me does not please me, it does not suit me."

"There were many it did not suit," writes Smith. "Yet despite incessant needling, he continued his 'noble silence.' His reason was simple. 'Greed for views' on questions of this sort 'tend not to edification.' "

My week of Buddhist retreat convinced me that not believing in God might very well be a plus in finding Him. If you don't believe in God, you don't have nearly so much baggage to deal with. And you don't have nearly as much to natter over. For people burned by organized religion, God brings up such negative emotion that they have to get over it before they can get on with it. Buddhism sidesteps the prejudice.

A no-God religion also has other advantages. It means believers look inward instead of reaching out to a Being whom many suspect is not listening or doesn't exist. They find the truths of existence inside themselves. That means they don't have to spend time debating whether they're praying to thin air or not. They don't have to beg God down or feel all abandoned when He doesn't seem to be around.

Buddha's reliance on experience to inform his followers about the best way to live without suffering means faith isn't an issue, either. "The Buddha had a tremendous insight experience that was not specific to him," Marty told me. "Anyone can take the same steps and come to the same understanding on their own."

"One of the things I like about Buddhism is that you are expected to measure everything they tell you against your own experience," said a woman I met at the retreat. Marty put it another way: "The idea is that everything is a rumor that you are invited to verify."

"What we teach is more direct than psychology," said Ralph McFall, one of the retreat instructors. "We teach people how to learn from their own experience." As a former student said, "It's not like studying a religion. It's like studying myself."

Buddhists don't think ultimate reality can even be put into words. It can be experienced, but it can't be conveyed accurately by the blunt instrument of language. I wish someone had explained that truth to me when I was a teenager struggling with the preachers' admonition to smile all the time. Only recently have I come to understand that my upset about not being able to smile constantly was a completely misguided interpretation. The preachers were trying their best to express truth about the nature of faith, which is that it lifts us into another plane of experience. The happiness they were talking about isn't necessarily conveyed by smiling, but it does occur to me that the smilingest people I know are Tibetan Buddhists. The Dalai Lama beams and giggles all the time. But my point is that anyone who tries to express religious truth is bound to bumble about. The literal interpretation I gave to their literal example compounded the problem. They didn't have the words to speak it, and I didn't have the ears to hear it.

Buddhists think intellectualization obscures the deepest truths. Description distorts them. Knowing that and knowing that people have to make their own journey, Buddhist teachers often deflect questions with other questions. They give answers that seem to contradict. Serious wisdom is often followed by an offhand negation. For me, that approach, which keeps throwing seekers back to themselves, is a good way to keep a search for God on track. It keeps us focused on ourselves and our own exploration of the mystery. Our experience works the magic we need—or it doesn't.

Buddhists set out exactly what you need to do to grow. Guilt and faith aren't part of the equation. The path is much more concrete. The goal is implicitly stated: to alleviate suffering. The way is difficult.

Retreat classes began at six forty-five A.M. and ended at nine P.M. Fifteen minutes of free time was a luxury. Concentration on meditation and other Buddhist practices was so constant that when the week ended, I felt as though I was surfacing after a long dive into deep water. Everyday life left me slightly dizzy.

One goal of Buddhism is to integrate mind and body. In that way, the teachers seek to bring students into what they call awareness or mindfulness. To help Westerners, a Tibetan master named Tarthang Tulku adapted exercises taken from traditional Tibetan healing practices. They are called Kum Nye. Standing, sitting, and lying down, we would perform the exercises at a snail's pace. The goal was to feel each tiny motion and to recognize any pain. For instance, we would extend our arms and raise them without pause but slowly enough to feel every motion. Holding them over our heads, we would bend to the right and hold. Bending to the left, we'd hold. Stretching up, opening the chest, opening the mouth, breathing slowly. Bending toward the ground, feeling every vertebra slip into place.

I wouldn't have to do the exercises long before my upraised hands were so bloodless they felt icy. Rarely used muscles would tingle and cramp. I would fight the urge to speed up as my mind turned toward lunch. Finally we would stop, stand, and then sit cross-legged on the floor.

Our feet fell asleep. Our backs ached. A giggle sometimes started in one corner and was echoed about the room. Sniffling was followed by the soft tearing of tissue being pulled from a box. Don't worry about any emotions you feel, our teacher said. One Brazilian, a gifted musician, always cried. For ten years she had come to Kum Nye and meditation classes. And every time, she cried. No one knew why. But she had the most beautiful laugh. And when she laughed, her face was luminous, as though her tears had cleaned the conduits of her joy.

Each day of the retreat included two and a half hours of working at a seemingly menial task. I made cakes and worked as a kitchen helper. Others stuffed envelopes, helped in the kitchen with me, or worked in the garden. We took whatever task was assigned. "Life doesn't always allow us to choose," one teacher said.

Tarthang Tulku calls this "work practice." What makes it important is the calm concentration and purpose of the worker. Part of the magic is that people who are working well are in the present moment and aren't suffering. As you pay attention to what you do, you learn who you really are, the teachers said. Most people don't have any direct experience of who they are because they define themselves not moment by moment but by what others have told them about themselves.

We talked little during work. Meals were eaten in complete silence. People sometimes passed without greeting or smiling. Conversations were in low, often hushed tones. At first, the silence seemed strange and isolating. But by the end of the first day, the permission not to be focused on others began to be a luxury. It allowed total concentration on one's self—a definite taboo in the Christianity I once knew.

Chapter 26

I Confront the Big Questions: Death and Hell

"**W**HAT ABOUT DEATH?" I asked the teacher at a Buddhist workshop on impermanence. "What can Buddhism do for us in helping us accept and face the pain of losing those we love?" Some people talk about the innocence of childhood, before they knew that death and loss were human destiny. I can't remember such a time. I have always feared loss. So, for me the hard test of any belief system is how it deals with my ever present, always gnawing sense that loss is right around the corner.

The teacher threw my question back at me.

"Are you speaking out of your own experience?" he asked. No, I wasn't. My only encounter with death had been the death of my grandmother. I had feared her death long before it came. Even when I was in college, not yet out of my teens, I made a pilgrimage to see her every winter. Every year as flu season approached, I felt her mortality and mourned the loss that I feared would come.

But to my surprise, when she did die, I looked at her body and felt perfectly assured that her existence was continuing. I was so sure of it that the fuss everyone was making over her body puzzled me. When I told him so, the Buddhist pointed out that reality—even my own reality—was far different from how I was portraying it. The message was clear: Don't live in an illusion. Touch what is real for you and don't be misled by what you imagine to be real or by what other people tell you is real.

One of Christianity's big sticks is its assurance that only following traditional interpretations of Christ's teachings will get you to heaven. Among the fears I had to deal with to move into a new relationship with God was the idea that I might go to hell for my effrontery. Going to hell didn't trouble me much when I rejected everything about religion. But once I opened the door again, I had to consider the old questions. If I stayed out here depending on a God I might just have made up out of my own imaginings, would I find that as I lay dying He was nowhere around? Pondering that, I went to a woman who was both a Christian and a person intimately acquainted with the last stages of life.

The Reverend Melissa Graham is a chaplain who has worked with the sick and dying through Dallas's hospice program. Ordained by the Christian Church and the daughter of a preacher herself, Ms. Graham told me that people with a literal, solid, churchgoing faith don't necessarily do any better when facing their own death than people without any kind of formal religious faith. They don't necessarily do any worse either. She believes that how well people do with dying depends on how much they believe that God loves them and will take care of them—no matter what happens to them and no matter how they have acted. Some people who never go to church, who don't even believe in the concept of God, have a faith in the goodness and rightness of life that sustains them. Others who've spent their lives pursuing God can't summon that reassurance when they need it, she said. "Some people think they have to be good to be loved by God, and I think the church sometimes encourages that, without meaning to," she said. People who buy into that idea often find that on their deathbeds, they don't think they have been good enough.

She thinks our differences are often not so much in faith but in vocabulary. Some people use religious language and other people don't, she said. Some of the dying agnostics she has worked with have just as much or more faith in eternity as lifelong church members have. And some of them have all the character traits that we look for in people whose lives have been molded by God, she said.

Working with the dying has reinforced Ms. Graham's belief that life goes on after death. It has also caused her to think that traditional ideas about beliefs and declarations of faith aren't what separates those who will go on to eternal life and those who won't. She explained, "I don't think how we talk about things is enough to keep us out of the family of God."

Chapter 27

Buddhism Begins to Seem
More and More Christian to Me

❦

ONE OF OUR two teachers at the Buddhist retreat, an ebullient Brazilian named Eleonora Furtado, often started class by asking, "So, what are you feeling?" People talked about the petty emotions that dog us daily. They talked about being angry when a teacher hadn't praised them, wanting to boss their coworkers, feeling resentful when forced to change a recipe.

Our teacher urged us to submit—to feel our emotions without necessarily reacting and without judging. "Submitting is not accepting," she said. "Submitting means being one with them." In fact, the best way to treat a bad emotion such as anger or confusion or embarrassment is the simplest way: Laugh at it. Those feelings are often nothing more than the ego's way of trying to take control of our lives. But our goal is to be in control ourselves, and laughing at our emotions allows us to slip free of the buffeting that life administers when the ego and its self-centered desires are in charge, Ms. Furtado said.

That sounds exactly counter to what Christianity teaches. In Christianity, we're supposed to forget ourselves, take up our crosses, follow Christ, sacrifice, love others. It was a great relief to stop nagging myself about all that. But notice what we talked about during our classes: feeling angry, wanting to boss other people, being resentful. Our problems were exactly the kind of petty, daily "sins" that I had prayed to get rid of. They were precisely the habits that robbed my life of joy for so long that I turned to religion for relief. Can it be that when Christians talk of sins and Buddhists talk about needing to let go of desire they're talking about the same urges and miseries?

As for guilt, we were also told to let go of it. Definitely not a Christian notion. Or is it?

If you harm someone, you must do what you can to make it right, our teacher said. Then you let it go. As Ms. Furtado put it, focusing on the wrong after the restitution keeps you living in the past and prevents you from knowing who you really are in this moment. That's Buddhism. Christianity says that Jesus lifts your sins and you are white as snow, free to go on with your life, to make it right and live free of the past. Not too different.

Judging yourself or anyone else is considered an obstacle to insight, according to Buddhists. Judging, ah, yes, I'm working on that already. Buddhists go a lot farther. Achieving compassion for yourself and others is a primary goal. This all sounds very familiar to a person raised in bedrock Christianity.

But here's a difference. The first step, according to Tarthang Tulku, is to have love for yourself. "Be kind. Be gentle with yourself," Ms. Furtado said. Human are thought to be essentially good, and once they open their hearts through relaxation and meditation, they will begin to care deeply about others. Evil isn't a concept Buddhists talk about.

This is a long way from the doctrine of original sin, from a God who demanded the sacrifice of His Son for man's awful misdeeds. But watch where we've ended up. "There are actions and consequences. Whatever you do bears fruit," said Mr. McFall. "It's exactly what the Bible says, 'As you sow, so shall you reap.' Anger always leads to anger and love always leads to love."

Now listen to the words of Catholic priest Henri Nouwen talking about the necessity of Christian discipline. Christian discipline isn't control, he said, but rather "the effort to present some space where God can act." Solitude is the first discipline, the priest said, because it allows us to be with God. "To pray is to listen to the voice of the one who calls you my beloved daughter, my beloved son, my beloved child," he said. "To pray is to let that voice ooze out to your whole being."

Nouwen said that hearing the unconditional love of that voice allows us to be free of the commands that all the "other" voices, strong voices of the world, are giving us. Those voices say, "Prove that you are worth something. Prove that you have any contribution to make.

Prove! Do something that is relevant. Be sure you make a name for yourself. Be sure at least you have some power. Then people will love you. Then people will say you're beautiful, you're wonderful, you're great."

Buddhists say we must reach that inner, good part of ourselves. The Christian says we must be quiet enough to let the love of God ooze out of us. Buddhists say we must separate the voice of the ego with all its striving from our own true voice. The Christian says we must hear the voice of God so strongly that it quiets the voices of the world that tell us we must attain power or prestige in order to be beloved.

Let me tell you about Abbe Blum and what she came looking for in Buddhism. See if you agree that she was looking for the same thing most of us look for in God.

Her first glimpse of Buddhism's power came when she and a friend happened upon a man's body in a New Haven, Connecticut, street. It was dark and the person looked dead. As they drew nearer, Ms. Blum's mind skittered like marbles dropped on a table. But her companion was perfectly focused. Without a tremor, he reached out to touch the still form. She asked how he could command such ease. His answer was in a word: Buddhism.

Ms. Blum's commitment was cemented years later when her father was dying with Alzheimer's. Before every nursing home visit, she did exercises and meditation based on Tibetan tradition. They helped clear her mind and settle her emotions. Then she went to be with her father. "It made it possible for me to be there with him as he was dying," she said. "I could feel my feet on the floor, and I could be there and not resist the experience."

In these two stories, Ms. Blum, a literature professor at Swarthmore College in Pennsylvania, pinpointed two of Buddhism's greatest gifts: calm and the ability to be content in the present—no matter what it is. But let's use different terminology. Let's say she got peace and a sense of well-being. Let's say she got a feeling of being protected no matter what happened. It's the same feelings, just in different terms. One is talking about a no-God religion. The other is talking about a very traditional God.

There is, however, one more important thing that a God-based religion does for us that most of us would miss. It lets us pray. Our prayers have the potential to make an impact on the world. They comfort us. They give us an outlet for the sense of thanksgiving that sometimes drenches our senses like a cloudburst. So, okay. Let's see what the Buddhists do.

One morning after breakfast, our teacher urged us to pitch in on the breakfast dishes. No talking allowed. Full concentration required. Scrape those dishes like it matters.

"We will be a team," she said. And we were. The cleanup moved so swiftly and with such grace that it felt dreamlike. Once it was done, the teacher gathered her group in a circle. "We hold hands now," she said, elated, "and we dedicate this good energy." She raised her arms high and proclaimed: "To all sentient beings."

It looked like cleaning. It felt like a dance. And it counted far beyond the kitchen. A nice package.

Buddhists who come from the Tibetan tradition also address themselves to the "force for good" in a way that Westerners can't understand as anything but prayer. They make what we call prayer wheels, which are revolving cylinders with tightly coiled pieces of paper inside them. On the paper are written good sentiments. They walk around the prayer wheels in a ritualistic way that they believe affects them and the world.

Buddhists believe their good deeds strengthen the force for good. They believe their actions influence it. In fact, their godless religion seems to me to be set up to do everything for its proponents that God-filled religions do—only it requires far less faith. So why didn't I just become a Buddhist and give up my struggle with Christianity?

Not all of the people who follow that path give up the God of their childhood. Most of my fellow retreat members had Christian backgrounds. One who studied Buddhism for years grinned and shook her head wordlessly when I asked if she intended to give up her own faith. Several people referred to Buddhism as "a path to knowledge" or "a way of life" rather than a religion. So I guess one answer to the question of why I didn't give up Christianity for Buddhism is that Buddhism doesn't ask anyone to give up anything. One Buddhist who has spent two decades building a temple complex in California for no salary tells his relatives that he still considers himself Christian.

But the other reason is more complex. Christianity is deeply embedded in my heart. As much as I may rail against some of the Baptist teachings of my youth, I never go into a group of Baptists without thinking how much I like them and how at home I feel among them. I say that I'm willing to give up Christian orthodoxy in order to go my own spiritual way, but I don't want to renounce the foundations of my childhood. I may never go to a church, but to give up Jesus is not something I would do willingly. Why? The answer can be captured in one word, a short word with incredibly complex meanings: grace.

For a while I thought that Christian prayer and Buddhist meditation were the same. But at one point when I was struggling to change myself, to wrest my emotions away from some sinkhole they had fallen into, I tried to meditate. It helped. I felt more peaceful, more centered, more in control. I told myself that I didn't need prayer.

But I did need it, perhaps because I'm so weak. I wanted a God to direct myself toward. I wanted a God to thank, to feel loved by, to wrestle with. I know these yearnings don't mean that there is such a God. And even if there is, I know that I am quite likely making an incomprehensible force into something like a warm, fuzzy pet molded into my own image. Even so, when I returned to my rather desultory habits of prayer, I did so with a rush of relief and happiness to be back.

I am reminded of an interview I did with a Buddhist monk who left his tradition to become a Christian preacher. I couldn't imagine why he would do such a thing. So I asked him what Christianity could have possibly given him that Buddhism didn't. He said that it gave him help. He was a refugee at the time, and he felt utterly hopeless. The Buddhists had told him to look within himself for comfort. "You're on your own," he said.

But the Christians said, "We'll help you and so will our God." It was an offer he couldn't refuse. I guess I feel the same way. One of the old hymns we used to sing in church has a line about standing on the promises of God. I like Buddhism. I still meditate. I think its wisdom is greater in many ways than the Christianity I knew as a child. But if I have to stand somewhere, I'm reluctant to move from the promises that my family has stood on.

SECTION 6

My theology

Chapter 28

Who Is God?

I AM NOT in this quest for love of God. I don't even know the guy. How could I love Him? I'm in it for my own benefit. I'm willing to be captured by a higher calling. I'm willing to entertain the notion that a closer acquaintance with God would change my focus to something more noble than self-interest, but my present motivation is entirely pragmatic. I want to live a good life. I want less fear, more peace, a sense of deeper meaning. If I am willing to scrape away the gilt of life's illusions, it is only because I hope that something better is hidden underneath.

But it does occur to me to wonder just exactly who it is I'm talking about when I say I'm looking for God. I guess you can look for someone without any notion of how he appears, and that's pretty much what I am doing. But it does make things more difficult. Reverend Dykes believes that one of the first tasks for a person trying to form her own theology is deciding who God is.

When I was intent on leaving God behind, I thought of Him primarily as the rule maker. He was the standard that I failed to reach. In prayer and in church services, I felt a number of pleasant feelings that I associated with Him—peace, a sense of well-being, joy, sometimes even ecstasy. I also felt a deep remorse for my shortcomings. I associated that feeling with God's presence and His call for repentance. For me, God was often the Great Guilt Giver.

I sometimes had the feeling that God was close, even inside me. People in the church of my childhood talked of Jesus as though he was very much our buddy. In other ways God was far away. He was up there judging, expecting people to be always reaching and yearning toward Him. More than anything else, God was static. All the preachers agreed that He was unchanging. What that often translated to was the notion that new ideas about Him were wrong. Having the "faith of our fathers" wasn't just a nice idea; it was essential. Anything else was fraudulent. I grew up hearing that God never changed and that people who didn't think of Him in exactly the way their grandparents did were trying to make Him fit their own sinful notions. The most sinful idea of all was to think that God might seem different to different people or that faith might be different to different people. That would be giving us wiggle room for our bad old sinful selves; that would be "cutting God to fit the fashion of the day." It would also mean, of course, that authority would have vastly less authority.

These days, however, I'm wondering if giving human authority less sway might not give God more. It's just a thought. But like a lot of thoughts, once you have it, it's hard to get it to go away.

The idea that faith might be radically different for different people and that what we need from God might be different according to our individual natures first occurred to me in a somewhat rude way. I was talking with one of those boundlessly enthusiastic young Christian men who approach faith in so much the same way they approach football that they often use the same terms in explaining them. He was chatting away about his relationship with God when he said, "God just told me to get my butt in gear." I must have looked shocked because he stopped for a moment. I was having some doubt about whether God would really speak in such an unholy way. But my Christian friend wasn't backing down. He knows God's voice when he hears it. "That's the way God talks to me," he said, as firm and cheerful as ever.

As a reporter I learned that people of strong faith can disagree completely about the nature of God. I always knew that people disagree about God, but, like a lot of other Christians, I was happy to write off the faith of those who disagreed with me. They didn't really know God, we said. But as a reporter without a faith to defend, it became clear that there wasn't any evidence to show that one faith was more true than any other.

So I looked at some of the versions of God. Some of those versions are bold enough to say God changes. There are even those who think of Him as being less than entirely blameless. Rabbi Burton Visotzky, the teacher who inspired Bill Moyers's series on Genesis, told me he thinks the story of Noah and the flood demonstrates that God is altering his behavior as He and humankind attempt to figure out how to make their covenant work. In a covenant, both sides have to learn to communicate. This means God must learn to listen, and because God has given humans free will, He may have to listen to things He doesn't like, said the rabbi. The flood God sent to drown all living things (except Noah, his family, and the animal pairs) is an example of a time when the "clunky" covenant between God and humans became so frustrating to God that He just started smashing things— or flooding them, as the case may be. But at the end of the story, God changes and promises that He will never again destroy all living things.

That is an astonishing reading of Scripture to me. Many Christians would think Rabbi Visotzky's ideas are heresy, although I don't know if Christians go so far as to accuse Jews of that particular sin. They might rather simply ignore them. But if you believe, as I do, that we can't really know more than a smidgen about God, then why not consider various ideas? God's reality doesn't hinge on our thinking. To get all upset about how someone thinks about God seems to me to be giving far too much emphasis to human reasoning, which is pretty puny.

The rabbi's interpretation of the flood gives God a much lower place in terms of His being fallible and changeable. So you lose something in his reading. But it opens up some very compelling spiritual ideas. If God is learning as we are learning, if we're in a contract with God and the outcome depends on both sides, then our part in this deal is quite a bit more important than I imagined. And if that's so, then the universe might change enormously if we did our part. To me that is a far more exciting, empowering idea than the old cringing, dirty, filthy sinner model. Maybe God isn't supposed to be exciting and empowering. But it's a nice idea to think that He might be.

Philosopher Alfred North Whitehead believed in "process theology," which said that God can't see the future and therefore He changes in response to what humans do. Charles Hartshorne, who elaborated on Whitehead's theories, says that God's ongoing evolution as He and humanity move through time together explains how the vengeful God of the Old Testament becomes the loving, forgiving God of the New Testament.

Finding out about these theories caused me to realize that perhaps the preachers who railed against the notion of the changing God knew more than I understood. I thought they were merely trying to box me in, when in fact they were aiming at far more lofty targets. Once again, what the conservative preachers see as threat, I see as opportunity.

Charlotte Perkins Gilman had a radically different idea about God that could have been put together yesterday. She based her life on what she called rational religion, believing that much of what the Christian churches taught came from the clergy's desire to protect their status, according to historian Jody Potts. God, Gilman wrote, is the force for good in the universe. "We have felt love, seen it at work, so we may know God is . . . just as we know other facts."

To know God, people should actualize the love within them, Gilman said. She didn't believe a personal relationship with God was possible, and she thought reverence for God was misplaced, writes Potts. "God is there working all the time, not angry or jealous or any of those things that the limited intelligence of the Hebrews discredited Him with, but a steady lifting force, always to be relied on, bearing no grudge against the last and highest form of his creation— Humanity," according to Gilman.

To bow down to God, to supplicate or beg for forgiveness, insults the force by implying that it is capricious and that it debases humankind, according to Gilman. "A Force does not require reverence; has no use for it. One may heartily respect the power of electricity or the power of steam; but this respect leads to earnest study and wise use—not to the swinging of censers and the singing of hymns," she wrote.

You don't have to do much interpreting to back up the notion that God appears to different people in different ways. To Moses, He is a burning bush. To Jacob, He is a wrestler. To Abraham, He is three strangers who come trekking across the desert. No one who encounters Him finds Him to be as He was in the last report. But those examples of God's presence don't seem to have convinced people who are intent on requiring that everyone else agree with their version of Him.

I believe God is vast enough to encompass the diversity of human personality and changing times. It is not He who changes but our ability to perceive different aspects of Him. Like a lot of other people, I think the blind men and the elephant analogy is an apt one. We stand in a certain place and we feel a part of something far too huge to be encompassed. The blind man at the tail says the elephant is skinny like a snake. The blind man at the side says the elephant is vertical like a wall, and so on.

Alan Watts uses another analogy. He writes that God is like a cat passing on a fence. We are looking through a knothole as the cat passes and can only see parts of his body. One person sees the nose and whiskers; another sees only the brightly blinking eye. Jalaluddim Runi casts the matter somewhat differently. His story tells of the man who gives a dirham to four people. The Persian decides to spend his on an angur. The Arab says he will spend his on an inab. A Turk says he will spend his on an uzum, and a Greek says he will spend his on an istabil. These differences so disconcert them that the men begin to fight, never realizing that each plans to purchase a grape.

The more I know about life and the more I hear about God, the less likely it seems that the conformity organized religion often demands from believers is something that comes from God. What kind of sense does it make to believe that in a universe of incredible diversity, everyone who has commerce with God must fit into a few rigid molds or He won't deal with them? If God loved us as a father loves his children, as most religious people claim, He wouldn't require that we all be alike. Even a human father would know that is an impossibility and not the requirement of love at all. We are like a bouquet of flowers, says Archbishop Desmond Tutu. Each one of us has our own color and scent and cannot be replaced by any other. Other religious thinkers put the same respect for diversity and its place with God another way: "All roads lead to God."

My own idea of God is, of course, merely one I made up. I started with the idea that God understands my heart, as my mother said, and from there everything fell into question. But once again, I made up my theology, gave up on having anyone else agree, kept quiet about it, and then began to see it reflected in unexpected places. I've already mentioned that Nouwen said God is the one who calls us beloved. That's fairly close to being the one who knows my heart.

Then I read that the late A. W. Tozer, an evangelist and Christian mystic, believed that God sent Jesus to show us His own true nature. "From Him we learn how God acts toward people. The hypocritical, the basically insincere, will find Him cold and aloof, as they once found Jesus; but the penitent will find Him merciful, the self-condemned will find Him generous and kind. To the frightened He is friendly, to the poor in spirit He is forgiving, to the ignorant, considerate; to the weak, gentle; to the stranger, hospitable." In that idea is a God who not only knows my heart but responds to me differently according to what is in my heart.

Ten years ago I read a short story by Karel Capek with a concept of God that so intrigued me that I have repeated the story to numerous people in different conversations over the years. It's about a murderer who went to heaven to face the final judgment. God was called to the stand to tell the truth about the man's life. He gave details about each of the man's nine murders, about his greed and his indifference to the suffering of others. When the judges left the room to debate the sentence they were about to hand down, only God and the murderer were left in the courtroom.

The man asked God who the judges were and why He wasn't among them. The judges are people who were judged on earth, God said. Why was He not a judge? "Because I know everything. . . . Because my knowledge is infinite. If judges knew everything, absolutely everything, then they would also understand everything. Their hearts would ache. They couldn't sit in judgment—and neither can I. As it is, they know only about your crimes. I know all about you."

I have to admit that despite my antibelief doctrine, I can't help but try my hand at shaping some image of God for myself. So here are my ideas.

I think God is that which we call out to, the one who understands us as no one else does. I think He is inside us and outside us. I think we make Him over in our own image because that is the only way we can understand Him. And I think He may sometimes oblige us by being what we perceive. But in my slight experience He is always a surprise. It is intriguing to think about who God is, but I'm not sure it's necessary. The point is to try to touch Him or to hear Him or to feel the effects of His presence in such a way that we become more what we were meant to be. If we stay humble and pure and follow

Buddha's advice about letting go of desires, I think we know what we were meant to be without too much preaching about it.

At least these are my thoughts as I write at this moment. I'm increasingly comfortable with the idea that my concept of God is such a rough sketch that He might not even recognize Himself if He were to see it. So I hope to keep refining or erasing if need be.

Chapter 29

What Is Faith?

THE GREAT EMANCIPATOR of my spiritual life is a Methodist minister and professor. I have only talked to him on the telephone. His name is James Fowler, and he freed me with two ideas. The first idea is that faith not only can change but must change for many people. The second idea is that belief and faith are not the same. His first idea allowed me to hope that I might not be the stubborn and prideful God rejecter I thought I was, but rather a stubborn and resourceful God seeker. The second idea allowed me to hope that even as I reject most of what other Christians believe to be fact, I might still have faith.

In the seventies, Fowler was a young Harvard scholar who set out to map the land of faith. It was terrain that human beings had talked about for thousands of years, but it had not been explored with the social science tools and perspectives that the theologian could bring to bear. Fowler and his assistants interviewed 359 people, asking them a series of questions that took about three hours. Using his analysis of those interviews, Fowler came up with six stages of faith that many people in complex, literate, industrialized societies may go through.

Correlating those stages with the work of human development pioneers Jean Piaget, Erik Erikson, and Lawrence Kohlberg, Fowler concluded that cognitive development is necessary for faith to mature. By that he meant that as reasoning, intuition, and perception mature, so does faith. It matures and it changes.

Young children have a different form of faith from adults, he wrote. As people mature, some move to different stages of faith, and others remain at the same level. Those who remain at the same level may do so because the faith they have meets their needs. But other people—perhaps in response to outside forces or crises in their lives or merely the way they process information in the world—may move to other levels.

Fowler's ideas began creating a buzz well before his work was finished. The six stages had such resonance for nuns at Boston College that they photocopied pages from his unfinished manuscript and sent them around the world long before *Stages of Faith: The Psychology of Human Development and the Quest for Meaning* was published in 1981. His ideas are now the foundation for much of the Christian education given in mainstream Protestant and Catholic churches.

Fowler's theories liberated me because they asserted that my failure to stay in the church of my youth might not be the lapse I thought it was. Instead it might be the necessary step for me to go forward into a more mature faith. Later I found others who said the same things in different ways. Sam Keen writes, for instance, that people who want to grow up spiritually must reach the "outlaw" stage in order to break free of other people's notions and find their own truth.

Fowler's first stage of faith development occurs in children from three to seven years old when they imitate what they see and hear. They may tell Bible stories and talk about Jesus, but in his view they don't yet have the cognitive ability to truly integrate spiritual ideas their parents give them with their own reality.

About school age, children in the second stage take on beliefs for themselves in a literal, one-dimensional way. Some adults and denominations stay at this "mythic-literal" stage.

The third stage may be brought about by the struggle of young people or adults to integrate faith into a complex world. This faith is a basis for identity and outlook, and it is deeply felt. Concern for others tends to be concentrated in one-on-one relationships.

Many Christian church members stay at this stage throughout

their lives, according to Fowler. Fundamentalist groups are characteristically at this stage. People in such groups may easily resolve conflicts or feel none between their faith and their perceptions of the world, but those who do feel such conflicts may break away and come to see themselves as being outside religion. In later life, however, they may return with a different appreciation.

The last three stages show increased questioning and openness to wisdom from other traditions. These styles of faith are likely to depend on inner confirmation more often than outside authority. People are likely to see themselves as responsible for helping to bring about social justice. A stage four, for instance, can see that people may be poor because of a system. So to work for social justice you have to be at least a four. Unitarian-Universalists are almost always at this level, said Fowler, and so are some evangelicals and fundamentalists. Many mainline churches are a mix of stages three and four, he contended.

At stage four, people tend to see one side as right and the other side as wrong. They still rely on categories to get a fix on reality. At stage five, that begins to change. People move beyond either/or as a way of seeing the world. Here the person of faith "lets go" more completely. Reality is allowed to speak for itself. Contradictions and paradoxes are more easily accepted as being simply part of how reality presents itself. These people celebrate, revere, and attend to wisdom of many kinds without having to control it, shape it, or make it fit into categories.

The sixth stage is such a high level of spiritual development that Fowler didn't find any examples to interview. He put Mother Teresa, Gandhi, and Martin Luther King, Jr., at that level, and likened that "universalizing stage" to some aspects of Buddhism and Hinduism. Their sense of being in a community that includes all humans allows them to "create zones of liberation from the social, political, economic and ideological shackles," Fowler wrote. That doesn't mean that they won't have personal problems or faults, but their concept of the world and the purpose of humankind in it will be spiritually far advanced beyond most people's.

His analysis also gave me some tools for understanding why the faithful have so much conflict within themselves and among one another. It was a window into how people's faith can grow. And it explained something that I often struggled with in talking with Christians. All the Christians I know say that Jesus, represented by the Holy Spirit, comes into their lives and changes them. They are "born again" as new creatures. So here's a question: Why is it that the new creatures are so much like the old?

The question only occurred to me after I heard it posed by a former Church of Christ minister. He had been in the church all his life. He believed fervently that Jesus saves souls. But he couldn't help but notice that people don't seem to change as much as the Bible seems to promise they will. They may go to church more. They may separate themselves from the world. They may talk differently. They may sing in the choir, tithe their salary, show up every Sunday—but almost none changes into the kind of people Jesus seemed to have in mind. A few of them *are* radically different from other people. They live lives of poverty in order to serve the poor or adopt handicapped children or exhibit such a loving spirit that other people get a strong sense of comfort and joy just being around them. But some nonbelievers are also like that, and most believers aren't. They drive big cars, buy expensive houses, go along pretty much as other humans do. I once heard Professor Martin Marty say that religion makes good people better and bad people worse. I thought that was about the most dismal observation I ever heard.

People of different faiths had convinced me that God might be saying different things to different people. But the basic principles of the religions are all the same: Love your fellows as you love yourself. Fowler's theories showed that even if God is saying the same things, we won't hear them alike because we simply have different ears. Some of us will take God's word to mean that we ought to vote for government food programs and others will be convinced that the good Christian thing to do is to make sure people work for whatever they get. It isn't so much that God is saying different things but that we hear according to who we are. Just as some people understand physics and others never will, just as some people hear meanings in a conversation that others never do, so some people move into different levels of faith that others never reach.

People before Fowler recognized that faith grows over time and they set out a progression. But Fowler used actual stages, and that has been problematic for some. One professor suggested that "styles of faith" might better convey the idea Fowler is going after. Thinking in stages, "We all can get worried about whether we are far enough along on the faith spectrum," he said. "That deforms faith into something we have performance anxiety about."

Other people criticized Fowler's ideas because they said he didn't give enough credit to the notion of God's grace. People can't progress in faith by themselves, they said. It's a gift from God. But, in fact, Fowler didn't say how people grew. He just noted that they were arrayed along a spectrum.

Fowler, too, was uncomfortable with the elitism implied by stages, but he said, "These are not stages in getting saved or in the degree or depth of your relationship with God." A person can have a deep and significant relationship with God at any of these stages. What he is describing are stages and changes in thinking and understanding that come as a person deals with complexity, deals with paradoxes, deals with the tensions that life provides us, he said.

People at the earlier levels might be happier people, he said. Their faith might very well get them through life better than the faith of people at the higher stages. They might be more comforted during grief and illness. They might have a stronger sense that God will be there for them. They might have a greater sense of well-being and peace. Nevertheless, he did not give up the idea that the stages were a progression. The faith that reaches beyond one's self and one's relatives and friends to a vision that applies to all of humankind is a deeper faith, he told me.

That brings me to the second point of Fowler's book, which challenged a common understanding of faith. Borrowing from theologians Paul Tillich and H. Richard Niebuhr, he said that faith is not the same as religion or belief. Belief, he said, is the content of faith. But faith itself is something deeper, something universal in human beings. He said faith is the process of making meaning out of life.

It is "what you set your heart on," Fowler said. It can be seen not in what you say you believe but in how you act, what you spend your money for, and how you use your time. Under Fowler's theory, a person might have faith in friends or work or family or God. Even an atheist might have faith, he said. In his view, most people are "practical polytheists." In other words, they base their faith on a variety of sources.

His theory was a great gift. It helped me move past the idea that believers are inevitably separated by what they believe about God. It said that what we believe is a sideshow, so to speak. The main event is deeper. It also explained something that puzzled me in my reporting. I was quite separated from the beliefs held by many of the religious people I interviewed, but I almost always connected with them on another level. I got along quite well with people whose beliefs sometimes appalled me. The reason is that our beliefs were different but our faith was the same, at least in Fowler's terms.

We asked the same questions. We believed that ultimate value resides in something outside secular experience. We might have disagreed on the answers but we had faith in the value of the questions.

Chapter 30

Who Are the People of Faith?

AFTER ABSORBING FOWLER'S ideas about faith, I went looking for four people who illustrated different stages. Once I found them, I wrote the following stories. I didn't put religious labels on the types. I don't see the point of that. The stories make their own points about faith and its different styles.

Elizabeth

You've got to wrestle with God if you want to grow in faith, says Elizabeth Blessing. "First you've got to tell God the truth." Such as? "I don't want to love my neighbor."

You must tell God the truth about yourself, Ms. Blessing says. "Only God and you know the truth about who you are. Everything else is just opinion."

And then, of course, God may very well issue a directive that will send you out into the world to face even more wrestling. Many evenings, as the seventy-six-year-old director of the East Dallas Co-operative Parish goes to her car, a mentally ill man presses his face close to hers to demand, "When you going to give me that Cadillac?"

Once in a while, she comes back at him just as aggressively. She tells him to get away, to leave her alone, to forget about that Cadillac. When that happens, she's likely to confess later, "Dear God, I've made a mess again."

Ms. Blessing works in some of Dallas's poorest, roughest neighborhoods, running a social service agency supported by twelve churches. Once, she and her husband were prominent real-estate developers. She was the second woman to serve on the Dallas City Council and the first to run for mayor.

"To work in this place takes all the courage I can muster—to do the right thing," she said. "And I don't always know what the right thing is."

She has a laugh that comes easily and often. There's a kind of delight in her hazel eyes as she talks of God and her life. Sitting behind the long table that serves as a desk, she shifts in the chair like a schoolgirl, resting her chin on her hands and then jumping up to fetch a book that has a quote she likes.

Her energy comes from having balance in life, she says, and from the Holy Spirit.

"Energy is definitely divine." Ms. Blessing has a hundred projects, a thousand ideas for projects, and she's in a hurry to get all of them done.

She says her minister sometimes tells her, "Oh, you're just in a hurry because you're old, and you don't have much time left." Ms. Blessing, who isn't above adding a year to her age for effect, says that's right, but it's not all. "I'm in a hurry because we're so far behind."

For Ms. Blessing, one of faith's rewards is a perspective that differs from that of many other people. She feels different about inner-city churches, for instance, from how many middle-class people feel: She doesn't believe in leaving them behind.

Munger Place United Methodist Church, where the cooperative parish is located, is the church Ms. Blessing grew up in. Her brother, who died at eleven, was the first person from the church to die. She was married there; her four children were christened and confirmed there. She's never belonged to another church. As the neighborhoods around the church declined and middle-class Dallas moved north, Ms. Blessing never considered leaving.

"I believe this is exactly where God wants me to be," she said.

Ms. Blessing says she has never doubted God's existence or even his presence. But she is no "head-in-the-clouds Christian," as she puts it. She has not always believed in events that many other Christians believe in absolutely: the six-day creation or the virgin birth, for instance.

After some years of such doubts, however, she's come back to believing in the whole package. "It's tradition," she said.

Ms. Blessing can't point to a time of actual conversion in the way many evangelicals can. She believes it takes lots of conversions to fulfill the Christian mandates.

"Maybe daily," she said. She believes in praying constantly, both consciously and unconsciously. She also believes that repentance and the acceptance of forgiveness have to occur often. With that comes the need to forgive others—which puts her right back where she started with God and wrestling.

But after all these years, she has some victories to reflect on. And as is often the way of faith, some of them came allied with defeat.

Her sixties mayoral campaign was one of those. She ran against J. Erik Jonsson, one of the city's richest men and most honored patriarchs. "He promised to send me back to the kitchen, and he did. But not for long." The campaign was rough, and she came out so battered that she wasn't sure she could forgive.

She prayed that God would keep her from having to face one of her adversaries. For a year, she didn't see him even once. When she finally did run into him at a wedding, she said, "Tom, do you know what my prayer was for a year after the election? 'Dear God, don't let me see Tom Unis.' But today I can say I'm glad to see you."

"Oh, Elizabeth," he said, laughing as if she were joking. "You don't mean that."

But she did mean it, she says. And she also meant that God had supplied. First the time. And then the grace.

Vincent

Vincent Hall works behind a desk all week. He wears a tie and pressed shirts to the office. He is chairman of the board of the $80 million Dallas Telco Federal Credit Union and a manager at Southwestern Bell. But on weekends, he's a warrior.

Marching up and down the street, taking baby steps in the crosswalk so drivers have to stop and read the signs he carries, Mr. Hall is one of Dallas County Commissioner John Wiley Price's group of protesters who call themselves the Warriors.

(Price is a flamboyant, outspoken man who has landed in jail a number of times for his activities, which usually involve protesting racism. He and Hall are both African American. Price is so despised by some white Dallasites that the mere mention of his name is often a code signaling that the speaker is about to launch into a racist diatribe. It will begin, as such soliloquies often do in the South, with the assertion, "I'm not a racist but. . . . ")

As Hall marches, people yell insults, denigrating his parentage, his race, and his intelligence in the most vile way possible. Oddly enough, Mr. Hall landed in this cacophony of abuse by being still and knowing God.

It was a thousand sermons, a heap of Bible verses. It was every Sunday—and most all of Sunday—when as a boy he listened to a stern grandfather who wore white shirts with French cuffs and had all the dignity of a righteous man. It was salvation at eight and renewed dedication at nineteen. It was one sermon in particular he heard ten years ago.

The preacher said that there are three kinds of believers: if, because, and regardless. Jacob was an "if" believer, the preacher said. He loved God if God did good things for him. David was a "because" believer. He loved God because God did good things for him. Job was a "regardless" believer. He loved God regardless of what happened.

"Ever since then, I've been trying to be 'regardless,' " the thirty-seven-year-old said.

One test of his faith was in 1990, when he was charged with criminal mischief for painting over liquor and cigarette billboards. Before charges were dropped, he spent his first and only time in jail.

"That's the only blemish on my record," said the father of two girls. He doesn't regret it.

"The first one we painted over had a scantily clad woman riding a beer can," said Mr. Hall, who won't allow cable television in his house because of the portrayal of women on MTV.

"One good thing about having grown up in such a pristine environment," he said, "is that you know what trash is and you know the damage it can do."

In the last Dallas City Council race, Mr. Hall believed God was calling him to run against incumbent Don Hicks.

"I had to do it. I'd prayed about it and tried to get around it but I couldn't," he said.

Mr. Hall lost that election, but he believes God was with him "regardless."

"Just because I didn't win doesn't mean I wasn't called," he said. "It just means God had another purpose. He might have had me run for my children."

Mr. Hall's wife, Regeina, is the daughter of a deacon and deaconess. Even so, she isn't always enthusiastic about her husband's decisions to follow where he thinks God is leading. "She thinks I'm crazy," he said. Some people at Southwestern Bell think the same thing.

And that's fine, says Mr. Hall. "When I get so small that I can't let other people have their opinions, I'm pretty small."

He believes in a balanced life. So, although he has picketed the police department, he also serves on two police advisory boards.

He's a leader of the Peavy Road Education Coalition, formed after school trustee Dan Peavy was tape-recorded making racial and antigay slurs. He also works with inner-city kids and is a deacon at New Hope Baptist Church.

He finds that his theology has changed over the years. He doesn't have many absolutes anymore, and he thinks about abiding by the spirit of God's law more than the letter. Mr. Hall also says God gives different people different directives.

"Your God ain't like my God," he said. "God is different to each of us."

What his God tells him to do isn't always his first choice. "I do a lot of things I'm scared to death to do, but my God calls me to do them," he said. "I couldn't do them if I didn't know my God was behind me."

The Warriors have a saying that Mr. Hall holds close: "Your prayers ought to have feet."

The protesters never march without first praying, and they never disband without praying again. "The ones who don't pray don't last," said Mr. Hall. Anyone fueled by anger won't be able to withstand the fusillade of insults for long, he explains.

Talking about how he lives his life and why, Mr. Hall may quote a Tower of Power song, Danish philosopher Søren Kierkegaard, his grandmother, or his friend Mr. Price. But most often he quotes the Bible. "There's a verse in Micah 6," he said. " 'But what does the Lord require of you but to do justice, to love kindness and to walk humbly with your God?'

"That about gets it."

Rebecca

For as far back as Rebecca Sklaver can remember, faith has given her life a sense of richness and wonder, and even magic. That sense was never stronger than on the day her mother died.

Mrs. Sklaver believes her mother knew she was about to die. Although she was perfectly healthy, a month before her death she began reassuring her children about her love for them. Her last day was a Sunday. Mother and daughter planned to eat together as their families did each week. But on this day, Mrs. Sklaver's mother insisted on bringing the food herself.

Twelve years later, her daughter still remembers. "The hamburger we ate was just hamburger, but it was wonderful. She was eating some bread, and she took it from her mouth and said, 'I give you this bread.' "

Mrs. Sklaver took it, and told her mother, "You are always taking bread from your mouth."

Her parents went home, and a few hours later her father called to say her mother was not feeling well. Rebecca looked at her husband, a physician, and said, "I am not ready for her to die."

She says she knew—and more than that. "Looking back, I know

God was with us," she said. "I didn't pray, 'God don't let her die.' I prayed, 'God, I am in your trust, whatever you want from us.' I just wanted to have the strength."

Faith begins Mrs. Sklaver's every day. "When I wake up in the morning, the first thing I am aware of is that I am a Jewish woman with responsibilities to my family, to my community, and to my world, and that gives me the strength to go on," said the fifty-two-year-old mother of three.

Elegant in slim black pants, an embroidered white blouse, and heels, Mrs. Sklaver still has the lilting accent of Colombia, where she was born. Listening to her is like stepping into a Gabriel García Márquez novel. The quality of her faith permeates even the most ordinary moments. She didn't choose it, she says. It chose her.

She says she has never, ever doubted God, or felt out of touch with Him. "I don't hear God talking," she said, "but I know what God demands of me."

What is that?

"My righteousness. I can only judge myself, not my neighbor. If you look at the Ten Commandments, you know what to do."

That includes visiting the sick, the frail, the elderly. One of the friends she concerns herself with is Rose Horowitz, who lives in a retirement home. Mrs. Sklaver calls Mrs. Horowitz three times a day.

"I want to make sure in the morning that she is awake. I want to know later that there is something good in her day. In the evening, I'm curious. What did she eat for dinner? Was it good?"

She does this out of friendship and because she sees such acts as part of being Jewish.

"This comes out of my Jewishness. It is my responsibility to say that she should not despair, that there is no room for despair."

Mrs. Sklaver's younger son once said of her that when assessing any course of action, her first questions were likely to be, "Is it ethical? Is it moral?"

Although not all her children observe Jewish traditions and holidays as she does, Mrs. Sklaver is well pleased with them because they have compassion. That alone is enough for her to call them successful, she says.

Her daughter's first drive in the first car she ever owned was to a home for the aged to visit a friend there. When her son was at Dartmouth, he also befriended someone in a nursing home. The other son chose to observe Yom Kippur a few years ago by giving sandwiches to the homeless.

The Sklavers have what her husband jokingly refers to as a mixed marriage. Although he is Jewish, he is not religious. Mrs. Sklaver, who calls him a holy man because of his compassion, says they don't have conflict over religion and admits that may be because he is so often willing to go along with her devotion.

Keeping kosher is among the acts Mrs. Sklaver, a member of Congregation Shearith Israel, believes is important. That practice restricts her life somewhat in that only a few Dallas restaurants serve food she can eat, and she calls ahead to let those know she's coming.

But the rewards outweigh the sacrifices, she says. The discipline reminds her that food is holy. And that what she does with her mouth matters.

"What I put into my mouth I have to watch. But very important, I must watch what comes out of my mouth."

Faith is everything, she says, and everywhere. "I truly think without faith we could not face the ugliness in ourselves and around us. It offers to us the chance to have that behavior of holiness that we all want to have."

Jon

Jon Cobb committed early. He was saved at eleven.

He committed often. "The decisions you make to be faithful every day determine a person's character," he said.

And he committed to a simple faith, the one his mother passed down to him.

Widowed with two children, she was in the pew every Sunday— even when she didn't feel up to it—and she gave money to the church even when she didn't have it to spare. She prayed constantly, and she believed the Bible to be God's literal truth.

"She taught me I was third—God first, others second, me third," said Mr. Cobb.

At sixty, he can look back over a life lived with a faith that has never changed, except to get stronger.

"I've been able to test his promises, his commandments," he said, "and I've found them to be true."

Mr. Cobb is an oilman, a Dallas native, married thirty-seven years in a relationship that he says has never had a hint of infidelity. On Sunday mornings, the Cobb family is and always has been in church. "Success as a parent is to raise responsible Christian citizens," he said.

He has an open-faced, easy manner. Not loud, not bombastic, a Texas businessman with not a bit of J. R. Ewing about him.

He has been "moderately" successful, he says. "I give Him all the credit," said Mr. Cobb, referring to God. When Mr. Cobb was studying geology and petroleum engineering at Texas A&M, he took a good look at his faith. He weighed his Bible against the scientific theories his professors were teaching, and the Bible won, for once and for always.

"I believe the first verse of Genesis is entirely correct," he said. "God created, and so He is in control."

Mr. Cobb seems to be a straight-ahead kind of guy—in conversation, in business, and in belief.

"A person has to decide in his own life: Is there a God or isn't there a God?" he said. "That's the big decision. If God does exist, then God must have come to the human race in some way."

The Bible lays out that way, he says, and if taken at face value, it puts down a good foundation for life.

"If you accept the Bible in that fashion, it comes alive," he said, "and it's a guide for your life. It's the blueprint."

Two of the pillars of his life are John 3:16—"For God so loved the world, he gave His only begotten son"—and Matthew 6:33—"Seek ye first the kingdom of God and all these things will be added unto you."

He said God called him to be an oilman and showed that calling by providing opportunity as Mr. Cobb proceeded in that direction. To some, that may sound like a rather secular calling for God to issue, but it fits well with Mr. Cobb's belief that God made man to manage the earth.

That belief gives him firm ground to stand on. If it leads to conflict with environmentalists, that's okay. "You're going to be in conflict with the nonbeliever," he said.

Mr. Cobb, an elder and chairman of the board at Scofield Memorial Church, an independent Bible church, said he believes Christianity is the answer to a good share of the world's problems. Racism, for instance, concerns him, and religion gives him a clear answer. God doesn't see race; he sees only believers and nonbelievers, said Mr. Cobb, demonstrating his point by drawing a biblical genealogy chart on the paper table covering at an Italian restaurant. The chart takes a while to draw, but he perseveres.

"This may not mean much to you, but it means a lot to me," he said. The answer to racism isn't social action; it's evangelism. "It's our responsibility to get out there and convert people."

Mr. Cobb sees his own success in life as a testament to God's faithfulness to the faithful. But God is also a good security in the hard times. "People of faith can go through medical crises, through loss-of-life crises, and they seem to have the ability to succeed without a lot of emotional distress because they have the peace of God in their heart."

If Mr. Cobb were to offer advice to young people, it would most likely come in biblical form. One of the verses he would include sums up his own life: "As for me and my house, we will serve the Lord."

Chapter 31

Models of Faith

ER HAIR WAS gray, a little longer than chin-length, but thick and neatly kept. She wasn't elderly, fifties or sixties maybe, but she had a face so wrinkled that her skin was among the first things I noticed. She walked like a young person. I would have asked her name if I had known that I was going to think of her for years afterward as an example of the kind of spirit I wanted. But it took me a while to realize it.

Philip and I were coming back from a short vacation in Santa Fe. It was summer, a bad time to come back to Dallas. The Dallas–Fort

Worth airport is in the middle of a prairie. It's so hot during the summer that everything burns up—grass, flowers, people. As you drive home watching the heat shimmer off the road, you wonder for the thousandth time why you didn't pick a better place to live. I also had the going-back-to-work blues because a few days away had been enough to remind me how nice life could be when you weren't constantly being squeezed by a deadline.

A young, loud Texan was on the plane. When he got up to stretch his legs, he also exercised his mouth. He announced to the plane at large that he had just bought himself a pretty nice little ol' place in Santa Fe. He had about all the money he needed, and he was going to retire to that beautiful country and live the good life, he said, full of himself and his own good fortune. I looked at him with loathing. I couldn't help it. My envy was so intense that I hated the guy.

But the woman with the wrinkled face was listening, too. She smiled at him. "That's wonderful," she said. "I hope everything works out the way you want it to." She meant it. Her expression was full of goodwill and peace. She was so content with life, so totally at ease that the good fortune of others seemed lovely to her. I looked away and said nothing.

I don't think her peace came from money. She wasn't as rich as he was. At least she didn't look it. She looked not poor, but like someone of simple means. When we got off the plane, I watched her. No one met her. She slipped through the terminal, walking quickly, lithe, supple, and so alive. I never spoke to her. But I think of her all the time. That's who I want to be. I want to be not just forgiven for my base desires, but free of them. I want to be gracious and generous right down to my heart. I don't want to be those things because someone tells me I ought to be. I want to be those things because I think they are the way of freedom. I am looking for God because I think He can help me.

Not long ago, I read a poll that said the reason people aren't more interested in Christianity is that Christians aren't different enough from other people. Few people are impressed with religious people because of their churchgoing habits or their religious pronouncements. We're only impressed by evidence. We want to know that belief makes a difference, that it changes people into something better, higher, more self-assured, more happy, more self-sacrificing, kinder.

It could change them into all sorts of things, but it ought to change them and the change ought to be better. Religious people sometimes make a big deal about the evils of situational morality and how people don't know right from wrong anymore. Maybe that's so. But most people do know what a deeply spiritual person ought to be.

I think a relationship with God ought to give a person different values and change that person so that she exemplifies those values. That's why I have never forgotten the woman in the airport. I was so knotted up with my unhappiness. And the young rich Texan had so much that I wanted. Just listening to him caused longing to shoot through me. But the woman in the airport was not vulnerable to such base feelings. I don't know whether she was religious, but I think of her as profoundly religious. And she never said a word to me.

A good way to move forward in a spiritual life might be to look toward people who are like you want to be and then find out how they got that way. So I've done that. One of the first things I found is that what touches me most deeply in people is often not anything I would expect. Perhaps extreme holiness is too far beyond me. When I interviewed the Dallas mother whose four children and father were killed in a car accident, she kept telling me, "Anyone can have what I have. It's a free gift." She meant that anyone could become a born-again Christian as she is. I knew what she meant, but I didn't believe her. She is so focused on a particular type of God. And it isn't one that I really believe in. It must be a powerful one. But she seemed too unlike other people, too foreign, too holy. Certainly unlike me. I would like to have that kind of faith, but I don't think it's reachable. I look for quieter changes. I usually find them in an odd moment.

One of my early assignments as a religion reporter was to write a profile on Professor Martin Marty. I knew Dr. Marty's name long before I had any idea what exactly he did in religion. He may be the most famous religious scholar of our time. He is certainly the most famous church historian. I was ready to be awed by him, and he had plenty of stories about conversations with important people that did awe me. But what made me like him and believe in his Christianity wasn't his fame or his work or his reputation. It was a quirky little thing that happened as we entered an almost deserted restaurant.

A woman was sitting across the room, alone and about to order. Dr. Marty is a fast-talking, fast-moving person, renowned for his organization and precise scheduling. He was talking fast as we entered, but he spotted the woman right away and decided that we ought to invite her to join us. After asking if I was willing to share our meal, he scuttled right over to her, stuck his hand out, and said, "Hello, my name is Martin Marty, and I wondered if you would like to have dinner with us."

When I mentioned the moment to him later, he said, "Anyone would have done that." No, not anyone. I wouldn't have. I especially wouldn't have if I were Martin Marty. And most people wouldn't have if they were Martin Marty because being someone so important would have changed them, given them rights, made them aware of how important they were. Most successful people wear their success in some way. It sets them apart. You can hear how special they are in their voices, see it in how they move, the way they sit. It's not obnoxious usually. It just is. It's the way human beings are.

But Dr. Marty is not like that. Later I heard about many good works he has done. People told me how gregarious and kind he is, how efficient and brilliant. But nothing impressed me as much as that moment in the restaurant. *That* was what made me curious about Dr. Marty's faith; nothing else. He is a Christian, by the way, a Lutheran minister.

I've met other Christians I wanted to be like. Foremost among them was Danna Whorton. I met her some time ago when doing a story about hospice workers. She is a founder of Dallas's oldest hospice programs and a steady volunteer. She's a down-to-earth woman who summed up her contribution to the dying by saying that mostly she has just been there to hold their hands and listen. Everyone who meets Danna is impressed by her unassuming goodness and almost everyone wants to spend more time with her. I was no exception.

She didn't make a big point of it in our first conversation, but Danna is also a longtime Baptist. She's not a sock-it-to-'em-and-save-'em Baptist like those I grew up with. She's more a quietly faithful, live-it-through-service kind of Baptist. In her work with hospice, she never tries to push Christianity on someone as they lie dying. She doesn't quote Scripture or bring the Lord's name into everyday conversation. But something about her spirit so impressed me that when I wanted stories about people of faith, she came to mind immediately.

Her theology can be summed up pretty simply. "God takes care of us and He expects a certain response from us because of all we're given." A Christian's marching orders are the Great Commission, she says. "Go you therefore into all the world, preaching and teaching and doing all that I have taught you." Lots of people concentrate on the teaching and preaching aspect of that command.

Danna doesn't. She thinks religion is a fairly personal matter. She would talk to anyone about being a Christian if the subject came up and she thought she could do them some good. "I don't jump to the conclusion that if people don't believe like I do they are going to hell. That's not my business." Instead, Danna stresses the "doing all that I have taught you" part of the Great Commission.

"That means to feed the hungry, help the poor, comfort the dying," she said. Her many good deeds and volunteer work have made her a legend among those who know her. More than that, anybody who is around her feels better just by being there. She's nonjudgmental and calm, funny and self-effacing in a way that makes you think the world might be a better place than you previously thought.

On an end table in her living room is a photograph of an African American young man. I'd listened to Danna, who is white, talk about this grandson many times before I realized that the picture *was* her grandson. Danna is from North Carolina and her late husband was from Alabama. They taught their children that everyone is equal in God's sight. When their daughter took them at their word and married a black man, they threw her a nice wedding. Some of their relatives didn't come and haven't been friendly since then. Danna considers that their loss. Her grandson recently wrote that his grandmother was the person in his life who has taught him the most about living.

I thought Danna, with her lifetime of Bible reading, would turn out to have a pretty simple, literal faith. But I was surprised. When I asked whether she believed the earth was created in seven days, she said that she didn't know and she didn't much care. Her business is to respond to the Lord's blessings by helping other people, she said, and that's what she does. Did she think about the rewards she would get in heaven? No. God had always taken care of her and she figured He'd keep on doing so.

It doesn't take any imagination at all for Danna to envision the worst. At ninety-three, she has seen every bit of how bad death can be. She's seen how lonely old age can be. She knows how cruel life can become.

And yet she is not afraid. She read somewhere that one of the most repeated phrases in the Bible is "Be not afraid." And so, she isn't.

If I could pick up anybody's faith and make it mine, I'd take Danna's. So when I asked her how she got to be the way she is, I listened carefully for what I might do. But I very quickly came to understand that Danna is the way she is not only because God changed her, but at least partly because it's simply in her nature. For instance, she's never been a worrier. As a child, she was perfectly trusting. As an adult, she moved through life calmly, even when her husband had a stroke that left him bedfast for many years. Men from his Sunday school class and employees he had befriended over the years helped her get through. She hasn't ever worried about what the future would bring, and life has borne her out. "You're going to have pain in life, even if you hide from it," she said. "I don't figure my thinking about things is going to solve it. I can go out and hold someone's hand and make them feel better. That's my talent."

As for her own future, she figures she can face whatever it brings. "When you're the one who has to face it, to do it, you do it." She gave up driving three years ago, and she stopped taking hospice patients two years ago because she can't lift people as she used to be able to.

Danna knows that death could come anytime. "I don't spend a lot of time thinking about the afterlife. I think if God said He would be with me He will be." She likens the anticipation of death to what it feels like before someone marries.

"They're afraid because it's something new," she said. But in her case marriage worked out wonderfully. She imagines death will be like that, too. Of course people are apprehensive, she says. "It's something new."

Danna knows that her quiet, steady faith doesn't fit everyone. "Maybe it's being foolishly optimistic," she said, "but it's a great way to live."

I would love to be like Danna. I might even sign up at the Baptist Church if I thought it would make me be like her. But I don't think it would. Danna is naturally optimistic, good-natured, even-tempered. She doesn't fret or question her faith. She doesn't get all riled up when people in her church say things she doesn't agree with. I am not like that. I could be a Baptist, but I couldn't be a Danna. Her makeup from birth lent itself to a different kind of faith than the one I can reach. So where does that leave me? Still looking.

Chapter 32

Looking for Faith Outside the Usual Suspects

FROM THE MOMENT I saw Sue Smith, I knew I wanted to be friends. I'm usually a cautious person, slow to get to know people. But Sue has a kind of easiness about her that I found hard to resist. Every time we went to lunch, I'd talk so much that afterward I would apologize for monopolizing the conversation. But the next time I saw her, I would do the same thing.

It was as though some spell had fallen over me. I couldn't shut up. "I did this . . . and then I did that . . . and here's how I feel about this . . . and here's how I feel about that. . . ." Yammer, yammer, yammer. I hardly knew the woman, but given an hour of her time, I would start pouring out my self.

Over years of friendship, I've calmed down a bit, and she has finally been able to talk a little herself. Once I asked her what she wanted out of life. She is successful in a hard-nosed, competitive business. I expected that she would reveal some ambition for advancement. Instead, she said she wanted more than anything else to be the kind of person with whom other people felt perfectly safe.

I was stunned. I had never thought of such a goal. Most of the people I knew were interested in being the kind of people others were afraid of. The whole thrust of the business world is figuring out how to posture and bluster and make oneself into someone others would see as a significant force. Most of us are so scared of being run over that it never occurs to us to put energy into making others feel safe.

But, of course, that is exactly what Sue had done for me from the very first moment. When I asked what she thought about God, she smiled and shrugged. She knew what she was about to say would not suit me. She simply believes God or the universe or whatever has a plan for each person and that if we listen to our inner selves, we can follow that plan. She believes everything happens for a reason. She thinks good is rewarded and bad is punished, right now, here on earth. She was raised a Christian, but going to the Bible for spiritual sustenance would never occur to her. For that, she goes to a book-store and browses until something speaks to her and she buys it. She understands that her theology sounds absolutely softheaded. She doesn't even try to defend it.

We've talked about God many times, and I always point out examples that go against her theories, especially about everything working out to the good and bad being punished. I ask her how she can live by ideas she just put together herself from various sources. When she gives me examples of how she thinks life works, I sometimes laugh and shake my head. Refuting her is so easy that sometimes I don't even bother. She always responds in the same good-humored, self-effacing way: "I know it, but that's what I believe."

And here's the odd thing. I don't know anyone who lives more steadfastly by their faith than she does. I've watched her set goals for who she wanted to become. I've heard her outline ways that she was going to change her life so that it came more in line with the force for good that she thinks rules reality. Her religion is integrated totally into her life, and she learns lessons about it through the ordinary course of a day. She is good-humored, forgiving, buoyant, generous, ready to face her faults. She is exactly how I want to be.

Once Sue was having a hard time with a colleague. When he was demoted, someone mentioned that she looked particularly happy that day because of his downfall. I hadn't seen her. I hadn't talked to her. But I knew without any doubt that she had not rejoiced in someone else's misfortune. I didn't have to see her. I didn't have to ask her. I just knew it.

Whenever I tell a story like Sue's, I always hear voices of the God limiters in the back of my head. Some are saying that Sue may be a good person, but being good isn't enough to get her into heaven. To get into heaven, the God limiters say, you have to be saved by Jesus. That's a claim I can't refute since I haven't been to heaven to see who is there. But it's also a claim they can't prove. They can bully and scare and guilt people, but they can't prove a thing. The God limiters' other claim gives me more trouble. They say that her faith won't hold up when the hard times hit. But I wonder if that's true.

Sue is a pretty close match to the kind of religious person that Karen Armstrong writes about in her book on Genesis, *In the Beginning*. In one passage, she compares Abraham (who is the father of the Israelites, you'll recall) to his nephew, Lot. Lot, you will remember, was the man who chose the best land when offered the chance to take whatever he wanted. Later he lost it. He was the guy who ended up having to be rescued from Sodom. Afraid to face the future, he ended up hiding in a cave with his two daughters. Equally fearful, they became convinced that they would never find husbands. So they got their father drunk and seduced him as a way of having children.

Armstrong compares Abraham, who had the imagination to see a good future even when things looked bleak, with Lot, who always took the easy way out but wasn't able to adapt when misfortune came his way. "Without the imagination of Abraham, he was unable to live robustly and confidently. . . . Religion has often been used to stunt a person's growth or encourage a wholly other worldly vision. But Genesis indicates that a function of faith is to make us more productive and at ease in the world. God should not be experienced as a wholly ethereal panacea but as a mysterious accompanying presence that helps us make sense of the bewildering circumstances of our lives."

I might want to be like Sue, but once again, that doesn't seem possible. She, too, is simply a sunnier kind of person than I am. She always has been. She looks on the bright side, trusts people, thinks the world is a pretty good place and that God is probably a pretty good fellow. I could be more like Sue by watching her and following some of her advice, but I can't be her by mimicking her. There's too much difference in us, at too basic a level. Maybe I could be like Abraham, though. Maybe I could look toward the future with more vision.

So now I'm back to what Reverend Dykes said about faith. "You can't have mine," he said. "You have to find your own." The best way to know God, writes Neil Clark Warren, is to become authentically yourself because then you are the person God created you to be and His love can flow through you unimpeded. And the way to become authentically yourself is to learn to make your own decisions—about life and about God, he writes.

"Churches who try to tell you how you can or cannot find God are interested in controlling you," he says. "And that was not what Christ was about."

Yale professor of the philosophy of religion Louis Dupré believes religion was once integrated into our lives through tradition, but that that is no longer so. To survive as a believer, he believes we must "personally integrate what religion did in the past." He defines a religious life as a personal response to the call of the divine. It originates within the self. "To attain the religious life, the believer must be alert to the inner voice," he writes.

Chapter 33

What About Doubt, Guilt, and Self?

I T MAKES ME feel a little silly to be earnestly importuning God with all my soul and then suddenly hear a wry little voice in my head suggest that I might be talking to nothing but the ozone. It's a lot like sitting down in a chair that turns out not to be there. As you flail toward the floor, you feel not only injured but foolish to have been so trusting.

I am newly returned to this whole idea of seeking God, and so lack of practice may be the problem. But I often doubt. If God knows my heart, what's the point of denying it? Some people may be able to banish it. But I can't. My new commitment to God seeking isn't that I will be faithful and brain-dead, but that I will be honest—even and especially with God. Under that rule, doubt is just one more feature of the landscape.

I was raised to believe that doubting God's existence was a terrible sin. It meant you didn't have faith, and not having faith meant going to hell. But now it seems to me that it is completely natural to have doubts about God. It's human. We can't see Him and we can't hear Him. We can't touch Him or smell Him or taste Him. Even if we think we do, we can never know in a provable way that it is really Him. We are creatures who rely on our senses to perceive reality, and He is an entity who cannot be apprehended in that way. He forces us to reach beyond our senses for a different kind of knowledge, one that can hardly be expressed in words. Our ability to do that is, in a word, transcendent. Since that quality is not our natural state of being, perhaps God might not expect us to be totally comfortable and sure of ourselves in matters that reach so far beyond who we are and how we were made to be.

Richard Elliott Friedman believes the modern sense that God is far away is no accident. In *The Hidden Face of God,* he writes that the Bible clearly shows God withdrawing from humans. In the early part of the Bible, God walks and talks with people. They see Him. Later they merely hear Him. And finally they stop even hearing His voice. Friedman writes that God has hidden His face and that we must look within to find Him. The modern task is to rouse ourselves to take our place as the gods we were created to be and thereby be worthy of a reunion with Him. In Friedman's theory, God has not so much abandoned us as He has withdrawn so that we may recognize and use our own powers. To bolster his point, Friedman quotes theologian Dietrich Bonhoeffer, who wrote that "God would have us know that we must live as men who manage our lives without Him." In other words, we have come to a time in God's relationship with humanity when humanity is ready to grow up.

That means leaving behind easy answers, facile certainties, and organized systems that allow us to live our lives according to the dictates of others. Seeking God means looking into the void. That is something all humans fear doing. It involves risk and insecurity and fear that the unknown is the unknowable. As we peer into the darkness, we see fantastic shapes that become visible and fade away. Are we imagining them?

I suspect even the most devout people have doubts about God. I once asked the Reverend W. A. Criswell whether he ever doubted God. At the time, Criswell was an old man, pastor emeritus of what has long been considered the biggest Southern Baptist church in the world. He was a man so conservative that he delighted in calling himself a fundamentalist or, as some would say, a fun-damn-mentalist. A large number of Baptists so revered him that he was often jocularly titled "the Pope of the Baptists"—even though, of course, that term itself is a heresy to Baptist thinking, which is fiercely independent and almost always fractious. Other Baptists think of Criswell as a symbol of exactly the kind of wrongheaded, bullying theology that elevates a pastor far beyond his true station and can keep people from really hearing what God has to say to them.

To my question about whether he ever had doubts, Criswell replied yes. "Sometimes along this pilgrim's way, I think I'm an infidel." Despite more than fifty years spent thundering certainties from a high pulpit, he has doubted that God exists. Why didn't he just give up the faith if after all this time it still can't stand without a wobble? I asked.

He answered quietly and in a way that ended my questions on the subject. "The reason is very obvious. One is that I have no place to go. If I turn aside, I don't have anything to turn to. It's just ultimate despair. And second, I don't care what, it is a blessing to love the Lord and trust in the Lord, and even when we don't understand, we believe that He'll make it plain in the by and by. So we'll just trust Him for it."

I think we can push our doubts away. We can cover them up so quickly that we convince ourselves they aren't there. But we can't really kill them. Doubt is such a human trait, so constant in most areas of life, and so valuable. Our skepticism protects us in everything from eating poisonous berries to believing all the nonsense we're told. It might have some virtue even with regard to God. It can spur us to keep looking for evidence of His presence. It can keep us questioning whether the messages in our heads are really God or merely the persistent voice of our own ego—or fears. It can also keep us linked with the rest of world, since the rest of the world is far more comfortable with doubt than with belief. Those "fruits" of doubt seem like good things.

At the same time, I'm finding that it isn't wise to pay too much attention to doubts. As Buddhist teachers say when dealing with both personal faults and errant thoughts that arise during meditation, "Note them and let them go."

Just as we are tempted to forbid ourselves doubt, we also tend toward giving those doubts we do entertain more room than is profitable. We worry our doubts like a kid with a hangnail. We are reluctant to leave them alone because they cut to the heart of faith. The question of whether there is or isn't a God is pretty central. We like to believe that if we struggle with a question long enough, we will figure it out once and for all. But that's not always true.

Doubting God is a lot like questioning whether you're in love. I once did a lot of that. I'd become enamored, and I'd immediately begin to question whether what I felt was really love. If the feeling was strong, I'd marvel at it and delight over the rush. When things began to be less perfect, I'd debate with myself over whether it was the "real" thing. When the affair would end, I'd try to analyze why this hadn't been genuine and how I should have known it.

None of my intellectualizing ever got me anywhere because love isn't subject to intellectualizing. Love is defined through time by actions as well as words. Much of what gives love its force can't be verbalized or even known. Love is often most clearly itself in wordless ways that go deeper than intellectualizing. I'm suggesting that faith is much the same.

Nobody would doubt that love is a real force. But, as with God, we can't see it, we can't define it, and we can't ever truly know what its effect on us will be. Once I stopped worrying over my doubts about love, I found that my love life went a lot smoother. I still had ups and downs, but when I learned not to stiffen in the face of them, a lot of the uncertainty just went away.

Love—and maybe our relationship with God—has something in common with playing in the ocean. The waves are always rising and falling—sometimes gently, sometimes with great force. If you want to enjoy the ocean, you have to give up having your feet on solid ground and let the waves carry you. Worrying about them, wishing they would rush like a stream or lie calm like a pool, doesn't alter them at all. You can fight them until you are utterly exhausted, but they will still rise and fall just as they always have. Better to simply let the vastness envelop you, and float.

C. S. Lewis, who believed a much more circumscribed Christianity than I am ready for, also thought scrutinizing belief was counterproductive. "The moment one asks oneself 'Do I believe?' all belief seems to go. I think this is because one is trying to turn round and look at something which is there to be used and worked from—trying to take out one's eyes instead of keeping them in the right place and seeing with them. I find that happens in other matters as well as faith. In my experience only very robust pleasures will stand the question 'Am I really enjoying this?' "

So I have resolved to allow myself my doubts and not feel guilty about them. It may sound self-indulgent, but one of my God-seeking goals is to jettison as much guilt as possible. If I don't, I think I'll be too heavy to float toward God. I'm not saying guilt doesn't have its purpose. But in my life, it has cost more than it has been worth.

I've felt a lot of guilt, a truckload, a mountain, enough for two lifetimes. Guilt was one of the reasons I broke off my relationship with God in the first place. It was part of why I had so much trouble seeing my own strengths. My faults loomed so large I couldn't see around them. As I move tentatively toward a God who was once such a negative experience, I have resolved to resist all guilt until I've scrutinized it enough to be certain that it comes with God's stamp on it.

The Reverend Michael Beckwith says guilt is often just a way of focusing on our egos and trying to control our lives. "Self-forgiveness is a discipline," he writes in *For the Love of God*. "So often people don't feel alive unless they're experiencing emotional drama. They get caught up in feeling that they are a bad person and thinking that God will punish them. At some point, as you begin to mature spiritually, it's the connection with God that lets you know you're alive."

One of my quarrels with guilt is that it doesn't reflect reality accurately. Much of the guilt I've felt was a waste of time and a discouragement. Some was over faults I couldn't help, slips I didn't intend, and ways of being that turned out not to be the terrible flaws of character I thought they were. I've felt guilty over things that turned out not to be even remotely as I perceived them to be.

A second problem with guilt is that it isn't reliable in motivating me. Guilt has occasionally stopped me from doing things I shouldn't have done, but probably not that often. More of the time guilt has muffled my thoughts and feelings until they went underground, where they gained strength and waited until a better time to ambush me.

For me spiritual seeking contains two particular sources of guilt that have little to do with the Ten Commandments. The first is guilt about doubt. The second is guilt about being myself. I learned that humans are sinful and therefore what is human is not good. Pleasing God was mainly a matter of resisting the urge to think for myself, trust my own experiences, and think my own thoughts. I could have myself or I could have God—not both.

But I have come to believe that finding God and finding our best selves are closely interrelated. Haranguing and bullying and nagging ourselves sets up a kind of inner clamor that can cause our true nature to withdraw like a rabbit to its hole. Henry David Thoreau thought similarly. "The finest qualities of our nature, like the bloom on fruits, can be preserved only by the most delicate handling," he wrote. "Yet we do not treat ourselves or one another thus tenderly." Being willing to claim your own doubts about God and life and yourself and not feel guilty while doing it is part of that tenderness, I think.

It's popular in some Christian circles to say that we must reach out for God and forget ourselves. But I don't think we can do that. Certainly I can't. Not now. I'm not holy enough. I'm not strong enough to even want that much holiness. It's too foreign to what I know. Every time I've tried to reach too far beyond myself, I've lost my footing and ended up doing something painful and stupid. Like many people lost in this noisy world, I feel a great need to withdraw into myself for sustenance.

Carl Rogers wrote that the mystic who reaches into himself discovers that what is most personal is most universal. "That which is most personal and unique in each one of us is probably the very element which would, if it were shared or expressed, speak most deeply to others," Rogers wrote in *On Becoming a Person*.

Some religious people fear that if we turn toward ourselves too much, we will forget our responsibility to others. Nouwen didn't think that seeking self and serving others were mutually exclusive. First the mystic touches himself and then he touches a place where he realizes that all people are equal and deserving of compassion, he wrote.

Perhaps it's the Western tendency to turn everything into a dichotomy that causes these problems. We think that God must be outside us, something we reach for, or He must be inside us, something we find already present. But He can't be both. Likewise, if we turn toward ourselves, we must necessarily be turning from others, because there is a clear separation between ourselves and others. But this way of looking at the world is not the only way.

In fact, many religious people believe that the great religious truth is that we are united—God and humanity, self and others. The idea of separation is merely an illusion that keeps us from knowing the true state of existence. With regard to whether God is "out there" or "in here," Huston Smith writes: "Transcendence and immanence, in absolute tension. If we lose our grip on either, the tone in our spiritual life collapses."

Bailey McBride, a columnist for *The Christian Chronicle,* believes the search for God and self are so intertwined that he says relationship with God is the way to find who you are. "I am firmly convinced that we can grow in understanding of ourselves only through careful and deliberate processes, and many of those processes can occur in the normal course of life, if we are looking at life through the eyes of God." He believes you look at life through the eyes of God by reading the Bible. I'm not so sure about that. I can say with more and more certainty that nobody owns God, and I can find out who He is in my own way. But I still have a grudge against the Bible. I quote it, but it has been so owned by others that I can't quite deal with it.

Chapter 34

Nobody Owns the Bible

ALAN WATTS BELIEVES the Bible needs to be put away for several centuries so we can hear it with "clean ears." I've already noted that I have trouble relating to the Holy Scriptures. To tell the truth, I would just as soon ignore them. I've had them used as a club against me so many times that I cringe at the word *Bible.* That book seems to have led as many people away from God as toward Him. I'm overstating the case . . . but the Scriptures are so problematic to me. Although verses rattle around in my mind frequently, I'm inclined to identify with one of my sources, a church member who is seriously searching for God. She told me she has a "grudge" against the Bible. Like God, the Book has plenty to answer for.

I have listened to thousands of sermons that drew on the Bible but few dealt with the real problems the text holds for me. I gave up on the Old Testament long ago. That bloody, immature, jealous God isn't someone I want to deal with, much less emulate. There's nothing admirable about Him. It's blasphemy to admit thinking that. So people just pretend He is perfectly reasonable, and the problem is in our interpretation or the sinful folks who so raised His ire.

I tried sticking to the New Testament. But even it gave me trouble. For starters, Jesus is supposed to be perfect, sinless, and pure. So what's so great about a kid who tells his mother to get lost when she comes worrying about him? Nobody would call me sinless if I blew my mother off in such a way. Does Jesus have a different standard? I never knew, and because church sermons rarely include question and answer sessions, I never was able to ask.

For a while I thought my attitude would cut me off from Christianity forever. But two things happened. One is that I found religious thought to be less monolithic than it often appears from the outside looking in. Even within the more conservative branches, there are radical differences of opinion about the Bible and even about the role it ought to play. "I am deeply distressed by what I only can call in our Christian culture the idolatry of the Scriptures. For many Christians the Bible is not a pointer to God but God himself. In a word, Bibliolatry. God cannot be confined within the cover of a leather-bound book. I develop a nasty rash around people who speak as if mere scrutiny of its pages will reveal precisely how God thinks and precisely what God wants," writes Brennan Manning in his book, *Signature of Jesus.*

Jack Deere, a former Presbyterian pastor and now a charismatic, includes in his book *Surprised by the Voice of God* a chapter entitled "Confessions of a Bible Deist." In it he writes, "Bible deists preach and teach the Bible rather than Christ. . . . Their highest goal is the impartation of biblical knowledge. . . . Actually, they use the adjectives 'biblical' and 'scriptural' more often than the proper noun 'Jesus' in their everyday speech." He writes that pride, personal wounds, and a fear that intimacy with God would bring pain led him to "Bible deism."

"If I had a question, I could ask the Bible, I didn't have to risk asking a God who might give me a painful answer," he writes.

Henri Nouwen also had trouble with the tendency to rely too much on the Book. In *The Wounded Healer* he tells this story: One day a young fugitive came into a village to hide himself from soldiers. The people gave him shelter and refused to tell where he was when the soldiers came for him, but the soldiers threatened to burn the village and kill every man before dawn if the young man were not handed over to them. The people went to the minister and asked him what they should do. The minister went to his house and began reading the Bible in hopes of finding an answer. In the early morning his eyes fell on these words: "It is better that one man dies than that the whole people be lost."

The minister closed his Bible and called the soldiers to tell them where the boy was hidden. After they led the fugitive away to be killed, the people celebrated. But the minister did not join them. He withdrew to his room in deep sadness. That night an angel came to him to ask what he had done. He said, "I handed over the fugitive to the enemy." Then the angel said, "But don't you know that you have handed over the Messiah?" "How could I know?" the minister replied anxiously. The angel answered, "If instead of reading your Bible you had visited this young man just once and looked into his eyes, you would have known."

Once I was able to build a case against the Bible, nicely buttressed with authority, I relaxed a bit. And the same thing happened with the Bible that happened when I began to spend time with the conservative Christians. I went in perfectly prepared to dislike, and found myself coaxed out of my corner before I quite knew what was happening. Richard Howard's words on why Scripture is a best-seller caused me to wonder if perhaps I had turned the Bible's openness to interpretation into a fault, when in fact, that was its brilliance—the essence even of its sacred nature.

The Bible has a secret, Howard writes. "Because on every page in every line, it hints at something that it does not reveal but that tempts us, arrests us, fascinates us all the more . . . the secret is that Scripture is addressed not to everyone but to each one, not to the public but to the individual."

Yale's Louis Dupré was another influence. I let down my guard when I read in an interview that he believes Christians are confused about what to believe because they have found that much of what older generations believed is not true. I can second that. Then he maintained that Scripture is still of help to people who seek God because they need the symbols of transcendence. "Religion cannot survive on mere feelings or moral intentions," he said. Private needs and feelings need the analogies that the Bible provides in order to be expressed in a wider context, he believes.

Bailey McBride writes for *The Christian Chronicle* that only the Word of God reveals the mind and will of God. Our spiritual lives were created in the image of God, and so as we learn more about the vast and infinite nature of God, we learn also about ourselves. If we study that Word it can be like a mirror held up to ourselves, he says. "We earnestly need to live in the shadow of God's mind and being. The sense of his presence can fill our hearts and minds even as we rush to keep an appointment or burn the midnight oil to complete a project." My friend Ray Dykes puts it more directly: "I read the Bible and it reads me."

Ron Somers-Clark, director of pastoral care at Dallas's Children's Medical Center, believes the stories of the Bible are so powerful that they comfort children and help them heal even when specifically religious language is never used. He and his staff deal with children and parents of all faiths and no faith in the worst, most frightening circumstances. One of the chaplains' primary tasks is to encourage the sense of hope that such families desperately need, Mr. Somers-Clark says.

One of his techniques is to use "parable boxes" as a way of letting children enter into the tale of the Good Shepherd. The box consists of felt cutouts that include sheep, a shepherd, a sheep pen, and dark dangerous rocks. As the story is told, children are invited to place the figures on a green felt background. The Good Shepherd contains certain images and certain signs that have a universal resonance, the chaplain told me. They are so core, so key, that the child interacts even in situations where families are falling apart. The name Jesus is never used. Instead they talk about a good shepherd who knows all the sheep and calls each one by name. No one tells the children that the story comes from a holy book. But it does its work anyway. The parables can do that better than a thousand sermons, Mr. Somers-Clark says.

"These parables are stories that people of faith have passed down for generations," he tells the chaplains who come for internships at Children's Medical. Tell the story: Let people interact with it, he tells his staff. And then trust, he says. Trust that God will work through these sacred stories as he has for thousands of years.

The strength of biblical parables was also amplified by psychiatrist Robert Coles's book *The Spiritual Life of Children*. He tells of a Catholic family in which two generations, father and son, had hit a point in their young lives where they were so focused on rebellion that their teachers and parents despaired of reaching them.

In the father's case, a priest began to take him for ice cream sundaes. While the boy ate, they talked. The priest told him the story of David and Goliath. He emphasized how David had controlled and directed his anger and so was able to defeat a much larger opponent.

The story did its work and the boy's life began to smooth out. Two decades later, his son was having the same problems. This time the grandmother took him for ice cream. Advised by the priest, she also told the David and Goliath story. Once again, paired with the love and example of people with faith, the old story worked its magic.

As I've worked through my problems with the Bible and watched its stories open up when told outside the narrow interpretations I was accustomed to, I've come to think of it in the same faintly defiant way that I think of God. Just as no one owns God, no one owns the Bible. Old Testament scholar Walter Brueggemann contributed greatly to my understanding.

When I first heard the renowned teacher and scholar was coming to town, I wondered what in the world someone who studied the Old Testament might have to say to a modern world. Then I began researching what Dr. Brueggemann believes. It was not only relevant; it was completely in tune with the times I see myself in.

Chapter 35

A Bible Scholar Speaks

IT WILL TAKE me years to grow into a full awareness of what Walter Brueggemann told me during an interview that lasted about thirty minutes. We had little time, but as I started researching this preacher from a Southern college, I knew I had found someone who could speak to my most pressing questions of faith.

In many ways, I had come full circle. I had rejected the Bible-oriented Christianity of my youth and, along with it, the preachers who taught it. Now I was going to question a man who represented much of what I felt I had to throw out in order to have God. By the end of the evening, I would feel doubly affirmed. The very authority I was in such rebellion against would have spoken—far more forcefully than I could—for the very tenets of my new personal faith.

He would reconcile me with the Bible. Soothe my anxiety about the anger and confusion I felt toward God. And he would point me toward an answer to the most important question of my new life: If you follow God, where do you go? By that I mean, who will you be? What will you do? What vision will inform your life?

Each time Brueggemann answered one of my questions, I felt that mysterious grounding of religious life that so many people inside and outside the church refer to. I felt a resonance within me.

Here is the interview.

Q. I love this quote from you: "The conversation on which our very lives depend requires a poet and not a moralist; the deep places in our lives—places of resistance and embrace—are not ultimately reached by instruction." Then you say that the "dangerous" stories of the Bible are a way to reach those places. Can you tell me such a story?

A. I'm going to talk about Elisha tonight. There is a story in Second Kings that says the Syrians were fighting the Israelites. They always are, still today, and the Syrian government had a leak in their military plans.

Somebody was giving information, and they said, "No, it's not a leak. It's the prophet Elisha."

So they send a whole army to arrest this prophet, and they ride up to his house, and the prophet is alone except he has this little kid to take care of him. And the little kid looks out the window and he sees the army and he's terrified.

And the prophet says, "Never mind. Never mind." And then he prayed and he said, "Oh Lord, open this boy's eyes so he can see."

And that's where the phrase chariots of fire comes from. The boy looked around and the mountain was filled with horses and chariots of fire.... Now the reason that's a dangerous story ... is what it says is that the world is filled with allies for people who work for good things like freedom and peace and justice.

But if you don't have the eyes of faith to see, you always think you're outnumbered, and you don't try because you don't have any energy, and you wind up in despair.

So the reason those stories are called dangerous—a German Catholic theologian coined that phrase—the reason they are dangerous is if your imagination is fed by those kinds of stories, you refuse to accept the definitions of reality that the power structure gives you and . . . you start doing crazy, unsettling kinds of things.

And if enough people start to act on that, the power system starts to give in.

Q. You really believe there are such chariots of fire around us?

A. I'm very ambivalent. When I'm in my faith mode, yes. But a lot of times I fall out of that, and I start thinking like a cunning, frightened kind of person. I think most people move in and out on those stories, and the purpose of worship and teaching and instruction is to try to get people to sense more and more of their lives through these kinds of narratives.

Q. You have said that the church has lost formal privilege, and that loss is a rich opportunity for the gospel ministry. What do you mean?

A. As long as the church is simply the chaplain of the status quo, then it has to maintain middle-class morality. It has to buttress the way things are organized. But when the church is no longer dominant, then it doesn't have that responsibility anymore, and nobody expects it to.

Nobody in Romania expected the church to defend the dominant values of the communist system. So if they had courage, the church in Romania was free to think and talk and act very differently.

I don't think we're that far along in the United States. But the church is increasingly marginalized from the dominant socioeconomic structures . . . and so it can get into its own story and its own way of imagining the world in terms of the gospel.

What we're talking about is the process of secularization. . . . The church's position in society is being radically shifted. That's a scary time but it's also a time of opportunity.

Q. Here's another thing you said. "Let me offer this as the way the Bible thinks about justice, 'Justice is to sort out what belongs to whom and to return it.'"

A. That's one of the best things I've ever said.

Q. Are you telling me that what I have is not mine, if I have more than I need?

A. Yes. What that means quite correctly is that the standard of living I have—which is inordinate even in the United States, not even

to speak about world standards—I have that standard of living because I am living off of the cheap labor of other people. . . . Justice
biblically conceived means a redistribution of resources.

Q. But what you are saying, and what Jesus sometimes seemed to
be saying, is very radical.

A. It is radical.

I think the church has to operate at two levels. It has to keep
showing the radical vision without toning it down, and then we have
to talk pragmatically.

What are we able and willing to do? That is a long way from the
vision, but we make the moves we can make. So I don't think that
people like me are going to give stuff back, but we could conceiv-
ably have universal health care so that poor people out of my taxes
could at least see a doctor when they needed it.

It would cost people like me very little to fund universal health
care in the United States. But you would think to raise taxes on people like me seven hundred dollars, you'd think I was being castrated.

Seven hundred dollars, that's two good meals at a restaurant for
five people.

We have few church leaders and we have no politicians who talk
about our having responsible membership with each other. And if we
don't have responsible membership with each other, I can't think of
any reason that my neighbor ought to get any of my stuff. It seems
to me that that is the church's peculiar insistence in society—that we
really belong to each other.

Q. You see that in the Bible?

A. It's everywhere. It's everywhere. In the Old Testament, they're
always talking about their neighbors.

Then Jesus radicalized it and said, "Now, who do you think your
neighbor is?" And he says, "Your neighbor is whoever is in need."

Q. For many of us the church already has no authority. We may
even wish it did, but it doesn't. How are we to proceed?

A. I read somewhere that the pope is like a wonderful grandfather. You're so glad to see him but you don't intend to take any of his
advice.

I think the key for the church is baptism. Baptism is a decision to
try to live your life according to this vision, rather than some other

vision. So I don't think that a pastor or a bishop or a pope has authority. The vision has authority, and pastors and bishops are people who keep explaining and bearing witness to that vision so that I have materials out of which I can imagine my life differently.

That's a very different notion of authority. I like to think of it this way: It's not authority in the sense that you must do something, but it's authority as a force that authorizes me to live my life . . . as a neighbor.

I believe the work of maturity is to say I'm going to move a little more of my life away from this commitment, which is kind of childish, to this commitment, which is more adult and more costly. It isn't that somebody can hammer me and coerce me. It is that there's something about me that wants me to be an adult.

Q. Tell me what you mean when you talk about the evangelical imagination.

A. Christian fundamentalists think that Christian faith is a package of certitudes. And Christians of a more liberal bent think that people like that ought to get nineteenth-century liberalism that says, "Well, you know everything is kind of evolving and nothing is absolute."

So what I think is going on in the church is we're having an argument between eighteenth-century conservatives and nineteenth-century liberals, none of whom is living at the end of the twentieth century. So that it's not nineteenth-century relativism and it's not eighteenth-century conservatism [we need]. But at the end of the twentieth century it's an ongoing dialogue in which people who disagree take each other seriously. [As an example, he begins to talk about the church's disagreement over homosexuality.]

The two sides never talk to each other, which is absurd because conservative Christians and liberal Christians elementally have everything in common. We ought to be talking about what we share and then let people in on what we differ on. What it means is that I have to admit that people who disagree about that question or any questions are really serious and are speaking in good faith.

The liberals do not believe that the conservatives on this question are in good faith, and the conservatives certainly do not believe that the liberals are in good faith. I believe that our sense of each other's good faith is sacramental. It's not ethical but it is the mysteriousness of God's presence and God's grace to which we all subscribe. We ought to create a context in which we can listen to each other.

Q. You mean God might indeed be speaking to us all but he's saying different things?

A. He's saying different things because God always speaks to us in, with, and under our experience. I think people who are really hard against homosexuals are essentially frightened people, and what they do is make their fear into a virtue.

My own sense is that what tends to convert people from a hard no to a kind of a gentle yes is when you have somebody in your family who you find out is a homosexual. All of a sudden you've got to recompute everything in light of that experience.

So I think we've got to honor each other's experience and to call all of us to move through our experience to a new place, but that takes a lot of patience and we live in a society that just wants things settled. Martin Marty says the church always takes about three hundred years to get its big quarrels settled. That goes back to the Trinity.

Q. But what do you mean when you use the word *evangelical*? It is usually taken to denote a group of conservative Christians who believe only Christians are saved and that the primary purpose of a Christian life is to bring other people to Christ.

A. By *evangelical* I simply mean *gospel*. The reason I use the word is I'm not going to give the word to radical conservatives. That means I believe the gospel. By *evangelical* I think we mean the work of reimagining our lives through the prism of the gospel, which means there are horses and chariots of fire all around us and so on and so on.

If Jesus is a living lord among us, then we have to imagine in the world that many things are possible. There are things that scientific absolutism declares are impossible.

Q. Such as?

A. Such as in Atlanta we've got twenty thousand homeless people. It's pretty easy to conclude it's not economically possible to deal with the homeless in Atlanta. Well, we Christians don't accept that. All that's lacking is the will to do something. The Bible is essentially the story of God doing things that the world thought was impossible. The primal one being Easter. The world thought you could not raise people from the dead, but there are many others.

Q. Tell me the difference between these preacher-poets you talk about and the kind of preacher I might be familiar with.

A. Preacher-poets open things up instead of closing them down.

The Bible is a document that is always running rhetorical risks and using funny images and saying crazy things. The primary examples are Jesus' parables. Jesus' parables are just rhetorical explosions, and often after Jesus tells a parable the disciples say, "I wonder what he meant by that."

And he doesn't tell them. They have to think about that, and so my idea is that in a society that is shutting everything down technologically, the church ought to be a place where we can communicate poetically in ways that are opening and inviting people to imagine that there are possibilities that we never thought of.

The problem with clergy is that we're not educated that way, and by and large we're paid to provide absolutes. That's what church people want pastors to do.

Q. But will what you're talking about—this no-answers faith— will it build sturdy Christians?

A. Well, there are answers but they're provisional answers. The problem with absolute answers is that they will crack right away . . .

Q. Under the onslaught of . . .

A. Of experience, of reality. What I think is that our society thinks it wants certainty. That's a cognitive category. Certitude is not what we want. What we want is fidelity. We want people who we can count on to stay with us in the places where we do not have certitude.

And certitude is no substitute for fidelity. What happened in the eighteenth century with the Enlightenment is that fidelity got siphoned off for certitude. But certitude isn't worth a damn because tomorrow something's going to happen to shatter that.

I teach in a Calvinist seminary. So the great certitude is that God is sovereign. Well, all you have to say is "Holocaust" and the whole question of the sovereignty of God is on the table and nobody knows what to say about it.

So you can either lower your voice, or you can holler sovereignty louder and pretend that the Holocaust didn't happen.

Q. So what can we know about God?

A. We understand bits and pieces of God. The way we understand each other. We never understand each other. Husbands and wives do not understand each other fully. Just bits and pieces. We're inscrutable.

Chapter 36

God's Voice

ALMOST ALL SPIRITUAL people talk about the importance of listening to God. I'm especially interested in the notion that God might communicate directly with individuals. If He does, then we can all trust our hearts and our own experiences with Him because we can all reach Him. If He doesn't, we have to take other people's word for who He is and what He does. It's going to be a lot harder to have faith under the second plan.

So when people say that God has given them certain messages, I have wanted to know what the voice says, what it sounds like, and how they know it is God. I've heard quite a range of answers.

Some people believe God sends them dreams. Others say they have seen visions and heard actual voices outside their heads. But most people who talk about hearing God are referring to a voice that speaks only in their thoughts. Some say the voice is distinguishable from their own because of the quality of what it says. Its insights are comforting or illuminating or compelling in a way that seems unlike the rest of their thinking. This voice seems to have a resonance not of timbre, but of meaning that satisfies in the way that logic doesn't. Sometimes the tone of the voice has a special quality of calmness or authority. In other cases, people say they believe the voice is God's because of the effect it has on them. They feel suddenly peaceful or comforted.

When Henri Nouwen looked toward his own death he called God's voice "the inner voice of love." As his friends and family began dying in ever increasing numbers, he wrote in his book titled *The Inner Voice of Love: A Journey through Anguish to Freedom* that the voice was getting deeper and stronger. "I want to keep trusting in that voice and be led by it beyond the boundaries of my short life, to where God is all in all," he wrote. As I read his words, it occurs to me that I don't have nearly so strong a sense of any force, but hearing him say that he does gives me hope.

I once asked a conservative Christian how she knew that the voice she was following was God's. She said that she checked it with Scripture. If it lined up, she knew it was God. If not, she knew it wasn't. Lots of people probably use such a test. I'm not sure it would work for me. The Bible is so full of contradictions and lends itself to so many interpretations that it seems to me people could back up all sorts of things.

When the young born-again Christian man said that God told him, "Get off your butt and do something," he was absolutely sure. "That's just how God talks to me," he said, shrugging and looking quite happy about it. Many born-again Christians seem to have a friendly, casual sort of relationship with God in which He talks frequently and sounds a lot like they do.

But that's not always so. In one of his books, former President Jimmy Carter mentions in a lesson about prayer that his sister, evangelist Ruth Carter Stapleton, seems to have a much less formal relationship with the Deity than he has himself. She addresses God throughout the day, continually and without preamble or careful phrasing. The former president himself is less spontaneous, he says. His approach appears to be more awestruck and formal. Mr. Carter doesn't say in that lesson whether God speaks to him and how, but I'm willing to bet that when the voice of the Almighty sounds in the former president's life, it speaks in much the same way it was spoken to.

That's not to say that God says only what we already know. I'm willing to consider that what we think of as God telling us something is only some surfacing of what we know at our deepest, wisest, most-tuned-in-to-the-universe level. Having conceded that, I have to also say that my experience and what other people tell me of theirs convince me that often it is the very unpredictability of what we think God is telling us that most convinces us it's Him we're hearing and not just our usual mind chatter.

Sometimes people are convinced God is speaking simply because what He says is so different from what they wanted Him to say and is different from anything they could have imagined He would say. One story stands out in my mind particularly because what God said was so undramatic and because its wisdom was then borne out by events.

A friend recently told me this story about the evening when her fourteen-year-old daughter ran away. She and the child had quarreled over the girl's failure to come home on time after school. As both tempers rose, my friends realized that things were getting out of hand. She told her daughter to go upstairs and cool off. Instead the girl screamed that she was leaving home and wouldn't be coming back. Then she turned and ran out of the house.

My friend, not as light on her feet as she once was, knew she couldn't outrun the girl. By the time she got the car out of the driveway, her daughter had disappeared. All night, she waited for the girl to return. She called the police. She called the girl's father, who lives in another town, and asked him to fly in immediately. She called all the child's friends. But no one could locate her.

In the kind of despair and terror that only parents understand, my friend prayed. As morning began to break, she found herself face-down on the carpet, praying as hard as she ever had in her life. "What do I need to do to get my daughter to come home?" she asked God.

The answer came. "Nothing." The word entered her head with clear, calm authority. She was certain it was God speaking. And all He said was, "Nothing." She got up from the floor. She walked through the kitchen and as she did, she felt a strong sense that her daughter was present. She looked in the garage. No one was there. She walked back into the living room. No one. Then her daughter walked through the front door.

Was it God my friend heard? I don't know. But knowing her as I do, I can say that she prefers action in almost every situation. I don't think "nothing" was the answer she expected or would have conjured out of her own head. I like the story for its everyday nature. No thunderbolts. No drama. No deus ex machina. Instead the simple, quiet, calming feeling that God was there with her, and then the confirmation of her daughter's return.

Okay, so it's not exciting. It doesn't prove that God has any real power or intervened in any way. I guess I like this example for those very reasons. It doesn't require any great suspension of the intellect. Just an openness to the idea that Someone might say something kind when you need it. That's a good place to begin, I think. If God could be depended on to do nothing more than that, it would be something valuable. You can't always get a kind word when you need it most.

The chance of having God speak to you does seem to increase if you ask Him a question. People who meditate receive certain understandings when their minds are totally clear. But most Westerners seem to have a more talky kind of relationship with God. Many don't even approach God unless they want something. So they yearn and sometimes God seems to respond, either by talking back or allowing them to have what they want.

Yearning may be the most common way of tuning in to God, but it has an obvious pitfall. If you know what you want to hear and God says just the right thing, you can't know that you aren't just supplying what you want. Former President Jimmy Carter has a funny story on that topic that his father liked to tell about a boy who worked from daybreak to dusk on his family farm.

"This boy got it into his head that he was destined to receive a call from God. Sure enough, one morning, as he worked in the field, he looked up at the sky and seemed to see clouds forming the letters 'G-O-P.'

" 'That's my call from God!' he said. 'It's telling me that I need to Go Out and Preach.'

"So he left the farm and began preaching. But no one wanted to listen to his sermons; he was just no good at it. Only then did he figure out what the message in the clouds had really meant: 'Go On Plowing.' "

God's messages don't always affirm what people want to hear. In my own stories, which I tell in the next chapter, I believed God was talking because the messages were so different from the harsh pronouncements and judgments that I usually hold myself to. My beliefs about God tell me He will nag me and shame me and push me toward whatever is most difficult and repellent to me. But my experience with words that seem to come from Him is entirely different.

Another hallmark of God talk is that it seems to occur in short utterances. One or two sentences sum up the issue, and that's it. I don't know if that means that God is stereotypically male and so doesn't go in for long gabfests or if it means that He just knows what He wants to say and says it so well that it doesn't take long. Maybe it's a cosmic trait. Even people who say they've talked with the Virgin Mary at some length come back with pretty pithy summations: The world needs more love or abortions are causing her great pain or we're heading down the wrong path and are about to be smitten for it. She is said to come back again and again to certain locations and certain people, but she doesn't seem to add much to her messages. The people who believe she's speaking say that's because humanity isn't paying the kind of attention they should to the simple messages she is giving, and so she repeats them hoping people will snap to.

When she and God tell people to broadcast their words to others, they often seem particularly focused on calamity. Those messages are often of the "Do what I say quickly or else" variety. That makes a kind of sense, of course. Calamities, especially ones as pressing as the end of the world, would be what the rest of us are most interested in. They're attention getters. But private messages I know about—the ones people keep silent about because they don't have anything to prove and don't want to seem nuts—are more likely to be reassuring or enlightening in a day-to-day way.

People sometimes have specific words they attribute to God. But often it's not the words that matter so much as what they mean to that specific person in terms of the feelings they inspire. When repeated the words aren't usually earth shaking in their originality. I've heard people say God gave them plots for books and hints about what to do next. I've heard God get the credit for sports victories and business deals. But nobody I know of has given God the credit for tipping them off about a cure for cancer or the final word on the big bang. Big discoveries do come through a mysterious process—the apple that bopped Newton on the head, the updraft that blew mold into a petrie dish and led to the discovery of penicillin. But people involved in such demonstrable breakthroughs usually credit hard work, their own brilliant intuition, coincidence, or just blind luck for those kinds of victories.

God seems to get His due only when the message is specifically spiritual or when something happens that science can't explain. That kind of message from God has a result that convinces some of the people around it. I've prayed for some things and had them happen. It's gratifying, but I've also prayed for things that didn't happen. The ones that did happen usually had a boost from me. I prayed and then I followed up by doing something that helped the process along. I don't want to steal any credit from God. I tend to think a concentration of energy in certain directions makes a difference—somehow. I'm not convinced that God steps in directly, favoring one person over another.

I tend to be most impressed with the God messages that cause a change in perception. So far, changing the human heart is about all that I feel fairly certain God can do. And I'm not even certain that God is the force that causes such changes. It could be universal consciousness or a deeper realization of self. It could be age or education or just the eventual reward of plodding along on life's muddy roads. But whenever I start chasing those rabbits, I pull myself back to the idea that I ought to deal with what can be known and leave the rest alone.

What can be known by a journalist is what people say. I can't know that they're telling the truth. In fact, I can be pretty sure that at best they're telling a version of the truth that could change over time and isn't complete even when they think it is. Situation has a lot to do with how much I believe what I'm being told.

Some situations lend themselves to out-and-out lying and others beg so shamelessly for some shading of the truth that people can't be expected to resist. An example would be polls of how many people go to church. Everyone quotes those polls but I don't know many people who really believe them. If the almost 50 percent of all people who say they went to church last week actually did go, the churches would have people spilling out their doors. People would be standing in the aisles, hanging out the windows, splintering the pews with the sheer weight of their numbers. But that isn't happening because those people aren't in church.

When some stranger calls on the phone and asks whether you've been in church in the last seven days, there is absolutely no reason to tell the truth. In fact, telling the truth is going to make you feel as though you've positively misrepresented yourself. If you're a person who thinks going to church is a good idea and who goes to church whenever possible, you don't want to come across as some kind of heathen God hater. So you give yourself the benefit of your good intentions. Maybe you weren't actually physically there in the last seven days, but you certainly were there in spirit.

That's an example of where it's naive to think people aren't lying. But the accounts are usually believed simply because they are couched in statistics. Anything with a number next to it seems to impress people as having some great veracity. I tend to tilt the other way. What I believe more often are individual accounts from people who have told their stories, to me, without obvious motive or big audience. I like to hear the tone of voice, see their faces, and then I can have a bit better sense of whether even they believe what they are saying.

Chapter 37

I Listen for God's Voice

I T DOESN'T SEEM quite fair to examine other people's spiritual experiences as though they are bugs under glass while holding my own back. So here are some stories of my own messages from God. These are stories about events that changed my perception of the world. I won't say they changed my life. Doing that may be a bigger task than can be accomplished in any one moment.

The first message from God that I paid attention to came when I was visiting Switzerland with my younger sister. We were at the largest waterfall in the country. The day was sunny, cool, perfect. I was feeling fine. People were all around. Suddenly, for no reason I can remember, I began to think of a young woman who had died some months ago in a house fire.

I never met the woman but I had talked with her on the phone two years earlier. She was in her early twenties. A nerve disorder made it impossible for her to walk. So hour after hour, through long nights alone, she listened to radio. She was an especially fervent fan of a popular all-night radio deejay I was profiling for the newspaper's Sunday magazine. I only talked to the girl on the telephone, but she had a plaintive sweetness I've never forgotten. One of the things she told me was how she hoped for a van so she could go to school. I remember wishing I could inspire someone to donate one, but I didn't think that I could. Some reporters have a talent for writing the kind of stories that move readers to great generosity. I have never had that knack. I already knew that. I've written a lot of sad stories and none of them has ever caused a great outpouring of money. Even more to the point, this story wasn't about the girl's needs. If I skewed it to include her plight, the editors would cut it back.

A photographer who visited her house came back with stories about how the house was filled with too many animals and too many people. He told a depressing tale. It made me sad, but I didn't do anything to help her. A year or so passed. I heard the girl had died when a fire broke out in the house. She hadn't been able to get out of her bedroom. When I heard the news, I was crushed with guilt. I hadn't driven to the neighboring town where she lived and checked out her situation myself. I could have reported what the photographer saw; maybe I could have raised a ruckus until she got the help she needed. The high sweet tones of her voice as she told me of her hopes for a better life still rang in my head. I had done nothing for her.

I suffered for a while. Then I let it go. I forgot the girl completely until that day in Switzerland. I hadn't been thinking about her. I hadn't been praying or thinking about God. I was probably thinking about nothing more weighty than how many inflated Swiss francs we would have to spend that evening to get a decent dinner.

Perhaps it was simply that my life had slowed enough for hidden thoughts to resurface. But suddenly out of nowhere images of the young girl's life and her death flooded over me. I thought, "Maybe I was meant to help her. Maybe the whole reason for the story on the disc jockey was to put me in contact with that girl who needed help. But I didn't help her." Maybe I had been the hand of God in that circumstance, but I hadn't acted. I could have gone to her house. I could have complained to the authorities if it looked unsafe. I could have taken her into my own home. But I didn't. I didn't do anything. I just went on with my perfectly nice life.

Out of nowhere, the horror of her death fell over me, and I despised myself for my indifference. This continued as I hiked up the mountain and back again. I said nothing to my sister as my gloom deepened. We were heading for the boat that would take us across to the falls when a voice in my head said calmly, "You couldn't have done the things that would have saved her. They are beyond your strength. You haven't stayed close enough to me for your nature to be changed that much."

It was true. I hadn't had the strength or the will to wade into such a mess. Even in the midst of my guilt, I felt helpless in the face of all I would have had to do. In the voice's message was relief, a sort of forgiveness, and a promise of hope. If I did stay close to God I might eventually become the person I so wished to be at that moment.

We got into the boat. I was still feeling pretty ragged, thinking that I'd conjured up that voice to let myself off the hook. "Typical," I thought, "cowardly and self-serving, as you always are." Then I looked toward the falls and saw a rainbow. The Bible says God sent the rainbow as a sign that He would never flood the world again. It is God's promise of hope, and it seemed to me that it fit right in with my need for affirmation. It was as if God's voice had spoken again. I laughed aloud. But, my relief didn't last long. Within moments, I was discounting the rainbow's significance.

The odds that I would see a rainbow at a waterfall were pretty high, I thought. This was no reason to feel as though I was God's special little darling. By now other people in the boat had seen the rainbow and were exclaiming over it in several languages. I looked away. I climbed out of the boat and was trudging up the hill when the voice in my head came again.

"It's true that everyone else saw the rainbow. But it didn't mean anything to them. It meant something special to you only because you were paying attention to another level of meaning."

What the voice said was true. My guilt and despair had made me want to hear and see God's presence, and so a commonplace event had been transformed. Maybe that is how it always is, I thought. Maybe God is constantly sending us messages as Sister Aloyius said He is, and the people who hear them are the ones who tune in. The more you tune in, the more you hear. If you never tune in, you might be getting messages all the time, but you will never receive them.

By this time, we were at the top of the falls. I looked over them to the other side of the river. And once again, there was a rainbow. A new one this time, arching higher and wider.

I turned away, laughing but still shaking my head. My sister and I went through the gift shop and then climbed some more. At the end of the trail we came to a plaque set in a monument. This place had been dedicated to peace and understanding of love's power, the plaque said. Everywhere I turned, something affirmed the message of forgiveness the voice had offered. I stood at the side of the mountain for one last look at the falls, and there was the third rainbow.

Three is a special number for Christians. God is the Trinity, three in one, God the Father, God the Son, and God the Holy Spirit. The apostle Peter denied Christ three times. Christ rose after three days. The first rainbow was usual. The second was somewhat less so. The third one? Was it rare? Maybe so, maybe not. But what was clearly true was that I had come to some sort of understanding that informed my life, and I had picked up signs in the natural world that seemed to bolster it.

What should I make of this message? Was it really God or just my own desires? John Dominic Crossan says that people who get messages from God in trances and mystical experiences always stay within the context of what they already know. Confirmed and undeviating Christians, for instance, may see incredible sights, but they won't see the god Krishna or the prophet Mohammed. "They will not learn anything they do not already know in their fondest hopes or deepest fears, but they may well know it thereafter with an intensity unobtainable in other ways," Crossan wrote. My three rainbows were definitely within my own frame of reference, and so was the message they seemed to confirm. I could argue with myself forever over whether the experience was all of my own making, but there's no way to know. Maybe it was merely an ingenious way for me to assuage my guilt. But even if that was all it was, it seemed to point toward a solution to my lack of action. Maybe getting closer to God would change me.

Chapter 38

The Teenage Cheerleader Prophetess Speaks to Me

L OOKING BACK OVER the years I spent listening for God's voice, one experience stands out in particular because it shows how far off the deep end one can go with this God business. It seems to indicate that my God-meter is wildly inaccurate. Whenever you start believing that God can talk to you, you're always moving toward the nut fringe. It may sound harsh to say so. But I'm not trying to judge anyone else's experience. I speak only from my own.

Trying to track God is likely to lead you to the kind of swampy terrain where it's easy to lose your footing. Start thinking too much about God talking, and you're likely to start listening to every utterance and every little thought as though it's coming right down from the Kingdom. Church people call that being so heavenly minded that you're no earthly good. My fear of that may keep me from ever becoming a woman of great spirituality, but it also tends to keep me sane. And once again, experience confirms my caution. Every time I get too far out there, something happens to bring me back.

Meeting the fifteen-year-old cheerleader prophetess was one such experience.

I found out about her from a news release. The Louisiana native was visiting Fort Worth. By the time I called, her church appearance was already over. I figured I would just chat a bit over the phone and make plans to catch her next time she was in town.

I envisioned someday doing a light feature story that wouldn't make fun of her and at the same time wouldn't affirm her claims. I planned to listen, watch, and write. I didn't plan to get involved in making judgments or applying any of what she said to myself.

The voice on the other end of the line was childish, unsure, somewhat shy. She kept calling me ma'am. She said she had discovered her gift when she was five. An ambulance was passing when she asked, "Why did they cut that woman?" Without any prior knowledge of the accident, she simply knew that the woman inside had been cut in a knife fight, she said.

Since that time, her knowledge had increased, and she had begun using it for God. She never takes money, she said, but she freely tells people what God has in store for them, and what she says always comes true, she told me. I questioned her with my usual mixture of friendliness and skepticism.

Then she asked if I would like to hear about myself. The question startled me. I laughed. I didn't particularly want her to do that. But I didn't have a good reason for the feeling. So I said, "Okay. Tell me about myself." She said she saw a little blond-haired boy in my life. I told her I have no children and don't live with any child that matches that description. She said she could see a black Mercedes-Benz. Did I have one? No. She said I would be getting one. Not likely, I said.

She wasn't doing too well so far. But I noticed that her tone had changed the moment she began giving me my own fortune. It wasn't anything dramatic, but the girlishness fell away. She spoke with a calm sense of authority. She was wrong about everything, but she didn't seem ruffled by that at all.

She told me I needed to spend more time with my husband, and I needed to call my mother more often. Those things were true. But what married woman doesn't need to pay more attention to her husband? And what adult shouldn't call her mother more?

She said I had been waking up at night. That was true. I am usually a sound sleeper, but for the previous week, I had been awakening deep in the night. I would lie awake for an hour or so and then go back to sleep. It wasn't dramatic, but it was odd. She said God was waking me up because He wanted me to spend time with Him. He wanted me to read my Bible more and support His causes with my money, she said. I waited for her pitch for money. But she didn't pause.

She also told me that I could stop worrying so much about dying. I was going to live to an advanced age, she said. It's true that I am horribly fearful. But aren't a lot of people? What sentient adult isn't afraid of death?

Big changes were about to happen in my life, she said. I was about to reap the rewards of all my hard work. She saw a job change in the near future. Now she had my attention. I could slough off blond-haired boys and Mercedes Benzes, but who wouldn't want to believe they were about to be rewarded for hard work? And even more to the point, my life seemed to be bearing out what she was saying.

My husband was a finalist for a job in another state. My newspaper was entering my work in just about every awards contest in the country. Maybe something was about to happen. If it was something good, I'd be a believer.

Not long thereafter, I heard from Ann Garner, the woman who had prayed for the bathing suit. Ann is a believer in prophecy and signs from God. She told me that she, too, saw changes in my future. "Something good is about to happen. You're about to get the recognition you deserve." The Spirit was speaking to her, she said, and she is hardly ever wrong. Changes and rewards. These were alluring thoughts. Something could happen, I thought, my skepticism cracking under the weight of self-interest.

But nothing did. Nothing. Not one of the prophecies came true.

My husband didn't take a new job. My job didn't change. What's more, I didn't win one award that year. Not one. Stories that had garnered praise from journalists and readers all over the country sank without a gurgle. Maybe I was getting the recognition I deserved, but if so, the prophecy meant just the opposite of what I had been gullible enough to hope for.

As for the Mercedes, I didn't even ride in a Mercedes that year. Nothing that girl said came true. I didn't even keep waking up at night. If God had wanted to talk with me, He must have gotten bored and decided to wake up someone more interesting.

Ann and I didn't talk much that year. I was busy doing an international series on peacemakers. I had started writing this book. Some people might have said those two events—the international trips and the book—were the changes the teenage cheerleader prophetess saw in my future. But I didn't think so.

My thoughts were as far from visions of glory as they had ever been in my life. I was doing so poorly in contests that I didn't even want to enter. Recognition and rewards were not coming my way, and I didn't expect them to. All I wanted was some time to live a normal life. I was working so hard that my fondest fantasies were about how I might escape. I was looking with longing at toll booths, fantasizing about how nice it would be to do the same simple task all day.

Chapter 39

A New Take on Prophecy

W HEN I FINALLY talked with Ann, it was at the end of the year when she had prophesied so much success for me, and she was jubilant. From where she sat, it seemed as though I was flying high. She had seen the international series and thought of it as a great triumph.

"All those changes came about. I knew the Lord was telling me that things were going to change in your life," she said. Ann's voice had the soft tone of wonder that she often uses when she talks about what God has done.

"No. They didn't," I said flatly. My voice had the stony quality it often has when I'm refuting her. "It looks that way to you maybe. But I have the same job. Nothing has changed." The travel had been nice, but it didn't mark any big alteration in my situation. Within a few months, I would be back covering church meetings.

As usual, Ann wasn't ruffled by my reality check. "I was sure that what I was getting was from the Lord," she said, musingly. Then she told me a story of prophecy that came true in her own life. One of her relatives had been murdered, along with his girlfriend. A seer in Fort Worth had told relatives exactly where to find both bodies, Ann said.

Ann's story didn't convince me. I didn't doubt her account and I didn't particularly embrace it. The central motto of my life has been "get more information." On this matter, I didn't have nearly enough facts to know what I thought. And, as I discovered in my first encounters with Ann, other people's miracles aren't enough for me. I have to have my own. It's not what touches the outer world that convinces me, it's what touches my soul. Ann, on the other hand, feels God's blessing no matter what the outcome.

"The purpose of prophecy is to give us courage," she said, not at all nonplussed by my attitude.

The wonder of prophecy is not whether physical events happen or don't but the effect believing them has on our lives, she was saying. It sounded like a cop-out, just another excuse for a God who promised much and delivered little, but I must admit that something in Ann's assertion tugged at me.

Had the girl's prophecy given me courage? Perhaps. I had pursued bigger, more complex, and more frustrating projects in that year than ever before. So the prophecy had helped me move forward.

I hadn't been rewarded in the ways I'd hoped, and I no longer expected that I would be. And yet it wouldn't be exactly true to say that I hadn't gotten a reward for all my hard work. In fact, perhaps I had gotten the reward I most desired and least expected. The year had been rich in understanding. I'd worked hard to move forward in this peculiar, idiosyncratic faith that I was patching together, and I was having some success. As I heard a preacher say once, growing in faith is sort of like the growth of a child. If you watch it day to day, you can't see that anything is happening. But if you compare it from one year to the next, you see astonishing differences.

What are the differences I've seen? I'm more hopeful. I'm not sure that I'm more loving. I'm at least a little bit more confident in the idea that there is something else out there besides an empty void. I'm a little easier on myself, and at the same time, I'm doing a little more good. Most striking of the changes is that I'm more confident that I can follow my own way to God. I've long been unwilling to declare myself a believer. The other day, I found myself unwilling to declare myself a nonbeliever. I'm learning to trust a bit more. What does that mean? I'm not sure, but it's letting me go forward without so much fear.

Maybe those are rewards of my hard work. Certainly, they mean more to me than the awards I hoped for. So was the cheerleader's prophecy fulfilled? Maybe. And maybe I'm just getting more agile when it comes time to excuse disappointment. When I started writing that sentence, I meant it to imply that I am learning Ann's cop-out skills. But by the time I finished writing the last words, I was wondering if I hadn't just outlined some spiritual grace that might make life a much richer experience.

In Karen Armstrong's book on Genesis, *In the Beginning,* she writes that the story of Abraham shows a man who "had the imagination to look beneath the unpromising surface of events and to realize that blessing is not always found in the most obvious places." He had learned to look at life with the inner eye of the soul. Imagination may be the chief religious faculty because it allows us to conceive of the apparently absent God. "In the quest for blessing, human powers need to be engaged to the hilt if we are to achieve enhanced life," she writes.

One of Ann's most endearing qualities, from my standpoint, is that no matter how I poke and scoff at her theories, she steadfastly maintains her belief that God has singled me out for special work. Every time she tells me that, I recall my mother's letter and my grandmother's long walk to the church dedication service with me in her arms. I took in too much religion too early to resist Ann's idea entirely. The idea that God might have special tasks for me is a strong vision. I'm vain enough to like the idea.

But I'm also sufficiently familiar with God's work to know that doing it isn't likely to include me getting rich or famous or particularly respected. She's probably wrong about me and God, and even if she's right, God is unlikely to have anything good in store for me. His work is often some hard, unrewarding task. It seems to me that contrary to the gospel of wealth and happiness Americans like so much, Christ's life points to a grim lesson: If you do God's work, you're likely to be crucified.

But that's bluster mostly. I yearn to believe God has a plan for humanity. I want the universe to be a place of justice and mercy and purpose. I'd like to have a part in that being true. Even a bit part would be nice. Ann believes with all her heart that we are living in just such a universe. During the year of the cheerleader's prophecy, I did look especially hard for the hand of God. At one point I wrote a column about what hope I had found. This is what I wrote.

One of the most compelling of religious ideas is the notion that a separate—better—reality exists apart from our everyday perceptions. In this hidden world, which only the spiritually fit understand, truth and justice prevail. Rewards come from right thinking and right doing. Greed and meanness, lying and self-serving behavior never pay off.

Some Christians link this religious reality to "Kingdom values on earth." Buddhists talk about it as the truth under the illusion. Hindus call it karma. Some talk about it as a world that comes to fulfillment only after death. Other people talk about this world as a sort of underlying truth that actually rules our lives.

I like the on-this-earth version and am always happy when something happens that seems to bolster that view. Some people use miracles for that purpose. They look for healings and heavenly appearances. They testify about narrow escapes and give God the credit.

Those things might be of divine origin. But I prefer more prosaic proofs. I like to see evil fail. And if I can't find anything truly evil that's failing, I'll settle for lying that doesn't pay off, greed that doesn't satisfy, or even simple rudeness that gets its comeuppance.

The reason I prefer these simpler wonders to their flashier cousins is that they seem to back up other observations about the world that are pretty much common wisdom. And they apply on a wider scale than most miracles, which only affect individuals. What I'm after here, you see, are not exceptions but some indication of universal laws.

For instance, religions say that gluttony and greed are bad ideas. But to many of us they seem like fine ideas, the kind any good, smart American could base a life around. We often reason that if a little of something is good, then a lot will be much better.

But here's the universal law for you: Nothing that you have a lot of is as wonderful as what you have a little of. Now, children and dogs might be an exception here. But with regard to food, too much cloys the palate, and with regard to possessions, too much, too easy makes everything seem worth less.

To find such lessons, you have to look all the time.

What's hard about this is the world so often seems to be proving just the opposite. Downsizing, for instance. For the last dozen years, it has seemed as though business people were learning that the more ruthless you were with employees, the better you would fare in the marketplace.

This has caused me much consternation. About ten years ago, I did a series of stories filled with examples of people who were being tossed out after having worked for companies all their lives. It looked as though businesses were doing what they had to do to survive and that's just the way the world is.

It was in that gloomy frame of mind that I learned of the American Management Association's study of downsizing. The study, which is done every year, indicates that most of the time downsizing doesn't do what managers thought it would do. Since 1990 fewer than half of the downsizing companies have increased profits or been rewarded with better productivity.

Larry Spears, executive director of the Robert K. Greenleaf Center for Servant Leadership in Indianapolis, shared my feeling about this development. His center is dedicated to helping business realize that it pays off to treat employees as though they are more than cogs in a wheel.

"Short-term solutions often have bad consequences in the long term," he said.

Exactly. Commonplace wisdom and not a bad religious thought, either.

SECTION 7

Into the new reality

Chapter 40

The Peacemakers

I've ALREADY ADMITTED that my vanity makes me wish to be part of some divine plan. The teenage cheerleader prophetess played into that vanity. Although her prophecies of change and great acclaim didn't come true, my life in 1997 was far more adventurous than I had anticipated. As the year began, I had no bigger plans than meeting deadlines. When the year ended, I had traveled to three of the world's saddest places—Northern Ireland, Eastern Germany, and Cuba. I also had covered what many called the year's saddest event, the death and funeral of Princess Diana. I didn't see these trips as being part of my own spiritual growth, but by then I was getting better at arguing with God and listening for whatever answers life might deliver. And if I was attentive, it delivered fairly regularly.

By this time the tenets of my personal theology were shaping up. They looked something like this:

- God is abundant.
- Grace abounds.
- Faith doesn't hinge on belief.
- Reality is not what it seems.
- You can find your way to God through the experiences of daily life.

Northern Ireland brought it all together. Germany addressed the angriest, most despairing of my quarrels with God. But first, here is how I came to be in such places.

For three years, I had proposed writing an international series on how people were using religious ideas to help bring peace around the world. The proposal did nothing but gather dust. No editor with any money was interested in it. I couldn't blame them. Peace is much harder to write about than war. Peace tends to mush into platitudes.

By the beginning of 1997, I had lost enthusiasm for the idea myself, but my editor included it in a list of possible projects, and for a reason I will never understand, one of the bosses suddenly found the whole idea fascinating. The word came back: "Flesh out the details. Figure out what it will cost."

Plenty of other editors were ready to say the project would never work. The foreign editors feared that I would be too naive to make the stories plausible. They seemed baffled by project proposals that seemed utterly clear to me. I assured them a hundred times that I wasn't naive enough to believe these religious ideas really worked, but the world was full of people who were. The stories would be about them. Whether they were successful was a question we could let events judge.

Finally they found the money. I bought airline tickets for two pieces in the series—Northern Ireland and Eastern Germany. My friend Ann saw the hand of God in all this. I didn't, but I didn't rule it out either. Many of the peacemakers I talked to ended our conversations by saying, "This is a.good thing you're doing. This is important work." No newspaper had ever put this story together in the way I proposed to do it.

Northern Ireland was my first stop. There I met Sister Aloyius, who assured me that God's love and care are so abundant that we can't move without brushing angels' wings. There I attended evening services in the Reverend Ian Paisley's church, where I shook off another big chunk of fundamentalism. It was in Northern Ireland that I met Peter Hannon and his wife, Lady Fiona. Their lives are exactly what I think Jesus had in mind when he talked about followers.

They are also prime examples of religious peacemakers working in the world to heal the wounds that cause war. Their work rests on the idea that—as absurd and unlikely as it seems—Jesus was right: Forgiveness is the way to freedom; love is stronger than hate. Such peacemakers believe that wars, fought over land or power, can't be truly settled by treaties that deal only with land or power. Wars can only be truly settled when the wounds and the bad relationships that caused them are attended to. People who feel victimized and trapped by old animosities cling to them even when times get better. They pass bitterness and hatred to their children, even if their children have no experience with the original reason for hatred. It's a cycle that has ruled the world forever. To prove their point, the peacemakers need only point to Bosnia or Rwanda or Northern Ireland.

If all these peacemakers had were lofty ideas and good intentions, there wouldn't be much of a story. But amazingly, world leaders who may or may not be religious are putting such ideas into practice for the most pragmatic reason: They believe they work better than the alternatives. The most obvious examples come from South Africa, with its commission designed to find the truth and reconcile victims with the people who preyed upon them. But there are many other, less well known examples all over the world.

In many cases, people are being asked to forgive what was unforgivable. But religion is in the business of healing souls. It addresses itself to reconciliation in ways that no other discipline does. And it claims to be able to draw on a greater power that can cause people to leap across the darkest chasms of existence.

The Hannons have given their lives to peacemaking, and agreed to help me find other people in the movement. They are what the Northern Irish call big house Protestants. Lady Fiona's grandmother was a Scottish baroness. Peter's father was one of Northern Ireland's foremost Protestant ministers. As young people, they joined a group called Moral Re-Armament, which works for world peace by espousing personal purity and selflessness. Moral Re-Armament adherents pledge themselves to meet such standards personally and then dedicate themselves to reaching world leaders who might also be transformed by the influence of such values. The Hannons have lived their entire adult lives without ever making a salary.

Much of their lives was spent in South Africa, where they were supported by a group of families who asked them to work on peace and pledged money for their support. The Hannons now live on reduced pensions outside a town called Coleraine, which is near where Peter grew up. The lovely house they own is direct evidence of God's hand in their lives, according to Peter.

They had returned from South Africa to Northern Ireland so their two daughters could continue their education. When they were looking for a home and were in despair because they couldn't begin to afford anything on the market, they heard of an unoccupied house on an overgrown piece of land that could be had cheaply. Someone else was just about to buy it when the Hannons came along and snapped it up. No one will ever convince him that God's grace wasn't at work, Peter told me.

I relate that story because it shows quite clearly how differently the Hannons and I think about God. I could concede that God might have brought them a house, but I didn't share Peter's wonder and gratitude. I thought, "Isn't that just like every story you ever hear about God? He lets us worry and suffer and feel totally wretched and then, maybe, just maybe, He does something. Poor Peter and Fiona dedicated their whole lives to Him, and when it came time for Him to give them a hand, He took His own sweet time about it just as He always does." I didn't share my jaundiced attitude with Peter and Fiona right away, but I didn't try to hide it from God. Toward Him I felt considerable exasperation.

Every morning, Peter and Fiona get up an hour early to sit with God, to read the Bible, and to listen for what He might want them to do. In his book, *Whose Side Is God On?*, Peter tells about how he started that practice fifty years ago when as a student at Oxford he pledged that he would give his life over to whatever God wanted from him.

One of the bonuses of the Hannons' early hour with God was that they would think about our day together before I was even awake. I'd stumble down to breakfast, still thick-headed and caffeine hungry. On a number of days, something was waiting for me by my plate. One morning it was copies of articles about an event I was interested in. Another morning it was a map of the route I needed to take to get to the airport. Once it was a list of the names and phone numbers of people I could interview. Sometimes the breakfast conversation itself would reflect the Hannons' earlier moments with God. No one mentioned that the two of them had been up spending time with God. But I knew it, and in quiet, unobtrusive, totally positive ways, I felt the effect of that daily commune.

I had the sense that I was rushing breathlessly through every day, while the Hannons were taking time to look ahead. It seemed as though God was sending them messages and ideas in the cool of the morning that smoothed their lives like a hand pressing the wrinkles out of linen. Peter refers to that hour as giving God a chance to tune the instrument before the concert begins. It is part of his search for "a core of tranquillity, a pool of silence at the heart of one's being."

One of the mysteries Peter ponders on those mornings is why life's trials seem to get so much harder as time goes on—even for those who've tried as hard as they can to live by God's will. Peter decided that such incidents might come our way because as we grow, God gives us harder tests in much the same way that students' tests get harder as they advance in school. I hadn't complained about God's tardy performance when Peter told me about finding the house, but after he told me about God's plan for tougher exams, I balked.

I have heard Christians say similar things all my life. And it seems to me that if God is going to single out those who love Him most for special punishments or tests, as Peter called them, then it only makes sense to stay as far away from God as possible. God ought to be on our side here, not sitting around dreaming up new ways to give us pain. Peter, of course, doesn't agree. He thinks life's tests, like school exams, get harder in order to build our confidence and ability.

I admire Peter and Fiona. I think they have something special. I think they and their counterparts in Moral Re-Armament make a great difference in the world. Despite my quibbles with the material rewards that God had been so slow to provide and my doubts about God's "tests" for those He loves, I knew clearly that the Hannons had received the rewards of spiritual life I was after. I could see it in their lives. I wanted those rewards far more than I wanted acclaim or praise or money. They were both so wonderful and generous and sweet that it was a joy to be around them. The Hannons don't have the kind of faith that makes you preach at folks all the time. They have the kind of faith that guides life into larger vistas. I did want that kind of faith.

I couldn't think of anyone I would rather be like than the Hannons. And still . . . was I willing to let God have control of my life?

One night sitting on my bed after having reread the account in Peter's book of his decision, I put to myself the question Peter had faced: Would I give control of my entire life to God in the way the Hannons had? The answer came back as clear and cold as winter rain. Nope. No way. Not going to do it. I wasn't interested. What sane person would be? It seemed pretty clear that God would mess things up, especially if His idea of a good time was to devise worse and worse tests for me. I could do that on my own. Listening to the Hannons made me realize that I still didn't trust God at all.

There was a time when I would have been afraid to let God know that. I'd have tried to jolly Him along by saying that I was considering the idea and would get back to Him later. But not anymore. I was through lying to God, and I was trying to stop lying to myself. I didn't trust Him enough. And I didn't trust myself to stick with such a vow.

It had been seven years since I prayed that God would open my heart. I had been working my way toward some kind of faith all that time. Now I had met exactly the kind of people I wanted to be. I knew what it had taken. And I wasn't willing—or able—to do it. That realization was one of the worst moments to come out of my foray into faith. A dead end, you might say. God wanted all, just as the preachers of my childhood said He did, and I wasn't going to give it.

Too bad, I thought. A sad ending. Oh well, it was fun while it lasted. I felt sad thinking that the next morning I'd get up and face the world on my own again, but that's the way it had to be. I had done it before. I could do it again.

I sat there feeling pretty lousy.

And then it was as though I heard a new message from God. Not a voice in the air, just a thought, a question that shafted through my mind with such surprising clarity that it didn't seem part of me.

"Okay. If you can't give up control for the rest of your life, how about for the next ten minutes?" I can't tell you whether God has a sense of humor, but I laughed. Ten minutes? All you're going to ask of me is ten minutes? What a comedown. Peter and Fiona make a lifelong pledge, and from me, you're willing to settle for ten minutes? What kind of wimp do you think I am?

I stood up shaking my head and got into bed. The despair was gone. God had my number. Or maybe I finally had His. This was a new kind of God, not at all the Big Nag I had always thought He was. Anyway, it was all right. I could do ten minutes. Sometime. I just wasn't sure when exactly.

Chapter 41

More Peacemakers

DURING THE WEEK I stayed with them, the Hannons took me to see Alastair Kilgore, director of Corrymeela, a retreat center that is among the most well-respected bridges to peace in Northern Ireland. Each year, thousands visit the lovely retreat in Ballycastle where Catholics and Protestants live together, trying to make Christ's loving community a Northern Ireland reality. When a neighborhood blows up—Catholic or Protestant—Corrymeela workers go in to work with the young people.

"We have to go in. If we tried to bus kids out, the paramilitaries would blow up the buses," said Alastair, who once did relief work in Africa and was a teacher in Belfast's toughest neighborhoods.

Corrymeela workshops break down stereotypes. Romance is often their ally. "You get kids who are fifteen and sixteen years old. They're interested in the opposite sex. We use that interest, and then," said Alastair, laughing, "we try to keep the interest under control."

Alastair was one of the most compelling persons I ever heard talk about Christianity. He saw it as a way to freedom from what society tells us about ourselves. This wasn't a new idea for me, of course. Peter had said that his hour with God gave him a new freedom of heart. I had felt new freedom as a result of my prayer on the way to work. Marcus Borg wrote that Jesus' central message had to do with being free of the bounds that separate us from one another. But Alastair was living the freedom in a place where that can cost you your life.

He grew up in a Protestant neighborhood of Northern Ireland. Until he was in college, he didn't even know any Catholics. Religion meant something to him when he was a boy, but as he grew older he cast his old ideas off in favor of humanitarian and intellectual pursuits.

When the Troubles—as Northern Ireland's conflict is often referred to—heated up, Alastair was in Africa.

There he met a group of Catholic priests called the White Fathers because of the white vestments they wear. Their dedication to helping others impressed him so much that he wanted to learn more about their faith. They introduced him to the notion that Christianity wasn't at all what he had grown up believing it to be. From them, he learned that in many places Christianity is so intertwined with the culture that it has become not much more than a way of shoring up cultural identity.

But that wasn't what Jesus had in mind. What Jesus intended, Alastair told me, was for his teaching to free people from the divisions that keep them separate. Being a Christian means being free to challenge the wrong things that our society pushes us toward—greed, narrow-mindedness, pride, clannishness, fear of others. He and the people at Corrymeela struggle every day to live past the boundaries they grew up with.

It isn't easy, he said, but it is the path to freedom. I grew up hearing preachers talk about Christianity as freedom. But I thought they meant freedom to be bound by the strictures of the church. I thought they said freedom and meant captivity. That was not what Alastair was talking about. He meant the freedom to have new visions of a better world.

At one point, I mentioned that my editors feared I would be naive in my portrayal of Northern Ireland. "Oh," he said, a look of delight on his face. "Are you naive? I'm so glad to hear it." When my editors said the word, they meant it as a warning against being soft-headed, too easily taken in by lofty ideals and big visions. Alastair meant it in the same way. But what they saw as a fault, he saw as the world's best hope.

Alastair called his work putting "the rat in the skull." I'd never heard the term. "It came out of the Vietnam War," he said. Soldiers used it to talk about the idea that the war didn't have a real point. Once the notion dawned, they would push the thought away. Then it would come creeping back. They could never get rid of it entirely. It was like a rat in their skull, always gnawing away.

Alastair's rat in the skull was the cross-community friendships Catholics and Protestants formed at Corrymeela. "First they learn it in here," he said, pointing to his chest. "They learn it up here," he said, pointing to his head. "They may forget it up here," he said, still pointing to his head. "But once it's in here," he said, pointing to his chest, "it can never be forgotten."

I had my own rat in the skull. It was the Hannons' morning hour and their willingness to let God take over. Their way of life had chipped away at avarice and ambition, arrogance and pride until all that was left was a sureness of purpose—and peace. They talked about their faults and their fears. They told the truth about their lives. But they were comfortable with people who disagreed with them totally.

When I returned to Dallas, I tried giving an hour of my time to God each morning. I'm not a morning person. But for the first week, I stuck with it. I would drag myself out of bed, sit on the couch, and try to keep my mind clear. It was something like my days of Buddhist meditation, but I didn't have to sit in a certain position, and instead of trying to keep my mind perfectly clear I put myself in a listening mode.

The result was the same calm clearness that meditation had given me. On the best days, that hour set a sweet, peaceful tone that lasted into the day. I felt content and sure of myself, in tune with some wonderful rhythm. Once again I was listening for the voice of God. And once again, when I heard it, it wasn't what I expected.

The voice didn't boom or announce itself with thunderclaps. It didn't burst into my consciousness. It was more a matter of some new awareness that came easily into my mind and seemed obvious once I realized it.

As usual, I expected God to nag. I hadn't wanted to present myself before Him because I was pretty sure He would have some outrageous, impossible plan that would involve me failing and feeling guilty. But that's not what happened.

On my first hour with God the message was that I ought to stop worrying myself about work all the time. I ought to take a break and pay more attention to my husband. So I did, and I realized that while I had been off proving how grand I was, having big revelations, my husband was having a fairly tough time. He hadn't complained and until I began to really listen, I hadn't realized how much he needed someone to hear him.

Did God really have an interest in the little details of my life? I don't know. It still seems unlikely. But my early mornings steered me into healthier patterns of living. Once again my little bit of God wasn't goading me toward shame and guilt. That had been my experience once before, with the morning prayers that I said on the way to work. It had been my experience with Buddhist meditation. And now it was confirmed again.

My idea that God was out to get me was being challenged every time I turned toward Him. I wasn't ready to give it up yet. But as Alastair would say, I was beginning to have a new understanding, not just in my head, but in my heart, where it might stay even when I forgot what my head knew.

The morning hour was a good experience. But I didn't keep it up. I was lazy. I was busy. And most of all, I was unable to make that hour the kind of priority it has to be. The rest of life pushed it out of my day. Why did I let that happen? I don't know.

I believe that some regular time of silence is central to spiritual growth. Everything seems to confirm that you must have some space without distractions to reach within yourself or outside yourself to God. "We are victims of overstimulation," says the preface to a book by James Fowler and Sam Keen called *Life Maps*. "The bombardment of the senses, information overload, and stress from constant decision-making cause us to move from fatigue to hypersensitivity and over-reaction to emotional exhaustion to literally, a deep psychological and spiritual numbness." I believe every bit of that. But it's hard for me to keep time free to be silent and listening. Life crowds it out. I don't know why.

As often happens, a Bible verse keeps rattling around in the back of my head. "Thou shall have no other gods before me." I know the god I put before Him and before myself. Work. Years ago I made a list of the top values in my life. The first value was my spiritual life. The last value, number eight, was work. And yet I live my life as though work were number one.

During a recent conversation with Reverend Dykes, I mentioned that fact. I asked him if many people said they were living their lives by their own lesser values. He said he didn't hear people say that very often. "But you know what that's called, don't you?" he asked. No, I didn't.

"That's called being a hypocrite."

Chapter 42

Lessons from Princess Diana
and Mother Teresa

LONDON—Katharine Norbury smelled roses Saturday morning as she opened the window of her apartment on Brompton Road. Although the vast sea of flowers left at Kensington Palace to honor the life of Princess Diana was a mile away, the scent easily made the journey.

The air of London, usually heavy with the gassy breath of buses and raucous with the rumble of motorcycles, was sweet and silent on the morning of the day that the Princess of Wales was to be buried.

IN THE MIDDLE of my research in Northern Ireland, Princess Diana died. Never having followed the royals, I was not at all prepared for the level of mourning that the world would plunge into. My editors called for me to go to London as backup for our European correspondent. When I arrived, I was feeling a bit jaded already. The media hypes so many events into so much more than they really are. I expected this was to be just such an example.

But I was wrong. Over that weekend, I was stunned to see the level of grief. Here is the rest of the story I wrote about the day the world mourned.

From before dawn, solemn-faced people carrying flowers filled the sidewalks as they hurried toward the funeral route, a three-and-a-half-mile journey from Kensington Palace to Westminster Abbey. Roads were blocked to traffic, and drivers had been warned to stay away from the central zone. Despite the largest gathering in a half century, Londoners said they could never recall the city being so still.

Ms. Norbury had flown in from Northern Ireland the night before.

"As we passed over the city, I could see Kensington below. There was a kind of glow in it from the candles and the flashbulbs and the cellophane on the flowers," said the thirty-three-year-old film producer.

Acres of bouquets were piled before the gates of Kensington Palace, where Diana lived and where her coffin rested in private the night before the funeral. Trees all around adjoining Kensington Gardens had become little shrines as mourners placed candles and flowers on the ground, taped photographs of Diana on the trunks, and hung cards from the branches.

At midnight, Ms. Norbury found the park filled with hushed people wandering from shrine to shrine.

"The wind was so still that all the candles stayed burning."

Further down Kensington Road, nineteen-year-old Verity Stevens, her mother, and three of her friends had been sitting all night. The women wore corsages of white lilies.

"They were Diana's favorite flower," Ms. Stevens said. "They're selling big boxes of them back home, sprayed so they'll last."

The group had come 110 miles from Leicestershire.

"I'm freezing and I haven't had an hour's sleep all night," she said, reaching for a Mylar blanket that she called her silver wrap. People all over the park, folded into the shiny coverings, looked like lumpy packages of tinfoil. Ms. Stevens said she was never a particular fan of Diana's.

"But when it happened, it hit me like it did everyone else," she said. All through the night, she and the other mourners shared their food and their stories. For retired painter Richard McLoughlin, the stories counted most.

"We've shared our food, our feelings, even our problems. It's nice you get to talk," said the sixty-one-year-old man, who traveled to London from Ireland's Sligo on Monday. "Unfortunately, it takes something like this."

Most people heeded police requests to leave their small children at home. The park would usually be filled with cyclists and skating children on such a warm day, but on Saturday the paths were taken by somber walkers hurrying for a view of the street. Talk was subdued. Even the dogs didn't frolic.

Radios, turned down low, also were full of death. "Calcutta is mourning," one announcer said, speaking of the death of Mother Teresa. "Georg Solti was eighty-four," another intoned, memorializing the conductor who also died Friday.

Once they had taken their places, most people just stared into the street, standing for long periods without speaking. At 9:08 A.M., a bell tolled, mournful and muffled, to mark the beginning of the funeral procession.

Only the draped coffin and its guards, wearing scarlet tunics and tall bearskin hats, emerged from Kensington Palace for the final journey. Diana's two sons, her brother, Prince Charles, and Prince Philip would join later, walking the final mile behind the military carriage.

Clarissa Palmer and her thirteen-year old daughter, Hannah, had places right at the Kensington Palace gate. As the princess's coffin appeared, a few people wailed and shrieked.

"We love you, Diana," someone shouted.

But the rest of the crowd remained stoic, much to Ms. Palmer's relief.

"Whether that was all they needed to do or the good British public just made it clear that this just wasn't the way to behave, I don't know," she said. "But people mostly watched. No one pushed or shoved. I've never been in a crowd like it."

Ms. Palmer hadn't particularly wanted to attend the funeral, but Hannah convinced her.

"It's a historical event," the girl said.

Ms. Palmer agreed but was puzzled by all the grief. "Perhaps it's just that there's some big lack in people's lives. I'm not a fan of organized religion, but maybe if we had more of that, we wouldn't need this."

The Palmers also had visited the park during the night. Ms. Palmer found the scene a bit eerie.

"I felt very uncomfortable with the whole icon thing," the teacher said. "But now I'm thinking, what the hell. It's not hurting her now."

Further down the road, the cortege's slow approach was announced by the hollow clop of horses' hooves. At each point along the route, a patter of applause accompanied the coffin's arrival. Then it went past, and for people lined twenty or thirty deep behind barricades, it was over.

People stood for a long moment, as though they could hardly believe there wasn't more. Then they turned away, wiped their eyes, and began converging on two large video screens set up in Hyde Park, a huge grassy plain in the center of London.

They rose to their feet to sing "God Save the Queen," setting aside resentment over what some regarded as the royal family's initial indifference to Diana's death. They also clapped when the screen showed the Union Jack atop Buckingham Palace being lowered to half-staff.

By the end of the eulogy given by Diana's brother, Charles Spencer, sniffles were coming from all sides. Some were openly sobbing. Though she hadn't even wanted to be here, Ms. Palmer's eyes were glistening as she leapt to her feet to cheer the eulogy, which included criticism of the royals and the press, unprecedented for such an occasion. When it was all done, people lingered, holding on to the sadness and the feeling of unity.

Before heading home, Ms. Norbury mused about what it all meant.

"It's a catalyst for something," she said. "Diana represents the underdog. It's sort of like the Statue of Liberty."

Paraphrasing the statue's famous words, she added, "I think that's who came to mourn—the tired and huddled masses."

Everyone was talking about the good deeds Diana did. People were praising her kindness, her innocence, her devotion to motherhood. The largest charity in history was formed out of money donated in her memory. She was turning out to be a kind of secular saint. People were truly and apparently deeply affected by having lost her. Even journalists back in the states told me they had cried upon hearing that she was dead.

I didn't understand what was going on. Diana was a lovely woman who had some bad breaks but no more than many other people have had. In many ways she had far more than her share of life's rewards, and she hadn't done more than a middling good job dealing with them. The truth was that her main occupation and chief claim to fame was her own narcissism. The good she did looked to me very much like a hobby that she had done little more than dabble in. And yet, she had inspired the greatest charitable outpouring in history.

Mother Teresa's death made the picture even more confusing. The media made a fuss about the Catholic nun's demise, certainly. People felt bereaved. But the contrast between the level of hoopla was astonishing. A casual reader could easily avoid details of Mother Teresa's life and death, but no one could escape Diana's saga. At first, I made bad jokes about the difference in how the two deaths were being treated, pointing out that Mother Teresa hadn't kept her figure. She hadn't had her face lifted. A good dress designer, a little makeup, a few confessions of torrid love would have given us real reasons to miss mother. But underneath the cynicism, I was really puzzled.

My colleagues tried to reason my disillusionment away. Mother Teresa was old and her death was expected, they said. Diana was young and about to start a new and better life. Diana was a symbol for some deep archetype within us. Yeah, maybe. But since I was in this new habit of basing my interpretations of the world on the premise that God was in control, I looked for what kind of lesson might be drawn from the differences.

Could the disparity in the world's grief say something helpful to us? I think people grieved over Diana more greatly than they did over Mother Teresa because Diana was more like us. Mother Teresa belonged to God. Her holiness was untouchable, unfathomable to most of us. What she did was admirable but hardly attainable.

Diana, on the other hand, did so many things wrong. She had eating disorders. She had an affair. She failed at her marriage. She told tales. She cared intensely about her clothes and her hair and her figure. She was beautiful and rich and flawed. And despite it all, she did some good. She gave what she had. It wasn't much compared to what Mother Teresa gave. She was no saint.

But she could hug children that other well-dressed people might not want to draw so close to them. She could reach out to people with AIDS when everyone else was afraid. When she promised to help people, she did. Her role as princess gave her a forum. She didn't change the world with it, but she tried to be open, and she tried to do the good that was available to her. Her most gutsy campaign, the one against land mines, did make a real difference in the world.

If someone as weak as Diana could grow into a woman admired by the world, maybe there is hope for us all. The charity in her name will do an enormous amount of good. Reflecting on that good as I continued to ask myself what living a spiritual life means, I couldn't help but think that Diana had turned herself to doing the good that was at hand, and it had made a tremendous difference. If she could do it, perhaps the rest of us could, too. Maybe the lesson for me is to stop flagellating myself for not being willing to make great sacrifices and to try doing what I can do. Make a start.

Chapter 43

In the Heart of Darkness, a Faith Too Good to Be True

I WENT TO Germany to do a story on peacemaking among victims of the Stasi, the largest state spying system in history. The East German government kept millions of secret files on its own citizens. Husbands had spied on wives, children had spied on parents, teachers had spied on students. The Stasi even had an elaborate system to recruit teenagers so that they would give information on their classmates. When Communism fell, the people of Eastern Germany were left to grapple with a society that was riddled with mistrust. That kind of trauma cuts to the very core of who people are. It destroys the trust that community requires.

In Germany I met Pastor Martin Kunze, a Protestant minister who spied for the Stasi for almost thirty years. When the Berlin Wall came down, Mr. Kunze confessed his secret life to the world. It cost him. But it also saved him, said the sixty-year-old Protestant minister.

"It revived me," he said, using the German verb often applied to resuscitation of a dying plant. "I wouldn't have survived if I hadn't told the truth. No way." Mr. Kunze stands as a testament to a promise his Christian faith proclaims: The truth will set you free. The truth is a pillar of the process many international peacemakers believe is necessary to bring about reconciliation within the world's most troubled countries.

While in Germany, I also visited a medical center for the treatment of torture victims. Some Germans were imprisoned and tortured by the East German government during the 1950s. Once released from prison, they were forbidden to tell anyone what had happened to them. And so the psychic wounds inflicted by the state had been hidden and festering for decades by the time these people went to therapists. But the center also treated immigrants from other countries whose wounds were more fresh and whose memories were sometimes even more horrific.

I've already mentioned that one of the great stumbling blocks of faith for me is the Holocaust. God's silence in that event, and in so many others, is certainly enough to make any reasonable person throw Him out. People who insist that God is love must do desperate gyrations, shut their eyes to horrible realities to avoid the realization that His love doesn't seem to have any power against evil.

Americans love to think that if you do God's will, you will be rewarded. We're currently in a time when football players trumpet their faith as a way of winning ball games. We hear prominent preachers promise great wealth and good fortune to those who love God. But the world's great stories of faith don't show good fortune at all. Read any book about the saints. Doing God's will often means suffering terribly. God doesn't save the faithful. He doesn't step in to rescue those who do His will. He lets many of them perish in great torment.

More than that even, many of the stories show Him drawing them toward a terrible fate.

Anyone who looks at faith honestly must confront what Karen Armstrong calls "the dark mystery" of the world's pain. I got a glimpse of that on one morning after my visit to the torture center. It was Saturday. Unlike Americans, my German translators didn't think working seven days a week was in order. So I was on my own for the weekend. I planned to do some sight-seeing. But it was a cloudy day and I was slow to start.

Sitting on the side of my narrow white bed in a Berlin hotel room, I picked up a booklet from the torture center to read about a Bosnian woman. The story refers to a Mrs. U. "A plain-looking woman, she is of small stature, dressed in black, with a peaked face. She looks helpless and without any strength, holding on to one of her care givers. . . . Her body posture and her slightly bent head could be signs indicative of depression. Her hands are restlessly in motion, her left hand clasping a handkerchief. When she raises her head, we notice a nervous flickering in her eyes as well as a slight tremor in her facial muscles; from time to time her entire head trembles. Her breathing is flat, her voice is hardly audible, at times the only thing we can hear is a choked moan." She is thirty-seven years old, but she looks like an old woman marked by death. She has been sent to the center because her abusive behavior toward her children horrified her caretakers who can't seem to help her transcend the terrible things that keep her body and mind in constant pain.

The booklet describes her many debilitating symptoms in detail. Only after a month of treatment is Mrs. U even able to tell what happened in Bosnia. Then she relates this story:

"May 1992 in Mrs. U's home town. It is early evening. She is at home with her husband and her two small children when Serb Chetniks storm into the building, forcing all inhabitants to go outside. In the street men, women, and children are lined up against a wall. In the hours to follow, all men are killed. Two women are with the Chetniks, approximately seventeen years of age, who act with special cruelty. One of them is the daughter of a colleague of Mrs. U. The killing instruments they use are knives and sickles mounted on long handles. The men are dismembered and their genitals are strung up on wire like a 'chain.' This kind of 'spoils' brings quite a bit of money for the killers, Mrs. U tells us. They cut the men's tongues, crosses are burned into their skin, and their throats are slit. Blood is everywhere. No word is spoken. No screams of horror are heard. The children do not whimper. Only the sounds of killing and dying are cutting the gloomy silence. Mrs. U is trying to spare her children this sight by hiding them under her skirts. However, she herself loses consciousness several times. At the end of the massacre all women and children are led away, the dead remain behind. For seven days, Mrs. U is unable to speak, she is frozen in silence." Mrs. U is taken to a detention center where she and other women are raped many times by many different men over the next months. She often thinks back to her husband's dying look, which she interpreted to mean that she was to care for the children.

The writer of the booklet comments that the human mind is simply unable to arrange or place such horror. Mrs. U says again and again, "God was absent. Why?" She asks her counselors. She asks herself. She asks God. But there is no answer.

After reading the story, I sat on the bed sobbing, the same question in my own mind. "Why? If there is a God why would He allow humans to suffer so much?" Mrs. U's story is just one fragment of humanity's suffering, and it is too horrible to imagine. My fragile faith can't deal with God's faithlessness. Is He helpless? Is He unconcerned? Or does He even exist?

Hours later, I leave the room to walk in the streets of Berlin. I no longer care about sight-seeing but I need to move, to walk as fast as I can until some of this terrible feeling dissipates. I've tried to stick close to my own puny experiences with God. I've built my own happy imaginings into a rickety kind of faith. But now my efforts seem like silly evasions of life's true nature.

I get on the subway and end up in one of the city's residential neighborhoods. It's a beautiful area where massive old buildings with apartments and shops are intermingled. I walk past a shop that sells war memorabilia. The Germans have fought so many wars that such artifacts are easy to find. I'm listless, worn out by my own emotions. At first I confronted God bitterly. Now I'm past that. I just feel wrung out, hopeless, and full of sorrow.

The shops are not yet open. I pause at the window of a jewelry shop. Among the display is a black onyx ring with a tiny diamond in the center. It looks old. As bad as I feel, the ring strikes a chord within me. My mother once gave me such a ring. Among my first memories is seeing her long-fingered, white hands with that ring on them.

The man I refer to as my father is actually my adoptive dad. My birth father left when I was five years old. On the day I last saw my father, my mother had left us together while she worked. When she returned home, she found him alone in the house. When she asked where I was, he said he had taken me to the park and left me there playing. My mother was enraged by such carelessness. After she brought me home from the park, they argued. He jumped into the red convertible she had recently bought him and drove away.

The ring was the only thing he ever gave her that she kept. When I was in my thirties, she passed it on to me. I lost it. It was a bit too large for me, but one evening I couldn't resist wearing it anyway. It fell off my finger. I don't know when or where. I looked for it for hours, but it never turned up. I so regretted losing the ring that for years afterward I dreamed of it. Sometimes I fantasized about finding it. But I never did. It's gone.

I rarely see a ring like it. The one in the Berlin shop window wasn't exactly like it, either. It looked older and more delicate. It was prettier than the one I'd lost but enough like it to remind me of my own lost treasure. At first I stared at it dully. I was in no mood to shop. And then out of the teary fog I was still in, it was as though a voice spoke in my head: "All will be restored and even more than before."

I stopped breathing for a moment. Could that be true? Could it be that God would heal all the pain, restore all the losses, comfort all the afflicted? No. It's too much to hope for. It couldn't be done. Even God couldn't do that. Then I remembered the story of Job. God's desire to prove a point had let Job in for terrible suffering. Even his friends had gathered to condemn him in his misfortune. But Job was blameless and at the end of the story the Bible says, "The Lord made him prosperous again and gave him twice as much as he had before. . . . The Lord blessed the latter part of Job's life more than the first. He had fourteen thousand sheep, six thousand camels, a thousand yoke of oxen and a thousand donkeys. And he also had seven sons and three daughters." All was restored and more.

I walked away from the window. This message was too good to have come from God. It must have been my own feeble attempts to make some sense of the world. I didn't believe it. Not with my intellect. But some kind of hope had sprung up in my body. I could feel it even though I didn't believe it.

As I started back to the hotel, I was doubtful, but some of the despair was gone. A little sprig of hope had greened inside me. Job had received new children and new flocks and new lands. They didn't replace the old ones. Nothing could do that. But they had been a comfort to him. He had had new joy. His suffering had changed him so much that the Bible says he made sure that even his daughters inherited some of his wealth. In the sermon on the mount, Jesus reaffirmed the idea that suffering might not have the end we think it has. "Blessed are those who mourn for they shall be comforted," he said.

I'm hesitant to offer my little imaginings as an answer to the world's pain. Maybe they mean nothing. But I can't deny them because they created, not belief, but some sense of reassurance and hope that I had never felt before. The end of the story, however, must also be told. It complicates the niceness of the package a bit.

When I reached my hotel, I thought again about the ring. I could go back and buy it. If I did, I could look at it every day and be reminded of the message that comforted me. This ring was even prettier than the one I had lost. It would be the seal on the message. Its existence and my ownership of it would remind me that pain will be soothed, all the lost will be replaced with greater blessings, if not in this life, then in another one.

You can reject my little vision. I wouldn't blame you. But even if you do, surely you can understand my desire to believe it. If Karen Armstrong is right about imagination being one of faith's great attributes, then it doesn't matter that it might have been only my imagination. Even if it was a fabrication from my own need, it gives me courage to face life.

So I decided that I would go back to buy the ring. A few days later I returned to the shop. The ring was still there. The shopkeeper took it out of the window. I could afford the price. I tried it on. It fit perfectly. But it wasn't at all what I expected. My old ring had been large and dominant on my hand. This one was smaller. In contrast to my hand, it looked puny and squashed into my flesh. It wasn't better than what I'd lost. It was worse. If I bought it, I would not be reminded that God's blessings were greater than what was lost. I would be reminded that what I'd lost could never be replaced with anything as good.

I didn't want that message. So I gave the ring back. Where was my delightful meaning now? Perhaps I had been wrong. Seeing a ring with so much symbolism seemed to mean something when I saw it, but when I reached out to take it, the meaning changed. Or did it?

I didn't want to be a sap about this story. I was accustomed to being disappointed in God and fearful about life. Maybe the story of the ring was only a personal parable about the desperate gullibility I was capable of. I wanted to harden up again. But somehow I couldn't. I felt the hope that was too good to be true and I couldn't forget it.

Maybe I was wrong only about the last part of the message. Maybe God can heal us and restore what we've lost. But we have to learn to let go. Maybe I got part of it right but not all of it. Maybe we can't own God's blessings. Maybe the key isn't in grasping for physical tokens but in letting go.

I would be extending myself too far to say that I know for sure what all this means. Maybe it means nothing. I offer it only in the spirit that Nouwen commended in pastors. He said that the best pastors are those who share their own stories. They are like the spies whom Moses sent to the promised land. They went over to where the Israelites had not been, and they brought back the lay of the land.

I, too, traveled to that strange land of faith. I saw these things. I heard these messages. I'm coming back with the tale. You have to judge whether it has value.

May 22, 2005

To Diana
Thank you for
participating in the discussion!
Best wishes to you,

Nancy C. James

STANDING IN THE WHIRLWIND

STANDING IN
THE WHIRLWIND

PHOTO BY RALPH NEBEL

THE RIVETING STORY OF A PRIEST AND THE
CONGREGATIONS THAT TORMENTED HER

NANCY C. JAMES

THE PILGRIM PRESS CLEVELAND

for my brother, FRANKLIN

The Pilgrim Press, 700 Prospect Avenue, Cleveland, OH 44115-1100
thepilgrimpress.com
© 2005 Nancy C. James

All rights reserved. Published 2005
Printed in the United States of America on acid-free paper

09   08   07   06   05   5   4   3   2   1

Library of Congress Cataloging-in-Publication Data

James, Nancy C., 1954–
    Standing in the whirlwind : the riveting story of a priest and
the congregations that tormented her / Nancy C. James.
        p.   cm.
    ISBN 0-8298-1619-4 (alk. paper)
    1. James, Nancy C., 1954– 2. Episcopal Church—United
States—Clergy—Biography.   3. Women clergy—United States—
Biography.   I. Title.

BX5995.J26A3   2005
283'.092—dc22
[B]   2004062805

contents

ACKNOWLEDGMENTS

I thank Elly Sparks Brown, Hugh Brown,
Roger Nebel, Bill Buchanan, and Judy May for
their friendship and support. I very much
appreciate Ulrike Guthrie's help in editing.

I also thank the Very Reverend David Bird
and Grace Episcopal Church, Georgetown, for
their support. Their work with the homeless
in Washington, D.C., is a light in our world.

To protect their identities, I have changed
the names of parishioners, persons I supervised
through the courts, and prisoners I taught.

one

THE HORRIFIC PRISON

*Rest assured, it is the same God who causes
the scarcity and the abundance, the rain and
the fair weather. The high and low states, the
peaceful and the state of warfare, are each
good in their season. These vicissitudes form
and mature the interior, as the different
seasons compose the year. . . . God loves you;
let this thought equalise all states. Let him
do with us as with the waves of the sea, and
whether he takes us to his bosom, or casts us
upon the sand, that is, leaves us to our own
barrenness, all is well.*

— Jeanne Guyon, *Spiritual Letters*

What is a priest? The question danced in my conscious-ness. What does it mean to stand before God, or to revel in the spirit of the divine? And how do we love unconditionally? All of us are chosen to love, all are called to be part of the priesthood of all believers. Throughout my life these questions beckoned to me, and I yearned to follow where they led.

I had known the divine through the wild Alaskan nature as a child. My father said to me one winter evening, "Come outside, Nancy. I don't want you to miss this." I turned my head to see Dad in his green flight uniform, ready to go out once again in his B-47, the jet engine streaming through the night skies of Alaska. So we went out into the dark Alaskan night. And I saw the northern lights, the skies dancing with joy, the colors, blues, greens, passionate reds, mixing and separating, loving, entrancing, calling us to them. And my mind, soaked with joy, looked at the dancing skies and worshipped. I knew my dad would soon crawl into the B-47 and fly into this wonder—and I felt humbled that he cared enough for me to want me to see this dance of color, me, his third child, his only daughter. I looked at him and laughed, "The skies are dancing, Daddy." He smiled at me and said nothing. A little later I heard our front door quietly shutting as he left for another day of flying through the arctic skies. The divine alleluias of nature sang in Alaska.

This search for God, this journey towards the divine, begins in our hearts at birth and continues eternally. Like pilgrims in Chaucer's *Canterbury Tales*, we all journey differently and yet how similar are our passions for God. Come, be a fellow traveler in this story of our adventurous pilgrimage towards God.

2

I moved to Culpeper County in 1985 with high hopes for a successful ministry in this beautiful area. The gentle rolling hills of the rural Virginia countryside mount gradually west until they grow into the peaceful Blue Ridge Mountains. I moved there with plans of contributing what I could to helping others. I felt needed there, for Christ Church, the small Episcopal Church in Brandy Station, would likely close its doors without me there as priest.

I remember my first trip out to look at the church, about sixty miles southwest of Washington, D.C., and I recall experiencing premonitions of something amiss when I saw the property. Paint was peeling on the older, white building, and a rusty sign merely stated it was Episcopal with no worship times announced. The scene was of a decaying structure: a white, wooden church with a large steeple topped by a cross announcing its existence to the world. No trees or flowers decorated the one-acre field surrounding this unkempt property. I wondered if the local culture, like the church building, was falling into disarray.

Later at the church I met with some of the vestry, the church board of directors. Betsy greeted me at the door. Her delightful offerings of hot coffee and fresh pastries were refreshment for weary travelers arriving after a long journey. Betsy was a statuesque woman with a shock of dark brown hair piled on top of her head. John, a local businessman, looked at me with his piercing eyes, and announced meaningfully and abruptly, "I finished fox hunting in time for this meeting." Relaxing, Betsy smiled with understanding and asked sympathetically, "So your gout is not bothering you anymore?" John shook his head in dismay at even the thought of the gout, saying, "I saw this doctor and he gave me some medicine—but asked me to avoid rich food and wines. I try but . . ." We laughed, identifying with his struggle against fine Virginia ham and local Chardonnay.

3

Love and comfort splashed all around us as we settled down to discuss the future of this historic Episcopal church.

John sized me up, cutting to the chase immediately with his statements and question: "We want to keep the doors open at the church. The bishop said you are a capable woman. Can you do this?"

I reacted with confidence. "I can do this. I'm working with the juvenile court in Culpeper during the week." We went through details about the church and its weekly service. Then John announced, "We want you to begin this Sunday."

And a deal was made. I was now the female rector of a church.

Waves of shock rolled through me. How had I come to this place, this call? In my life I had experienced a persistent sense of calling, to "Leave all that is familiar behind. Follow Me." And somehow I wanted to answer this gracious feeling. So, I followed. I trailed behind ineptly at times, and angrily at others, but I sought God enthusiastically.

Pondering these memories, experiences, and questions as part of my divine search, I walked slowly around this small town of Brandy Station. John had explained to me the significance of the colorful name, Brandy Station: the train used to stop here to allow the sale of this popular beverage, the availability of which was announced by a large sign. Beyond the train tracks, picturesque, rural homes dotted the landscape, separated from each other by green fields and grazing cows. About one quarter of a mile away from the Episcopal church lay the local Methodist church, which had been sold and turned into an antique store. This was also a white, wooden edifice, with a steeple. Clearly the glories of this church were long gone. I wondered, was this the future of Christ Church also? A church that metamorphosed into a store?

Walking inside this unusual store, I saw that this old church was filled with aging furniture. I listened to the friendly proprietor tell me about the Civil War cavalry battle of Brandy Station in 1863. It had been a bloody and violent battle, the largest cavalry battle of the Western Hemisphere, resulting in the deaths of more than a thousand men and countless horses.

When I asked the antique store owner about the battlefield, a frightened look crossed her face. "Your church owns a graveyard there still," she said, choosing her words carefully.

"In the battlefield?"

"Yes, right in the middle."

I wondered why this hadn't been mentioned to me, but the obvious uneasiness of the woman cautioned me from pursuing this conversation. Quietly I strolled back to the church.

So in 1985 I became both the priest at Christ Church in Brandy Station and a juvenile probation counselor for the Commonwealth of Virginia. My duties for the court included supervising young men and women who had gotten in trouble with the law, as well as recommending possible sentences. This was not a new circumstance for me. I had started this cor-

4

rections work earlier as part of my seminary studies. Mine had indeed been an unusual journey to ordination.

I attended Virginia Theological Seminary from 1981 to 1984. In 1982, during my second year at seminary, I had chosen as a place for a year's fieldwork the Washington, D.C., jail. Two days a week I left the cozy, luxurious surroundings of the beautiful Virginia seminary, located in the old, river port town of Alexandria, across the Potomac River from Washington, D.C. The seminary occupies a large tract of land, filled with delightful gardens and trees, which in its pre–Civil War days had been an isolated, rural location. Now in this garden haven in the midst of an urban setting we studied, discussed, and enjoyed many social activities. These days, like all the others, we had many choices for our lunch—hot pasta, sandwiches, desserts, and fruit, eaten while we engaged in conversations about the latest church news in a refectory whose glowing oil paintings of the church hierarchy beamed beneficently on us. Feeling full of the delicious lunch and enjoyment of this life of privilege and intellectual stimulation, I descended into the subway station, traveling forty-five minutes away to emerge into a starkly different world. Here, in southeast Washington, D.C., I heard of hungry children going to the zoo, not to see the exotic animals, but to eat out of the garbage cans plentifully filled with stale popcorn. In this world, women shook with fear at the presence of the powerful men in their lives: the heartless pimps who controlled their money and told them with whom to sleep and when, or the dissolute boyfriends who came home intoxicated, knocking them down if they got in the way. In this world, I felt their desperate, interior struggle to survive, knowing that tragically many women and children would lose the deadly battle for survival.

I received quite an education at that chaotic jail, where the way people were packed in reminded me of Dante's hell. I worked mainly with women charged with prostitution. One morning I sat in my dirty, noisy office, listening to the sounds of caged humans cursing each other and banging doors, when

5

a frightened young woman walked in, wearing her bright orange jail jumpsuit. She stood, unnaturally quiet, her long, lustrous blonde hair sparkling in the garish jail lights. I asked her what had brought her here. She paused for a long time. Then she answered in a voice colored with embarrassment and a shrug of her shoulders, "I am a call girl." Her frightened eyes asked the question, *Are you going to judge me harshly for this?*

"Where do you live?" I asked, trying to change the subject to deflect her obvious distress.

"Do you know where the Church of the Resurrection is?" she asked, referring to a local Episcopal church. She lived directly across the street from this prominent edifice.

"Yes," I said sadly, and I wondered, had the church ever tried to reach out to this woman and had she ever been told of God who cared enough to show her a different way of life? Had the church left her at the mercy of her pimp and wealthy clients, and now thrown her on the mercy of the legal system? I believed in my life that we were to trust God and God would guide us, like a cloud by day and a pillar of fire by night, as the Old Testament described God leading the Israelites. Yet this beautiful woman had the worst of guides, a self-interested pimp.

The comfortable life of the Episcopal Church seemed disconnected from this raw human suffering. The Bible was so obvious in its meaning in the gospel of Matthew when Jesus calls some blessed, "For I was hungry and you gave me food, I was thirsty and you gave me something to drink, I was a stranger and you welcomed me. I was naked and you gave me clothing, I was sick and you took care of me, I was in prison and you visited me" (Matt. 25:35, 36). The sheer number of suffering women at the jail overwhelmed me, and increasingly I questioned, why wasn't the church helping to address these horrifying problems? That I frequently invited one of the seminary supervisors to visit me on site and he refused, finally admitting to me that he didn't want to go into such a dangerous environment, only exacerbated for me this sense of disconnection. Did no one care about these human beings who were begging for help with no one to answer them? And so I grappled, attempting to remain faithful to my beloved Episcopal Church, while serving what I perceived as my vocation to the poor.

Through all this I still knew the intense joy in life that I had learned as a child living in Alaska, a place of primeval bliss. We had lived in this unfinished end of the world, this strange Alaska, this ancient place. For who could define Alaska? It was as if God had been weaving a beautiful tapestry with huge California redwoods, the powerful Mississippi River, the steady Kansas plains, and then at the end of the tapestry, God scratched the divine head in perplexity and said, "Darn! What am I going to do with these ends?" And so the Divine left the ends dangling, unpolished, unfinished, sublime in their godly, unfinished, primal beauty. Gold dazzled in the rivers, glaciers glittered in the sunlight, colors danced in the skies. And animals, strange and fearful, walked in this primeval wonderland as confident as in that first Garden of God, the one we still seek in our hearts. Baby moose, gangly and adorable, struggled to coordinate their legs while the mother moose protectively gazed around, overlooking these mere humans, these interlopers in their paradise. They had allowed us humans to see this raw handiwork of God and we felt this amazing honor bestowed upon us to see them.

7

Honored by the privilege of a theological education, my friends and I loved debating the ideas we studied. The seminary experience was a varied one, including excellent professors as well as overly pious ones. One Wednesday evening, my visiting California artist brother Tim accompanied my husband and me to the weekly church service. The preacher gave a long-winded sermon interpreting Jesus' temptations in the wilderness as "dull, dry, boring days such as we all have." The analogy between our twentieth-century boredom and Jesus' suffering in the wilderness seemed farfetched to me, but I didn't say anything about it on the way home. We drove quietly down from the seminary hill, back to Old Town. As we neared our home, Tim turned, looked at me with his bright, blue eyes, and said mischievously, "Yes, those long, dry, *boring* days when Evil Incarnate appears to us." We burst out laughing and chortled about that for a long time. Then we improvised on the theme. Tim would start, acting nonchalant, "Those long boring days . . ." I would enthusiastically finish, "when Satan himself stands before you in the desert." Enjoying ourselves immensely, we continued, "Those dry, dull days . . ." my husband Patrick laughingly interjected, "when Evil Itself interrogates you about your life." I started, "Boredom and ennui sets in . . ." Tim finished, "when evil confronts your very existence." Weak with laughter, we walked in the door refreshed by our private joke, and settled down to large amounts of ice cream. Little did I know that my quest for understanding evil had begun.

I was ordained in 1985 but, instead of working in a parish, chose to work at the Washington, D.C., prison, Lorton Reformatory, located about twenty miles south of the District of Columbia in Lorton, Virginia. The first day, I shakily walked to my copper-colored Honda to drive out to the prison. What could I expect, going into a building packed with men who had committed violent crimes, including murder? But the entrancing call to do this lingered. I felt encouraged, as if a living spirit were gently guiding me to this strange place, pointing me in this direction, and promising me nurture in it.

Much of what I knew about prison was what I had learned from Dietrich Bonhoeffer's *Letters From Prison*, which Bonhoeffer had written while incarcerated by the Nazis in World

War II. From them, I gained a sense of Bonhoeffer's immense suffering, isolation, and yet the fragrant, fragmented moments of grace he described. But as I drew nearer the tough D.C. prison, I wondered if I had been too trusting by trying this work.

Still reflecting, I drove south, circling through lovely Virginia farmland till I was confronted with the menacing, gray prison buildings. "What a contrast," I murmured to myself, leaving behind the pastoral setting to enter buildings with guards, guns, and imposing walls. I felt intimidated by the sharply glistening, rolled barbed wire. A corrections official who patrolled in a birdcage-like structure on top of the fence pointed his rifle in my general direction and demanded, "Who are you?" Shakily I announced, "I am the new teacher." I walked timidly into the checkpoint, which looked something like a rundown security station at an airport. A corrections officer thoroughly searched my belongings, while a female official patted me down to make sure that I didn't have any contraband on me, such as guns or drugs. This was the way I was to begin every working day for the next two years.

9

My assignment was the teenage youth offenders who were in Protective Custody. Walking into the cellblock, I was overwhelmed by a cacophony of yelling, cursing, and slamming doors. As prisoners saw me for the first time most stared, shocked that a white woman was coming in here. I heard the loud, taunting call, "Hey, white bitch." Others, though, reacted with respect as I introduced myself as the new English teacher. As my supervisor gave me a tour down the two long corridors with cells on both sides, each crammed with several men, mirrors popped out of the small openings on the doors so they could see who was approaching. I was relieved that my classes were to be held in a trailer, separate from the prison building, and that it had windows allowing in daylight. I made plans to put posters on the walls to brighten this cheerless and dangerous place.

During my orientation, I learned that I had been hired with money that Senator Specter from Pennsylvania had worked to get for a prison education program. Specter money, they called this new program. I would work with those who were in direct danger from other prisoners and needed protection. Some had only committed minor property crimes but had ended up incarcerated with hardened criminals. Inside the prison walls the stronger ones preyed on the weaker.

During my first week, I met with every prisoner to review his educational test results. The scores were pathetically low, but I struggled in the smelly, dark room to maintain an attitude of hope for the sake of these young men who came to see me one by one, their heads bowed, struggling with feelings of guilt and shame. I hoped to offer an open door to a different existence. But to hope in that brutal environment was difficult.

The prison was located directly next to a garbage dump. We endured not only the horrors and stresses of prison life but the odors of decaying garbage. Corruption confronted me day after day: the corruption of young lives decaying and dying before their prime combined with the horrendous reality of a giant mountain of rotting waste in their nostrils every day.

Death accompanied us at the prison, with occasional murders and frequent stabbings. I showed up for work on several occasions to see FBI agents swarming around looking for clues about the latest stabbing or beating death. Yet these were very infrequently solved because of the dangers of being a snitch and the terrible retribution against those who cooperated with the authorities. My terrified students frequently told me about their brutal rapes, beatings, and knifings. I was told that prison officials commonly looked the other way while these acts of violence occurred, and that a prison official actually perpetrated some of these acts. When I begged the young man with long, light brown hair who told me of the sexual abuse committed against him by the official to report the crime, he responded aghast: "You don't understand. I don't have any power here. Nobody's going to listen to me."

And indeed I didn't understand what was going on around me. Abuse, illness, and injustice reigned at Youth Center One.

Along with the daily struggle to survive, several men in Protective Custody were dying of a strange form of pneumonia. We wondered about the unusual deaths when a staff meeting was called in late 1985 in which we were told more about the strange, new disease called AIDS from which my students regularly perished.

As time went by, I worked diligently at my teaching, trying to make it both effective and fun. Every Monday we had a spelling bee, which after a few beginning, uncomfortable moments turned out to be a good-natured game. Many of my students bordered on being illiterate, and I claimed every chance I had of increasing their reading skills. One day I was writing on the chalkboard in my classroom, "Tomorrow is the Halloween Spelling Bee." Mark Proctor, a prisoner I had heard about, walked in just then with a message for me. "What is a *Halloween* spelling bee?" he asked me quietly.

A little timidly, I said, "I'll give out candy to everyone who participates."

Mr. Proctor said, "These men need their education, Ms. James. It's their only hope."

I recognized that he had the same attitude I did. "Yes, Mr. Proctor. I think you are right."

He left after giving me a look of respect. I sat down nervously. Mark Proctor was known in the prison for having much influence with both the inmates and officials, apparently because of his power in the gang community in Washington, D.C. I knew instinctively that was an important moment for me at Lorton Reformatory.

I tried to recall what I knew about Mark Proctor. He had grown up in the toughest area of southeast Washington, and had never known a safe community. But a loving grandmother raised him, instilling in him respect and care for others while he continued to live in abject poverty. As many did, Mark turned to illegal activities as a way of making money. Even as he participated in this, he continued to care for and love others suffering like him. Mark possessed a personal authority that commanded respect from others, an authority born from his own struggle with poverty and despair.

A few days later, Mark Proctor visited my class again. At the end, he stood up and rather deliberately announced: "If anyone hurts Ms. James, he's coming to me." Another gang member said quietly, "Me too." I was surprised by this and talked to some prison officials about it. They answered, "With Mark Proctor's protection, you'll never have a moment of trouble here." The other teachers expressed envy. After that, I walked carefree around this dangerous place, frequently overhearing people say, "She's protected by Proctor"—a protection for which I was indeed grateful since it freed me to do my work.

I taught English at the prison, as well as making parole recommendations. One day I needed dictionaries for my students and had no hope of getting them through the prison hierarchy. Following the recommendation of my bishop, I made an appointment with an Episcopal priest to ask for his assistance. I was newly ordained at the time.

"I need dictionaries for my students. Nobody deserves the life they have at that prison," I explained. "For the last year, I have read their social histories and I can tell you, these teenagers were victims. They desperately need our help."

The priest looked at me coldly. "My parishioners wouldn't want me to help that prison. The prison shouldn't be in our neighborhood. No, I won't help you," he said abruptly ending the appointment.

Suddenly I felt nauseated, remembering Richard who had recently been gang raped and Louis who shook with fear all his waking moments. This priest felt comfortable denying help to people in crisis, people who were suffering dreadfully. I picked up my purse and walked slowly out, shocked to tears. I wondered, from what level of hell did this reality come? Did a demon design these Conditions of Being, to use a phrase from Paul Tillich. Alone, beaten, raped. Beside a stinking mountain of garbage. I felt disgust at a world that makes and hides away places like Youth Center One.

The fortunate prisoners were those who were released. I received a note from one such, named Ralph, whose note was carried to me by his friend. It started, "I wouldn't be telling the truth if I were to say I wish I was there for the spelling bee." I laughed, thinking of all those spelling bees and newspaper articles and book reports. But the students worked hard, and with gratitude I learned that many passed their GED tests.

One cold, winter morning the heat in my classroom trailer failed. The guard announced the cancellation of classes, but I said that I was willing to leave my down jacket on and teach whoever wanted to come. To my delight, in trooped Mark Proctor, who sat and read his book, along with Ronald, Louis, Richard, and Robert. They lined up at the chalkboard and we worked first on math problems. With my hat and gloves still on, I began, "A man has $98 in a bank, earning 4.5% annual interest. At the end of one year, how much does he have in the bank?" The teenagers, hidden under gray prison jackets, raced to the chalkboard, working to the correct answer, and then yelling, "I got it!" The first to accomplish it would explain his answer. I sat, feeling like the Queen of Sheba presiding over an earnest search for wisdom. After many math problems we moved on to spelling. I said, "Please spell the word 'ancient.'" They groaned, not remembering the "i before e" rule, as well as the exceptions to the rule. We cheerfully practiced all of that. More words followed. "Now," I said, "what is the scientific idea of phototropism?" as I looked at one of the many beautiful plants in my room. A slender, young man started to respond, "Plants grow towards light . . ." when an older, uniformed prison guard walked in.

"Time for the count. They need to go back to their cells."

"See you tomorrow," I said, while they quietly picked up their GED books and walked out. And, Lord, I prayed, please protect them from violence tonight.

I remained contemplatively at my desk that winter day after they left, savoring the lovely feelings of good work accomplished. I remembered being a child on Eielson Air Force Base in Fairbanks, Alaska, learning many of the same things these teenagers were now studying. In the cold, dark winter evenings, my pilot father would drill me on my spelling words, while my mother listened intently. I sat drinking the chocolate milk and eating the candy bars he saved for me from his flight lunches, listening carefully to the spelling challenges. My dad deliberately pronounced word after word, with me yearning to please him by spelling what seemed to me impossibly difficult words. My mother would laughingly groan if I missed the same word too many times. After a particularly good evening, he would smile and say, "You're smart, Nancy. Keep up the work!" Yet this joy I had found sharing with my parents my scholastic achievements throughout the years was one that I knew many of these young men in prison had never had access to.

My students and I became close as we studied for their tests. We laughed as we practiced multiplication tables. We chanted rules about grammar, sometimes using rap beats. One student, Steve, who came from the general prison population and was part of an advisory committee for the administration, asked me if he could sit in all of my classes and walk around with me. Unsure about his motivation, I asked him why. He said he wanted to make sure that I was safe and taken care of. He knew about Mark Proctor's protection, but he didn't want me to be alone. I accepted his gracious offer. He was a teenager with a minor charge on his record. I quickly discovered that he was emotionally supportive of me. "How are you feeling today, Miss James?" he would ask cheerfully. Or, "Do you want me to go ask Major Peed up at administration about getting more light bulbs down here?"

When we walked from Protective Custody to the main school, Steve would tell me about his committee's plans for improving the prison, such as scheduling movies and educational activities. He himself had successfully completed his GED and was now enrolled in college classes at the Maximum Security facility. I tried to talk to him about his life. "My mother has been sick for years," he said sadly, offering no more information. "I want to try to get some more college before I leave," Steve said looking at me with determination and hope.

Day after day Steve met me, shooing away any prisoner who looked unstable. Now I no longer heard anyone cursing or yelling at me, as I had at the beginning. Instead, as we walked places, my students would call out a continual stream of pleasantries, "How are you, Miss James?" or "I passed my test, Miss James! I got my GED!" in response to which Steve and I would offer congratulations. Other prisoners, respecting Steve, brought problems to him. "Man," they would say, "my cell-mate has someone after him. I need some help." And Steve, the angel of mercy, would figure out an effective way to approach the problem, helping prevent violence in this over-crowded, dirty facility.

One day I decided to go read Steve's record in hopes of fig-uring out how he had become so caring toward others. Sitting down with his file in the large, comfortable record room I saw that he had correctly presented his charges and biographical information to me. The court official wrote that Steve com-mitted a minor property crime because he needed rent money and had little family support. Then in the social history, I read, "Steve has had a sad history, starting with his mother's victimization on the streets of Washington, D.C. His mother was taking good care of Steve until he reached the age of eleven, when she was violently raped on a street in Washington, D.C." I held my breath in shock as I continued reading the court document. Steve's mother spent some time in the hospital recovering from the violence, but then had a nervous breakdown as she struggled to deal with this dreadful assault. Steve's previously happy life now fell apart as his mother spent lengthy periods in St. Elizabeths [sic] Hospital, a federal mental hospital. With no one to care for him, Steve was shuttled back and forth between foster homes. Although he continued to visit his mother, her formerly warm personality disappeared and she had to remain living in this hospital. Left without mother or family, Steve's unstable existence finally led him to crime.

The next day I talked to Steve. "I read your record yesterday," I started quietly. "You never told me about your mother." He looked at me with sorrow, but said nothing, "Steve, I want to thank you. I understand now," I said. "You want to make very sure that I don't get raped or hurt, right?"

Tears filled his eyes. "That's right, Miss James. My mother was never okay after that happened to her."

I started to cry also. This young man's sweet character was like a godsend. Obviously his mother had done a very good job of nurturing him before the tragedy.

Conditions at the prison continued to shock me. I sat at my desk one afternoon, going over test results with a recently admitted inmate. He was shifting uncomfortably in his seat, clearly experiencing some discomfort. Finally I asked, "What's wrong?" He looked down and started crying. "I got raped in the shower stall last night. Two prisoners watched at the door while several others did it to me." Outraged, I asked, "Do you want me to report it?" "Oh, please don't," he begged. "That will make it worse. They'll rape and beat me again as punishment for reporting it."

I left work that day feeling sick. What a terrible place, I thought, and complained at length to my husband that evening, as we sat talking over a drink. Before this job I didn't have any idea that there was such rampant violence in our prisons.

Shortly thereafter, everything became worse at the already hideous Youth Center One adjacent to the garbage dump. An inmate was burned and seriously injured in an explosion. Had he been innocently burned, I wondered? "Miss James, he was freebasing cocaine," a parole officer informed me, "He got what he deserved." I listened, not having any concrete reason

16

to question his assessment of the situation, only feeling a growing uneasiness.

Then two more explosions happened, leaving more young men severely burned. Finally, the prison officials investigated the possibility that the problem was in the prison itself. They discovered that methane gas existed in the ground, possibly exacerbated by the garbage dump. When these young men had merely lit a cigarette, their rooms had exploded. The complacent prison officials had apparently let this situation continue uninvestigated until several men lay in the hospital in agony, severely burned. How could human beings treat each other so callously? How could our society allow such a dereliction of duty? Judged unsafe, Youth Center One was closed. The men were shoved into other, already overcrowded facilities.

Desperately needing a break from the mayhem, I took a vacation in the wilderness of northern Idaho, which reminded me of Alaska. In the Alaskan spring, the snow started melting gradually, first a hint of softer snow, and then a promise of slushy snow. Finally, in a monumental act of creation, the Earth's powers harmonized, producing the first drops of pure, fresh melted snow. Refreshing water transformed from the hard ice, the frightening cold now turned into streams of water that pooled in the ground, dancing, rushing, rollicking, as if they were in the know with the divine joke—the Earth lives and breathes and skips with the pure ecstasy of cleansing streams of delight.

God, our ecstatic God, accompanies us on our journey. Without this knowledge I would never have returned to Lorton Reformatory.

Back at the newly reopened Youth Center One, I struggled with how to inject some health into this dreadful situation. Patrick suggested that I invite a poet who had spoken to one of his classes at George Washington University. I followed up on my husband's idea and invited the poet, Ethelbert Miller, from Howard University in Washington, D.C., to speak at Protective Custody. Mr. Miller spoke quite eloquently. After reading his poetry, he turned to the very attentive young men and said, "Do you know what they are calling you? The underclass." He then encouraged them to do whatever was in their power to change this horrific situation.

Eventually, the unjust state of affairs at Lorton became unbearable for the inmates. The ongoing abuses and poor living conditions finally provoked an explosive reaction. One morning I showed up at work only to learn that during the night another riot had broken out and the officials had used tear gas to stop the men. When I reached the guards surrounding the gate, I was told, "The mood in there is pretty funky. Be careful." Trusting in my protection, I entered nonetheless and walked towards my classroom, with inmates standing around everywhere, looking like alert, unhealthy statues. In the unnaturally quiet environment, some still said a somber, "Good morning, Miss James." I stopped at my office, opened the door, and tear gas came billowing out: what a horror not to be able to breathe.

One of my students, Thomas, came to talk to me that week. Cleaning up around me, he said very quietly so the guard would not hear, "It is not safe here anymore for you. I'm afraid something will be happening here. We think you should probably stop teaching here. I was asked by others to give you this message." After reflecting on the riots and untrustworthy officials, along with this man's kind warning, I sadly gave my two weeks' notice at work, realizing that indeed this dangerous prison was out of control. I saw no prospect that safe conditions would return to Youth Center One.

My last day at work, in May of 1985, I was alone, cleaning out my room, when I heard the door open behind me and shut firmly. Alarmed, I turned to see I was alone with the six prisoners who had gathered with me that particularly cold, heaterless day when we had studied our schoolwork together. I knew they were breaking the rules to be here and was quite aware that I was defenseless: no guards, no telephone, and a closed door. For a moment I was afraid, and then I looked at their eyes, and I relaxed.

Steve spoke first, "Miss James, we don't want you to leave. What are you going to do?"

"I'll be working in Virginia with the juvenile court system. I don't want to leave here either. I've grown to love you all."

Another prisoner spoke up, "You'll be helping kids stay out of places like this?"

"I hope to, Louis. But I'll never forget you."

"The children," he said insistently. "You will help them?"

I realized that all of these men had suffered so much as innocent children that they wanted more than anything that children be protected from things such as happened to them. I had read their charts full of their personal histories of child abuse, neglect, living in parks, and going hungry. I respected their concern for the children.

"I will do what I can for the kids. And you write me, please."

Another student said, "We'll let you go, but we needed to say good-bye. We won't forget you."

They gave me a hand-made card that read:

There once was a lady who lived in a shoe
She had so many children, she didn't know what to do.
One day she had to leave them,
She was feeling blue
Miss James don't take it so hard,
We all love you!

On the cover was a hand painted, colorful shoe with a picture of me looking out, and students climbing all over and through this large shoe. All the students had signed it, with personal notes of thanks. I cried. The students solemnly lined up, shook my hand, kissed me on the cheek, and left as quietly as they had arrived.

A few weeks later, I opened my morning *Washington Post* to see pictures of fires burning at Lorton Reformatory after a night of violence. Horror had enveloped the prison, as we had expected. I said a prayer for those left behind, still enduring the chaos, and thanked God for those inmates who had warned me to leave. God, through the ministering hands of the inmates, had delivered me from the dangers of the position.

Before my husband and I moved to rural Virginia, I preached a final sermon at a Virginia Episcopal Church called the Falls Church. I climbed into the colonial pulpit shaped like a communion wine glass. I started the sermon. "Jesus knows the world in which we live. Jesus understands the crimes and outrages of which human beings are capable. He understands the violent rapes and bloody murders, as well as the overwhelming, degrading poverty so prevalent in the world." I continued, "Where is God? we wonder. How do we trust God? Where is Jesus? Are we alone in this confusing world? And yet," I paused as I looked down at the packed, attentive church, "Jesus has heard us and he knows us and he cares for us. He binds our wounds and looks upon us with affection. I learned that in the violent environment of the prison. I learned about the affection of Jesus through men such as Steve and John, who protected me. I learned about Jesus in redemption that I saw firsthand. I experienced God's new and marvelous energy as the young men struggled for a new and faithful life."

After the sermon as I removed my church robes and stole, adorned with the ancient symbols of the divine, I pondered again the mysteries of my prison experience. I had gone there to help and found myself overwhelmed by the sense of God's fresh goodness experienced in the bowels of an overcrowded prison. What a powerful God we worship, is all I could say.

two   THE RURAL LIFE

O God, when you are the absolute master
of a heart, it can have neither trouble nor
anxiety; it is you alone who fill all desires.

— Jeanne Guyon, *Autobiography*

I left Northern Virginia with some regret but looked forward to my new life in the horse country of rural Virginia. As a joyful beginning to the position of rector of a church, we boldly started with the service of Celebration of a New Ministry.

A vivid sense of the importance of this new phase in life danced around us that cold January evening. Cars from all over Virginia drove up to the white frame country church nestled among horse farms. The church windows glowed with warmth from the candles burning in every window. Betsy stood at the door, in her deep Southern accent cheerfully welcoming all who entered: "Thank you for comin'," "How're you?" "Put your coats in there," "Why, Jackie, I haven't seen you forever!" Christ Episcopal Church, Brandy Station, site of a large Civil War battle, now welcoming a *female* rector—what a shock this was! ("Why, honey," Betsy had said to me, "we were going to close our doors without ya. We'll get used to this.") Handsome and chivalrous gentlemen took the ladies' coats and the church itself seemed to glisten with pride. Filled to capacity with about one hundred people, everyone in the church prepared busily for his or her part in the service.

During the celebration I knelt and prayed out loud the traditional words from the Episcopal prayer book, "Grant that, by the clearness and brightness of your holy Word, all the world may be drawn into your blessed kingdom." The elegant Bishop Lee preached a sermon about love saying, "Sink your roots more deeply into love." My friend, Tony, an African American opera singer who taught at Lorton Reformatory, sang a beautiful rendition of "This Little Light of Mine, I'm Going to Let It Shine." We courageously asserted: I'm *going* to let it shine.

After the service, a large supper was served by the Women's Guild of the Volunteer Fire Department of Brandy Station. Huge slices of roast beef, mashed potatoes, and apple pie were served with iced tea while I'm sure some partook surreptitiously of the ever-present Virginia beverage, bourbon. Brazenly, John told the bishop, "Sundays are for foxhunting." Other snippets of conversation I overheard bothered me: "Was that colored man with a white woman?" demanded Pearl, an older woman, but I tried to shake them off, thinking that this attitude was definitely in the minority now. Patrick sat there quietly, watching the festivities with interest. What a lovely place, I thought. The community seemed to support and care for each other in gentle ways. Next to me, Maxine insecurely said to Betsy, "I've gained twenty pounds this year," to which Betsy blithely responded, "And *most* becoming it is!" Maxine's face beamed with relief at this delightful thought.

Did we realize what we promised that wintry evening? Would anyone have continued the journey if we could have seen our future as a congregation?

None of us anticipated what happens when God is manifested. A theophany, I had learned in seminary, is when God appears and reveals Godself, such as when Moses encounters God in the burning bush in the desert. Or when Jesus converses with Elijah and Moses and becomes transfigured into a supernatural presence. At the theophany of Pentecost the Spirit descended like a living flame, a fire resting on the heads of the apostles and yet not consuming them.

Yes, in this rural hinterland, we experienced a theophany that was like a fire and a burning. God was there. But like the first Pentecost, doubts and troubles eventually emerged, and the community became divided. That night, however, I saw only that God was among us, feeding us, caring for us, and sheltering us. That evening we humbly prayed for God's presence among us, as we embarked on a new journey in Virginia: a *woman* with her own Episcopal church.

And how do we bear spiritual fruit, I wondered? The mystery of God creating something in our midst cannot be unraveled. The fruits of the spirit are love, hope, faith—as beautiful as our mysterious, tangible, sweet delicacies, Alaska blueberries. Why blue? What a color! Do they harmonize with their green leaves and scratchy branches? Does the Earth hide the berries in its low-lying bushes, chortling at us poor humans walking tall looking at the trees and other humans and thinking of our lives and our plans, when at our feet lie succulent delights, juicy jabs of joy? Is the Earth teasing us to realize we can't produce a wonder like a blueberry? Can we produce God and spiritual fruits? No, but faithfully we assert that the Spirit moves and acts within our hearts. God creates and we marvel in amazement at the sheer goodness of these gracious actions.

23

The whole adventure at Brandy Station started off so beautifully. As the new rector, I loved the work of ministry and being there for people at difficult times. Now I had the authority to live out my vision of the church as a community that worships God, while reaching out to the poor and needy. This was essentially St. Paul's understanding of the church in the Acts of the Apostles. He developed worshiping communities in which he encouraged them to be mindful of the needs of others. I enjoyed encouraging the church to participate in the ancient, life-giving tradition of caring for others.

Before the first Sunday I prayed: Help me know how to do this, help me love. I heard my acolyte approaching. She smiled at me, braces glittering, freckles sprinkled on her nose, long, gangly legs sticking out of her white and black robes. I realized that the purity of children cried out to the living God naturally. I smiled at her and joyfully started the opening hymn, "Holy, holy, holy . . ."

At the same time, I continued to find my work in corrections rewarding. Among other tasks, I supervised a young man, Andy Hucks. The first time I drove the ten miles to his isolated, mountain house, I marveled at the beautiful, gradually ascending hills, covered with lush trees, with small raccoons, foxes, and woodchucks rampant. I approached the area with directions such as, "Turn left at the brown house, go until you see a small trading post . . ." When I found their property, I saw hand-painted "No Trespassing" signs everywhere.

That I was accepted by this mountain community pleased and surprised me. When Andy's cousin, Linda, decided to get married, she came and shyly asked me to perform the ceremony. The sunny day of the wedding, crowds of people showed up at the church, neatly dressed in plain clothes, and carrying themselves with great dignity. Linda walked down the aisle, her lustrous brown hair hanging thickly to her waist, looking with joy at the blonde-haired man awaiting her at the altar. She said her vows to her beloved tenderly, an air of holiness hovering over the assembled community.

The church at Brandy Station experienced an explosion of growth. New people started visiting the tiny congregation: persons came from association with me at the court, from the town, and from the surrounding county. Because of the influx of people, the church vestry started sprucing everything up. We had a cleaning day, washing the windows. We raised money for a new, red carpet. The church building reflected the new life growing within.

To my delight I discovered that I was changing under the good influence of the people I knew in Culpeper. The first hot

Sunday I showed up in the non-air-conditioned church with my professional clergy outfit. Betsy took one look at me, smiled, and laughingly told me to put my clergy robes on after taking off my street clothes. "Honey, you'll faint like that. No one here cares what you wear." I took her advice, realizing that freedom from social conventions was a good thing. Life for them was expressed in a panorama of glorious, fun activities.

Patrick and I enjoyed some new friends together in Culpeper. One new friend was Albert, who worked at the Culpeper courthouse. A handsome, gray-haired ex-Marine who had served in Vietnam, I heard his stories about that war with an interest I had picked up from my military father. He in turn asked me about my father's career.

"Dad was a Strategic Air Command pilot, flying in World War II and Korea, making a career in the Air Force. He started in the Army Air Corps and switched over to the Air Force when this branch of military service began. He was particularly proud of having flown in the Berlin Air Lift."

25

Albert exclaimed, "What a career!"

One day, Albert's sparkling eyes seemed more serious. He met me in the parking lot and said, "There are lots of spirits in Culpeper from the Battle of Brandy Station." Trying to laugh this odd thought off, I said, "Oh, Albert, you're kidding me." "No," Albert said firmly. "Lots of violent deaths cause spirits to hang around. You know, Nancy, I think we might have known each other in a previous life. Everyone is brought to a place for a reason. We both came to Culpeper and I am sure each of us has something to learn and do here." I made an unbelieving noise. He continued, "Don't dismiss it too quickly. There are a lot of spiritual influences in this area. Wait and see what happens."

Albert was always encouraging, as if to say, "Come on, believe, the journey is an adventure!" I took seriously his ideas of spiritual realities but didn't know how to proceed with understanding his thought. Little did I then know that I didn't need to have a plan for understanding everything. Life itself would guide me through these most difficult passages.

The time came for the annual Montpelier horse races. Held at the home of President James Madison, horse owners brought their fine, thoroughbred horses for cross-country races. The competition was stiff, and the winners went on to larger, more well-known races. But, although the Kentucky Derby and Preakness brought instant name recognition, as far as the sheer passion for horses goes, nothing could beat the Montpelier races.

Patrick and I were invited for our first time and asked to bring some food and champagne. Dressing casually for the whole-day, outdoor event, we drove out to the elegant, isolated mansion of James Madison. Large, spectacular gardens adorned his estate. President Madison grew beautiful cedars, which swayed and rustled in the gentle wind like the ancient, mystical cedars of Lebanon. Expensive cars pulled in from everywhere, parked in designated spots, and opened up the back of their cars. It was as if a potent *bon vivant* had ordered, "Time to live well!" Champagne corks popped and the bubbly flowed extravagantly into crystal glasses. Fine Virginia ham from peanut-fed pigs rested on fresh biscuits baked early that morning. We drank bourbon and water, bourbon and coke, bourbon straight, only interrupted by gourmet potato salad and crackers—all making us thirstier for yet more bourbon. Cheeses from around the world lured us, hinting of the luxuries of countries such as France and Denmark. This was the day in which "life is as it should be."

People strolled around, chatting about Virginia news and seeing who was there. Was that Sissy Spacek, who owned a nearby estate? Or was that Senator Warner over there? For who would miss the Montpelier races? The gentle glow from champagne nourished by the elegant tidbits combined with the warmth of friends greeting each other to hint at a tantalizing prospect of the passion yet to come. Names of horses were circulated and we settled to serious contemplation: which horses would we bet on? How much? Turning to friends, we would ask: "Does the horse have stamina? How is the horse's heart?" But behind it all were the haunting questions: Does the horse love it? Does the horse hunger for the victory? Does the horse know the sheer joy of becoming one with the jockey and sailing over the posts, turning to lunge up the hill, yearning to be the first to race across the line, tail high, jockey yelling with glee, people cheering? Can the horse taste it now: victory, mastery over itself, its jockey, the field, and, yes, mastery over the power of ecstatic life itself?

And as soon as our bets were made, the horses and jockeys nonchalantly strolled to take their places in the lineup. Then the announcement: "They're off!" The horses charged, legs extended as only thoroughbreds do, running on the large circular track surrounding our partying place. We ran to the sides to watch a sea of horses streaming by, loving it, charging, heading for the climax, the colors of the jockeys' silks seducing our eyes with grand and glorious reds, green, golds. As we watched, we knew that soon one horse would pull ahead of the rest. This was the horse with vision, the horse who had seen, who understood the allure of the glorious achievement. This horse would leave behind more pedestrian horses and cast aside all care to plunge into the full command of which it was capable. When we saw the passion take over this individual horse, the horse who most yearned for victory, we saw pure magic. The horse's heart ruled, dominating all of its other forces. That horse, as if on wings, flew, danced, and jumped to the rhythm of Being. That horse became one with the Ultimate, the jockey merely letting the horse use its passions and its love. Flying across the finish line, the horse would rear back its head as if to say, *Let us do it again. Let us do it often. Let us love it, for it is good.*

And we cheered and we loved and we exulted in the grandeur of the horse and its command over all of us. Give in to the passion, give in to the love, let your heart lead. And win the race towards the ecstatic center of life.

Afterwards in the winner's circle, the jockey and owner of the horse stood humbly next to the horse who was the true

27

possessor of a passion we admired and emulated and longed to have ourselves.

Resting, we reached for another bottle of champagne, pouring it recklessly into the glasses now, drinking it deeply, casting aside the previous dainty sips, lustily ingesting it. For we had learned from watching the horse, we had learned from its passion and its love and its sheer magnificence.

All day long the horses came, running, prancing, tempestuously throwing their heads as if they pitied us poor human beings. Submerging ourselves in the love of the horse, we experienced an ecstasy like no other. I thought of Walt Whitman, "I sing the Body Electric . . ."

Refreshed, satisfied, and content, we allowed quiet to reign in the car on the way home as we submerged ourselves deeply in the wonder of life.

28

three   THE MOUNTAIN PEOPLE

Yesterday morning I was thinking. But who
are you? what are you doing? what are you
thinking? . . . I have to apply myself to know
if I have a being, a life, a subsistence.

—Jeanne Guyon, *Autobiography*

onders abounded in Brandy Station. I read my theology
and sought God. Everywhere I went in Brandy Station,
people greeted me and I responded with warmth. Life felt full
and good.

But I heard warning signs of danger that pointed to possible trouble in this pleasant society. One evening at our short
story group, we were sitting around reading *The Little Prince.*
The doorbell rang and a neighbor strode in. We greeted him
warmly, and then he said jovially, "Is this the Klan meeting?"
My blood ran cold, remembering pictures of lynched bodies
hanging from trees that I had seen in history movies about the
South, the horrid reality that I hoped had passed. I wanted to
scream out, "The Ku Klux Klan is not a laughing matter,"
when the hostess jumped up, kissed the man, and said,
"Honey, would you like some cake?" The horrendous moment
passed and we were soon immersed again in *The Little Prince.*
More and more I was dismayed at the acceptance that racism
and the Klan still had in this society.

At times, juggling the two roles of Episcopal priest and court
official was difficult. One day I was going through court records

and ran across a report about the son of parishioners. The record contained a long account written by a Charlottesville court employee complaining of local officials tipping them off that an arrest was imminent. The story went like this. The son was suspected of dealing drugs. An out-of-town surveillance team was being put on him to catch him in the act of selling drugs when a member of the sheriff's department alerted his parents about the danger. They immediately communicated this to their son. The arrest was stopped because the evidence for dealing drugs had been destroyed. The report from Charlottesville detailed who had leaked the information to my parishioners.

I sat down in the general office, upset at such stories of favoritism in the justice system. And yet, the silent, interior questions began to haunt me. The God I worshipped was one with a passion for justice. Where was justice in this situation, where the rich could avoid arrest because of their connections with the leaders in the community?

30

One spring day, I sat on the picnic table in front of the historic courthouse, with its huge, white pillars. I was eating my lunch in the park next to the statue of the looming, pensive Confederate soldier. The sheriff's department and the antiquated county jail were built on the other side of the park. Albert would sometimes take a break and come out to offer a needed education about the rich history of the area. "The Union troops took over this area for the long winter of 1863–1864, building huts all over this county. Ulysses Grant himself lived in Culpeper, actually setting up his headquarters in Brandy Station." I took a bite of my apple while I listened intently. "That long winter the Union troops drilled and prepared for the final year of the war, the culmination of it all. The Union Army left here on May 4, 1864, for 340 days of military action in which the two armies dogged each other until the end of the war. During the next two months, 65,000 men from that Union camp died. Culpeper was the last home they would know. A Union soldier said that there was a trail of blood running from Rapidan to Appomattox."

Albert continued, "Remember all of those plantations you drive by as you come here? Officers of the army lived in them, planning, hoping, working towards the final battles of that tragic war."

I took a drink of my bottled water, glancing at the people strolling around. This town looked so deceptively peaceful, but after reading the court records, I knew otherwise. We ended our lunch, and Albert and I walked back into the courthouse, I to once again face the many cases coming my way.

I worked and watched, trying to intervene as much as I could for these teenagers in trouble with the law. Sometimes the work seemed endless, but there were victories along the way. I loved it when some of these young people started communicating with their families again, or when they started back to school. Before my own personal crisis hit, I had been in the job for over one year, achieving some victories and feeling fulfilled that I could offer help.

Then the horror happened. I woke up one night at 2 A.M. to the sound of my phone ringing. I sleepily picked it up, only to hear Mrs. Hucks's sad, mountain voice, saying "Miss James." "What's going on?" "Andy is dead," she said simply. "I just heard from the sheriff." "Oh, my God," I moaned. "What happened?"

Andy, whose cousin's wedding I'd performed not long before, had been picked up, taken to the town jail, and several hours later, was pronounced dead. I called the sheriff's department and asked what had happened. They immediately said Andy committed suicide by hanging himself when he was in the drunk tank. They told me that I didn't need to be involved with this because Andy had just turned eighteen. I retorted that I would be down there shortly. The image of Andy hanging there dead haunted me as I drove the five miles to the county jail in the middle of the night. When I walked in through the darkened park outside the jail, the deputies were eerily quiet, displeased at seeing me, keeping to their story that Andy had killed himself by hanging, using his T-shirt as

31

the weapon. My mind kept flashing the image: Andy, blonde, young, dangling from an old pipe in this unkempt building. His head hanging crooked now because of the freshly broken neck, like a broken bird fallen from the nest. His eyes staring vacantly, never to see the beautiful child his pregnant girlfriend was carrying.

The harsh deputies stared intently at me, saying the mountain community was dangerous and I shouldn't visit the Hucks's home. An uncanny quality hung around the deputies and their hardened eyes glinted coldly. Outside in the dark, tree-filled park, weird shadows played on the statue of the Confederate soldier from the bright lights of the jail. Wind lashed the tree branches back and forth, whistling around the buildings. Everything was out of whack and seemed weirdly misproportioned.

Deciding to ignore these deputies and praying for guidance, I drove to the Hucks's home. Both parents greeted me with hugs. Amidst the deep sorrow that hung everywhere, the thought kept breaking into my consciousness: Was it really suicide? Andy wouldn't do that. Sunny was near her delivery date. He had so much to live for.

Mrs. Hucks wept, and said over and over again, "Andy didn't die a normal death." Something was very wrong. A terrible feeling of vulnerability enveloped us as we sat through the dark hours of the night, overwhelmed with the possibility of suicide or murder. My mind raged. What happened to cause death and suffocating? The Hucks's cousin Linda came in, weeping, trying to look brave, saying how awful it was. And I remembered her beautiful wedding when evil seemed impossible and love sheltered us all. I sat frozen: how could the sheriff's department let this happen?

I made it through the next few days, knowing I was in the midst of an ethical dilemma. Sheriff Peters called me and said. "We've got this under control. It was suicide. Don't trouble yourself about it anymore." I retorted, "He is still on my caseload, and I will trouble myself." Sheriff Peters said threateningly, "Don't get involved with this, Miss James." Suicide? Murder? I knew the horrendous possibilities of this situation.

I could not dodge the moral ramifications of the highly questionable death of this teenager while in the custody of the sheriff's department.

I remembered reading the writings of the mystic Catherine of Siena, and her analogy of a conscience to a barking dog. She said that when we engage in immoral actions our conscience wakes up and begins to alert us by barking. The dog warns us that our soul is in danger. We need to take action against the peril by relieving ourselves of unethical behavior. In this situation I heard my barking conscience, telling me over and over again that if I didn't thoroughly register my disapproval, I would be participating in allowing Andy's young and untimely demise.

My dilemma deepened as I increasingly read reports about this, some suggesting the suspicious nature of Andy's death. I kept remembering his engaging smile and his enjoyment of working on trees that needed care, pruning off dead branches. He had said, "I can just look at a tree and know how to keep it alive. Then I knock on doors and tell people what's wrong with their trees. I help their trees." This young man, connected to earth and nature, should still be alive. Part of me wanted to ignore this situation because I knew how unpopular my stand would be in a society that said, "These people are just moonshiners and woodchucks. Why worry about them?" But my internal dog kept barking. Could I be honest with the parents? Finally, one afternoon in my office, I knew I had to break my silence. I reached for the phone.

"Mrs. Hucks," I said when she answered. "What are your plans?"

Weeping, she said, "We are thinking about getting a lawyer."

"Why not get a lawyer from Charlottesville?" I suggested.

A long pause from both of us. The magnitude of the situation stunned us.

Innocent blood cries out, I thought. We can numb ourselves and pretend not to listen. But Andy dying alone in that jail was a horror from which I could not turn. This unjust situation needed to be addressed. I knew God loved justice and I wanted to align myself with the good of this situation, in spite of what it might cost me.

The Hucks found an out-of-town attorney and sued. The newspapers announced an out-of-court settlement with an undisclosed monetary settlement. But no amount of money could bring back Andy's engaging grin, his joy in life, and his unfulfilled fatherhood towards the beautiful boy born after his death.

And what is ministry? How do we truly help others? Is it in recognizing another's pain and not looking away? The burning bush of Moses came after he recognized the innocent suffering of the Israelites in bondage and pondered this dreadful mystery. As humans we flinch at the sight of a new Job, sitting and suffering. Yet we watch with respect and step closer. What is this heat we feel? It is the living flame of love shooting through our being, awakening, restoring, God healing as we stand and silently offer ourselves for ministry.

The sight of this innocent suffering had left me seared, burned, shocked. I began to yearn for a life free from the problems that were rampant in the corrections system that I had witnessed. As a committed Christian, the whole problem of the innocent suffering I had seen bothered me immensely. Patrick, absorbed in his studies, expressed that this life was too different from his own for him to understand the situation or my feelings. Increasingly I questioned, where was God in all of this? The question burned within me.

One day my oldest brother, Dr. Franklin James from Denver, visited me. Franklin teaches at the Graduate School of Public Policy at the University of Colorado. Together we visited the University of Virginia in Charlottesville. During the hour-and-a-half drive south to Charlottesville, I relaxed at leaving the Culpeper problems behind. The Blue Ridge

Mountains calmly presided over the horizon. Gentle hills and placid rivers graced the land, occasional restaurants and antique stores inviting us for times of quiet, intimate conversations. Walking around Thomas Jefferson's university, I began feeling my deep love of knowledge and wisdom reawakening.

Franklin looked at me intently as we walked by the classical Rotunda, which seemed to hover pacifically over the entire university. He said, "Why not attend here, Nancy? Working on a new degree would be good for you."

I appreciated his thoughts and realized: I could study this problem of innocent suffering that concerns me so deeply. "What a great idea, Franklin!" I exclaimed.

And so the grave decision was made. I spent a few more months working for the juvenile justice system, then left my position sorrowfully, yet feeling that after all I had seen, I wanted some time to think about my theology more carefully. I resigned that position and started taking graduate classes at the University of Virginia, working towards a Ph.D. in Religious Studies, while remaining in my role as priest at Christ Church, Brandy Station.

I knew that St. Augustine said that questions come from God and I knew I must honor my questions. Indeed, the signs of God within us are our questions. Yet questions cannot live in the same heart with complacency and self-congratulation. They are calling to us, saying: *Seek me in the nakedness of your questions. Take off the illusion of control and domination and realize your nature. Our first thoughts and words are questions. Seek, inquire, interrogate life. The answers you receive will give you rest.*

four   P E R S O N A L   S T R U G G L E

I let others think what they please;

for me, I find security only in abandoning

myself to the Lord.

—Jeanne Guyon, *Autobiography*

During my first year at the university, my personal life was turned upside down. My father, the brave fighter pilot, now battled with cancer. My older brother Tim called from Sacramento, California, to tell me that I should come visit my parents immediately, for his prognosis was uncertain. I left for an emergency visit.

I'll never forget seeing my father, frail and thin but very happy to see me. Sorrowfully, my brothers, Tim, Franklin, Robert, and I discussed medical plans, hoping that some treatment would heal him. The doctors weren't hopeful, but still searched for a way to extend his time on earth.

For a lighter moment, my family went together to an airplane museum on McClellan Air Force Base, where my father had been stationed. What a treasure of planes we saw! Large hangars, filled with carefully restored planes, with histories of when they were developed and how they had fared in stressful situations. My father engaged us with his observations, his eyes revealing layers of meaning and satisfaction as he looked at each plane. History buffs all, my brothers clustered around him, gleaning information about when he flew the planes, in what battles, and how they handled. I stood back, marveling at the scene, soaking in my father's philosophy and his stories about his adventures. "The Berlin Air Lift," he said, his voice resonant with the satisfaction of having flown those missions.

"Daddy," I said, laughing from a happy memory, "Do you remember the time we saw the missile site being loaded at Eielson?" He looked somber, "Yes. We were driving up to the hills to pick blueberries together. And suddenly rounding the corner on the isolated hills, there they were, men marching around with the missile, heading to load it in the site." I finished the story, "Yes, I vividly recall them coming to the car and checking our identification and asking us to leave the area quickly. You know, I think they have missiles in my part of Virginia, in Brandy Station. I've seen similar facilities there." He shook his head, still looking serious. "I bet they do." Then he added, "What a day that was: seeing a missile with my daughter!" But I had other memories with Dad, too: of picking blueberries with him, while friendly moose grazed close to us. My father glanced at them occasionally, saw they were relaxed, and we stayed. Later, my mother made blueberry pies and we ate them, while my childish mind drank deeply of the adventure of missiles and moose and an ecstatic earth giving birth to innumerable bushes of blueberries.

I said, "Remember, Daddy, when Mom used to bring me and I would watch you land your planes when we lived at Wichita, Kansas? I used to think, 'My daddy is flying those big planes.'" His face suddenly glowed with pride and happiness at this thought, and I could once again see my father, young and healthy, leather flight jacket on, striding authoritatively towards the door. I would watch him return later, always bearing gifts, dolls from all over the world, or a strange, foreign book. He would stroke my cheek with affection, saying "And how have you been doing?" In our family we lived planes and flying and adventure—and yes, love surrounding it all. Love for our country and for each other and for God who looked down upon all of us.

Then it came time to go to the airport to return to Virginia. In the bright Sacramento sunlight, my father walked me to the

37

car, saying, "You turned out well, Nancy. Come back soon." With tears in my eyes, I said, "I want to see you get well, Daddy."

As my brother Tim started his old Yugo to take us to the airport, my father leaned down and spoke through the window, "I love you."

Crying, I responded, "I love you." And looking at him I realized he was glowing with love, sparkling with a beautiful affection I had never seen before. Something like a halo of light surrounded him. Entranced by this, I knew he experienced a heavenly love that even then embraced him. Tim started backing his car out of the driveway, shifting gears clumsily because we were all crying.

I was never to see my father again. Two weeks later, my brother Tim called, crying, and choked out the words, "Dad died today."

I wept profusely when I heard the news, remembering my father's many kindnesses to me. I walked outside in the beautiful Brandy Station night, looking at the luminous stars, and then I saw it: a gorgeous, full moon, reddish, glowing brightly. I remembered as a child my father taking me outside to look at the northern lights and the stars in the brittle, cold Alaska nights. He had explained to me about the moon when I was scared about the lack of sun because of our closeness to the North Pole. I remembered him gently saying, "Nancy, as we go into December we won't see the sun much anymore except for occasional glimpses. But the moon will stay with us. The moon's light will guide you to and from school. There's nothing to be afraid of just because you don't see the sun." He had told me about flying his large B-47 planes in the night and described the moon as a solid and reliable companion.

And now on the day of his death, in Brandy Station, Virginia, I saw the same dependable guide, a full moon. And suddenly I sensed, with a feeling of wonder, that my father was fine. As usual, I felt he had planned well. For he died the day of a blue moon. And the moon didn't desert him but guided, supported, as he attempted his last flight, the flight to leave his body.

I went to California and performed his funeral at the request of my family. During the months following his death I was grieving intensely. There seemed to be no relief from the sorrow until my cousin Harry Pierce sent a beautiful note saying, "Your father always loved to fly—now he has angel wings."

That fall I started a class, "Medieval Mysticism," taught by Dr. Carlos Eire. I was looking for something different, for I still struggled deeply with my loss. A wonderful thing happened. I began to comprehend what the mystics write about as pure love. I started doing research on a little-known French mystic from the seventeenth century, Madame Jeanne Guyon. In her *Autobiography* she writes, "Mystery of love and sweetness! Who will understand thee?"[1] She wrote that the experience of pure love was a possibility for strong souls. Pure love came in a person's life, offering not only a warm comfort but a real experience of the divine. This love demanded rigorous self-control and discipline. But the outcome of this process of annihilation (as she called it) was a soul in union with God.

I lingered over Guyon's words promising union with God. Yes, I wanted intimacy with God, the perfect love and creator of all wisdom, but what was the cost of enjoying this union? According to Guyon, the price was great.

But as fascinating as my academic work was, I needed first to turn my attention to a very real difficulty, problems in my marriage.

For another unhappiness awaited me. My husband, who had once been my best friend, had become increasingly distant and cold. We went to marriage counseling but nothing worked to restore our relationship. My husband had trouble living with the pressures of being the spouse of a female priest, feeling deeply how unusual this role was. These conflicted feelings about my unusual role we explored during counseling. He respected my professional abilities but also felt intimidated by them. He humorously said, "Why, in Culpeper she has the

39

power of the state to arrest people, as well as the power of God to grant absolution."

I took Patrick to the airport as he left for a separation. I felt torn apart, miserable. Our unified emotional life had died. Sadly, I realized that there was no marriage.

The grieving consumed my life for months. Memories of Patrick, the teenager I had met in California, now gone. Like a chill wind blowing through my soul, I yearned for this not to be. And I cried out over and over: Why? But I knew this question could only be answered by time, by that power carrying us through and offering gentle consolations. Learn to listen, I thought, listen to the caring of others who recognize your suffering, listen to nature as it too experiences its yearly death in winter, and, I hoped, listen for a spring coming when life will feel good again.

As I entered into this grieving, I trusted that pure love would carry me through this transition. I preached a sermon saying that, "In life there is a gap between what we know and what we would like to know. We can never totally fill that gap. But as Christians, we don't despair, for we know Jesus stands firmly in the gap for us, extending his hand to us. We don't have full knowledge now of life and the sorrows it contains, but we have a person, Jesus Christ, the same yesterday, today, and tomorrow." I had so many questions about this divorce and so few answers. But I had a person I needed, Jesus Christ, who carried me through all the changes that came with the marital separation.

Overwhelmed, I was left with a feeling of mystery at my failed marriage. Yet somehow through these specific mysteries the consummate mystery began to intrigue me: the mystery of life itself. Why are we here and how do we love?

In Alaska it was the ice blue color of the glaciers that surprised me. They weren't crystal clear, pure, lovely incandescent white. But they gleamed blue, glowed icy blue as they lay majestically certain. The uncanniness of life, the wonder of life, the intangible graciousness of Being, lay unconcealed in the Great Surprises known as glaciers. Drive around a particular corner in Alaska and there is the Whale of the Land, the Gigantic, Glorious Glacier, presiding, holding court. I felt as if I should sit down in hopes of a confidential talk with Queen Glacier. "Tell me," I would say, "How did all of this Life happen? Were you there when it began? Was it wonderful?"

five

T W O   C H U R C H E S !

Believers who are dead to self-love become

kings. They reign over themselves and all

others. They have become priests giving unto

God a continual sacrifice of praise.

—Jeanne Guyon, *Christ Our Revelation*

I returned to my life's endeavors following the divorce, finding solace in the rhythm of my existence. My first parish, Christ Church, Brandy Station, thrived, and a job offer came from another congregation: Emmanuel Episcopal Church in Rapidan, which I joyfully accepted. I was now in charge of two Virginia parishes! I moved from Brandy Station ten miles south to the town of Rapidan. A river curves itself through the town of Rapidan and fruit orchards grace the surrounding fields.

As I reflected on the new church, I compared the two churches in my mind. Brandy Station's congregation included more farmers and horsey people who loved the wild extravagances of fox hunting. Several people from the Rappahannock Fox Club came to the church. Under their influence, I had enjoyed riding a white, racing thoroughbred named Candy. One day I think Candy became disgusted with my inept riding and tried to scrape me off on a tree. I clung to her neck and thought, "If I escape this, I will never again ride horses that are too adventurous for me!" Candy finally walked us both back to the barn and after that I enjoyed spirited horses from afar.

Society in Rapidan entertained lavishly. Antebellum mansions welcomed the admiring visitors, uniformed men and women served from a well-stocked bar to complement elaborate food. But sometimes—I shook my head at the nagging thought—sometimes I would notice that all of the workers were African American and the party-goers, laughing loudly, enjoying themselves—or acting as if they were enjoying themselves—were Caucasian. Was there ever any justice in this world? But who was I to make waves? A woman without a man in this society is considered a second-rate person.

I moved to a beautiful home offered to me by Emmanuel Episcopal Church. The house looked stately: a large white country home, with black shutters and a dark green roof. A front porch with four white columns provided a place of repose and promised mint juleps and iced tea. Large, healthy trees circled the house, offering shade and respite from the summer sun. Cows grazed peacefully in the pastures near the home.

A vestry member, Ted, talked to me shortly after my move into the beautiful, five-bedroom house. His enthusiasm about the church warmed my spirits. But he also warned me about tense political realities, telling me that divisions existed on the vestry that hired me. I asked about the divisions. Ted frowned and answered, "For many persons, a woman is too much, but a divorced woman is unthinkable."

I tried to shake the serious mood by admiring the view of Rapidan from the second floor of this isolated home. He asked me, "Will it bother you not to have any close neighbors?"

Reflecting on this, I said, "No. I don't think so. I have my dog, Cornelia, and I plan on getting a second dog."

Ted said kindly, "You can call me anytime if anything happens."

I nodded acceptance.

Troubles surfaced shortly after our conversation. A parishioner called me up and invited me to her grand house for dinner. She lived on an estate replete with servants' quarters and old, historic houses. On the evening of our dinner, rain poured down and thunder crashed as I drove toward the house.

"We are a very special parish," she announced, and then proceeded to start to tell me how much money each individual had.

Interrupting her, I said, "I don't want to know their financial worth. I am a priest, not a banker. Their money doesn't interest me."

Changing the subject, she went on to tell me how the parish was organized, and then pronounced, "I will start planning the worship schedule." This meant she would schedule who was involved and who was not.

"I'm sorry but you can't do that," I responded. "The vestry does that at Emmanuel."

She started walking out of the room, and then turned to face me and yell, "Change the [expletive] rules!"

I said, "I don't intend to push other people out for you."

She walked me to the door, signaling that the evening was over. As I left in the pouring rain, with no lights or stars to help me see, I stumbled several times in the wet grass, struggling to keep my umbrella straight in the strong wind. I thought, when I finally found my car through the black darkness, "This evening is straight out of a horror movie."

Driving home, I tried to make sense of the dreadful evening. This wasn't *her* church. I knew I needed to stand up to her so I could be fair to others. I ran from the car in the sheets of rain into my house, relieved to see my familiar dog Cornelia waiting for me.

The next day as I walked along the peaceful Rapidan River with the sun shining, the abrasive scene from the previous evening seemed far away. What is going to happen? I wondered.

My personal life was going well. After a time of solitude following the divorce, I had started dating again. I saw one man in particular, Michael Kaluta, a professional artist who lived in Manhattan, who drew *The Shadow*. I found both him and his work fascinating. I kept my personal life quiet, though, so that whatever choices I made would not be an issue for the parish.

One Sunday, however, Michael quietly visited the church for a worship service. I preached about Sören Kierkegaard and his ideas about the leap of faith.

"Kierkegaard emphasized the radical nature of Christian beliefs. The words of the gospel are not comfortable ones but ones of great challenge. Thoughts such as 'Seek ye first the kingdom of God' if applied to our lives require great sacrifice and discipline." I looked up and saw Michael's attentive eyes. "Kierkegaard wrote particularly challenging words to the clergy. He said, the words of the gospel say to seek first the kingdom of God, yet what do the clergy seek? He said they usually want something like a financially independent parish with a good pension plan." I knew how the clergy felt. The words of the gospel were so challenging. Sometimes I wondered whether Jesus knew the ramifications of trusting in grace for your life's security. Yet the challenges rang true and clear in my mind.

Michael said to me following the service, "I loved it." I stood up straighter. Michael continued, "These parishioners drink in every word you say. I'm amazed! You are talking about Kierkegaard at a country church and they are fascinated."

I laughed. "That's not me—that's the wonder of Kierkegaard. He takes life—all of our lives, whether they are rich or poor, educated or not—and describes our basic issues. We all seek for a faith which he describes so beautifully. And as much as we can, we all attempt to avoid the cost of maintaining that faith."

That evening we enjoyed ourselves at the home of Michael's friends in Culpeper. We sat and talked about the difficulties of making ethical choices. I explained two main theories about these decisions. "The first is that you follow ethical rules and standards despite the consequences of these actions. The second is that you behave according to what would be a preferred outcome." Michael enjoyed discussing abstract ideas. "The classic question," I said, "is would you lie to save someone's life? For example, someone asks you where a man is, wanting to go and kill him. You know where he is. Would you lie and say no? Or a less extreme example: Would you kill one person in order to save the lives of many? An enemy holds a group of people hostage, and tells you, shoot this one person and I will save the rest."

Michael leaned back, engaging these thoughts. "I think considering the consequences of action is crucial," he said. "What do you think?"

"After hours of considering these issues, I almost hate to say it, but I think we are to follow high ethical standards like the Ten Commandments, and trust the consequences to God. We're less in control of our lives that way, but I believe that it is how we experience our humanity most deeply. We discover more about life when we do this, as frightening as it seems. The cost is high, but the rewards are many."

As we walked towards the dining room table, we played with a lighter conversation, Michael entertaining us with stories of the art world in Manhattan. The lovely day drew to a peaceful end.

46

While enjoying this country existence, I took two classes on the philosophy of Heidegger and became fascinated by his concept of *Eigentlichkeit*, which translated means authenticity. I sat once in Michael's wildly decorated New York apartment with paintings, sculptures, and model airplanes everywhere, talking with him about *Eigentlichkeit* and what it meant to be true to yourself. Michael appeared moved by the concept, as was I. "To speak the truth always . . ." he said wonderingly, letting the words hang in the air. "Being authentic, honest about your feelings and thoughts—what a challenge," I stammered, humbled by the very dignity of the idea.

Michael called me after my return to Culpeper about a week later, saying quietly, "I went to a party where I met a philosopher and I asked him about *Eigentlichkeit*. The man became just as quiet as we became, paused, and then answered, 'That's not an idea. That's a way of life.'" *Eigentlichkeit*, authenticity, this became a connection, our word for Michael and me; *Eigentlichkeit*, bearing an authority in our lives. How should we live? *Eigentlichkeit*. With authenticity.

I saw this authenticity in radiant flashes in my parishes. My favorite times at Emmanuel Episcopal Church were the Christmas Eve services. Life glowed with warmth and joy. I remember at one service an elderly couple affectionately kissing in their car before the evening worship. The church was decorated with greenery and large red bows. The lights glistened on the stained glass windows, bringing out sparkling golden colors. Parishioners gladly worked inside the church, cooking, and caring for anyone who walked in the door.

After I came to Emmanuel, a new member, Kathy, renewed the custom of having a Christmas pageant. The children diligently practiced their favorite part as little angels hiding in the pews. The narrator would read from the gospel of Luke, "And suddenly there was with the angel a multitude of the heavenly host praising God and saying, Glory to God in the Highest . . .", and the small children bounded up out of their pews, smiling brilliantly, aware that they were the Sudden Angels. The congregation laughed appreciatively.

During the service, I sat in the front of the church, listening to the familiar Christmas carols. Looking out at the congregation, I knew the struggles of my parishioners. I knew the marriages that were unhappy but still together. I saw the family whose abusive treatment of their elderly relative had prompted an investigation. I knew those who kept their love alive, who instinctively knew that love was what this life was about. I remembered fondly the first time I celebrated the Eucharist, an older priest saying to me, "The joy comes when you pass out the bread and the wine, and you know the struggles that each individual is having. You pray for them as you give them the bread." I had found this to be true, for a deep love wells up within a priest as he or she passes out the elements, praying for the best for each individual.

Following the late-night service, one teenage girl, Mary, distributed her beautifully decorated Christmas cookies, along with gentle hugs. Echoes of "Merry Christmas" could be heard everywhere following the traditional singing of "Silent

47

Night." Life felt good as I drove back to the church manse. I mused on the wonders of the belief in the Christ child, this gift of God who was silently given centuries ago and could still be received today. I turned into my long isolated driveway, yawning. As I opened the door, my Labrador dog, Cornelia, greeted me, and John, the cat, jumped up on my lap as I sat down. I started munching on my gift of Christmas cookies. The coziness of my animals, the beauty of nature, and the gift of faith in my soul: what a beautiful Christmas, I thought, and fell asleep in my comfortable home.

The Alaska dogs pranced with pride, sensing that they were in Absolute Dog Heaven. Here, in the cold northern lands, they ruled, because their relationship with humans was turned upside down. In the lower forty-eight, dogs depended upon human beings. Here in Alaska, we needed them. We needed them for pulling sleds, for their sensitivity to nature and their communication to us about coming storms. And if we were to be honest, we needed them to reassure us vulnerable humanity that the cold would not destroy us. When we became anxious, we reached for a drink or a dog's friendly reassuring face, along with the husky's thick, abundant, life-giving fur. Dogs ruled us with grace and love.

six

PURE LOVE REALIZED

Oh, Love, only You can impart the perfect

love which is that 'gold tried in the fire.'

Only You can place in our soul pure virtues.

Only You can clothe us with this Spirit of

Faith which is a very pure gold. Only You

can produce in us these works so perfect

in love that fire cannot spoil them.

—Jeanne Guyon, *Christ Our Revelation*

L ife flowed along with its regular pattern of services and visits to parishioners. I still drove into Washington, D.C., when I could to lead a literacy program at several homeless shelters. I knew many of the men from their time at Lorton. Now they were moving in free society and I wanted to help. One day Thomas came in, the man who had warned me to leave the dangerous prison. We sat down and talked about life at Lorton.

"I'm so glad you are out of there, Thomas."

Averting his eyes, he said, "That was hell, Miss James."

Later, as we talked about people, he said, "Did you hear about Mark Proctor?"

Remembering my distant protector at the prison, I asked with some trepidation, "What?"

"This isn't good. He was gunned down in southeast Washington. He bled to death on the street corner."

With tears in my eyes, I remembered how secure I had felt teaching in that violent atmosphere because I knew he had publicly supported me. And I sent up a special prayer to God for the good that Mark had done for me. I remembered characters from Graham Greene novels who were like Mark, imperfect, struggling human beings who sometimes achieve goodness and then fall back. We all do that, I thought. We search for and find God, and then before you know it, we are once again full of doubts and fears.

The paradox of all my ministry was brought home to me: I had gone to the prison expecting to help, and surprisingly found a deeper, richer understanding of life, with brilliant, unexpected flashes of love. I remembered inmates helping each other, students studying together, men supporting each other in the most hellish environment I had ever seen. I felt like I had seen the best and the worst of human nature. The glory and mystery of human life was that love flowered in ways I could never have imagined, even in a hideous prison located next to a rotting garbage dump. My faith in God was nourished at Lorton Reformatory. God was in the contradictions and paradoxes of the prison.

And now at the homeless shelters I saw the same intense, fiery flashes of love. My students worked hard and cared about progressing in life, while they warmly supported each other's struggles. We became close and shared thoughts about life.

As a result of our sharing, the men began to express an interest in where I lived in Virginia. One day a retired judge who worked with the homeless, the Honorable Grover Small, offered to drive them down to Brandy Station for a party. The men could relax in beautiful, pastoral Virginia, and contemplate both the beauty of the scenery and their changing lives. Grover's excellent work with these men inspired me to want to try this idea.

I also knew that I wanted to share with my parishioners the joy I had found in my work at Lorton Reformatory. Through my relationships with the men I taught in that hideous prison, I had experienced God as I never have since. Truly, God cares for those who suffer and seek the divine. Now these homeless men and women demonstrated the same

holiness I had seen at Lorton Reformatory. They had an aura
of divinity, a depth of belief, an abundance of insights that
gave me a taste of what God is like. The God who is and was
and will be sparkled around these persons seeking healing
from various tragedies.

I took the idea to the vestry, which immediately said a
resounding, unanimous "Yes!" to the plan of parties for the
homeless. Instinctively we realized that God appears in grace-
filled moments of unity such as these.

I announced this party in church saying, "If you want to be
around a sense of personal holiness, come and meet these
men. There is something very special about people when they
try to turn their lives around."

We planned our party for Christmas time, the special time
of year when we wish happiness and prosperity for everyone. I
awoke early, anticipating something wonderful, drove to the
church and found Betsy bustling around the kitchen. Her no-
nonsense greeting, "Hi, Nancy, we're almost ready," intrigued
me. She avoided meeting my eyes and I silently walked to look
into the parish hall. Real tablecloths graced every table with
vases of tall red and yellow flowers leaping up to heaven. The
serving table against the wall already offered hors d'oeuvres and
plentiful apple pies. This was a banquet fit for the best company!

The parishioners started arriving early at the church, along
with smiling, friendly guests. "Pearl told me about this," one
neighbor offered. What a delight it was to see everyone turn
out for this event! Judge Small brought as many homeless people as he could and they piled out of the van with a happy
sense of anticipation. Wise men arriving on camels could not
have been more surprising than this van of inner-city guests.

I walked out to greet my inner-city friends. Dressed up in
clean, donated clothes and wreathed with smiles, one of the
men offered me his hand in greeting. "This is beautiful out
here!" he said in pure simplicity.

Inside the kitchen, John prepared delicacies. "Taste this,"
he called to me solemnly. I looked at it, hesitated, and then

said, "Is it chicken salad?" He laughed, saying, "It is my specialty. Squirrel salad." I laughed and said, "No, thank you." "You watch," he replied. "Our friends from the city will love it." And love it they did. The joke grew: "Hey, Rodney. Try some of this!" Chortling, most tried the squirrel salad in the spirit of a new adventure.

First we took armloads of Christmas greens and decorated along all the walls, doors, and windows. Then we enjoyed a magnificent lunch of fried chicken, local hams, sweet potatoes, and endless desserts. Many talked openly of how difficult it was to go through the deep changes of treatment for alcoholism and drugs. Our personal connections deepened and became stronger in our openness about our struggles. A woman who worked with the homeless in Washington, D.C., sat and watched the festivities. "What a nice church!" she offered. What else could be said? This was real: a church that gave a party for those who were going through difficult personal transitions.

Our group included men and women of all races, rural southern, inner-city residents, mountain people, professionals, and laborers. We sang rousing Christmas carols, and finished up quietly with "Silent Night, Holy Night!" which had a new reference after experiencing this day of holiness. Pearl prayed, "Thank you for sending our visitors to us today!" I thought about the wonders of the day and how we had accepted others in spite of our obvious differences. Christ is here, I thought. Our divisions ceased to exist. This was a taste of heaven, a unity, a oneness, a love so strong that our minds were drawn to the powerful reality of God. This must be the experience of pure love that Madame Guyon wrote about, I thought. Out of this glorious day, I sensed a truth that became more clear through the coming years. God doesn't honor our divisions and hatreds. We remember our hatreds between races or classes, but our overpowering and transcendent God will have none of that. God breaks down our prejudices and fears of those different from us.

I realized that in this afternoon of passionate love we had reached beyond old hatreds and fears: we jumped and jetted over the divisions between the races, we shooed away the no man's land that separated the rich from the poor, we laughed at the differences between inner-city and rural pastoral. In the magnificence of the afternoon we acknowledged a simple and beautiful truth: our hearts stand equally before our Maker. With the outer differences washed away, we immersed ourselves in the absolute joy that comes from living in the presence of the ancient truths. What matters about us is within; what matters about us lies in our hearts; what matters about us is residing in pure, sparkling love of others.

We invited the homeless men back several times because of the success and enthusiasm of their visits. Every occasion brought new experiences of the divine spirit. I became stronger and felt that my search for pure love was answered by refreshing moments in which I sensed the truth of this marvelous reality.

And I turned again to the mystics for wisdom about this reality of pure love. The delights of these parties, divine parties, lovely tastes of heaven, sparkled in my mind, encouraging me to seek more of these wonders.

I read more about Madame Guyon after I located a copy of her autobiography in which she described her life in seventeenth-century France. A physically beautiful woman, she wrote movingly about the mysteries of God realized in this world. I reveled in her distinctive vision of God as One who upheld, comforted, encouraged, while deeply challenging our respectability. Jeanne was born into the aristocracy and experienced the wonders of this world. I contemplated her life as she walked around Paris in her beautiful gowns, as she was welcomed to all of the extravagant parties. She told a story about her life that haunted me. I pondered this story one evening sitting next to a roaring fire I had built in my wood stove.

On a gray, chilly day in Paris, Jeanne was running to Mass at the Cathedral of Notre Dame, dressed in a long gown and

53

flowing veil. She saw the magnificent cathedral spires surging up to heaven, decorated with its frightening gargoyles and lively angels. As she quickly crossed the bridge over the River Seine, a beggar quietly moved into her path. She paused, stopping her rush towards the incarnate God present in the eucharist. Although Jeanne yearned for this Mass and the peaceful body and blood of Christ, she stopped and respectfully waited for the beggar to speak.

The peaceful, ageless beggar said, "Madame, I need to have a word with you."

Hearing the intensity in his voice, Jeanne stopped and pulled her veil aside to face him directly. "Monsieur, what can I do for you?"

He looked at her with compassion. "I have a word for you from God. You have a special place in God's kingdom. You will be asked to suffer for God; truly, you will suffer great agonies. But God will uphold you. God allows this suffering because he desires union with you."

Jeanne grew pale, looking intently at the man's piercing, powerful eyes. He returned her direct gaze, but somehow no questions were necessary.

Jeanne said with simplicity, "I accept whatever God wills for me." She let her black veil again fall in front of her face and continued walking to Notre Dame. After she walked up the massive front stairs of the awe-inspiring cathedral, she turned to look back. The beggar was no longer there.

Jeanne wrote in her journal, "I never saw him again, but the grace of that conversation lingered the rest of my life."

And I reflected as I viewed the fire crackling and burning: God as fire, God as one who calls us to suffer? Could that be? I snuggled down more deeply in my cozy setting. I knew that some situations in life demanded our strength as individuals. The beggar seemed to be confronting Jeanne with the knowledge that she would be tested. I knew about such testing because of my own trying experiences in Alaska.

The cold, dark Alaska winters forced everyone to become an individualist. No comfortable community could shelter you from the intense, deadly cold that tore at you. Even layer upon layer of wool and fur clothing could not hinder the still, intense, frozen Fairbanks air from shredding our feelings. At times, walking along in the pitch dark Alaska day, I felt entirely isolated. The only power I knew was bitter, desolate cold separating me from any hope of a humane, beneficent force.

This too was the meaning of the mysterious prophecy to Jeanne. One day Jeanne would be separated from all that supported her and be tested as few are ever tested. Somehow, the challenging image of Jeanne, beautiful, veiled Jeanne stopped by a mysterious beggar as she was running to God reached out to me over the centuries and clung to me.

55

seven

The Civil War Revisited

I can say tears became my drink,

and grief my nourishment.

—Jeanne Guyon, *Autobiography*

In Culpeper County, people lived and breathed Civil War history. Many of the people I knew spent hours with metal detectors looking for Civil War memorabilia and decorated their home with these discoveries. The Brandy Station chapter of the United Daughters of the Confederacy met regularly, giving talks with titles such as "Faithful Southerners."

And then one day, I received a challenge to allow a search for truth in my Brandy Station Church. One of the vestry members had contacted the Smithsonian Institution about researching the battlefield.

"This is Dr. Douglas Owsley from the Museum of Natural History of the Smithsonian Institution. We want to excavate your Brandy Station church's cemetery for unmarked graves of Civil War soldiers." Agreeing in principle to his request, I hung up the phone, stunned. Dr. Owsley had previously conducted excavations at the Gettysburg battlefield, as well as doing the work on murderer Jeffrey Dahmer's victims, and was a noted authority in his field.

The battlefield, I thought, wonderingly. An aura of mystery shrouded this land. The area was gorgeous: located in the midst of rolling Virginia farmland, the two-acre church cemetery was covered with original vegetation. The church had been destroyed by soldiers who had camped nearby. The ruins of the old church foundation were still vaguely discernible. Old headstones rested at strange angles because of the sinking of the ground caused by coffins decaying underneath. Residents, though, were reluctant even to *speak* about this area. It was beautiful, pastoral, yet unmistakably eerie and chilling.

While at Brandy Station, I had slowly pieced together the story about the property. The Battle of Brandy Station happened on June 9, 1863, when the Union cavalry surreptitiously advanced into Culpeper County to make a surprise attack on the Confederate cavalry. The Union troops, under the leadership of Major General John Buford, led the assault against the troops of Confederate General J. E. B. Stuart. The line of engagement was nearly three miles long. Both troops wanted control of Fleetwood Hill, which was the highest point of the battlefield. The two cavalries of nearly 7,000 horsemen charged each other in battle over this hill, hundreds from each side killed in the process. I remembered an elderly woman telling me that her grandfather had told her that the stench of the decaying bodies hung over the area for days.

The original St. James Episcopal Church had been built in 1842 on this land that became the site of the Battle of Brandy Station. It was a small church with hand-made wooden pews inside.

Following the war, parishioners collected money from the federal government for the church's reconstruction and built it on a different site several miles away, renaming the church Christ Church, the church that I currently led. They retained the deed to the original land.

The Christ Church vestry voted unanimously to support the Smithsonian plan for historical research. Dr. Owsley brought a team of twenty-seven research archaeologists and, using noninvasive techniques, he discovered one unmarked grave on the last day of his excavation. They carefully opened the grave and found the remains of a Civil War soldier. Dr. Owsley took the bones back to the Smithsonian for scientific study. In their excavation they also found the lock to the church's back door, bullets, horse gear, uniform buttons, and Civil War food ration cans.

After this excavation, community tensions were immediate and intense. Desecration of a cemetery, was what some people said, while others defended this research because of its historical value. A man fearfully said to me, "Don't you know you've released ghosts now?" Letters flew back and forth in the local newspapers, weighing whether our actions were justified or not.

But another real issue was now at hand. A California developer, Lee Sammis, had purchased rights from local farmers to about 3,500 acres around Brandy Station, including much of the battlefield, in hopes of developing it. Our small church cemetery was adjacent to Sammis's land. A fight over the development started. The Second Battle of Brandy Station was what they called it, and, to my dismay, I was right in the middle of it.

The Brandy Station Christ Church members were divided about the possible development. Betsy vehemently opposed it while most businessmen and women desired the change. I didn't want to take sides, but Sammis asked that our church property be sold to him. He wanted to remove the graves from our small cemetery and develop the church land, as well as much of the surrounding battlefield. A heated vestry meeting occurred, with members standing and yelling angrily at each other. The idea of selling the property was voted down.

All I wanted was out of this mess. But the anti-development side used the historical value of the land as an argument against the development. I tried to be fair to both sides. I awoke every day to fresh newspaper articles about this controversy. Headlines traced the progress of the fight: "Board Opposes Historic Area at Brandy and Preservation Fight Looms at Brandy Station."

I felt myself becoming weary of the rough realities of this priestly position. I wanted to seek God, and to have others seek God, yet I found myself in the midst of a community squabble. My professors at the University of Virginia had read about this community struggle. One sent me a note telling me of fall plans for getting together. He then added, "So you can go back to the war! (Keep it civil.)" I laughed, keenly aware how my studies at the university influenced my actions.

Dr. Doug Owsley, who had been analyzing the bones, called me up and asked me to come work at the museum for a week. Dr. Owsley's office was filled with bones of persons whom he was identifying. My first day in his office, he showed me the soldier's bones, handing them to me as he explained the work he had done. I grasped them firmly and then held them in my arms as we talked. As I nestled the soldier's bones in my arms, I felt once again a desire to help this soldier have the honor of a decent burial in a marked grave. Through research, Dr. Owsley identified two possible names of the dead soldier. Here they were, two young Irish immigrants, fleeing the poverty, famine, and hardships of Ireland. I pictured them on the ship to the New World, Louisiana, seeking the possibility of a decent life at about the age of twenty. They enlisted in the Confederate Army's Washington Artillery in New Orleans—expecting what? Excitement? Bravery? They traveled across our country to Brandy Station, Virginia, until their military encounter on June 9, 1863, in the Battle of Brandy Station.

Then a charge, a flash of a bayonet. Did they see it coming?—and pain, shock, surprise, falling, falling, falling . . . ?

Somebody picked up their bodies later, took church pews, fashioned a rough coffin by placing two of the pews together and into the Virginia ground they went.

Somehow now I sensed what the local people had warned me about. These awful realities of the Civil War arouse passions of sorrow, anger, and fear. In this battle happened everything you don't want to happen: young deaths, dismemberment, hatred between neighbors. And I understood how important it was to be very careful with this land. Violent, sudden deaths had happened all over the battlefield. Some of my neighbors were afraid of the spirit world—and who was I to ignore the spiritual dimension of the tragic battle?

This situation made me wonder about ministering to the souls of those departed. In the Episcopal Church we pray for the dead. I wondered if the dead from this awful battle didn't need our help in retaining dignity where they died. My ordination began to mean more to me: did I have a priestly responsibility for these dead young men? I prayed regularly for wisdom about all of these many issues.

I planned a burial service for the young man for May 16, 1992, knowing that the soldier had never had one. The Smithsonian had identified him, returned his bones, and now his remains would be honorably buried. The church became enthusiastic about this project. We invited the Washington Artillery, still existing in New Orleans, as well as Civil War reenactment groups.

To help me understand my role in this ceremony, I turned to the mystic Catherine of Siena. Catherine said that it doesn't matter what effects your actions have as long as you are obedient to what God is asking from you. She wrote that when we have the courage to do the right and moral action, we swim in a sea of peace, which is God. I wanted this godly peace. Somehow I felt that obedience to God required that I help serve these deceased soldiers, both Union and Confederate, who were still buried unknown in this vast battlefield.

I had begun to realize that the priestly role is to intercede for anyone who needs help, regardless of the consequences to the priest. The soldier deserved a funeral and I would do this for him.

Yet many wanted this funeral stopped. Because the sheriff's department anticipated some dissent against the church's actions, a deputy was assigned to the ceremony. And indeed, later that morning a group of men in favor of development confronted me at the scheduled time of the funeral, telling me loudly I could not perform this ceremony.

"You cannot go through with this!" one man angrily exclaimed.

"Yes, I can and I will," I said firmly. "Please remember that you are walking on holy ground." Their demonstration was not appropriate on the consecrated ground of a cemetery. The crowd was gathering and I felt the solemnity of the occasion.

Leaving the prospective developers angry and fuming, I went to start the ceremony.

I felt utterly respectful towards the occasion of this funeral. This soldier's death lacked everything: dying young, an immigrant, violent. But, as much as it was in my power, I wanted to set things right by giving him a burial with honors. His remains would be placed in a grave in our cemetery, with a handmade coffin and a head marker, properly honored with a funeral service.

A solemn drum beat announced the beginning of the ceremony, with a company of Civil War reenactors soon coming into view marching down the narrow lane next to the cemetery. I felt supported by something: that it was a combination of positive emotions, a good spirit, a divine influence, only partially describes how I felt.

The scriptures were read by a long-time leader in Culpeper who wore a suit and topcoat. I had chosen the scripture from First Corinthians 15:20–55. He read with great dignity. "But someone will ask, how are the dead raised? With what kind of body do they come? . . . What is sown is perishable, what is raised is imperishable. . . . It is sown a physical body, it is raised a spiritual body. . . . When this perishable body puts on imperishability and this mortal body puts on immortality, then the saying that is written will be fulfilled:

'Death is swallowed up
in victory.'
'Where, O death, is your victory?
Where, O death, is your sting?'"

I knelt and prayed beside the lovingly crafted coffin of the young Irish lad, knowing that a prayer from the heart transcends time and space as powerfully as a flash of lightning.

After I lifted up my hand to give the final blessing of the funeral, I took a small flask of Louisiana soil given to me from the Washington Artillery and lovingly sprinkled the coffin with this piece of land from the soldier's adopted home.

"Rest eternal grant to him, O Lord; And let light perpetual shine upon him. May his soul, and the souls of all the departed, through the mercy of God, rest in peace. Amen."

I prayed that we commend, "to Almighty God, our brother." Following a sacred silence, the solemn, timeless military salute of guns sounded, echoing powerfully throughout the beautiful Virginia land.

Following the ceremony, the women of the church served a luncheon, at which Dr. Owsley spoke. Together we had planned for the publication of his book about the excavation, which was placed in local bookstores shortly after the funeral. I wrote about our history:

62

> The story of St. James dramatically reveals the place of the church in the world. In the midst of destruction and tragedy, of chaos and death, the Christian faith remains resolute and strong. The church witnesses to an eternal presence, a quiet love, a strong place in which to stand, even when the powers of war rage around it.
>
> This same faith carried St. James into the future. The church was built again, grew again, and served again. Now, amidst the serene pastures and gentle breezes of Brandy Station, the church still professes the Christian faith in a world now transfigured. Transfigured by glory, we say, changed and rebuilt by our God.
>
> We are thankful for the strong souls who loved when hate seemed to rule. We are thankful to know our heritage, a heritage that shows love's power, even in the tragedy of war.[2]

Unfortunately the political struggle over the development of this land continued. I believed that the remaining graves in the battlefield needed to be found before any potential development occurred and I was committed to expressing these views. A bill was introduced in the Virginia legislature allowing the development to proceed. Traveling to Richmond, I met with some legislators to ask them to vote against this legislation, explaining my reasons.

I went to a hearing at which I had been invited to speak. The room was packed with those following this bill, media persons, and legislators. I sat there, dressed in my black clericals, when to my surprise Governor Wilder stopped by for a while. I was the final speaker, and I kept my message simple. I explained about my church land and what the study conducted by the Smithsonian reported. I said, "Dr. Owsley has stated that other anonymous graves lie in the Brandy Station battlefield. These dead soldiers deserve our respect. We need to look for these graves before any possible development happens." I ended by saying, "A civilized society honors its war dead. We must provide these soldiers the honor they are due." A poignant silence followed my talk before the hearing was adjourned.

I believed that I had fulfilled my duty in this situation. Driving home that evening from Richmond, Virginia, I felt utterly at peace.

eight   A BIG SURPRISE

We may gather from this that, though the

soul suffers greatly in the search after her

Beloved, its pain is but a shadow in

comparison with the bliss arising from the

possession of its adorable object. The same

thing is asserted by Saint Paul, who tells us

that the greatest sufferings of this life are not

worthy to be compared with the glory that

shall be revealed in us (Romans 8.8).

—Jeanne Guyon, *The Songs of Solomon*

With gratitude I left behind the busy political struggles and returned to my study of Jeanne Guyon. What a magnificent life she had lived! Her life changed rapidly after the prophecies of the beggar.

Jeanne left the Cathedral of Notre Dame after the surprise visitation by the beggar and returned to her spacious mansion where she lived with her three children and husband. She walked around her mansion, pondering the odd prophecy. She wondered, "A strange suffering will come upon me? How could this be? I have wealth, beauty, three healthy children. Yes, I have a strong passion for God that frequently puzzles me and leaves me hungering for God—but *agonies*? Maybe the beggar was confused." But somehow she doubted this; the strangely beautifully timbre of his voice resonated peacefully in her mind and the strong assurance in his eyes carried an authority she had never seen before.

Then one day as she moved around making sure that the servants were about their tasks and preparing for the day's dinner, she glanced at her son. His eyes glowed oddly. Instinctively she reached for his forehead and felt an unhealthy warmth. Immediately she put him to bed and called for a servant to fetch the doctor. In the next few hours, Jeanne experienced an increasing terror. Her other children also became feverish, hot, calling for a relief that she could not supply. Panicking, she waited what seemed endless hours. When would the doctor come, when would help arrive? Praying, crying out to God, she saw one by one all of her children grow ill, pale, and then red, screaming, crying. My God, she prayed, help me, help me. Her children, her joy, all suffered, crying, but then even worse, one by one they became dreadfully quiet, limp, lifeless. Jeanne knew fear like she had never felt before. God, where are you?

Finally she heard the welcome sound of a carriage pulling up in front of the house. The doctor walked in somberly and with few words together they rushed up to the nursery bedrooms where her children lay limp. The doctor compassionately inspected them and then turned to speak to her, saying the feared words, "Madame Guyon, your children have smallpox. You must leave here to save yourself."

Tears filled her eyes but she immediately rejected the doctor's idea. "I will stay here and wait upon my children." Jeanne went through several days of restless work, wiping them down with cool clothes, watching and waiting for the doctor's daily visit. The fever raged within the small bodies of her beloved children.

Then one day as she walked into the nursery, one of her legs gave way beneath her and she fell, helpless as a rag doll.

A servant ran from the other room to help Jeanne up. "Oh, Madame, what happened?" The servant cried, "You are hot! Oh, no. The fever has gotten you too."

Jeanne stared at her and then darkness descended upon her as she fainted. During the next few days, at times she was only dimly aware of tossing in bed, of crying for her children, of wanting and needing, of suffering, of hurting, of being hot, so very, very hot.

And one day, she became aware of someone sitting in her room, dressed in black. Slowly she opened her eyes to see her local priest sitting there. Confused, not sure what was happening, she slowly remembered her situation. "My children? How are they?" The priest looked at her, judging what to say. He recognized her need for honesty.

"Your second child, your son, has died. He received the last rites and has been buried. But the others live."

Jeanne felt sudden pain. The fresh grave in the family cemetery caused a dreadful void, a horrible sadness in her soul. One of her beloved children lost and dead. "The other children wish to see you, Madame, if you are up to it. But you must be aware—they will look different now."

Not quite comprehending, she nodded: of course she would like to see her beloved, remaining children.

They walked slowly in the room, still weak after the struggle through smallpox. As she looked her eyes grew wide. No more the beautiful, carefree children, but faces now weak and scarred by pox marks, ravaged by the disease. Beautiful smiles grew on their faces, as they saw their mama, causing their deep furrows of scars to become more apparent. But a beautiful, entrancing love enveloped them and Jeanne's heart filled with joy to see them.

Then quietly Jeanne asked the priest, "May I have a mirror?"

He answered softly, "Are you ready for this, Madame?"

Jeanne answered, "Yes."

He handed her a mirror and she saw the same ghastly marks all over her face too. Her beauty was gone forever, as was the beauty of her children. She said slowly, "My sweet child has died. It says in the book of Job, *The Lord has given, the Lord has taken away, Blessed be the name of the Lord.* I thank God that these live." And she warmly hugged her children even as her heart shrieked with pain at the loss of the one lying in the cold graveyard.³

I wondered: how had Jeanne accepted all of this sorrow? What had been the source of her peaceful resignation?

But events still drew my attention to external activities. The national publication *Episcopal Life* wrote about the Brandy Station Civil War funeral in September, 1993, using the headline "Ghosts of the Past Bring Parish Together." The article said: "What sets Christ Church apart from any other small-town church is that it has a sort of ancestral ghost, wreathed in the smoke and blood of battle 130 years ago."[4] How accurately they expressed the feeling of Culpeper being shaped by the violent past! This article reported that the parish felt some pride in its accomplishment after the peak experience of the funeral. But this didn't stop the local controversy about the use of the battlefield from continuing to grow after the funeral ceremony.

Some church members led a movement to fire me but failed. I prayed and stayed at the churches. I was pleased when the vestry of Emmanuel Church, Rapidan, issued an invitation to the homeless men to come for a church service and a luncheon. Some vestry members expressed their own feelings of joy about the visits of the homeless men. "I've never felt closer to God than during these visits," one vestry member said.

The Sunday arrived for the planned visit. When I walked into the church, I saw to my pleasure about twenty people, primarily African American. I realized how happy they were to be there; they had brought their Bibles and were reading, looking up with smiles when they saw me. But I also saw frowns on some long-time members faces as they entered. A female parishioner walked into the beautiful church. She looked angrily at the visitors and then stormed out of the church, muttering something. A woman walking immediately behind her reported that the parishioner had said as she reached the churchyard, "I'm not going to church with n_____."

Fervently I prayed for peace before the church service, horrified at the angry scene. I realized that the "ancestral ghost" of Culpeper included a long history of racist attitudes directed at African Americans. To my relief, a calm descended on me before the service. I preached about pure love and the glory of transcending our self-concerns, which enables us to embrace persons of all races and stations in life. "When we accept this powerful gift of pure love, we find ourselves gathered together in love. We adore God's entrancing presence, while we feel the abundant joy of our brothers and sisters." During our final hymn of "Amazing Grace" I looked around in wonder at the glowing, happy faces of both the regular parishioners and our inner-city visitors.

At the luncheon afterwards, I walked around cheerfully greeting everyone. Our visitors from Washington, D.C., clearly loved being in the country church. They ate heartily and then took an energetic walk by the Rapidan River. Later, Grover Small, the retired judge, put his arm around my shoulders saying in his pithy way, "Great sermon!" He briskly told the men, "Time to go," and they happily piled back into their van. They respected this authoritative judge, as did I.

As I drove through the town of Rapidan that Sunday, I reflected again on the fresh truth of the Christian vision. In God's presence our differences lose their significance, and people may come together in unity. A sparkling beauty reveals itself. This is life as it should be: when principles of justice and love are realized among us, we sense our compassionate God. Our lives are touched by the divine. I wrote it down in these words, *love divinizes our mortal clay, our bodies.* The gorgeous vision of pure love danced and laughed in my soul, tantalizing me with heavenly understandings of love, purity, and goodness.

I prayed before I nodded off to sleep, "Thank you, God, for Grover and for all the help he has given your people." Closing my eyes, I rested in my joy at realizing the realities of pure love.

I remembered a time from my childhood when my father was involved with a controversy on his Air Force base. In his pilot-training program he was supportive of a black pilot. He began to receive private criticism about this, but he wouldn't

68

budge, saying that the man was a capable pilot and should be recognized as such. I met this pilot when he visited our home, and even as a child could sense the respect and gratitude he showed toward my father. I believed that I, too, should make my stand now, and not change my behavior because of racial prejudices.

Yet criticisms continued to surface about this unusual ministry, making my life difficult. But as some openly criticized me, others started attending *because* of the ministry to the inner city poor. The church thrived. The active Sunday school became filled with the sound of singing, happy children. A Mother's Support Group met regularly to discuss raising children. Attendance had never been higher at the church.

One evening I received a long, unhappy call from a parishioner, openly telling me that a group was leading another attempt to have me fired. I pondered this situation and decided to leave this in God's hands. I wanted to obey whatever guidance God gave me.

How could I survive this unbalanced community situation? What would happen? But when I started worrying about this, I remembered wisdom I had learned from Alaskan nature: dance in the chaos, relish the uncertainty, learn from the precipitous edge.

Like the grand jetés of a dancer, we Alaskans learned the Dance of the Spheres. We luxuriated in the dangerous twirls of the winter, learning an inward balance. The externals sparkled brilliantly, bringing the possibility of snow blindness. How could we survive? We could only live by moving and trusting our still, small interior spot of harmony. Was Alaska a manifestation of this internal face of our soul? Who knew? We couldn't stop the divine dance long enough to ask, for none wished to miss the Steps of Ecstasy we knew. Let the dance continue!

Then the community situation escalated in an unusual way. I received a call from the Rev. Faulkner and his wife Mary, who had heard of the church's problems through their daughter, Ann, who attended Emmanuel. Reverend Faulkner himself had been priest at Emmanuel in the late 1930s and knew the community well. The Faulkners said that they wanted to have a "Nancy Day," a day just for me, and asked my favorite food. Shrimp, I immediately said, and it was settled. I was to drive to their home in Fredericksburg, enjoy a meal with them, and talk about the problems. A "Nancy Day," I told my friends. What a sweet and considerate idea. We planned our visit for the Monday of Holy Week, March 29, 1993, a few days before the observance of Good Friday and Easter.

The morning of my day, I dressed quickly, visited an elderly parishioner who was lonely, stopped briefly at Christ Church and drove off, munching on a piece of butterscotch candy. I wore my big, down coat and headed out along the two-lane country road. The day was drizzly and chilly.

I rounded a small turn in the narrow road, slowing down because a mail truck putting letters in a mail box was stopped in my lane. I was wondering what the "Nancy Day" would be like, when my car was suddenly propelled off the ground, moving through the air, and turning over and over. I prayed, Jesus, help me, Jesus, Jesus. Would I even be alive at the end of this? I landed in a destroyed car, crouching down on the passenger side of the car, praying the Lord's Prayer. Where was I? What had happened? Our Father, who art in heaven, Hallowed be thy name . . .

I heard men running up, saying in frightened voices, "Is there anyone alive in there?" I said, "I'm here," and heard the response, "You need to get out of there. I smell gas." I asked how to escape and the men said they didn't know how. They started quarreling among themselves about the best way to proceed. Then peering out of the crumpled car, I saw a large, calm man of African American descent standing quietly in front of the car.

"You need to get out of the car," I heard him say.

"There's no way out," I gasped.

He leaned down and tore off what remained of the wind-shield. "Why not climb out here?" he suggested.

Holding on to his hand, I pulled myself out.

"Are you okay?" he asked quietly.

"I'm fine," I replied, honestly feeling this way. "Thank you."

I started walking toward the front porch of the house and my benefactor was gone.

As my dizziness gradually disappeared, I saw the distressing situation. I had been rear-ended so severely by a woman speeding that my car had flipped over several times, ending up destroyed in the front yard of a small house. Then the woman had hit others cars, creating a massive accident. I believed I was fine, but the crowd gathering around me expressed concern in case I had internal injuries. I found my way to the front porch, sat breathing deeply, and was joined by the woman who had been driving the mail truck. The man who lived in the house came running out, and, to my comfort, he was a nurse. He quickly took my blood pressure, and I was relieved to hear it was normal.

An ambulance arrived and took me to the Culpeper hospital. As I was lying in the emergency room, a large state trooper came in and said to me gently, "You are one very lucky woman today. You were wearing your seat belt, weren't you? I said I always did, adding that the seat belt broke near the end of the accident. He smiled, saying, "I think it saved your life today. The woman who hit you will be charged with reckless driving."

The doctor on duty in the Culpeper Hospital emergency room gave me the welcome news that I was fine, except for soreness.

In court at the trial of the woman who hit me, through the testimony of witnesses I heard more details about what had happened. A woman had driven up behind me, speeding, and hit me, causing my car to turn over three times. She then hit two other cars, leaving traffic entirely stopped and congested in both directions. Witnesses saw the large, African American man help me out of the car but no one saw him arrive or leave. Since traffic was totally stopped both ways because of the multiple accidents, everyone questioned who this strong man was and where he went. The mail truck driver said slowly, "What a strange day that was."

A parishioner called me one evening a few days later to ask how I was feeling and then she started hesitantly to say something and then stopped. I asked her what she wanted to say.

"Nancy, you know the black man who helped you out of the car?"

"Yes," I said, feeling somehow shy about talking about this very intimate moment in my life.

"I feel like you should know something. Everyone saw that happen, him helping you out, but no one saw him get there or walk away. How did he get out of there since traffic couldn't move? He doesn't live around there. Well, my maid told me that people are saying that since you helped black people in Washington, God sent a black angel to help you and that God wouldn't let you down in your time of need." She sounded uneasy expressing this community news to me, and finished, "What do you think?"

"I don't know. I do know that he helped me immensely, whether he was a human or an angel. I've never felt more cared for in my life. He glowed with a peace that spread into me. And then he was just gone. Maybe one day we'll learn more about this." In the weeks I spent recuperating, the beautiful image of the loving man hovered in my consciousness, helping me overcome the weakness I felt as I grew back to full strength.

The car accident challenged all my assumptions about what was important in life. I wondered: What is the good life? And what is important? I talked to my brother Tim shortly after the accident realizing that, "Life will be over soon," understanding for the first time how quickly everything jets by. We feel like we have all the time in the world for the luxurious dinner parties, for the delightful hours of pleasant talk and superficial activities. After the car accident, I felt an internal warning that time runs out and is our most precious commodity.

I also understood that I had not dug deeply enough into life to create anything important. I wanted to stop avoiding the uncanny reality, the amazing idea that in this immense universe we exist at all and that there could be work for us to do, accomplishments that were destined by God for us to do. I remembered one of my favorite novels, *Momento Mori* by Muriel Spark, in which a mysterious character calls persons and merely says, "Remember you must die." Somehow, God's grace through this accident reminded me that I must die one day, but that before I died I had something to accomplish.

I experienced the car accident as a revelation of pure love. I understood that it was time for me to seek God entirely, to abandon myself to God's goodness, as Madame Guyon says. Abandon yourself and give yourself to God; take no concern for yourself, but only look at the divine goodness.

The crumpled car that was wrapped around me actually gave birth to me.

I decided I needed to be serious about Madame Guyon. Who was this enigmatic, powerful woman? I had written about Madame Guyon while taking a class on mysticism at the University of Virginia. I remembered what she had said about the intense joys of God. "I regarded myself as a little bird you were keeping in a cage for your pleasure, and who ought to sing to fulfill her condition of life. . . . My joy was based on your love, O my God . . ."[5] I felt amazement at how deeply this woman loved and desired God: how could she dare to have such passionate feelings toward the Divine! Somehow Jeanne had known that God came not to destroy her passion for life, but to fulfill it.

As I recuperated physically from my car accident, I read Jeanne Guyon avidly. Spiritually I had never felt stronger. I knew what I should be about: a deep search for intimacy with God. This renewed an urgent sense of purpose that transfigured my life. I wanted to live passionately.

In Alaska all I knew were passionate people. We were passionate about the fishing, the fresh salmon, the polar ice cap, the latest sightings of aliens, passionate about life incarnate, incarnate and inflamed by fresh divinity. This divinity danced with us, inviting us to love and to wonder and to nurture and to feel—to feel deeply the sheer magnificence of nature that twirled us and carried us and waltzed with us: the flame red passion of life!

nine

THE CHURCHES THRIVE

All I know is that God is infinitely

holy, just, good, happy . . .

—Jeanne Guyon, *Autobiography*

In my reading of Guyon I sensed that some answers about life were possible. Yes, answers seemed remote, but also as if they hearkened to me, saying, *seek and you will find us.* Somehow when I read the autobiography of Madame Guyon, I felt that I could receive some answers about the experience of innocent suffering.

I returned to Jeanne's life to see what happened to her next.

After Jeanne's disfiguring smallpox and death of her young son, she attempted to resume life, even as she deeply grieved for her lost baby. She worked with the poor in her community, often giving out food and clothing to help the very real needs of those suffering in seventeenth-century France. One morning Jeanne woke early and went to the corner of her bedroom to pray while her husband continued to sleep. "My divine God, lead me in your ways, let me know Your will, grant me wisdom," she prayed. Grief flowed over her body like a never-ending fire. Would this fire consume, destroy, annihilate her? Yet her passion for understanding drove her. What was her life like, she wondered. Like a dance with God, she felt, as if prayer lifted her into brilliant motions moving through inner space. She felt times of ecstasy when she leapt in the air with ease, the times of intimacy when the Divine Partner lifted her up and carried her. The moments of love, of passion, of dancing . . . But now, she paused, someone needed her downstairs. She sensed this without knowing that someone awaited her.

Putting on a heavier robe, Jeanne walked to her kitchen, opened the door, and saw her, a young, despairing woman with a crying child. The anguished mother stood mute, tense, not even having the courage to utter a word. Jeanne saw the intense hunger on the mother's face and felt the agony of the needy babe. She opened the door, and gestured for them to come inside, "Sit, sit, sit, my dear. Sit and rest." Tears filled the young mother's eyes as she sat and Jeanne rushed to the larder, pulling out bread, fruits, cheeses, jams, what else, what else, she said quietly. Then running back to the kitchen, she placed the food on the table, saying affectionately, "Eat, my sweet one. Eat, while I hold your child."

Jeanne took the suffering baby, cradled the child in her arms, and starting feeding her warm cereal. She felt the baby respond and Jeanne's heart leapt within her. With their suffering abating, Jeanne sensed her Divine Lover standing behind the chair, comforting them, as the famished mother and child knew for the first time in days the satisfaction of nourishment.

Later, in her journal, Jeanne wrote, "How does this work? My Divine Love comes to me, and forces are released, calling the innocent suffering ones to me. I thank you for the joy of helping and of caring. The power of prayer—I don't understand it—but I know it is real. Let us dance together, my God. Do not forget your desolate ones." Jeanne knew her prayers connected her with the poor, suffering ones. For this ministry, Jeanne thanked God.[6]

After my car accident, I continued my commitment to focus on the thought of Madame Guyon, while trying to live a life abandoned to God. God allowed suffering, Jeanne wrote, so that our self-interest would be annihilated. Our self-preoccupations would be torn from our lives, at first causing us extreme emotional pain. Following this agony comes the peace and serenity of the Divine Spirit filling the space left by the annihilated self-interest. In this process personal selfishness would be replaced with God's pure and perfect love. This healthy suffering enlarges our heart and expands our love to embrace all people, while challenging our limited understandings of life. Let yourself be annihilated through suffering, Jeanne Guyon encouraged, and you will find a germ of immortality inside of you. This germ grows into an abundant, wonderful life, leading us safely into eternity. Guyon's theology inspired my newly focused life.

Later that week, I talked to my brother Franklin about this place of suffering in our lives at a French restaurant in Georgetown. I had just left my work with homeless men where I had seen horrifying examples of human suffering. Franklin became frustrated with my choice of conversation topic, and suddenly said, "Suffering, suffering! Why all this talk about suffering?"

I laughed and pondered his outburst. Somehow the subject of suffering seemed a necessity. I responded slowly, "Many theologians think that Western civilization avoids both the topic and reality of suffering. They suggest that this is a weakness in our culture that causes problems in our lives. I think they are right." Franklin observed, "Why can't we just all seek to be happy? Why not avoid suffering?" I pondered his remark. "All I can say right now is what Guyon believes. She says that the center of life is the cross. That cross was not only meant for Jesus but for all obedient believers. If we refuse our personal cross and sacrifices, we refuse also the transcendence of God." Even as I said this I realized how difficult indeed these ideas were. The reality of voluntarily accepting suffering seemed impossible.

I looked at the parish situation directly. Some wanted me to stay, others to leave. I didn't know how to reconcile these conflicts until I applied Madame Guyon's ideas to my situation. She said that a person should always proceed with the good they can accomplish, letting God handle whatever barriers and problems arise. Focus your energies on God alone, she advocated. I followed her belief, trusting that God would handle the difficulties.

The controversy moved into frantic letter writing. Letter after letter flew between vestry persons, congregational members, and the bishop. Some defended me and my work, others castigated me for the very same actions. One person wrote to Bishop Lee saying, "Some I think even resent a woman being a minister."

A new member wrote Bishop Lee about her arrival at the church saying, "Initially, the congregation was friendly and inviting. I told friends about the church and they have come and enjoyed what they heard. But it seems the more new people that came, the more resentful and tense some of the congregation became. I am dismayed that the feelings that surface now are anger and resentment."

Then some of the parishioners started leaving the church and moving their membership out of Emmanuel, Rapidan. A feeling of relief prevailed among those remaining. Now, we thought, we could heal and rebuild the church. The worst had happened, we thought: an ethical confrontation between mature adults who disagreed. Some left the church, while many remained.

I attempted to regain a normal life, but some fresh sorrows confronted me. One day, my German Shepherd puppy, Gretchen, disappeared from my yard. I called her name over and over again, hearing only a desolate silence in reply. No golden-haired dog came bouncing towards me. I searched for her, and asked my neighbors, but she was never found nor was her body recovered. Then another day I returned home but did not see my Labrador, Cornelia, racing across the field to greet me. I called and looked, hoping desperately to see her lanky body charging home. And though I searched the neighborhood, I found no clues of what had happened to her either. I remembered with love her gentle, brown eyes. My dog, Cornelia, kind companion and guard, was unexpectedly gone.

The question plagued me about what had become of my dogs.

One Sunday in July, 1993, a young girl and her brother came racing up to me immediately following a church service, carrying a beautiful, black Labrador puppy, handing him to me while I still had my church robes on. "We brought him to you!" they exclaimed. I received him in my arms, thinking how sweet it was that the puppy was being presented to me in church. Looking at him, I named him Bear.

Simultaneous to all of this, I was aware that a major development was brewing in the Anglican Communion (which is the loosely connected group of Anglican churches throughout the world including the Episcopal Church). The then Archbishop of Canterbury, George Carey, supported the ordination of women in England. An immense struggle began in England as the day for the historic vote regarding women's ordination drew near. Many threatened to leave if the church ordained women, while many women who had already completed the necessary education for ordination waited expectantly to see if they would be allowed this crucial passage into priesthood. Unfortunately the vote was expected to fail.

As the day for the vote approached, I prayed and waited anxiously, fearing that the failure of the ordination of women in England would have dire consequences for all ordained women. Would England, the spiritual home of the American Episcopal Church, begin ordaining women?

The day dawned and I started on my round of pastoral visitations. I listened to the news on my radio as I drove places, with the announcers saying every half hour that the vote in England was expected to fail. My spirits began to falter. The acceptance of ordained women in the United States was still a serious issue; if this failed in England, many opposed to women's ordination in the United States would feel supported. Sadly, already in the Episcopal Church, if a parish wished to reject a female bishop from its annual visitation, they could do so, without any cause more than saying they didn't believe in ordained women.

My angst began to grow. What had I done with my life, I thought. Naively I had believed that most persons considered women to be equal with men, yet since my ordination I had received countless comments from persons saying that they thought that ordained women were unnatural. Why, one prominent parishioner had confronted me at the Christmas dinner, of all places, and said that a woman could not be a priest. I regretted the upheaval my ordination had brought into my life, including contributing to my divorce. Why had God called me to this, I wondered. I knew that I had experienced a strong call to ordination and found support for this, yet . . . The ordination had brought such turmoil into my life.

I listened again to the hourly news on the radio. The announcer said, "As the vote draws nearer, church observers predict that this will fail this time, but this divisive issue will be reintroduced in the future. We will let you know as soon as the vote is finished."

I sighed unhappily, turning off the radio. Walking into the house, I put down my purse and rather absentmindedly checked my messages on my phone machine. Then I heard a parishioner's excited voice on a message saying with great excitement, "Nancy! Have you heard? The ordination of women passed by two votes in England an hour ago. Two votes! We are all delighted."

I felt a shock of joy. Ordained women had not been left desolate. Now women would be fully recognized in England also. I called the parishioner. "How exciting! The church is now in a new era."

Our church had moved into an age of women experiencing the same freedoms and opportunities as men. Women and men could learn to relate as equals, learn to love without the shackles of historic oppression. We could be in a new time when the different sexes could appreciate their gifts and learn to apply them for the good of creation. Now women could dream and have visions of God in the organized church as fully as men had done for centuries. Women could now baptize, bless, and lead the church with power and authority.

I felt this new, abundant life in rural Virginia: the poor were attended to as we praised God in the community. The children were taught about our God who cared for the least of these. We came together week after week, seeking to know God's ways and hoping to understand the divine will. What a gift and glory to participate in this, I prayed thankfully.

As I prepared for bed that night, no more did I regret the sacrifices and suffering my ordination had brought upon me. I thanked God that I had been allowed to play my small role in this new and historic era in the Christian Church. My God had not failed us. Our divine Partner, whom I had known since I was a child, carried us, nurtured us, and gave us divine bliss.

We leapt across Alaskan mud puddles in the spring, joyfully tap-danced our way through the thick berry bushes in the summer. Through the long Alaskan nights our pas de deux with nature satisfied us. But our unseen Partner surprised us— no, actually shocked us—by the attentive care we felt. In the dark moonlight, was that our Partner's shadow? When we were blinded by the midnight sun, was that the supporting Arm waiting for our trusting reaction?

Eternity, time: all is eternity, all is God.

God is Love, and Love is God, and all

in God, and for God.

—Jeanne Guyon, *Autobiography*

Jeanne waited anxiously for the private Mass on her estate to begin. Yet another difficulty had surfaced in her life. Her dignified, aristocratic husband had grown increasingly ill and now lay weakly on his bed. With tears, she prepared for a final conversation with him.

Following her morning prayers, she approached the large bed in which he lay. "My husband," she began, when he motioned for her to listen. "I never deserved you, Jeanne," he said quietly. "I know I have put you through suffering and haven't cared for you well. I am sorry," and he grew quiet as tears started welling from his eyes. She reached up and gently caressed his face. "We all grieve for our shortcomings," she said compassionately. "God is with you, listening to you, loving you. You will ascend to the divine arms at the right time." He nodded, and closed his eyes, exhausted from the effort of speaking.

And Jeanne knew grief, pain as hot as flashes of lightening coursing through her body as she looked at her dying husband. Alone, desperate, she cried out, "What will happen now? How will I live?" And all she felt was coldness.

I pondered the story of Jeanne as I rejoiced in this new stage in the Christian church which brought its accompanying struggles and challenges. My bliss at the well-being of Emmanuel Church and the ordination of women in England brought me new strength. I needed this encouragement at this point, for what started as a small, seemingly insignificant problem in my church developed into a major storm.

A married and influential parishioner, Ted, started showing signs of too much personal interest in me and was known to offer his opinions about my job performance. He was in his late fifties, an intelligent man with an overbearing yet attractive personality. Ted exerted a powerful presence at Emmanuel Church, serving several different positions on the vestry. As a member of the church board of directors, Ted was among those who evaluated my job performance.

One day Ted showed up at the church office in the middle of the afternoon. He walked into my long office with its bright windows offering a full view of the gentle Rapidan River. Sitting down in the comfortable chair, he said assertively, "I want you to go to dinner with me on Tuesday evening. The restaurant is well known for its cheesecake, which I am sure you will like." I felt a sudden flash of uneasiness but he continued. "We can talk about the church budget, which we haven't been able to get approved yet in committee." I agreed to go to dinner to discuss church business, but I suggested we bring another church leader along with us. Ted said it wasn't necessary for her to accompany us, but I insisted on this. I called her later in the day, and she gladly accepted the invitation for dinner.

The next day, that church leader called, perplexed, saying that Ted had called her the previous evening, telling her she wasn't welcome at this dinner. We agreed that a dinner with only Ted and me was inappropriate.

I contacted Ted to let him know I was canceling the dinner. "You will go out to dinner with me," he stated coldly. "Oh, no. I won't go alone with you," I retorted. He became angrier, while I tried to be coolly professional. As I hung up the phone, I knew there was trouble ahead. With an already unsettled community, I knew that turning down even inappropriate advances from a supporter would provoke trouble.

Ted's interest, though, did not abate despite my obvious displeasure at his attention. He continued calling and pursuing me. He would call at eight o'clock in the morning and ask when I was leaving for work. I would be deliberately vague, and pointedly ask him not to call me so early. Or Ted would call at seven o'clock in the evening, asking, "Have you had dinner yet?"

During the day he would call the church, leaving messages on the answering machine. Yet since he was a member of the vestry, which supervised my job, I felt I couldn't completely reject his phone calls. Church members frequently called me at home at odd hours.

When I didn't respond to his attention, he started showing up daily at the church about ten or fifteen minutes after I would arrive. I began to be fearful. How could he predict when I would be there? He lived far from the church, so he couldn't easily see me arrive. And my schedule was different every day so he couldn't know the timing. Was he waiting for me? Was his timing mere coincidence? I began to dread seeing him arrive at my office. Yet he had a right to come to the church. I began to seek out literature about stalking, slowly becoming aware that his unwanted attention fell into this category.

Ted's behavior continued its downward spiral. He started calling me on the phone three or four times a day, from early in the morning until late at night. He began showing up at church every day, wanting to know where I was going and what I was doing. I began to feel smothered under Ted's oppressive behavior. I felt a fresh and cutting fear about this increasingly burdensome predicament.

Then one day he started discussing his romantic feelings for me. I cut the conversation short, letting him know that his feelings weren't reciprocated, and that this wasn't appropriate. I wrote Bishop Lee immediately, explaining the situation and stating that this form of harassment could cause serious problems in the church. Sexual harassment *by* priests was a concern to the diocese; I reported this harassment *of* a priest but at first received no guidance about it. I floundered through my days, aware that the more I resisted Ted, the more tensions grew.

Then on the night of November 16, 1993, things came to a head. Asleep in my large, isolated farmhouse, the nearest neighbor about one third of a mile away, I awoke to the sound of the back door being shoved open. The chain lock banged eerily as the door jerked to a stop. Quickly, I jumped out of my bed. My puppy, Bear, ran to me, the hair on his back erect. I crept towards the kitchen, saying, "Come on, Bear." To my surprise, the kitchen door was closed. I stared at it and heard no strange sounds. Then I assumed that I had misunderstood the noise, or maybe it had been a nightmare, or some wild animal outside. Picking up Bear, I returned to the bedroom and in a short while I was back asleep.

Several hours later, I woke up very cold. I once again walked into the kitchen, only to see that the kitchen door was unlocked, only a solitary chain preventing entry. I gingerly peeked through the kitchen door to find that someone had destroyed my back porch door; it hung eerily broken apart. Who had been there? Little did I know that my long odyssey into terror had started.

I called a neighbor to tell her what had happened. She drove over later that day, cheerfully running inside, bringing me a welcome gift of a can of hot pepper spray.

"It's legal," she told me energetically. "Spray it in his face. It will incapacitate him when it hits."

I felt hope rising that perhaps I could after all handle this awful situation. I also called the sheriff's department. They sent out a deputy who examined the door.

"Since this is a church-owned house, I wonder who has a key," he said. "I think that this sturdy chain might have saved you. It is put quite deeply into the wood here. But get those locks changed immediately. I bet the intruder had a key."

I breathed easier. A plan was developing. I had a weapon of hot pepper spray and the mission of changing the locks.

That evening Ted called me up, "Are you rattled yet?" Then, "You didn't need to call the sheriff. Why did you do that?"

Angrily, I replied, "What in the world are you talking about? Of course I needed to call the sheriff. Someone tried to break in here."

"Don't call the sheriff again," he responded and hung up. I sat, stunned, on the chair. As a priest, I wanted to keep Ted's problems quiet, yet I needed intervention and help against his bizarre behavior and the frightening things that had happened to me. And on top of all of this, technically he was one of my job supervisors. Yet here he was, telling me not to call the sheriff after a crime had been committed. How did he even know I had called the sheriff? How could I balance all of these opposing factors? Staring at my wood fire, I tried to read. Yet thoughts intruded: Where is the bishop? Why isn't he helping?

The next day I received a call from Kathy, who said with curiosity, "Ted called me. He is desperate to figure out your schedule. What is going on here? He wants to know where you are *in a big way.*" Trying to protect his privacy, I said that I was confused by this also.

I climbed the stairs and once again looked out the windows at the miles of pasture surrounding my house.

How could I stop this? I remembered seeing from this window a panicked fox running and lunging away from the baying dogs and colorfully clad hunters. Tears had sprung to my eyes at seeing the terror of the fox. This is considered sport? I'd shuddered. Now I too felt hunted.

My life became frightening and horrific. As public awareness grew about the problems, my relationships began to shift like a brilliant kaleidoscope moving into a new pattern. Before the colors would have been a peaceful blue, with flashes of yellows and greens. Now the background was a murky gray with vibrant flashes of red and gold. I experienced God's grace dramatically, but on a backdrop of unclarified darkness.

One day I returned home to find all of my plants lying broken apart on the floor and the long, cotton curtains in my bedroom ripped down. Then I noticed my dresser drawers had been pulled out. "Someone crazy has taken my underwear.

What is going on? How violent is this person?" My personal jewelry, including my favorite pearl earrings, had disappeared, while more expensive diamond jewelry was left untouched.

Then in quick staccato succession during the next week, someone pulled my typewriter apart. My telephone wire was cut. My Subaru was broken into and my personal papers taken. Horror filled me whenever I discovered fresh destruction. Was Ted doing this? Were others helping him? Pain filled my heart at the implied threat of missing undergarments and the destruction of my favorite belongings. Why was this happening, I prayed over and over again. Who would help?

Then more destruction. My church office at Christ Church, Brandy Station, was broken into and all the papers were wildly thrown around. The Rapidan church was also broken into and more extensively damaged. Once again, a sheriff's deputy came out, took a report, and said, "Someone is very angry here. This siding has been kicked off the church in a rage."

87

I slept uneasily, dressed in street clothes, ready to run. I kept Bear with me constantly, mainly worried for his safety. I went to the animal shelter to get a second dog, thinking I would get an imposing German Shepherd. But when I arrived at the shelter, I saw a sick puppy that the worker said would be destroyed later that day. I kept looking at the sad, sick puppy and decided to adopt him. He was a Belgian Shepherd who took days of care to get over his terrible worm infestation. I named the new dog Pogo, and found some relief in playing with the dogs, although I constantly feared their loss. The break-ins, the phone calls, and the loss of security felt like a hail of bullets hitting me.

I felt increasingly panicked. Who was doing this? Why? Where was God in all of this? What was I to do? No answers seemed to come. I listened to the radio, trying to calm down. I prayed, but I could find no peace. Should I run? Run where? Should I throw everything away I worked for and believed in? What should I do?

Then my friend Albert called me. "I've been hearing about the situation in Rapidan. I know you haven't talked to me about this, but I'm concerned how you are handling it. Can we talk?"

Feeling totally shaken up, I answered, "Of course. I don't have the faintest idea what to do."

"Nancy, sometimes I get insights and understandings. It's a gift from God."

I nodded, agreeing that these spiritual gifts were real. Albert said bluntly, "Someone is trying to destroy you. Look at you: you are obviously not eating and are rapidly losing weight. You're getting weird phone calls every day. Whoever it is might go down to one call a week, or even one a month so as not to get caught. But this caller won't give up."

Paradoxically a feeling of peace descended on me when he said this. I felt for the first time that someone else understood how I felt and was looking at the situation realistically.

Albert continued, "I have something to say to you and you need to hear it. Move out of your house and find a safe place to live. Do it quickly. You are in danger where you are. I know this is a nightmare. But get out of the house. Do it today."

I agreed with Albert and felt a deep peace in response to his words. I couldn't express my gratitude fully with words, but I tried. "I think you are right. I can't thank you enough."

How bizarre, I thought, but it seemed true. I knew I needed to follow Albert's advice.

I quickly found a basement apartment in the town of Culpeper. I rented the apartment, moved a few belongings and left my isolated house in the country. I now lived in the town of Culpeper, ten miles from Rapidan, surrounded by other homes and apartment buildings. I hoped that this would end the awfulness. It did not.

More destruction of my belongings in the Rapidan house followed: shattered dishes, belongings wildly thrown around as if a tornado had passed through my home.

One night, I tossed and turned, unable to rest or settle. Finally I fell into a deep sleep and started dreaming. I dreamed that I was sitting in a movie theater watching a film. I became aware that demons were dancing around me, trying to provoke me. They would pop up and leer at me, encouraging me to run away. They moved oblivious to material reality, becoming faster and more threatening. Then, in this vivid dream, I sensed a beautiful, calm, feminine presence saying, "Peace, Nancy. There is always magic. Call upon us to help." At the sound of the words, the demons immediately disappeared. And I woke up deeply comforted, murmuring to myself, *Hail, Mary, full of grace, the Lord is with thee. Blessed art thou among women and blessed is the fruit of thy womb, Jesus.* Who was this feminine presence in my dream, I wondered after I awoke. Mary, Jeanne Guyon, my mother, my grandmother Priscilla? What was this magic dream? I could not understand it but I enjoyed its very real comfort for months. An anointing dream was how Guyon classified a powerful dream such as this one.

89

My spiritual interests anchored me during this time. I read the Bible, prayed, and studied Madame Guyon. Her words of encouragement circulated in my consciousness, telling me that God draws closer to us in our afflictions. After the death of her husband, Jeanne believed that the worst was over. Now she thought that her life would adjust and she would become a quiet widow living in the country, doing good works. She had already suffered through the death of her child and husband. "Abandon yourself to God and know a spiritual purification during a time of suffering," she advised herself, thinking that maybe the worst was over. She could not have been more wrong about her life.

I believed her kind thoughts, yet, like her, I sensed that more horror might be coming my way too. I wondered if I would survive this blizzard of horror enveloping my life.

The snow started quietly in Alaska, coming down in peaceful clumps, blanketing the small trees and homes. But then the wind started playing with the snow, cavorting, gamboling, each new breeze adding delicious heights of play. We skipped in rhythm with the startling, dancing snow.

New gusts of wind came, opening up ancient depths of bewilderment, blowing stormy expirations of power, snow circling us, blinding us with brilliance, hiding the ground from us, yet enticing us with the play of power. Come, dance, come, surrender to my white Beauty, the beauty of unfettered power.

There are even sufferings so excessive that the

senses weep and cry, desire their deliverance,

without, however, taking from that central

depth of peace and unity with God's will . . .

—Jeanne Guyon, *Autobiography*

Local headlines still screamed daily about the fight over the Brandy Station Civil War battlefield. With my own life being destroyed, I could no longer pay attention to this intense and escalating struggle and turned to Madame Guyon for solace once more.

In desperation Jeanne sought comfort from a priest, explaining her numbness of feeling and the dreadful aloneness of her widowhood. What could she do? How could she live?

Father La Combe heard her terror and said, "Minister to others, Jeanne. Others feel as you do. Scared, alone, knowing that when people fail them, they have few resources. You are an intelligent woman. Help others and as you do so, God will reach out and offer you assistance for all the good you can do."

Jeanne left the church, musing on his words. He was right. People everywhere struggled to survive. Listen to them, the crying ones, and help. *Help them.* She felt these divine words echo in her soul, as if it were a call from God.

But my life continued its downward spiral. Ted's aggressive behavior and the attacks on me by someone yet to be identified, like dry kindling wood, lit a smoldering fire in Culpeper County: I was quickly inundated with a host of frightening, fiery situations. I struggled to lead the churches while tossed about by severe fright and terror.

It was on January 22, 1994, a bright, sunny Saturday as I was preparing for Sunday worship services at Christ Church, Brandy Station, that matters took another turn for the worse. I checked my voice mail and, to my horror, one whole message was filled only with the sound of Pogo barking. What did this mean? Was it a threat against Pogo? I had my dogs with me for their safety while I worked but took them with me for the quick drive down to the church house in Rapidan. On the spacious front porch, I saw my dogs' large, yellow ceramic food dish broken into three pieces. The weapon of destruction, a large stick, had been thrown down by the receptacle. The destruction oppressed my spirit, like a blight falling on a healthy tree. What should I do about all of this, I screamed to myself.

I met with a sheriff's investigator along with some vestry members about this series of crimes. He asked for many details about the crimes, including whether my undergarments had been stolen.

"Yes," I said softly.

"I thought so. I think you are dealing with some sex maniac. I need to ask you to do something I don't think you will want to do." The investigator paused. "Get a gun quickly and learn how to use it."

I thought about what he said, feeling a genuine reluctance to go to such extreme measures.

I continued to live at the small apartment, though returning regularly to feed some outside animals at the Rapidan home. On one of those visits, on February 8, 1994, a gray, drizzly Tuesday morning, I turned into the my house's long, meandering driveway, to hear at first only quiet farm sounds. I put Bear on his leash to take inside with me, leaving young, four-month-old Pogo on the front passenger seat. I started putting out the cat food, and chose some clothes to take back to the apartment with me.

Suddenly Bear started running around, barking wildly, and looking frantically for an exit from the house. Something was terribly wrong. I lunged for the door and ran to the car, Bear in close pursuit. Pogo cowered on the seat, whimpering. He was not the happy puppy of a few minutes earlier.

I climbed into my seat, reached back to put my seat belt on, and realized that the seat belt attachment which had been there for the drive to the house had been deliberately broken. Waves of fear flooded my being. I anxiously looked around and saw a maroon truck near the red barn. Quickly I started the car and sped towards Emmanuel Church.

I saw the parishioner Kathy's car parked at the church. "Kathy, someone just broke into my car while I was at my house!" I yelled, running toward her. A storm settled on Kathy's face. "They've hired men to harass you," she said in a loud, angry voice. I started backing away from her. Denouement, I thought. The community tensions were so great that someone had apparently hired men to frighten and possibly harm me. I ran to my office and called the sheriff's department, and explained to the investigator what had happened.

He responded vigorously, "It doesn't take a rocket scientist to figure out that someone is following you. Get out of Rapidan immediately and come back to Culpeper. Call me when you get back."

I agreed, struggling to keep focused and cool. I ran out to my gray Subaru, and had barely started the long seven-mile drive when suddenly the same maroon pick-up truck loomed behind me. Muscles tense, I memorized the license plate. I started driving very carefully, even slowing down, drawing on my inner strength. The truck clung to my bumper. The image of the driver was clearly reflected in my rear-view mirror: a white man in his twenties, wearing metallic sunglasses, coolly drinking something out of a cup. At times, he wove back and forth in his lane, acting out of control. When he did this, I drove more slowly and steadily, not speeding at all because my instincts told me he wanted me to panic and crash my car.

The cruel man and I continued this odd dance for three, immensely long miles: he solidly on my bumper, I possessed by a strange quietness that encouraged me to drive carefully.

When I got to the Route 29 overpass near Culpeper, he drove off the other way. The confrontation was over. Sweating, I reached over to pet Bear affectionately. Poor Pogo still hid on the floor.

When I reached my apartment, I shakily called the sheriff's department and we set up an appointment to meet the next day with an investigator. The rest of the day I sat enveloped by a cocoon of thankfulness for my military father and his example of coolness under pressure. Day after day I had watched him leave for work in his flight uniform, unflinching, even though he always faced danger in those giant B-47s. Yet realistically I could only see thunderclouds and a giant, raging storm ahead in my life. That day had been a denouement, a turning point: I had finally learned what was happening. It seemed that men had been hired to harm me.

Unexpected turns of events were also part of Jeanne's life. One day Jeanne was sitting in her study when a servant came to announce that a young nun had come calling, begging for a chance to speak to her. Jeanne looked up, surprised at the unexpected visit. She said, "Please show her in."

Soon Jeanne heard the gentle rustle of black robes as a young woman came in and sat down. Her eyes were red from crying. Jeanne leaned forward, and taking the obviously unhappy nun's hands, she said gently, "What can I do for you?" As she looked at the nun's steady gray eyes, she noted the beauty of the nun's unflawed skin and her sweet smile.

"Madame, it is the Bishop's assistant. He keeps asking me to visit him. And when I have gone out of obedience to my superior, he wants something from me I cannot give." The nun leaned over and started weeping. "I wish to be obedient to my order but I can't go on with this tension."

"Of course you can't!" Jeanne's eyes flared with anger. "I will talk to the bishop about this immediately. This will stop."

The grateful nun nodded with the beginning of a sense of peace. Jeanne gathered her hat and belongings and marched out with her to get this problem solved. Jeanne thought to herself, *I will confront this evil today!*

I knew the decisions I was making would form my character. I felt that I should remain and fight, trusting that God would grant me a strong mind and a will to do so. In awe, I recognized the peace I felt during the road confrontation as a gift from God.

Then more crimes happened. My lawyer's office was broken into. Before church services one Sunday, a tall man confronted me, yelling at me to not report anymore of this, and only leaving when a vestry member courageously walked over to us, firmly telling him to leave.

What was I to do? I understood how lepers and homeless persons must feel, forced out of normal society into insecure living situations. Would I ever find stability again?

How had I survived my own beloved Alaska? On a dark, winter, Alaskan afternoon, I had trudged out of Taylor Junior High School and immediately felt the wind tearing at me—pushing against me, turning me around. How would I get home? How can I push against this force? Could I make it to safety?

I struggled towards home, nearly bent over. This wind, my dancing partner, this immense raw power, led me in a grand allegro, pushing me along, blowing where she willed. The high-pitched shriek of the wind tolled in my ears. Was this nature screaming in anguish? Was she moaning and crying? In my all-encompassing numbingly cold cocoon, all I could hear was the world lost in dissonance.

My developing personal theology shaped the way I responded to the terrifying situation in which now I found myself in Virginia. One of Guyon's main ideas is that suffering is to be understood as a time of spiritual purification. When the pain about my situation became overwhelming, I turned to Madame Guyon for strength and consolation. Every evening I would curl up in bed, after putting on my peach-colored running clothes. I comforted myself by looking at Pogo and Bear peacefully sleeping on the floor. Then I avidly read all of Guyon's books, digesting them from beginning to end. I lost myself in her life when mine was too dreadful even to contemplate.

Guyon expressed the intellectual side of her personality in an era when women didn't do this. She sought knowledge openly, as well as developing her spiritual qualities in prayer and contemplation. She sought to be obedient to God, even when her Christian convictions came into direct conflict with her personal desires. She experienced God as an intimate, loving power in her life.

What happened next to Jeanne, I wondered late one night. Alone, widowed, struggling, yet still confronting corrupt authorities? The answer came as I continued to read her *Autobiography*.

Jeanne heard that her favorite priest, Father La Combe, was moving to Geneva to accept a position with the bishop there. She prayed about his departure, realizing that he mediated God's presence to her. Father La Combe told her of a nunnery near Geneva that could use the ministry of her presence, her love, and yes, her financial resources. After prayer and working this out with the Mother Superior of the nunnery, Jeanne and her daughter left for Geneva. "Just like that," I thought as I read it. How had she left everything behind that was familiar to her? But as I read on, I discovered that Jeanne found an intense, new life filled with both joy and persecutions in her new home. She reveled in the ministry and new people, though some responded to her with contempt. Jeanne continued with her ministry, though, and decided to write a book to help abused women. She wrote her book quickly, calling it *A Short and Easy Method of Prayer*. But the Bishop of Paris heard about the book and a great controversy grew. The gossip started, "How could a woman write a book? God would never reveal anything to a woman! This was preposterous. In fact, this was heresy. Everyone knew a woman could not be a theologian or a priest. Why, Jeanne Guyon was a witch! She should be burned at the stake!"

And one sad day, the church authorities showed up at her door and arrested her, accusing her of immoral behavior with Father La Combe and with the heresy of being a witch. Jeanne's half-brother testified against her. They locked Jeanne up in a nunnery, forcing her to live in an unventilated room without windows for ten months.

I ached with pain for her. Separated from her daughter, alone, and sick: despite all this, Jeanne steadfastly denied the charges of immorality and also asserted that God did indeed inspire her thoughts for the book. Finally, the authorities under the orders of King Louis XIV released her for lack of evidence. Many hoped that Jeanne would no longer speak about God, but of course, they were wrong about that. Jeanne lived for God and loved God and her words continued to flow freely.

When I read Madame Guyon's *Autobiography*, I thought, this is a real woman, a passionate, intelligent woman who sought an intense intimacy with God. In many ways, Guyon had known all that life offers, not flinching from any experience or any challenging truth. I thought as I read her, *Heidegger said we are afraid of the uncanniness of life: the shocking truth that we exist at all. Guyon faced into the uncanniness, celebrating it, loving it, dancing under the passion of Being itself.* And as I read, glancing down at my friendly dogs, I felt renewed strength flowing into my being. Life, the mystery, the intensity, the marvelous dance is to be welcomed and adored, even when life comes offering crimes and trouble. Look underneath this shallow level, I thought, and see the divine realities, the holiness and sacredness of our lives. I thought: *every step I take scalds me with living holiness.* Our lives, all lives, are lived in this holy cauldron. Welcome the uncanniness and love the hardships. Guyon had and so would I, I asserted.

How to fight ethically was the deep issue for me. Should I remain quiet about the harassment or speak up? And the hardest decision was, should I arm myself? The situation became clearly defined when I struggled over whether to accept a weapon from Dave, a talented photographer who regularly came to the church. I realized that the moment of decision had arrived. I could no longer avoid the fact that persons in my community meant harm against me. Was if better for me to declare myself a pacifist ready to accept death instead of defending myself, or to arm myself?

In order to answer these interior questions for myself, I thought about other women who had been stalked. Crazed men became obsessed with them and frequently killed these women in their own homes. What would I model for others if I turned down the offer of this gun? Would they see weakness, vulnerability, and unrealistic ideas of divine protection? I believed that the innate sacredness of life itself demands that we do all in our power to live life deeply and passionately. This would not be in harmony with accepting injury or death from sick persons who wished me ill. I breathed deeply, trying to draw on an inner strength, and said to Dave, "Yes. I will accept your offer of a gun."

This was the turning point for me when I symbolically said a resounding yes to life and to love, when I started to fight, knowing that I was willing to learn to shoot and to defend myself, if needed.

And so it was that one day, Dave gave me a cold, shiny handgun. Early the next morning, a sheriff's deputy taught me how to handle the gun safely. And the next day, I stood on a parishioner's farm, and taking the gun, I fearfully aimed at the target, and pulled the trigger. The immense noise of a handgun exploding unnerved me, but I shot again and again until I knew how to handle the gun. Yet I continued to experience qualms about this course of action. Good grief, I would think, remembering my quiet mystical studies reading Jeanne Guyon, St. Augustine, and Catherine of Siena, how could centering on these spiritual writers carry me to a place where I would be practicing with a gun? But even during that week of practice, I read in the *Washington Post* about a woman in Virginia who was murdered by a stalker who broke into her home. Women must protect themselves from crazy men, I decided.

It was March 3, 1994, that I went to the Rapidan house to feed the animals, accompanied by a neighbor. She noticed something strange in my kitchen, and pointed at my mixer: "Look at those cards leaning against that. Someone has put them there." I picked up the cards and they read in this order, "wood" "to wound" "to lower" "to finish" "bench" "to acquire" "work."

When I reported this to the sheriff's department, the investigators agreed that these cards represented a threat of wounding or finishing me off in the woods. The cards used were the French language flashcards I was using to prepare for my Ph.D. language tests.

I felt increasingly shaken up. I had no desire to be hurt, raped, or killed. What was I to do? The sheriff's department asked me never to be alone at the churches anymore, advice that I carefully followed. The image of being attacked in the woods was one that could easily become reality among the large trees that surrounded the Rapidan house.

As the harassment increased, so did community tensions and criticism of my values about racial relations. One day a neighbor strode into Christ Church to meet Darlene, who was waiting for her. She held an old, beat-up pair of men's work boots, handed them to Darlene with a hard look of satisfaction on her face, saying, "Give these to your colored man." "Oh, yes," said Darlene with a triumphant tone in her voice, "He will love these." I stood there, dumbfounded at the obvious feeling of ownership in her phrase "your colored man" when Darlene turned to me and said breezily, "Nancy, have you ever seen the lynching tree in Brandy Station?" I mutely shook my head. "Right on the other side of Route 29, that highway those New York Jews built so they could drive to Florida. Yep, that big tree still stands, a monument to when we knew how to handle our problems." Without waiting for a reply, they turned, leaving the church. I sat down, my knees shaking, horrified at the venom in their voices. Where was the warm, supportive community that I thought was here? Why were they making these horrendous racial slurs?

I wrote about this mixing of normal and bizarre experiences in my journal:

"How did this bizarre journey start? The beginning was a dissonant series of events. My dog Pogo barking on the phone message, Bear let loose, announced the arrival of evil. I had a long series of days of peace reading the saints and then broken dishes, destroyed doors, tough deputies. A rhythmic series of events including odd, bizarre, grotesque, and weird elements. I, who had never even liked thriller movies, who struggled to keep things normal and satisfying. Days streaming with peace and joy (*then a violent phone call*) driving by the Blue Ridge (*now your phone wire cut*) Mountains, giving piano lessons (*Help me, help me, help me, I begged over and over again to Bishop Lee and Sheriff Peters*), what shall I make for dinner, what is on sale (*will the dogs be there—who broke the seat belt?*)."

The horror, the desolating sacrilege—I was being suffocated in a bag of evil, unable to come up to feel the goodness, the godness, anymore, only oppressive evil. Was God stronger than this situation? My faith was being tested in a way I could never have predicted. And yet . . . And yet . . . I believed in God and the divine spirit.

What was this encounter with God like? The Sun blinded me, momentarily causing me to stagger like a newborn thoroughbred learning to walk. My head swam in an absolute darkness. The Sun, our dark God, our fearsome Father, our distant Patriarch, set us ablaze, left us to struggle in this encounter with the Orb. I tried to stand up straight in the intensity but stopped. Would I be crushed, annihilated in this encounter? Or would I brush against pure, divine gold? My heart failed me, doubting; I staggered, fell prostrate. Yet the Sun abided, unblinking.

Then the miracle happens. Melted, warm, gorgeous gold flows everywhere. Melted gold, touching our sad hands, strengthening our listless fingers. We reach for it and find the gold everywhere. Wisdom crying in the streets and we listen not until we see the gold swimming and we run to it and it is gone and crying we turn and see a mystery, a Man of Gold reaching out to us, without a word, and crying also until our eyes meet and we join together in safety.

Whom should I trust? My lawyer finally said to me, "All of these people with their sweet, smiling faces aren't to be trusted. We need to hire a private investigator." I numbly agreed. What would the future hold, I pondered yet again. I hoped Madame Guyon was right and that help would arrive to arrest this flood of terrorizing events.

But how to dance with God in this? How would this happen? The idea of the music of God entranced me. Worshiping prayer was like a divine dance. Dancing through life, I had visited prisons and hospitals and seen downtrodden inmates. And now as we danced, sweeping, turning, I saw angry men, militia men, calling me, stealing my dogs, chasing my car. Do I stop the dance with the divine? No. For now I sensed the utter passion of God towards me. What was it that Jeanne Guyon had said? That God was her Beloved. And this Beloved was everything to me. Let the dance continue!

twelve   F I G H T I N G   B A C K

But for those who give themselves up to
God without any reserve, and who are willing
with all their hearts to be the plaything of
providence without restriction or reserve—
ah, as for those, they are assuredly a spectacle
for God, for angels, and for men: for God,
of glory, by the conformity with Jesus Christ;
for angels, of joy; and for men, of cruelty
and disgrace.

—Jeanne Guyon, *Autobiography*

"One of your vestry members said his greatest sexual fantasy was to make love to an angel. He said he thought that would be the ultimate high—to have sexual intercourse with an angel." A feeling of shock and revulsion flowed through my body as the sheriff's investigator reported this to me. The investigator continued, "I've never heard anyone say anything like that. But to say that to criminal investigators is even weirder. This man's conversation was very strange. You have to be very careful. With your blonde hair and blue eyes, in your clergy robes I think you could look like an angel."

I sat, frozen. Burglaries for money at least made sense. But I was dealing with a parishioner on my vestry who had some power over my life, telling sheriff's department officials that he wanted sex with angels.

On the way back to the apartment, I hummed a spiritual song I had heard recently, "Jesus' blood never failed me yet." The instant I opened the apartment door I saw that someone had trashed my home again. A window had been forcibly opened. And the VCR, which was actually an investigative camera taking pictures of the apartment, was now broken with the tape cut and hanging out. My belongings had been shoved off tables and my books thrown around. As I inspected the destroyed camera, I felt that the criminals were mocking this method of detection. I called up the sheriff's investigator at home, distressed that this plan too had failed. He said, softly, "Nothing works." I stood rigidly, clinging to the phone.

Once again, I turned to Jeanne's life for consolation. When all had appeared lost to Guyon, a powerful defender, Archbishop Francois Fénelon, arose to help her. She had met this distinguished church leader one afternoon at a small reception in Paris. The archbishop had walked over to meet her, saying with concern, "Are you the celebrated Madame Guyon?" They talked at length about her difficult incarceration.

Jeanne later wrote in her *Autobiography* that "it seems to me that my soul has perfect rapport with him . . ."[7] Fénelon became fascinated with her theology, seeking her out frequently to discuss religious matters. They met and discussed the Spirit as the passionate lover of our souls.

But not for long did Jeanne's life remain at peace.

A few months later, Jeanne heard the news: the authorities were after her again. Her soul screamed in anguish. Running for her room, pushing everything away, she reached for a few belongings. She fled for the only sanctuary she knew, a poor section of Paris. Let them leave me alone, she prayed over and over again.

Jeanne found a small basement apartment and took new names for herself and a loyal friend. They stayed inside day and night, creeping outside once a week for food and a quick Mass at the Cathedral of Notre Dame. She prayed over and over again, "Please, God, I can't stand another incarceration. Please, please, protect me."

And I sadly wondered, how much suffering would God allow? Would they find her? Jeanne lived in constant fear and terror. She started reading the words of her friend, Archbishop Fénelon, on how to trust in God during suffering. Now, in turn, I too turned to this famous author for help.

Those days living in my own dark basement, I read avidly how Fénelon said we are to handle the loss of our reputation and severe disappointment. Fénelon says that God takes away from us our own wisdom, our own glory, our own interest, our own wills, and makes us content with the sight of our own frailty. He says that God makes us feel more afraid of disobedience to the divine than shame and punishment. I felt nurtured by his words and strove, however feebly, to live up to the example he set for me. Yearn for obedience to God, I heard through his words, and fear not what the world can do to you.

On March 24, 1994, I walked out to my car on my way to a morning swim. As I settled into the driver's seat, I felt my determination rising, and thought to myself, I will survive this. Then I saw them, waiting, like little demons lined up on my dashboard. More language cards. The words read this time: "Sweet" "to bare" "to lower" "opportunity." My whole being cried out for release from this hell. Who placed them here? When? I yearned to resume a safe and normal life. Picking up the cards, I frantically thought, what is he trying to say now?

Instead of my needed exercise at the pool, I drove to the sheriff's department, feeling claustrophobic. "What do they mean?" I said, my voice trembling, begging for words of assurance but knowing all he could give was his interpretation. Phil grimaced, feeling as disgusted as I did. "Probably, it is, 'Sweet, I want an opportunity to bare and lower you. To rape you.'"

Looking around at his cluttered office, I grimly gave the cards to him. I saw in his eyes that he felt as bad as I did. He waited and then said, "I'm getting lots of weird phone calls now. Every evening two or three times, someone calls, listens on the line, waits, and then hangs up. My wife is getting them also."

"I still get weird phone calls every day," I said, dismayed at how despairing I felt about all of this.

That's all he said. Someone is holding all of us hostage, I thought. When will all of this end?

I called Michael later that day. His voice sounded worried as he said, "The language cards lined up would be like something that would happen in my comic book, *Star Struck*. I think he is playing a very weird game here. But we don't know how violent he can get."

Phil brought two experts in to look at my apartment. They discovered that my apartment phone was tapped. In a discouraging meeting, the investigators told me to discuss nothing confidential on the phone anymore.

Phil arranged for two Virginia State Police investigators to help. We met with them and they set up surveillance cameras at the Rapidan home, which was still regularly being maliciously vandalized. One of the first times they came back to check the cameras, the policemen said in surprise: "There is nothing on this film. You've been here, haven't you?"

"Every few days I came in with a parishioner to feed the outside animals and pick up clothes."

"So at the very least, you should have been on this film. Either they weren't working correctly—which has never happened before—or they have been tampered with. These people harassing you must be real professionals to know how to do this."

Phil and the other investigators discussed with me the status of the investigation. The Virginia State Police investigators had additional plans to try to apprehend these criminals, if Sheriff Peters would approve. They named two male parishioners who they thought were behind this, either together or individually. I felt a cold, numbing chill when I heard the news. I also felt a deep appreciation for the efforts of these policemen; I knew they cared about my well-being. But I had also begun to wonder about leaks of information from the sheriff's department to the harassers.

A few days later, my lawyer asked me to meet with him. Seeing him, I felt reassured, but his words chilled my spirit.

"Nancy, two times last night the motion lights came on. Someone was here. I kept trying to see who it was but I was unsuccessful. Larry Peters, the private investigator, will be here later today. Why don't we all meet?" We agreed on this. He continued, "I've been around awhile, Nancy. I have never before felt such a spirit of evil. When the lights came on, I sat straight up in bed, terrified." I said quietly, yes, I knew what he was talking about.

Mr. Peters quickly gained my confidence with his intelligent ideas about what was going on and how it was accomplished. After the tour of Rapidan, he said with understanding, "It is easy to see why they are not getting caught. Look at your church and your home: where you live and work is down near the river level. I guarantee you, they can easily see all of your movements from their homes. This situation isn't good for you at all."

I felt a sad discouragement settle on me. How much more bad news could I endure?

Larry looked at me with gentle compassion. "You didn't know that people who went to church behaved like this, did you?"

"No," I said softly. "The whole point of Christianity is to love God and your neighbor." Responding to his sympathy, I continued, "Why do they come to church? Why do they bother with church if they aren't interested in being Christians?"

My question lingered in the air, reverberating in harmony with my anguished soul.

"Control," he said. "They want to control the community and you are an easy target out there living alone."

I responded, "Thankfully this hasn't destroyed my faith. Actually I've never felt closer to God. But this is so painful. I used to trust these people."

"They are out to get you," he said. "Don't forget that. And don't *ever* leave those dogs alone. If you do, one day you'll come home to their dead bodies, I promise you."

The day after Easter, April 3, 1994, someone left more cards, eerily lined up on my car dashboard. They read: "Enough"

"Choose" "Await violence." Easter Monday, I thought. As we celebrate the resurrection of Jesus, I hear from this crazy mind who designs this. Extreme anger filled me: yes, I said to myself. My harassers will choose. They should make up their mind what they are going to do and do it. As for me, I will trust in God and I will not run.

My whole being cried out for relief from this situation.

The investigator and I both believed that this crisis finally needed to be made public. We chose one Sunday in spring, April 24, 1994, during which Phil would speak to the Rapidan church. I had hoped with all of my heart that this could have been quietly solved and the perpetrator receive the help he so desperately needed. I put on my priestly robes and prayed for peace.

During the announcement time, I stood up and said, "I have been struggling with a very bad situation for several months now. Today a sheriff's investigator has come to talk to you about it."

Phil walked up to the front of the church, telling people a general history of what had been happening. Phil mentioned the stolen underwear, as well as the burglarized homes and offices. Then he said, "I count at least thirteen felonies that have been committed. I need your help solving this. If you know anything, please call me or the sheriff's department. I would appreciate your help."

A stunned silence followed his talk, and then a few questions were asked. An older woman asked forthrightly, "Can you guarantee that Reverend James will be safe?"

Phil paused, and then said, "No, I can't."

A shocked silence followed. I noticed the beautiful light streaming through the Tiffany stained glass windows. Phil and his family left the church, as I began to celebrate the eucharist.

On April 25, 1994, I walked to a meeting with a commonwealth's attorney, aghast at how the authorities could let this go on so long. I entered the small, ordinary office, only a floor below where my own office with the state government had been. The commonwealth's attorney asked me what personal items had been taken from me. I described pajamas, underwear, and my favorite jewelry, such as my pairs of sapphire and pearl earrings. He looked at me thoughtfully and said, "Probably this man has a shrine to you somewhere." The image the attorney described revolted me: a place where this man kept pictures and personal belongings of mine, a place which fed his dark fantasies. It was a perfect image of hell. What did he do in this demonic place decorated with my personal belongings? Did he plan the sick crimes he committed? As I reflected on this, I feared for other women: how many more would go through the agony I was experiencing? I yearned for freedom from this living nightmare.

I felt a corresponding hunger for a deeper closeness for God as I imagined this evil scene. God upheld women throughout the Bible, with women being the first to witness the resurrection of Jesus Christ. I too wanted to be one of the faithful women who clung to him, no matter the cost. My favorite story in the gospels was the loving woman who came to wash Jesus' feet, placing costly oil on his dry, dusty feet. She loved him so much that she took her long hair and wiped away the oil with it, a small act of personal devotion. I too wanted to love God and fulfill what work the Spirit gave me to do.

I knew this required my personal commitment and abandonment to God. Guyon had written about Mary saying that she too had to consent to her role in salvation history. Guyon wrote, "Did not the angel ask the consent of Mary to be the mother of the Word?"[8]

I felt good on a beautiful, spring day, five days following Phil's talk to the church. A Christ Church member had planned a softball practice at a Culpeper park. The blossoms on the trees flashed pink. The day was April 29, 1994, the day on the church calendar set aside to remember Catherine of Siena. I thought of her gentle words of comfort as she encouraged people to love honorably and decently, to have compassion for others, to care for one's neighbors as well as to seek

108

God. Another ball went whizzing by me, but I laughed with joy. Following the practice I romped with my dogs and watched a glorious sunset. This Catherine of Siena day had been a lovely day.

Back at my apartment, I checked my phone messages at both churches. At Christ Church, the message was of a man's ugly voice saying angrily, "The Devil will win!" Quickly I called the phone operator: "I have just received a harassing phone message. I have to be able to do something!" It had been such a lovely day and now, *The Devil will win,* in this ugly, rasping voice. Hell, no, I thought. The operator responded, "Go quickly to the phone where it was received. Dial *69 and if no other calls have come in, the call will be traced."

Walking into that darkened church at 10:30 P.M. took more courage than I knew I had. What if I had been followed? What if this were a setup? But I knew that I could endure no more and was willing to take risks—serious risks, if necessary. I jumped and startled at every sound—dogs barking, cows mooing, strange creaks. I couldn't see anything and knew I might walk into a vicious man at any second and be defenseless. But my soul screamed out for justice.

I walked down the long, gravel driveway, up the front porch, and unlocked the door. The only light I had was from the stars. Entering the dark building, I found the light switch in the Christ Church parish hall and turned it on. I was relieved to see I was alone. Running into my office, I picked up the phone and dialed the prescribed numbers. Then I heard a recording, "You have successfully traced this number. Contact us in normal working hours for more information." I ran back to the car, noticing how beautiful the stars were.

The next working day, I contacted the appropriate state agency and was told they would give the name to a law enforcement official. Phil contacted them and was given a name we did not recognize. Now, I thought, we have the names of two harassers: the name of the truck owner from the license plate and this name. Thank God!

The next incident came soon after. The Emmanuel altar had the ancient words, "I am the Bread of Life" in carved wood letters on it. The following Sunday, I, along with a member of the altar guild, discovered most of the letters broken off. Some of the letters lay on the floor, while others had disappeared. I felt breathless at this attack on the holy altar of God.

I thought of the large earthquake we had experienced in Fairbanks, Alaska, when I was a child. I had been lying in my bed on a Saturday morning, sleeping in late with my friend Karen Tucker, who had spent the night. The bed started shaking, and I sleepily said, "Stop it, Karen," thinking she was trying to wake me up. I heard her voice from the other side of the room saying with fright, "That's not me, Nancy." Then I heard my dad yell, "Nancy! Karen! Get outside fast!" Obedient girls, we ran for the front door, the ground starting to shake harder and harder. My father was trying to get Tim out of his basement room. My mother already stood outside, still holding her breakfast toast, but calling for my brother Tim in anguished tones. Then as I turned to look out at the field across the street from our house, I watched the ground with total amazement and awe, rising and falling like ocean waves traveling past our house. The nurturing, strong earth was transformed into a wild, ecstatic force of immense power, uncontrollable, raging, and tearing the very land apart. As the waves of land approached, I faintly heard my mother continuing to cry, "Tim! Tim!" He had not made it out of the basement yet: her voice sounded a mother's love violently torn out of her heart—her beloved child—where was he? I watched the spectacle of it all, the earth gone mad, or maybe just the quiet earth revealing its true, tempestuous nature, transforming our carefully cultivated lawn grass into giant mounds of rich dirt, left in chaotic clumps.

Then the earth stopped moving and an eerie quiet fell upon us. Tim emerged from the basement safely, my family stood together, not moving or saying anything. Silence, quiet, lull, a hushed world. But we still heard resonating in us the power of nature, gently chiding us for not knowing that all of our efforts to make life understandable and predictable are sheer foolishness.

The stillness engulfed our world. Slowly I became aware that our neighboring families were also hanging together, vainly seeking a familiar comfort or solace. But we still stood, the eeriness clinging to us like icicles hanging on a tree: frozen, solid, unmoving. Then slowly, gradually, we dispersed, going back inside, trying to regain a routine sense of life. But the eerie icicles continued to cling. Days of aftershocks reminded us that the majestic earth moves and lives, a magnificent, brutal force.

All of the harassing events affected me like that earthquake moving through my life: the routine and normal expectations of settled existence were destroyed like bland lawn grass now violently changed into huge, new constellations of rich, life-giving earth.

But as to personal ill treatments, I have

felt bound to sacrifice them, to sanctify them

by a profound silence . . .

—Jeanne Guyon, *Autobiography*

Then the authorities came to arrest Jeanne again. It was the look in their eyes that terrified her. A hard malicious glow enveloped their faces. She thought, my God, what do I face—rapes, beatings? They grabbed her as her beloved servant started screaming. She reached out frantically for this friend. My God, help us. She saw her friend knocked to the ground and heard more screaming, then she realized it was her own screaming, screaming not only for her plight but for her friend—stop—*leave her alone—don't touch her* and then the nightmare started. She disconnected with reality—as if she were floating over the violent situation—she saw them slap the sobbing woman, she felt her stomach flattened under repeated blows and she thought, *This will happen, I cannot stop it.* But the odd, high pitched screaming continued and intellectually she knew someone was begging for help. That someone was herself. A strange calm descended and she felt the blows but a deadly quiet reigned within her soul. Jeanne's second incarceration had started with her arrest on December 27, 1695, ordered directly by Bishop Bossuet and Louis XIV, king of France.

When I was a child, my family moved frequently, whenever my father received new military orders. My parents would put us children in whatever latest car they had, once a Thunderbird and another time a GTO. Off we would roar, heading for another state and a new life. I sat in the back seat, loaded down with maps that I picked up every time we stopped for gas. I waited for my signal to help, when my dad would say solemnly, "I need a navigator." Exceedingly proud that I had been chosen for this crucial role instead of my two older brothers, with great self-importance I unfolded my state map of Georgia or Florida or Kansas or whatever state we were in. After careful study, I announced, "In twelve miles we get to the town of Gainesville." Or, "We are coming to a national park in twenty-three miles."

But my favorite times traveling as a family were when my father allowed me to navigate us to the beaches. Georgia and Florida beaches were our favorites. As soon as he parked the car, we ran to put on our swimming suits. All of us were capable swimmers, yet after we were all decked out in swimming gear, my father would nonetheless greet us at the shower rooms with stern warnings about possible undertow in the area. "The undertow is a force that can pull you out and you won't be able to swim against it. *Don't go past the designated area,*" he commanded with all of the force of a military officer. I wondered about this unseen, powerful undercurrent: a strong, silent force that carries you into oblivion, into a space where you won't exist. The undertow: a danger to euphoric kids splashing in the gorgeous ocean, the waves rhythmically crashing, the sun shining. And yet: an undercurrent that harmed, that could drag innocent children away. Few words frightened me as much as *the undertow*.

One sad morning, as I again struggled with what to do about the harassment, I thought: I have been caught in a social undertow. The designated area for a woman was being married, caring for her family. But to be a divorced, female Episcopal priest was beyond the pale for many in this rural society.

The more determined I became to survive this, however, the more intense became the crimes. On June 2, 1994, a vestry meeting was scheduled at Emmanuel Church, Rapidan. On my way to the meeting, I briefly stopped at the church house to feed my outside cats. I pulled into my driveway and saw a middle-aged man wearing a pink shirt walking around my house with a white Chevrolet pick-up truck parked next to the yard. I rapidly wrote down the license plate number from the safety of my car.

"Get out of here!" I yelled, filled with outrage.

The man smiled maliciously. Then he got into his pick-up truck, quickly backing it up so I was blocked in my driveway. Instantly my outrage changed into fear, with this dreadful ominous atmosphere engulfing me. Grasping my gear shift, I quickly activated the four-wheel drive function on my Subaru. He walked directly in front of my car and stood leering at me. Jerking my wheel, I drove my car towards him—he jumped out of the way—and then I drove directly across the field. Gunning the engine, I headed across the field until I could safely turn onto the street. I sped to the church, where I saw vestry members entering for the scheduled meeting. I sat in the car, taking deep breaths, trying to calm down. I remembered one of my friends say, "Never let them see you sweat." When I felt sufficiently composed, I entered the church parish hall, and asked, "How are you all doing?"

The irritating harassment was like mosquitoes endlessly buzzing around me. I longed to focus my attention back on the sublime mystics. In Alaska the mosquitoes buzzed furiously in the height of the summer. What a paradox! The summer reigned sublime, in glorious ecstasy, in heights of splendor. Then the irritating insects landed, attracting our distracted attention. Wipe them off quickly; even a second distracted from the grandeur of the eternal, midnight Sun was a sorrow, a wasted moment.

The harassment intensified. On June 15, 1994, I told a parishioner, Lauren, that I would teach her daughter a piano lesson at my house in Rapidan later in the day. I pulled into the long driveway about fifteen minutes before they were to arrive. Lauren and her daughter were late for our appointed time. Five minutes went by, then ten minutes, twenty minutes. I anxiously listened to the clock ticking. I became increasingly uneasy at being alone in the house. This wasn't like Lauren: where was she? I paced around the large home. Was it safe for me to be here? Where was Lauren, I fretted. Forty minutes late . . . Forty-five . . .

Then I heard it. A long, low whistle outside close to my house, sounding like a subtle signal. No car had driven down my long driveway: it wasn't Lauren. I sensed danger. But I felt something like an aura of protection descend upon me, telling me precisely what to do. Instinctively I recognized that I had to act decisively and quickly, or I would be hurt.

I sensed the order: *Get Pogo inside,* and I obeyed. Then I locked the kitchen door, putting the chain on it. The next internal command came: *Close the living room window.* Quickly I walked into the living room, and firmly pushed it shut. *Get near the phone and wait.* For what, I wondered. My only phone was in the kitchen so I strode towards the kitchen phone, located immediately next to the back door. A tense Pogo stood beside me, looking like a furry ball of dread. Bear ran frantically from room to room, trying to guard us all. And then I heard them: two men walking up to the door. They started banging on my back door. "Let us in," they yelled. "Now. Let us in." I dialed 911 and waited for an answer. Hoping to stall for time, I said to them through the locked door, "Who are you?" Laughing maliciously they answered, "We are the enforcers." "Yes, the insurance enforcers," the other echoed. "We need to get in. Open the door now." I screamed at them, "Go away." They started pounding with increasing force and then rattling the door. I felt totally afraid, frozen in this moment of terror. As the old, wooden door shook, they yelled again, "WE NEED TO GET IN." I stood, terrified, waiting for someone to answer at 911.

A female dispatcher finally answered. I said, "Give me the Culpeper Sheriff's Department immediately. This is an emergency. Two men are trying to get in my door right now." To my shock she responded, "Your phone number shows that you need the Madison County Sheriff's Department." "No," I said. "I live in Culpeper County and I need that sheriff's department." I was aware that my 672 phone number was frequently used in Madison County and only a few Rapidan residents had it in Culpeper County. But the obstinate dispatcher continued, "You need Madison County Sheriff's Department." I watched my door shake and feared it would give way any moment. I frantically wondered how much longer it would hold against their violence. I yelled, "Give me the Culpeper County Sheriff's Department now!" Her curt voice responded, "No." I yelled again as I watched the door heave to and fro, "The men are breaking in right now. Give me the Culpeper County Sheriff's Department." The dispatcher hung up on me and the next voice I heard said, "Madison County Sheriff's Department." At that moment, the door stopped shaking and I heard the men start walking away, still talking loudly. I said, "This is Nancy James. I am in an emergency. I need the Culpeper County Sheriff's Department." The deputy responded, "I've heard about your situation. They've given you the wrong sheriff's department. Let me connect you." I now heard the men walking away, laughing loudly and eerily. Then they connected me with the Culpeper County Sheriff's Department, a man promptly said, "We are on our way." I walked over and got a glass of water, drinking it shakily, my legs trembling.

About ten minutes later, the sheriff's investigator came running up to my door. I rushed out to meet him, saying, "Two men were here trying to get in my kitchen door."

Phil stopped cold, putting his hand over his face, looking frightened. "That's what we've been afraid would happen."

"Phil, don't you understand?" I confronted him. "These rich people out here have hired people to do this. We've got to do something. They are getting away with this!"

His words stumbled out quickly, full of despair. "They decided to use their money to get rid of you."

The next day as I dressed, I attempted to shake off my numbing despair. Then I had a funny memory of laughing wildly with Tim and Patrick many years earlier, a memory that penetrated through my rapidly accumulating layers of discouragement. I remembered that seminary sermon about Jesus' temptations in the wilderness: "Those dull, dry days," the preacher declared. My sweet brother Tim had later finished, "Yes, those long, dry, *boring* days when Evil Incarnate appears to us." Or, "Those long boring days . . ." I had finished, "when Satan himself stands before you in the desert." "Those dry, dull days . . ." Patrick had laughingly interjected, "when Evil Itself interrogates you about your life." Evil was now definitely confronting and questioning me about my very existence and what was I to do? Run in fear and trembling? Hell, no, I thought. Socrates said you never run from evil; it will just turn and chase you. I picked up my purse, said a prayer, and off I went to chastise whatever office was responsible for that incredible telephone dispatcher. When Evil confronts, I thought, stand tall, and wait for the strength of God. Let Satan himself stand before me; I was not running. Somehow I had learned that when terror hits, the power of goodness is always stronger. My mind and spirit refreshed by the lighthearted memory of good times with Tim and Patrick, I put my dogs in the car, and off I went for another day of battling for my very survival.

The harassment escalated. My lawyer called with reports of new criminal offenses at his law offices. My car was broken into and damage done to the interior. A vestry member now led another attempt at a meeting to have me fired, saying, "The only thing that will help this parish is getting a new pastor." Once again, the motion failed.

All the bizarre events made me reflect on my first unusual experiences in Alaska. When we drove from Fairbanks to Anchorage I looked back to see the mountains, rolling and picturesque. The immense beauty dazzled us, strong trees, radiant light, infinite skies. With high spirits we looked forward to the experience of riding horses through this strange, unique territory. Yet somehow, the ghosts of the pioneers, the sourdoughs, called to us, reminding us of the immense danger in Alaska— the deadly cold, the steep ravines, the hungry, predatory animals. And I wondered, maybe danger and beauty are twins. Maybe to revel in the beauty, you have to face into the danger.

During the next weeks my lawyer and I spent time intensely lobbying Sheriff Peters to either arrest the suspects or let the Virginia State Police handle the case. The Virginia State Police had agreed to accept the responsibility for this criminal investigation but Sheriff Peters said he would never release jurisdiction. We continued to plead for justice.

One morning I walked into the church only to see Ted sitting in my office, waiting for me. I tingled with dread when I saw him. What else could I do? I had reported this to both the bishop and the sheriff's department. No one intervened.

Ted smiled at me. "I don't see why you won't cooperate with me. You have very special gifts that few persons have. You can preach excellently, play music, and write. Together we could be a good team."

I carefully stood up, reached for my purse and walked directly out to my car. Once in the car, I immediately locked the doors and drove out of the parking lot. But where would safety lie? Did Ted or someone else arrange to have someone waiting at my house? Was someone following me? I had to trust in God alone. And my life had become a sinking ship that could go down at any time. *Jesus' blood never failed me yet*, I hummed in an effort to comfort myself.

I went to stay at the home of another parishioner who had also suffered break-ins. We called the private investigator, Larry Peters. He came out the next day and found the freshly made path through the woods that the intruders had made. I could stand no more. My parishioner didn't deserve this harassment. I knew I was in a full-fledged crisis. Everywhere I tried to live attracted trouble. I had to think, I had to decide what to do. How would I survive? And once again when I needed a fresh input of strength, I remembered an experience in Alaska, my father's polar survival training.

One arctic evening my father showed his movies of flying over the polar cap, ice and snow extending for seeming endless miles, bright and white, with only the nose of the airplane breaking the brilliant white. My father talked occasionally of the polar survival training he would soon undergo because he spent hours flying over the North Pole and surrounding areas. Along with two other pilots, he would be dropped off in the cold Alaskan winter, with K rations and whatever gear they would have in a simulated plane crash. The group needed to prove their ability to survive in the extreme environment by burying themselves in the snow zipped up in their sleeping bags. My father jokingly said about the group ready to undergo this test, "We certainly hope the days that are chosen are warm ones!"

The three days arrived for their long, northern exposure. When my father left that morning, the thermometer read twenty-five degrees below zero. The temperature steadily dropped. The sun made a brief appearance about noon, with blackened skies enveloping us. Unbroken darkness and a still, deadly cold hovered around our house, intensifying our sad mood. My mother looked serious and bereft. We ate our dinner that evening with an air of concern hovering over all of us. My father was living outside *in this weather?* Why, it was thirty-five degrees below zero.

The three days dragged by interminably slow. I imagined him, zipped in his sleeping bag, buried in the snow. He had assured me that the blanket of snow would keep him warm and be his friendly life support in the desolate area in which they were to be dropped. But I wasn't so sure that snow would keep him warm enough.

119

Then my father reappeared, looking somehow saddened. He leaned down and kissed me. But I sensed a fresh sorrow within him. Later I overheard him telling my mother, "Bob went crazy out there. He crawled out of the snow and started walking around talking to himself. We heard him where we were still buried. I had to crawl out to help him. I tried to talk him back to reality and get him to bury himself again, but he wouldn't. Finally I had to radio someone to come pick him up."

I realized my father's empathy for his friend, seeing for the first time that when another person hurts, we hurt also. Our love for others binds us to them with very deep spiritual and emotional connections. Bob's troubles were shared by my father. I admired that as I grappled to understand these very deep issues of empathy and love. Yet at the time I felt mainly relief: my father was home again, out of that deadening cold.

During these episodes of harassment, I thought that if my father could survive three days in a bitter, cold Alaskan winter, I could stand this. And what was my friendly snow in this situation?

I was hemmed in and It (they made me into a Thing to be rid of) was getting closer. Everywhere I looked was Not Caring and Not Going to Help. It was like trying to walk on a greased mirror. Trying to get a footing, a place to stand, losing my balance again and again, not escaping from myself, catching glimpses of myself frightened beyond belief. Falling, I heard the church saying "we must be reasonable about this," and others saying, "it must be tough," and the man in the pink shirt leering at me. The terror of it—my ears buzzing with anxiety—my nerves ringing—my thoughts racing—how did this happen? Why won't anyone help?

Jesus' blood hasn't failed me yet.

I looked outside again and again for answers—bishops, detectives, parishioners, friends, yet the answers seemed to be only inside. How could I unlock them? I needed to make a real connection between my inner strength and the outer dangers. But what would mediate here? The patriarchy was dead and so were my illusions that others could save me. Salvation was from one source—the kingdom of heaven was from within.

I decided to go to Alaska, to go to where I had lived and think this through very carefully. I called about airplane tickets, ordered maps of the Alaska wilderness, and with great relief planned to visit the land of the midnight sun from July 18 to July 25, 1994. I felt nothing but peace as I planned this journey back to my spiritual roots in the northern land on the top of our planet.

fourteen ALASKA!

O my God, what pleasure to lose all

and quit all for you!

—Jeanne Guyon, *Autobiography*

The passionate goodness of life had been manifested to me as a child in Alaska. Now I was returning to Fairbanks to get back in touch with this sense of goodness and joy. Catherine of Siena called this the "same joy as the angels,"[9] when humanity touches the ultimate boundaries of the human spirit, only to sense a whole new world opening up to them. I had known this joy in Alaska and now returned to my childhood heritage, hoping to rediscover it. Memories and reflections flooded my mind as I flew from Washington, D.C., to Fairbanks, Alaska, in late July, 1994.

I had read in the Bible that God had made the greater light to rule the day and the lesser light to rule the night. But upon first moving to Fairbanks, Alaska, in my twelfth year, I discovered that this scripture wasn't true. For up there, it seems, God made the greater light to rule the spring and summer, and the lesser light to rule the fall and winter. They called this odd place the land of the midnight sun, the place where the sun never sets in the summer.

The greater light hung around for a much longer time than I had heard about in Sunday school in that routine place, that scheduled place, Georgia, where we had lived previously. Life was new, weird, odd, brilliant in Alaska. Gradually the initial fear we felt upon moving there turned to joy. I remember once flying to Seattle to see a dentist. The waitress said as she poured my mother's coffee, "So you live where the sun doesn't set. I don't think I could handle that." And I smiled my pre-teen smile, knowing that this life wasn't handled by us; it was given to us, a great gift, a gift of knowing that life was beyond our control but that that wasn't bad. Life was exploding up there, with bountiful goodness. But at the time I only said, "I like it up there."

For life beckoned in an interior, mysterious way in Alaska. The midnight sun seduced the earth into exploding with life. Ecstatically the world jumped into spring time. The snow melted, leaving streams of cool, refreshing water flowing through the open tundra. The temperature rose tentatively from forty below and crept up to the warm temperatures of thirty, forty, finally fifty or sixty degrees. Appreciating our freedom from the deathly cold, we ran all the way from school, sloshing through melting snow, jumping over puddles, our boots protecting us from the deep mud.

The sun presided elegantly in the summer. Every so often in the long, sun-filled evenings, my father would ask my mother, "Would you like to go see the bears tonight?" My mother would smile as if this were the best date in the world and would accept with pleasure. So after dinner we would pile in the car and drive out to the garbage dump, waiting for the arrival of the wild animals. And slowly the large, chubby bears arrived, their rolling gait most amusing, as they walked all over the small garbage dump, searching for their dinner. They soon covered that delectable garbage dump like children running for cookies, like fireflies buzzing in the darkened southern night, like Spanish moss clinging to the old trees in Savannah, like my heart clinging to the extraordinary beauty of Alaska and becoming one with its essence.

The bears sniffed out fresh delicacies, casually thrown out by the human community. First one bear waddled around, then another, and soon the entire dump was covered with bears, bears sniffing, bears looking, bears crawling, bears sitting back on their haunches and eating a particularly delicious treat. And my family sat in the car and giggled and smiled and chuckled at the sight of these beautiful creatures with their immense and frightening power, yet demonstrating their ability to enjoy the simple pleasures of life, such as this delectable pile of aging food that we humans with our short-sighted understanding of life had discarded. The bears ate and enjoyed themselves, while we humans delighted in watching their Bear Community having its nightly meal.

Winter came, though, with its burden of dark and snow. At midday, the sun appeared briefly on the horizon. The dark gathered us in, holding us close, as we struggled through the accumulating deep snow. This dangerous, twilight world smothered us with omnipresent cold, biting, bitter, and incredible cold.

One cold Saturday in this strange land we went to see the dogsled races. The dogs, in splendid physical shape, barked and jumped with joy. The human leader respected his highly competent pack of dogs, knowing their personalities and communicating in mysterious ways with them. All of us battled with the elements, wearing our parkas, watching the skies for signs of changing weather, but longing in our hearts to watch the dog team and the human merge as they raced around the track, heading for the goal. For the first time I understood the draw of throwing oneself into an activity with all of one's heart as I watched the sled team duel with the deep snow and rapidly changing winter weather.

The attitude of the day was utter reverence: reverence for the weather that could destroy us if we underestimated the power of fast blizzards; reverence for the force within the huskies that enabled them to run through the humongous drifts of snow; reverence for the native Alaskans who for generations had learned to live in harmony with this harsh environment. And, yes, reverence for humanity, knowing that we too participated in the Great Creator with our soul. Sometimes we held this inner force, this soul, in so much awe we did not name it at all, but just *knew* the Creator Spirit inside us. We humans gratefully participated in the mystery of the husky races, knowing that humanity is only one small part of the great, mysterious scheme of our universe that includes people, animals, and our beloved Earth.

We watched in wonder as the huskies ran. How would they react in the intense cold? In a snowdrift? In a blizzard? What would happen when the lead dog tires or the human becomes unfocused?

As the day progressed with each dogsled striving together with one soul, the real question became, how long can they stand the intimacy and unity of hearts working as a team, striving for oneness? The dogsled races dramatically broke us from our separated, mechanized existence, returning all of us to a primordial unity. The huskies' power combined with sheer strength of souls running and charging, the human watching and letting go of self-concern—they became one force. The dogs and leader surrendered their differentiation to join in a thundering One-ness, with flashes of fire in their eyes and the taste of glory in their hearts.

I felt as if I had seen life as it was before the fall into separation and disunity. It was as if life had whispered, *Stop and look. All the variegated forces around you are working together.* This revelation tantalized us; we wanted more and greater tastes of this unity.

And then the veil would fall again, shielding us from the vision of primordial oneness. Maybe it is God's mercy that knows our weak human frailties, sparing us from the sight of this passionate vision of unity. Our harmony with others inspires a powerful awe, humorously reminding us how little control we actually have. The problems of the postmodern world, such as alienation, the un-oneness, the nonself, the brittle lack of harmony, all glare in our minds. But in the dogsled races, we all mattered, and were one with matter, as if we climbed the Matterhorn together.

The Alaskan *pièce de résistance*, though, visited us at unforeseen magical moments, inviting our participation unexpectedly. One night a neighbor on the military base called us to say, "You need to go out and see them tonight," and we didn't need to ask, see what? We knew what she referred to by the awe in her voice. Them, the living force, the signs in the skies, the signature of unseen forces, the northern lights. We quickly walked out to the fields between the duplexes in which we lived, and there they were: reds, yellows, blues, sweeping around, dancing, glistening—as if an invisible artist brandished a paint brush, with quick and amorous strokes, decorated the darkening skies with colorful, abstract dances. The northern lights captivated us, while more persons quietly joined this growing band of people, standing still, looking up, for the skies skipped, entrancing us, making us long to join in this dance of the universe, this song of the ecstatic. And then the moment arrived when the moving colors welcomed the admiring human beings and we felt one with them, part of the giant movement of creation. We too floated in the mesmerizing golds and reds, knowing fulfillment, reaching the ultimate, participating in the world humbly, lovingly. We felt the kindness of the northern lights graciously offering themselves to the adoring band below. And then quietly they were finished, this exhibition of the divine power, leaving behind powerful traces in our souls.

I pondered these magnificent realities as a child, yearning to comprehend their wild beauty. For my science project one year I worked on the constellations, placing stars in the patterns on a poster, using different colors to show the age of the stars. For I had just learned that stars were not inanimate, but they lived, and had life, and they grew and changed, just as our universe grew and changed. My father took me outside one evening and showed me how to find the North Star, along with the Big and Little Dippers. I learned to recognize many constellations such as Andromeda and Cassiopeia. The stars of Big Dwarf, and dying stars and red stars, stars changing and growing, just as I grew older, and the friendly bears at the dump grew older, and the moose that grazed across the street grew older. The universe sparkled with life, animating, breathing, growing, changing, singing a paean of praise to Life, passionate and good in its essence. And what was time in this universe, centuries and eons and millenniums? Time was an empty vessel filled with the sheer goodness of it all, a breathing, growing, expanding universe, divinely harmonious and ecstatically filled with wonder.

One evening my friend Karen and I left the base movie theater and were walking home when an Air Police Car went by with the serviceman announcing through a megaphone, "Wounded bear alert; get inside immediately. A bear has been shot and wounded on our base and could be dangerous." He announced this over and over, *Wounded bear alert*. My parents drove down and picked us up and we felt the sadness of it all. Who would shoot a bear that lived on our base? We knew only someone inexperienced in Alaska would shoot such a marvelous creature—and that is who it was. A new airman with a gun panicked when he saw a bear near his barracks and shot the animal. What extreme foolishness and sorrow to shoot one of these innocent, lumbering creatures who inhabited our universe with us. Didn't he know the balance here, the harmony between the forces of nature and animals and humans? But, no, he was too new to Alaska—and we felt sorrow for him as well as sadness for the poor, dying bear.

127

Thus full of memories, I started my travels in Fairbanks. I stayed at a bed and breakfast in downtown Fairbanks. I enjoyed the large breakfasts and the interesting conversations. I happened to visit Fairbanks when it was celebrating the pioneer gold rush heritage, so activities filled this small city.

I attended the Eskimo Olympics that were currently taking place. These ritual, native Alaskan games were held in a huge auditorium, filled with hundreds of people. Most of the participants and observers were of Native Alaskan ancestry. I watched as the dancers participated in the time-honored dances. One young man started his dance ritualistically, as others before him had, and then, as if the Spirit had descended on him, he started dancing with new fervor, transcending his limitations, overcome with joy. The crowd grew quiet, as they watched his demonstration of spiritual power. I sat, absorbed in his elemental dance, seeing that the Spirit indeed blows where it will, blessing our human lives with a touch of ecstatic otherness. Following his dance, a pause ensued. Then the crowd roared with approval, its faith in the divine Spirit renewed.

The next day I drove out to a lodge in the surrounding mountains. I hiked around and joined in a guided horse ride. During the ride, we crossed rushing streams and walked up steep hillsides. On the way back to the barn, we walked past a large, friendly moose, and this brought back good memories from my childhood.

A couple of days later, I drove my rented car up to the gates of Eielson Air Force Base, wondering if I would be let in at this secure facility. I stood in line with others who also needed access. My turn finally came to talk with the airman in charge of security.

"I'm Nancy James. I want to visit my schools and see where I lived as a child," I explained.

The man behind me in line overheard me and made a surprised noise, saying, "Are you Tim James's sister?"

"Yes, " I acknowledged, smiling. Tim was a well-known musician in this area and had attended the University of Alaska, living in Fairbanks for many years past his graduation.

The airman, satisfied about my intentions, gave me a day pass for the base. As I drove around, I realized how the place looked much the same as it did in my childhood. I walked by my childhood home, saw the base chapel, and visited my schools. Then I sat near the base runway and for a long time watched the military planes taking off and landing. As I sat in peace, I communed once again with my father's strong presence in my life, watching planes that he had so loved to fly. Long, silver planes circled the air, comforting me with the familiar sounds of their powerful engines. As I sat and relaxed, I experienced a deep understanding about what was happening in rural Virginia, while also realizing what I must do to gain my soul in this situation.

I realized that the harassers were like the ignorant man who shot the friendly bear soon after his arrival in Alaska. The harassers didn't know that the ordained women living in Virginia were friendly, participating in the harmonious order of the universe. The harassers knew not that God in infinite kindness had prepared a place for them, if they only had the courage to trust. They didn't know that other human races enrich them, not threaten them. In their foolish blindness, they struck out wildly against that which is different, increasing their interior darkness, as they blunder around in a world they do not understand. The harassers saw only danger to their position in society. The harassers and many community leaders shared a racist way of thinking, which brought a deadened, violent understanding of life and led to cruel actions. Yet these evil ways are like twigs that will be rushed over the Niagara Falls of the divine goodness. As Madame Guyon said, the ways of God are very strange and different to humans.

I also began to fathom the depths of interior change within me that this harassment had caused. The earthquake of harassment flowed through my life, taking away easy answers yet simultaneously granting a new paradigm of pure love and the transcending Spirit. This earthquake had torn up my simplistic worldview, and I saw now that it was good that my complacent, facile understanding of life had been destroyed. I had learned something from the Eskimo games. I thought, "That's what we need to do in life. We need to dance, to love, to transcend even the worst situation." And in loving it, we transform the situation.

Humanity with its violence and hatreds lies like one slain, and to live again the divine Spirit blows upon it. Go with the wind, love the wind, learn from the wind, and fly.

This whole experience of harassment in rural Virginia was a crucible, a microcosm, an intensified version of life. It was like God said: *Look at it. This is it.* What an adventure and joy life is. But don't close your eyes to any part of life, even the suffering and agony you have just gone through. Love, even if harassers attack. Listen to all of life, knowing that even in the belly of the beast the Spirit still moves and loves, causing the transcendence for which we all yearn.

I learned to plunge the depths of life, love the highs, and know Being. For all of life is holy and sacred.

A natural deconstruction of my theology had occurred in this crucible, forcing me to think more profoundly about how life operates. I began to understand that God honors our self-sacrifice by splendid moments of transcendence that can occur in all cultures and religions.

The Spirit blows where it will, as the gospel said. The Spirit blows at times on homeless persons and those who suffer innocently—and this Spirit gives life.

When Evil confronted me, I stood my ground, believing that a universe so incredible that its stars lived and its northern lights glowed would not let me down. Even if Sheriff Peters and the commonwealth's attorney refused to help, I innately believed, *I will find help and live, because my soul inside sings with joy.* I believed that the Great Creator would hear my cries and help me.

As I sat on Eielson Air Force Base, contemplating the immense airplanes, my decision was made. I would go back to Virginia to stand my ground with dignity, and to listen reverently to the God within and to the universe around me. I would be true to myself in this situation. As a priest, I express the eternal truths in my life and in my words. Inviting the homeless persons to church was a good act. I could express no regret and render no apologies about it. In my reading of the Bible, both Old and New Testaments, God asks us to care for the poor. To worship with the poor was to experience a unity among persons I had never known before. I knew primordial unity when the rich knelt humbly next to the homeless, acknowledging that at our heart depth, we are one and we are alike, and we can love, if we have the necessary raw courage.

I also realized how deeply this situation had changed me. And listening, having now experienced my own personal homelessness as I ran from one abode to another, I heard the cries of homeless men and women, their sobs and their despair. And I wanted to run to them and to comfort them. I had needed to know how they felt. Now after the attacks by the harassers, I knew the pain of being homeless and of running from place to place. Maybe that was God's purpose in all of this, so that I could turn and truly empathize with those who suffer.

In hearing the harmony of the universe in Alaska, I heard more distinctly the cries of the victims, of those cruelly cast aside, marginalized by brutal, ignorant ones.

Life had truly taught me, saying: Listen to those who hurt, and help them. Offer them nourishment. That is Life's deepest wisdom. And though my recent lessons had been so painful, I understood: we are here to experience the ecstasy of pure love, which is as beautiful as those entrancing northern lights.

My theology now became one oriented to the power of the Spirit, rather than one limited to conceptual beliefs. I pondered this paradigm shift towards the Spirit, sensing that this was a good change. Throughout history, prophecies abounded about the coming age of the Spirit, through such mystics as Madame Guyon. She believed that one day a new age would arise, when the Spirit would fill the inner life of humanity. Others talked of the age of Aquarius, or of new age ideas. Who knew what was happening in our splendid universe? Many believed that during the late twentieth century we were going through a vast religious change, becoming more aware of the actions of God's Spirit. I realized, with gratitude, that through this awful harassment I was becoming sensitized to the deep and powerful actions of the Spirit.

I rose to leave my place watching the Air Force base runway, turning around to look longingly at one last military plane. I felt my inner spirit, strong, ready to return to the lower forty-eight. Driving back to Fairbanks I felt tremendous relief. Once again, Alaska had truly ministered to me. I had found the inner clarity and joy necessary to continue with the dangerous struggle in rural Virginia. My time in Alaska was now finished, but the goodness of creation was once again firmly established in my soul.

On the flight back, I faced into this dreadful community situation peacefully, knowing that once again I had a clear, inner joy. At a layover in Anchorage, I hungrily ate a sourdough grilled cheese sandwich, delighting in this simple pleasure as cheerfully as a hungry bear on a garbage dump.

The joy the soul then possessed is so great,

that she experiences the words of the royal

prophet: 'All those who are in you, Lord, are

like persons ravished with joy.

—Jeanne Guyon, *Autobiography*

The Alaskan nature taught me about the Spirit moving and creating, gently guiding me to the realization that life is an eternal dance of love between our soul and God. We can decide whether to participate and how to dance and whether the dance will be one of ecstasy and trust, or we can sit out the whole affair on the sidelines, watching for a security that will never arrive. For the only safe place, the only security in life is precisely in this passionate dance of love.

133

I arrived back in Virginia during the dog days of summer, with the heliacal rising of the dog star, Sirius. I returned with my connections to the natural universe renewed. I looked with anticipation into my future. What would happen in this bizarre situation? How could I continue this spiritual dance?

What had happened to Guyon I had learned while in Alaska. Jeanne was arrested and taken first to one prison, then to another, as the authorities tried to break her spirit. She suffered through long, brutal interrogations by the chief of police in Paris, Monsieur de la Reinie. This chief of police was well-known for torturing women and getting forced confessions from them for witchcraft.

But the blessed Jeanne suffered quietly. "I abandoned myself to God and refused to lie," she later wrote.

And then—and tears fell unbidden from my eyes as I read this—they took her to the horror of horrors, the dreaded Bastille. Jeanne lay in solitary confinement year after year.

Archbishop Fénelon tried to help her behind the scenes through church authorities for a while without any result. Then he unexpectedly took a public stand in favor of Jeanne while she languished in the Bastille. The Archbishop wrote a book called *The Maxims of the Saints* in which he said that God always works through despised and rejected persons, the unusual ones of God whom we call the saints. Bishop Bossuet told Fénelon that if he didn't condemn Guyon with the rest of them, Fénelon's career would be destroyed. Fénelon stood firm, saying that he needed to stand up for the truth.

As I read this amazing story, I kept skimming ahead to see what would happen. Would Fénelon lose his courage and deny the truth of Guyon's life and words? To my surprise, Fénelon never broke but, yes indeed, his career was destroyed. Fénelon was never allowed to leave his diocese again and never became cardinal as everyone had anticipated. He ended his days banished from Louis XIV's court. Yet Fénelon continued writing beautiful treatises about his pure love of God and the importance of following one's conscience. He continued to say this even as Jeanne remained incarcerated.

The glory of the honesty and authenticity of these two clung to me day after day, encouraging me to remain honest, to be true to myself, and to be true to God. I knew Guyon suffered through her lengthy incarceration and I knew that Fénelon's career was destroyed. But both survived with their souls intact; they both followed their consciences. But most important, to the end of their days, their love for God was fresh and pure. They still wrote about God as divine lover who passionately sought them and cared for them. In observing the lives of those around me, I could see nothing I wanted so much as a pure love for our compassionate God. No money or position or worldly situation could come even close to the wonder of dancing with God. But to keep this love fresh requires courageous acts. I was not naive about the cost of remaining faithful to the crucified God.

Now after having experienced once again the primordial oneness of Alaska, I made the crucial decision to move back into the church manse. I thought to myself, confront this situation and let the chips fall where they may. Or, to use a Guyon phrase, abandon yourself to God and trust in divine providence.

On July 26, 1994, I drove back to the church house, which now looked very desolate and misused. The broken dog dish still lay shattered on the front porch. Inside, curtain rods hung straight down with their ends pulled out of the wall, the piles of curtains on the dusty, wooden floors. I brought hammer and nails, and though it was a hot, humid summer in a house without central air-conditioning, I nailed every window shut. While I accomplished this needed task, Pogo and Bear clung to me, not leaving my side. The echoes of the pounding hammer resembled the powerful strength I now possessed.

I didn't have to wait long for a test of my resolve. The next evening, on July 27, 1994, I came home exhausted, after a series of routine parish duties. In the dark summer night, the cicadas sang their busy song, with only the bright stars providing light in the blue-black skies. After checking my phone messages and mail, I headed to the bathroom to get ready for bed. I took my clothes off and, lying in the bathtub, felt a tired relaxation flow through me. After a long journey, I had come home, had faced into the place where I felt that I should be.

Suddenly, in a flash, the bathroom went completely dark, the lights out, and I knew the powerful force of wanting to survive, as a power stronger than me sweeping through my body. Jumping up, I started pulling clothes on rapidly, images of possible rape and bloody murders sweeping though my mind. I pushed against the wall of terror: keep moving, moving. Get to the phone, find your gun, keep moving, Oh, please, God, help, don't let me stop, don't even think, just keep moving. Running into the kitchen, I found the phone, and called my friend Cheryl, who said she was on her way over. I grabbed the shotgun, loaded it, trying not to choke. I heard men moving around outside, talking loudly. I sat down and started to pray for calm, for help, for presence of mind.

Finally I heard Cheryl pulling in the driveway. She came running into the house. "I saw them leaving," she screamed.

I felt a dash of hope. "Did you get the license plate number?"

She turned pale. "I couldn't focus on it," she said.

I felt disappointment but also relief that we were both safe. I knew we were fighting against enemies too large for us. They had gotten away with it again. We searched around to see what had happened and found a fresh cut in an outside wall leading to the wires. Cheryl spent the night at the house, with no more incidents occurring.

The next day, I wrote to Sheriff Peters yet again, requesting a meeting with him, the commonwealth's attorney, Gary Close, and a representative from the Virginia State Police. I mailed the letter to him by certified mail. This was the third letter I had sent to him asking for a meeting in which to discuss this harassment. But Sheriff Peters had still not allowed a meeting with the Virginia State Police.

I spent that night at the house, feeling yet stronger about my decision to encounter this harassment head on. I knew, though, that I had to stop depending on friends. I could see the terrible stress being inflicted on them and resolved not to call to them for help anymore. I went to sleep awash in satisfaction that I had the spirit (or rashness!) necessary to face this hellish scourge.

An attorney from my parish called me the next day, having heard about my decision to move back to Rapidan. She said that the local authorities didn't want to solve this case and suggested that I talk to her friend in Washington, D.C., an official in the D.C. Bar Association. This parishioner suggested that I allow a newspaper article in the *Washington Post*.

"If the authorities won't stop this, I think that publicity about it will," she said quietly. I responded, "I will think about it."

I felt a terrible dilemma. The traditional Episcopal way was to avoid publicity and to settle things quietly. Yet I had exhausted my resources. I realized the church hierarchy wasn't going to intervene. Sheriff Peters clearly wasn't going to act. The sheriff's department investigators couldn't act without the support of Sheriff Peters. I could see no further avenues of help. Would I accept this offer of a *Washington Post* article, I wondered?

I called the Washington attorney and talked to her. She said that a reporter, named Marc Fisher, was interested in this story and would be calling me. She supported the idea that publicity would stop this, and possibly provide explanations. In the hot summer day, stifling inside my barricaded house, I listened to the attorney, sweating and numb. Later that day, I received a message, "Reverend James, this is Marc Fisher from the *Washington Post*. Would you consider talking to me about what is happening in Rapidan?" I didn't return his call until I felt certain about my course of action.

Later that day I felt a preternatural calm and realized the moment of decision had arrived. I lay down on my bed, as quiet and still inside as a motionless pond. I thought, you have three choices. You can fight and make this nightmarish situation public. Or you can run and move, probably back to California. Or, if you stay here and not speak out, you can commit suicide.

Pushed into a corner, no exit (why, Sartre was right—hell is other people!) should I kill myself—should I kill them—should I should I would I could I . . .

The Fairbanks trees surprised me. No towering pines here but pathetic short trees because their roots could not penetrate the frozen ground. Stunted, short, they only faintly resembled trees. They stood alone, desolate, bleak. I knew the harassers were like these pathetic trees without any foundation in love.

I knew I wanted to be rooted in pure love and to bear permanent fruit. I stood up straight and walked to the telephone. I dialed Marc Fisher's phone number and left a message: "Mr. Fisher, this is Nancy James. I have decided to speak to you." Surrender to God and let the divine harmony handle this, I thought.

On August 3, 1994, I heard a knock at the church door, and opened it to find Marc, an intelligent looking young man, with light brown hair and a quizzical look in his eye. I wondered what he had heard about me. He had already interviewed many in the community who publicly identified themselves as being against me. We sat down at my desk and I answered a whole series of questions. Then Marc said quietly, "Do you know what they are angry about?"

"No," I said.

"It's the black, homeless men coming to church," he responded.

I felt a rush of sorrow. "It wounds me to hear that. They would *say* that?"

Marc answered. "They not only say that—they are proud of it."

Shortly after this we finished the interview, and he said he would be back in touch if he had more questions. Watching him leave, I realized the seriousness of this article. Racism in rural Virginia was well-known, but usually not made public. I continued my regular duties, while grieving over the thought of black, homeless men, searching to build a life, being rejected by a group of wealthy, white Episcopal parishioners. Had these Episcopalians no compassion?

The night came for my baptism by fire. Two days after the interview, I was home alone in my Rapidan house on

August 5, 1994, ten months after the first break-in attempt. At about 12:30 A.M. in the totally dark summer night, I heard two men talking loudly outside my bedroom window. They then walked around the house and approached the kitchen door, the same old, wooden door at which so many confrontations had happened.

What would I do, I wondered, and I'm sure, they also wondered. Did they wonder, has she been worn down? Was she near mental collapse? This evening, it was as if a small, still, inner voice said to me: *Enough. Confront these demons.*

I quickly crawled out of my antique bed. They started pounding on the door, saying the now familiar, "Let us in." I thought, what a bunch of jerks, using my father's term for ignorant people. I walked to the kitchen, quietly picked up my shotgun, loaded it, pulled up a chair near the door, sat in it, and waited. "Break in," I thought, "I dare you to," remembering a childhood taunt my brothers and I employed. I felt wholly calm and peaceful as I waited to see what they would do. Now I would not scurry around like a terrified mouse. I faced into the situation, ready to let this confrontation with evil happen. I heard them walk to the kitchen window, and saw their shadowy forms looking into my windows. "Let's do it," I thought using an expression I picked up from Grover. But as I waited, I heard them leaving, walking away, like dogs, I thought, running away with their tails between their legs.

Both relieved and a tad disappointed, I put my shotgun on top of my beige refrigerator, and went back to bed; within an hour I fell fast asleep, listening to the rural country sounds of cows mooing and dogs barking.

But in that hour I confronted myself about many things. I realized that life had prepared me for this confrontation with evil, yet I had shied away from it time and time again, begging others to help me. Now I knew that in facing this evil directly, alone, I had won my soul. I now felt an inner strength I previously didn't even know existed.

I knew that I had seen examples of courage time and time again, but had never fully appropriated them for myself. This courage lived in my father when he walked out to fly planes in dangerous areas. This fiery courage lived in women fighting to care for their children as they struggled with poverty and abusive husbands. This courage resided in illiterate adults as they struggled to learn to read. Yes, I had seen courage: the prostitute standing up to her all-powerful pimp, defying him and saying a raw, existential "Yes" to her own life. Or the raped Lorton inmate focusing on studies when he knew the possible violence that awaited him that evening.

The courageous act calls down a true baptism, an authentic cry for life in the midst of a void. I learned that when I cried out within the privacy of my heart, saying strongly, *Enough*, I sensed the whisper of a response. I had not yelled into a void, a nothingness. I felt a presence and a hope. And that was enough. I had participated in humanity's eternal cry for freedom, freedom from harassment, freedom to be and to live, freedom needed within the depths of our souls.

Now I knew. Maybe Madame Guyon was right: there is no better place to be than in innocent suffering because once you rest, you lie down, you find inner peace in the hint and whispering of a spiritual response. "I am a couch, rest on Me," read a hidden Gnostic gospel. What could I say about this confrontation? I almost heard Michael's reverential voice saying again, "Authenticity, *Eigentlichkeit*."

I understood the passionate vision that God grants us a rich life of freedom, not a life lived in demeaning fear of others who intimidate and harm us. This vision awakens the cry for a life lived deeply and powerfully. This vision overtook me and made me say, "No, I will not participate in this dance of terrorism anymore." Call for the vote—cut to the chase—do what you will and stop your pathetic little threats. I will pay whatever price it takes to stand up for my freedom from this harassment. I want to live.

I realized now that I had spoiled myself with hopes of a pampered, comfortable existence. I had wanted to know God intimately, yet I also wanted a sophisticated, happy life. The two don't go hand in hand easily. But God in God's great mercy challenged my desire for comfort and leisure by putting me in this crucible. Somehow I finally had found here the great gift for me. I knew the gift of a soul that confronted her greatest fear; the threat of bodily violence or the horror of rape or the ultimate loss of life. I stood up to these forces threatening me, believing God would assist me. I finally modeled myself after those whom I had been so privileged to observe in my work: the single mother at the court, the incarcerated prostitute, the homeless persons struggling for survival. These persons had shown me true, raw courage. Their hearts had touched mine and had taught me how to have a soul that dances and sings.

I thought to myself before I peacefully went to sleep, "You spoiled brat. Now you can begin—just begin—to learn to live."

Yes, those dull, dry days when Evil Incarnate confronts your very existence had arrived, those dull, dry days when Satan stands before you in the wilderness. When Evil came, I at first ran, then I begged others for help, but now—finally—in a grace-filled moment, I stood my ground. My soul found her wings.

I remembered military ceremonies when my mother pinned wings on my father's students after they achieved the status of pilot, when they knew that they could handle competently those magnificent flying machines. I saw the look of utter pride in the new pilot's eyes with my mother in her finery helping them celebrate. My elegant father had schooled them in flying. And now somehow I realized that all through my childhood, I had been trained for a life filled with the ecstasy of flying spiritually, of seeking God, and, with humility, trying to stand up for what seemed right. This dark night, my soul's wings emerged and I felt sublime, inner joy. Resting on this spiritual couch, I slept happily without fear in that isolated Rapidan home.

sixteen   H E L P   A R R I V E S !

During the time I was at Vincennes and

M. de la Reinie interrogated me, I continued

in great peace, very content to pass my life

there, if such was the will of God.

—Jeanne Guyon, *Autobiography*

I woke up on Wednesday, August 10, 1994, thinking that the *Washington Post* article would be published on Thursday, the eleventh. I lay in bed wondering what my last day of anonymity would be like when the phone rang. I answered it.

"Hi, Nancy. This is Joe. I saw the article today and am sorry all of this has happened to you. How are you doing?"

"Oh, no. I haven't seen it yet!" I exclaimed.

"It's pretty shocking, Nancy. Has the bishop suggested you get a job as a waitress at Chi-Chi's?" We both laughed. Then "On a more serious note, Nancy, let me know if I can do anything. I'm here."

"Thanks, Joe. This means a lot to me. I appreciate you being the one to bring this news to me." As I got ready to go buy the paper, I felt a rush of love for my seminary friends. I knew they would be kind and supportive.

Running to my car, I drove into Orange to buy a copy of the paper. The first thing I saw was a large picture of me in the Style section, looking haggard and tired.

In Marc Fisher's article in the *Washington Post* the headline read "Preacher in a Bullied Pulpit. Many Have Left Her Congregation. And Now Nancy James Is Facing Some Very Unholy Ghosts."[10] Marc with his accepting, unassuming personality successfully elicited many revealing remarks from persons involved with this controversy. As I read the article, I appreciated his insightful understanding of this conflicted situation.

In his attempt to comprehend what had happened, Marc had conducted a telephone interview with the former rector of this parish, the Rev. Robert Elder, now in Newfoundland, Canada. "Nancy is a little more informal than I was," Elder was quoted as saying. "It wasn't off-the-wall stuff she did, but social action stuff that came in the '60s. Of course, we have to bring the word 'jealousy' into this."

"This is psychological warfare to get her out of town," said Larry Peters, a private eye in Winchester. "I found places in the woods outside Nancy's house where these people were hiding."

"Nancy is a brilliant person, a good teacher," said the Right Rev. Robert P. Atkinson, a retired bishop who was sent last year by the diocese to calm the waters in Rapidan. "There's a certain kind of naiveté and vulnerability about her, and that makes her an open, interesting person."

A former Washington lawyer was interviewed and among other remarks said, "Christians and women and people trying to do good works in society have always had detractors and persecutors."[11]

The day of the *Washington Post* article, I experienced an onslaught of media attention. Journalists from radio, television, magazines, and newspapers besieged me, asking for interviews. I declined most of these offers. In the days to come letters poured in from all over the country, the vast majority of which commended my stand and encouraged me to remain strong.

A Washington, D.C., law firm offered me pro bono help and tried to move the jurisdiction away from Sheriff Peters. They appealed for help from the Justice Department and the F.B.I. But the answer always came back the same: no one would intervene because of the issue of jurisdiction. The awful fact was that Sheriff Peters had jurisdiction, which he steadfastly refused to relinquish. Sheriff Peters essentially shut down the investigation, leaving my churches, friends, and me alone to handle these criminal offenses.

My local lawyer attempted to get Gary Close, the Culpeper commonwealth's attorney, to help remove the jurisdiction from Sheriff Peters. Gary Close wrote a letter refusing any help with these crimes.

And I began to sense the horrific truth of the injustice in our criminal system. I understood the horror of many African Americans in the South who had experienced this injustice. The legal system supported the powerful and mighty in the community, caring not a whit for justice and equality for all.

Finally, though, I turned to Guyon for solace in the face of this injustice. Jeanne spent nearly a year in an overheated, unventilated, isolated room. She felt torn from her children and worried about their lives. Then for ten years she suffered in the Bastille. Yet still, she wrote about her continuing love for God. This love was like a fresh river descending from the mountains, purifying, cleansing, powerful. This divine love carried and protected her soul.

Guyon wrote of her own time incarcerated, saying that those who mistreat us need to be left in the hands of Divine Justice, a power from which no human may escape. And although Sheriff Peters seemed to my short-sighted vision to have gotten away with denying justice, I know that one day God will provide eternal justice. But Guyon also asserted that in these unjust situations God is preparing the person for a greater spiritual authority and a more powerful ministry to others. Guyon gently advised those who suffer to wait and see the greater good that will emerge from the situation. I took her wisdom to heart.

The vestry of Emmanuel Church, Rapidan, invited the homeless men back again for a final picnic. On a Sunday in September, the men from the mission visited one final time, enjoying yet another glorious day. In the September 25, 1994, *Richmond Times-Dispatch* article the reporter interviewed one of the men who had worshiped in Rapidan. The visitor,

145

"his eyes full of wonder as he took in the majesty of Rapidan's hayfields and orchards, offered a quick assessment of the storm-tossed woman priest. 'She's standing in the gap,' he said. 'She's standing strong in the breach.'"[12]

The reporter interviewed the private investigator. "'The whole thing has the feel of an intelligence operation; it's all very much by design,' said Larry Peters, a private investigator who said he has a background in military intelligence. 'They are trying to let it be known that they can get to her anytime they want.'" The article continued, "Grover Small, a retired judge and former prosecutor in Maryland, has been a friend of James' for several years. He puts things differently: 'What has happened down in Virginia to Nancy is obscene and no one's doing anything about it. It's absolutely frightening.'"[13]

But even though the local law enforcement officials had failed me, the free press had not. As soon as the *Washington Post* article appeared, the harassment ceased. Kaput. Gone. And for the first time in a long while, I rested, sleeping, enjoying a normal schedule again. I relaxed and went for long bicycle rides through the lovely Virginia countryside. I continued my fulfilling parish duties. I knew the intense satisfaction of no more homes broken into, no more threatening phone messages, no more terrified friends who also suffered harassment. I breathed deeply again. This article gave me the gift of a life restored.

A local journalist and his wife, Norman and Wini Williams, contacted me in concern that the law enforcement authorities had done nothing about this dangerous situation. In late 1994, they made their first public stand. "We are friends of Nancy James who are alarmed by the on-going pattern of harassment and intimidation against her and others who are helping her— and by the failure (so far) of law enforcement authorities to find and prosecute the perpetrator(s)."[14] Then they gave information to join in this group, *Friends of Nancy James.*

To my amazement, people started joining the group. I felt supported and knew I had resources in this time of great conflict.

To my sorrow, one of the first times I went to Washington after the articles started appearing, I met one of the men who had visited the church. He stood looking at me, clearly very inquisitive, saying with a sad amazement, "You mean to tell me that those people down there didn't want us to visit?" Responding with a similar shock, I said, "I am sorry to have to admit that *some* of the people didn't want you to visit."

I wrote in my journal, "You are shocked when evil arises. You cry. But you know that evil is dependent on the good; evil is always a sign of weakness. When evil arises, you seek God and accept his virtues *more* deeply."

My life was a daily challenge of dealing with the intensely personal comments that were being made about me. Once again, I read Guyon, looking for wisdom. How do I handle all of these personal comments about me? Church bishops and leaders accused Guyon of being a witch and diabolical, so I turned to her as an expert about dealing with slander.

Guyon wrote that in a time of terrible calumny, God clothed her with a divine presence that was like the sun. She believed sources of power would open up and protect her against the slander and persecutions. Guyon stated that help would arrive from unexpected sources and waited patiently for this assistance, believing that God would provide needed assistance. The sun shone on Jeanne as she ministered to others, its golden rays protecting, leading, caring.

I found great hope in this story. Her description of those attempting to destroy her made my situation seem insignificant in comparison. Somehow, I felt that I would find the unexpected help if I would only stand and fight, as she so passionately did.

The controversy grew, engulfing my life, but hope arrived in the form of caring visitors. Maybe a controversy was needed in the comfortable Episcopal Church. The Roman Catholic Church had political theologians in Latin American reminding the church that to care for the poor and suffering is the mission of the church. Episcopalians needed this reminder also.

In early fall a couple came by the church, a sister and a brother, in their fifties. He said with reserve, "Have we been reading about you in the paper?" I said, "Yes." He said with dignity, "You don't *look* dangerous." I smiled, and then we all started laughing. After encouraging me to keep up the struggle, they left. I walked over to a pew in the beautiful, old church and sat down. I laughed again, thinking, *"You don't look dangerous.* Maybe God does have a sense of humor." Refreshed by the moment of playfulness, I returned to the parish duties.

The wonder of God still fascinated me. The mountain spires leapt up to the heavens in Alaska, piercing the crystal clear blue skies with their radiant glow. Mountain after mountain reigned in the Alaskan Mountain Range. A range, a line of mountains, each a testimony to what? Huge monuments to a land upheaval in ages past. The mountains circled the small town of Fairbanks, as if they protected the town. The mountains engaged us with their sublime beauty, their pure essence reaching a hidden part of our hearts. The mountains whispered a gentle testimony to timelessness, eternity, eon, the Alpha and the Omega. Yet even as the mountains presented permanence, against the brilliance of the Presence, the One, the Fire, the Love, the mountains became worshippers, as if they danced with joy, remembering the first moments of creation. In these moments God said, I create, and it is so. I create humanity with a soul that may love and a heart that may sing and a body, a beautiful body that may dance. Come, dance with me in the joy, come live with me in purity, sparkling, bright purity, that together we may be One.

And the mountains joined in, singing the praises of the Eternal.

seventeen THE BISHOP'S MEETING

The church is about to give birth to the

inner spirit: her true spirit.

—Jeanne Guyon, *Christ Our Revelation*

I now had a growing insight within me: authenticity calls down God's grace. Being authentic, being truly yourself, being openly vulnerable, brings immense spiritual power.

Albert called me up after reading the *Washington Post* article, offering me his help. "Honey, I have seen better pictures of you than they had in that paper. Let me come over and let's take a walk." Tears filled my eyes when he walked through the door and I saw his compassionate face.

He didn't say anything but we walked out to the river. Albert started, "Life always goes through changes. This is a low time, a very low time. But, Nancy, it won't last."

I started to say something, but he stopped me. "Just listen. The only insight I have is this. Be bold whatever you do. This is not a time for trying to patch things together again. The situation is beyond patching. What is that scripture—you can't put new wine into old wineskins. You are new wine, Nancy, full of love of life and wonder at God. I trust that God has a place for you but you will need boldness and courage to find it. Start right away," he warned. "This situation is getting more and more desperate."

I stood quietly, praying in desperation, recognizing the truth in what he said. Soon Albert gave me a brief hug and walked slowly toward his car.

As I contemplated moving out of the church manse, a flood of memories swept through my mind, bringing tears to my eyes. I remembered moving in with such joy, believing that God had called me to Rapidan. I remembered a hot, summer evening when some church members and I cheerfully made vanilla ice cream while their children frolicked in the large yard. We ate the quickly melting ice cream in cones, relishing every delicious drop, while the mothers and I talked of our struggles. Then a desolate memory sprang into my consciousness. With a cold shudder, I remembered the disappearance of my sweet and playful dogs, Cornelia and Gretchen. And with horror, I thought of men banging on my door, breaking into my world with threats of violence. But the stately trees that surrounded my beautiful home reminded me of a scriptural promise from the Old Testament: *those who believe in God are like trees planted by a river.* I remembered when I had baptized some children, saying as a blessing, "May you be like a tree planted by a river!"

I remembered now the beautiful sermon preached by Bishop Lee when I was installed as rector at Christ Church, Brandy Station. He had also used the image of a tree as a symbol of faith. *May you sink your roots more deeply into love,* he gently challenged. We had sunk our roots more deeply into this enchanting reality of love by inviting children, mountain people, new members, and yes, those suffering from homelessness to share our blessings. We had fulfilled the bishop's mandate. In that I took great comfort.

More help arrived. I had continued my work in the literacy program. Through these connections, I was offered a job in Washington, D.C., as the director of a women's shelter on Capitol Hill. I decided to accept this new challenge. My own gruesome experiences had certainly prepared me to listen to the cries of homeless women. And so the decision was made to leave Culpeper County. As Guyon said, my help had arrived from unexpected sources: I needed the protection of this women's shelter as much as any homeless woman!

I realized that now was my time to spread my spiritual wings and minister to the most destitute persons I had ever met, the homeless, those living on streets. I had seen these suffering women exposed to the dangers of the street, women who hauled all their worldly goods around with them in shopping carts. They might be forlorn, desolate, yet still they struggled to live in whatever way they could. I knew that homeless women frequently walked all night long so they would not be raped, and then tried to sleep during the day in public places in order to have some safety.

More help arrived from unexpected sources. My oldest brother Franklin had arranged a meeting at the Southern Poverty Law Center in Montgomery, Alabama. My plane landed the evening before the meeting and I took a taxi to a local motel. On the way I chatted with the taxicab driver about the Southern Poverty Law Center. I knew that this was the organization specializing in investigating and fighting the Ku Klux Klan and other white supremacist organizations. The African American driver gently murmured, "You are going to the Southern Poverty Law Center? Lots of good people there."

At the Center, a beautiful fountain adorned the front of the building with the scripture from the Old Testament prophet Amos, "And let justice flow down like a fountain and righteousness like a never-failing stream." The Center itself had been firebombed before and nearly destroyed. Hate groups such as the Ku Klux Klan would stop at nothing.

I met with the chief investigator, Joe Roy, and found him to be an intelligent, observant person. I described what had been going on with me, my friends, and my churches. Mr. Roy told me that this harassment was consistent with how the Ku Klux Klan would treat a white woman who was associating with black men. He also told me that their information said that a lot of white supremacist activity was happening in Virginia, including some in Culpeper County. Investigator Roy described possible legal tactics in dealing with the sheriff's department. Flying home after the meeting, I felt deeply concerned at the information that I had just received.

Interest in this strife-ridden community abounded. *60 Minutes* considered doing a piece on the situation. Interviews were set up with everyone after a representative from *60 Minutes* called people involved with this controversy. But I received a call from a parishioner late one night. The middle-aged woman said, "Did you know the interviewer interested in this is Ed Bradley?" I answered, "Yes, I did," wondering where this conversation was going. Then she said, "Some of the others just heard about this and everyone has canceled meeting with him. They said they wouldn't talk to a black man about this."

I wrote Bishop Lee in his Richmond, Virginia, diocesan office, as I always did, about the crimes happening in Rapidan. After I had reported my sexual harassment from Ted, Bishop Lee wrote back in a letter written on December 13, 1993, saying, "I see no necessity at this point of any further action and believe you have acted wisely." Now he continued the same policy of remaining distant. Finally Bishop Lee decided to lead two public meetings. Bishop Lee would listen and seek information in the first meeting. The second meeting would be a public forum. I was delighted.

I sat down and wrote notes to many of the persons involved with this conflict, inviting them to the meeting. I wanted everyone to attend with the hope that truth would emerge. I felt like we were heading into a showdown at the OK Corral. A throwing down of the gauntlet. *Ya'll come now, hear!* was the theme of every invitation I sent. I prayed fervently that God would come also. A confrontation. A meeting of the minds and hearts. But mostly I prayed for a theophany.

A theophany is when God reveals God's divine character. When a theophany happens, everyone's heart is tested. At the theophany at Sinai to the Israelites, some waited patiently for Moses to return with the Ten Commandments, while others made a golden calf and worshiped it. At the theophany at Pentecost, the apostles spoke in different languages. Some believed that this was of God, and others said they were drunk with alcohol. At the resurrection, some believed that Jesus rose from the dead, while the authorities said that Jesus' body was stolen. When God is present, no external criteria exist to test whether this is God or not. You believe or you do not.

God, like divine fire and storm, descended at the bishop's meetings. But like in any storm, people struggled to know how to survive. With wind whipping us around, how do you keep your footing? In a fire, how do you avoid burns? People's reactions differed widely. Love, anger, joy, humor, outrage. A theophany, a testing, a fire, and a revelation. My only concern was to remain true to myself and to be obedient to God.

The dark evening of the second, public meeting arrived. Brilliant stars shone brightly in the black skies. A large number of persons poured into the country church. The crowds of people arriving reminded me vividly of my installation as a rector of Christ Church, Brandy Station, almost exactly eight years earlier. People poured into the church, arriving from all over Virginia and Washington, D.C. I saw in the crowds my supporters, reporters, friends, and yes, those I'd invited who had bitterly complained about me.

Bishop Lee presided over the event. A man in his late fifties with thick, gray hair, Lee's presence exuded compassion that unusual evening.

I glanced around the parish hall. A reception preceded the event at which people enjoyed pecan pies, carrot cakes, and all kinds of cheeses and crackers. The intense conversation, activity, and eating was a picture of bustling activity and warmth.

At the beginning of the meeting, Bishop Lee made an opening statement in which he emphasized that all persons of any background and race are welcome in the Episcopal Church. Next Bishop Lee gave people a chance to make statements.

An African-American man from my work in Washington, D.C., stood up first and stated, "Nancy is a woman seeking the will of God. Leave her alone." Wini Williams stood up and with love reached out her hands to a young man from the ghetto of Washington, D.C. Tears filled her eyes. "We are all members of the body of Christ," she faithfully asserted.

Following this, others stood up and complained about the controversy, blaming me for these problems.

With the opening statements concluded, the group adjourned to the parish hall. Bishop Lee consecrated the desecrated altar. A parishioner had hand carved the new letters that read simply, *"I am the Bread of Life."* I felt the joy of life restored with the pathetic and broken altar made whole again.

Bishop Lee had written a letter to the congregation which he read aloud. The letter was dated February 20, 1995. It read:

"The harassment of the Rev. Nancy James must stop. A distinguished law firm . . . is working with Ms. James to help put an end to the harassment. . . . I have consistently supported Ms. James and will continue to do so. . . . So I ask you to worship regularly, to support your churches, to help stop the harassment, to attend parish meetings and to encourage your priest and your vestries. . . . Let others see that Christians, when they disagree, can do so with honor and respect. Faithfully yours, Peter James Lee."

Bishop Lee stood up in front of the church, looking confident and ready to respond to any questions. He read his letter out loud, "The harassment of Nancy James must stop." Norman Williams jumped to his feet. "I want to clarify something. You are publicly acknowledging that this harassment is real. You know that Nancy James is not imagining this."

Bishop Lee announced that he knew this harassment was real.

A parishioner then complained that Judge Small had brought some of the homeless men from Washington, D.C., to this evening meeting. He angrily said to Bishop Lee, "Outsiders shouldn't be allowed in here! When a family has problems, you don't invite outsiders in. Only church members should have been allowed in here."

Bishop Lee serenely stated, "A lot of this disagreement has been about what constitutes the family of God."

Then to my surprise, Jeff, a Rapidan handyman whom I visited when his wife died of cancer, spoke up and asserted,

"Nancy James is my friend and I have a right to be here!"
Bishop Lee smiled in agreement. A Rapidan cleaning woman
echoed Jeff's thought, stating confidently, "Nancy James treats
me like a person." Her son quietly nodded his head in agreement with his mother.

"This is not how the Episcopal church works," Pearl said.

Albert said, "Jesus loved poor people. Only hypocrites
wouldn't want homeless people to come to church." A pause
followed his strong statement.

Another parishioner stood up and started an angry speech
to Bishop Lee, her voice becoming louder and louder. "I want
the media coverage of this controlled. I want *you* to stop it."

She shrieked, "Get it stopped! I want the media attention
stopped!"

Bishop Lee flushed with anger, "I cannot control the media."

"But you *can* control Nancy James!"

Bishop Lee started laughing, and rolled his eyes, obviously
questioning his ability to control me.

Laughter exploded throughout the church and went on for
a long time: I laughed also. We laughed because all of a sudden
we recognized how no one of us felt in control and maybe that
was God among us. A theophany happens when humans reach
the limits of their control.

A theophany, I thought. Protected by God's presence,
Bishop Lee standing firm in support of me. I had never seen a
blue-collar worker standing up to wealthy members of this
community, saying he had the right to be in the church. This
was God in action. In the kingdom of God, no distinctions exist
because of wealth or social position or race. All God looks upon
is our heart. I felt quiet within me. The power of the divine
erases all class distinctions, all cultural signals of who is more
important. Maybe this is the reason we fear God. We fear the
nakedness of losing our comfortable signals of who we are and
avoid the understanding that God loves all races. But in avoiding this leveling of social and class distinctions, we avoid God.
The inner heart is all that God looks upon and cares about.

What a stormy evening in Rapidan! I saw the fire of right-eousness: "The harassment of Nancy James must stop." I heard the wrath of God: "The poor man declares, 'I have a right to be here.'" We were in a cloud: "How did this happen?" asked the local reporter. Can we see, can we understand in this storm? Can we stand in this storm?

This was a community changed, a community turned upside down, a community where love brought in the poor, the sick, and the homeless, a church where the first were last and the last first, a place of God caring for God's people.

The evening ended calmly. We shared hugs and went home quietly reflecting on the evening's events.

Following Bishop Lee's meeting, a devastating whirlwind of harassment escalated again.

Both Albert's and the Williams' houses were broken into. A dog was tied up and left in the hot sun with his owner find-ing him after the dog became ill from heatstroke. The church struggled to continue, planned a lunch, and showed up to find all of the church locks destroyed so that the doors could not be opened. And so on and so on and so on . . .

I finished my move to Capitol Hill in Washington, D.C., recognizing that I could do nothing more.

Was this a tragedy? Philosophers have written that suffer-ing and sadness must remain the dominant impression for a tragedy. Yet I knew that even in the midst of this situation, joy was my major experience: joy at the sight of mountain people leaving their alienated state to ask for the blessings of a church marriage. Joy when a young man dying with AIDS knows the gentle splendors of an outdoor, country picnic before he dies. Joy at seeing the acolyte children bearing the cross with love in the processional hymn. And my joy at God's great mercy that I would be allowed to handle the body and blood in the eucharist.

I remembered Virginia Theological Seminary's motto: Seek the truth, come whence it may, cost what it will. Yes, this had been a costly situation for me, but I had remained faithful to the call of seeking the truth. This insight brought me great joy.

No, I was not left with an overwhelming sorrow at the state of the world, but joy at realizing that at special moments we call theophanies, we know the Ultimate Power is present. God is here, when the hungry are fed, when strangers are received, when those who are in prison are visited, when the children praise him, casting flowers at the glory of God's spirit, as God, the Holy One, walks among us.

And the silence . . . the silence as the grandeur settles in our minds. That grandeur is God among us.

eighteen

THE STRENGTH
OF THE HOMELESS

Divine providence constitutes all the rule

and guidance of a soul lost in God . . .

— Jeanne Guyon, Autobiography

Bishop Lee invited me into his office. Leaving the door slightly ajar, he started the conversation asking me about my welfare and hopes for the future. We sat formally facing each other.

"Nancy, I think you would be happier working in Washington, D.C., than in Virginia. I could see you working with a large parish in D.C. and teaching about medieval spirituality."

I looked at him numbly, feeling torn apart. Yet I saw the truth in what he said.

The Bishop spoke compassionately about my future while I sat wondering whether anything good could come out of this situation. Yet I had kept my integrity, spoken truthfully, and lived out my principles. Would my life now be destroyed? *Jesus' blood never failed me yet.* Would God's wisdom, God's truth fail me?

And so it was decided. I quickly acted on the decision. I gave my resignation notice at Christ Church, Brandy Station, the following Sunday. I talked with the vestry at Emmanuel, Rapidan, and they asked that I wait a few months before leaving, a request with which I complied.

The last Sunday at Christ Church, Brandy Station, the vestry gave me a small reception at the parish hall. As at our first meeting, delicious pastry and fresh coffee were served. But now the atmosphere was uncomfortable, tense, as everyone avoided *The Subject* of the harassment and lack of arrest.

Pearl talked jubilantly about me leaving as she proudly announced, "Now those colored people won't be coming here anymore." Another younger parishioner pulled me aside, saying, "I am sorry if I caused you any trouble by bringing my black friend to church." I felt a moment of great sadness and responded, "I am glad you brought friends of other races to this church." The local journalist, Norm Williams, came and took my picture in front of the altar, congratulating me on a successful ministry.

This situation had granted me new gifts. I had gained my new sensitivity to homeless women in this fiery crucible of harassment in Culpeper County. I now was the director of a women's shelter housed in a large, old, comfortable home donated for charitable use. Lots of light shone through the large windows. I had a small apartment in the back, just big enough for my dogs and me. Down a flight of stairs was the shelter, which housed about fifteen women. Soon the house was full of women needing physical shelter, emotional support, and spiritual solace.

I wondered how the poor and homeless persons the shelter served would respond to the recent publicity about me. The men who moved in my furniture stopped for a break and told me they appreciated the stand I took. One helper, Ray Paylor, said, "You've suffered like we have. We consider you one of us now. We say about you—that woman is from the hood." They were right. After my experiences in rural Virginia, I could identify with many of their life experiences at a personal, emotional level.

Shortly after my arrival in Washington, D.C., I was invited to speak at a church women's group. I knew they were interested in my harassment, which they had read about in the newspapers. For the evening's address I took a message dear to my heart: that of all the women in trouble in the Bible. Soon the formerly quiet group was speaking with intensity about all of the women in trouble portrayed in the Bible. Images sprang quickly to mind: the Old Testament Hannah, weeping and praying to God, while the attending priest didn't recognize her intense grief and accused her of being intoxicated; Mary, the mother of Jesus, pregnant and unmarried, fearing Joseph would desert her; Mary Magdalene weeping at the tomb of Jesus a few days after his crucifixion, having lost her beloved friend; Martha running to see Jesus, bereft about the death of her brother Lazarus; the bleeding woman, suffering for many years from a hemorrhage, who reached out secretly in faith to touch Jesus; Ruth and Naomi searching for a home after the death of their male relatives; Hagar, the mother of Abraham's first son, sent out alone to the desert to die along with her hungry child; Sarah, the wife of Abraham, sad, childless, desperate, laughing, when the angel brought good news to her of a son she was to bear. Women throughout the Bible suffered and yet found help and consolation.

I had learned this from—whom else?—Jeanne de la Motte Guyon. Finally I understood her strength, her peace, her love. For I had read about her time in the Bastille.

Jeanne woke up again in the cold, stark, brutal environment of the Bastille. Years of deprivation had taught her not to fight back or cry out. A numbness enveloped her. Instinctively, she started quoting scripture. "My God, my God, why hast thou forsaken me?" she said over and over. Then on this day, the day that would change her life, she sensed a different light, an enveloping quality and she thought, what is this? And looking up she saw her, the divine her, a woman dressed simply in a loose, light, blue dress but looking at her with simple, gray eyes expressing unfathomable compassion and love and kindness. The woman reached out her hand, and said to her, "So you are the brave one my Divine Son has told us about. Suffering, my poor little one, while others look away from you. We look toward you, my Jeanne; the divine heavens never forget you." And Jeanne suddenly realized that tears were coursing down her cheeks, not tears of sorrow but tears of joy, the wetness soothing her dry, aching soul. "Sing, my Jeanne, while you are here. You will be released one day. But what you gain here will never be lost—for you have gained your soul. I can speak no further—words are not necessary. Sing, write poetry, love, experience the heavens—and know that God never takes his gaze away from you."

And just as simply, the heavenly woman was gone but Jeanne felt new hope, new life. Words, lovely words, danced in her soul, words about pure love, perfect love, divine love. Her words flowed out, as lovely as delicate, carved crystal and as soothing as pure, fresh water. She wrote: "Oh, blessedness, all bliss above, / When thy pure fires prevail! / Love only teaches what is love: / All other lessons fail: / We learn its name, but not its powers, / Experience only makes it ours."[15]

I knew what scholars called Jeanne's experience: the beatific vision that Thomas Aquinas asserted was the ultimate search in life—the vision for the haunting loveliness, the piercing beauty, the ecstatic sublimity of God. Jeanne knew the feminine God we call Maria, Mary, the blessed one among women.

During this transition time I continued to help at Emmanuel Church in Rapidan. A thick, uneasiness hung over the church members. How would we shake the sorrow over these experiences and move into the future? A sense that something evil had happened in the church lingered among us.

The evening before my birthday on June 28, 1995, I walked outside late in the evening on Capitol Hill and felt a light, gentle rain on my hair. Little did I know that what was a light rain in my area was even then becoming a whirling deluge in the Blue Ridge Mountains! The rain poured down in Culpeper County, not stopping, creating a tempest, a vortex of power. The water collected in the mountains and finally roared wildly down the sides of the mountains. The Rapidan River flooded and rampaged, creating new paths for itself, and eventually burst into the Emmanuel Church sanctuary, sweeping everything out of its raging path. The river destroyed our church buildings, leaving furniture overturned and broken and a foot of mud everywhere, and ripping a wall from the church offices. This storm's groundswell pushed into our lives and hearts,

pivoting the entire situation out of human control. The mael-
strom created havoc within our ordered communities. Nature
spoke in power, revealing its true omnipotence over our lives.

When I first saw the church after the flood, I could not
believe my eyes. The church pews had been thrown apart like
the children's game of pick-up sticks. The church pulpit was
upside down and nearly destroyed. My church robes were covered with mud and dirt up five feet high. All of the papers in
the church offices had slid out of the opening where the wall
had been. The floor of the parish hall was a foot of slimy, dark
mud. Members of the community came from everywhere to
see the damage. A county official came out and nailed up a
sign on our church property: *Condemned.*

But in the destruction came seeds of hope. The first Sunday
following the Flood of 1995, the congregation met to discuss
the future. The commotion of a flood gave this community a
new beginning. The previous tension was now broken. Now
the evil crimes against the church buildings were finished. A
cleansing had occurred. The tempestuous storm had overwhelmed our church.

As we started the process of rebuilding, many gathered on
the steps of Emmanuel Episcopal Church, Rapidan, Virginia, on
July 30, 1995, to talk of our perceptions of the flood. A teenager,
Mary, captured the freshness of the moment. "When I first saw
the church I was shocked. I thought of the flood in old times
and Noah's ark. That was a fresh start and so is this, not a second chance but like a baptism of a place, a people, a time."

One phrase summarized how we felt about the experiences of the past year, culminating in the powerful flood: this
was a "baptism of a place, a people, a time." A cleansing, purifying baptism.

The governor of Virginia, George Allen, issued a procla-
mation ordering support for the victims of this flood and sent
a capable representative to help us.

We started the process of cleaning up the church buildings
and applying for insurance. A fraternity from the University of

Virginia came and worked all day, helping us clean up. A construction company came in and took out the destroyed walls. They checked the foundation of the church sanctuary to ensure that it was safe enough for us to hold church services. After several months of clean-up we started worshiping there again, in the midst of dirt and dust and cold. But the warmth of the church services kept us aglow!

For now our small church group became solidified and unified. When we gathered on Sunday, a haunting, wild beauty encompassed and filled our church services. We sat in the dirt and dust, accompanied by my flute, singing the words of Henry Baker, "The king of love, my shepherd is, / His goodness faileth never" ("The King of Love, My Shepherd Is," 1868).

We gathered every Sunday as an intimate, loving group. Looking out at the congregation, I would see sweet Mary's puckish grin and Albert's fortitude. The church was a spiritual home again. The freshness of our love and vision was like the petals of a rose beginning to unfold. After the flood, after the theophany, we were left with a remnant, "we few, we band of brothers" and sisters, as Shakespeare might say.

Support poured in with checks arriving from everywhere. We raised enough money to have the church moved to higher ground.

The *Washington Post* wrote an article on July 13, 1996, about the flood's effect on the church. The headline boldly read "The Rainbow after the Flood. In the Virginia Piedmont, A Tiny Congregation Restores Its Building and Its Spirit."[16] Bishop Lee was quoted in the article saying, "One year and two days ago the river rose, wind blew, the rains came and nearly destroyed this building. But the house of God is not a building, but people like you and me. You have demonstrated that a church built on Jesus Christ can survive any storm." Indeed, we had not only survived, but we were newly created with a spirit of love.

My own life started flourishing again. Memories of the agonizing harassment began to fade and were replaced with

163

good experiences of helping homeless women as well as helping the church establish itself. I planned for my final departure from rural Virginia.

What did pure love mean to me? Why had I clung to this mystic idea? When I first learned of pure love, I had thought of it as something holy, something that cloistered nuns and priests might experience. Somehow I had missed an essential characteristic of pure love: that pure love was found by the mystics when they became more deeply involved with the world, not less. Madame Guyon discovered pure love when she took courageous stands for abused women and children. I realized that authenticity, *Eigentlichkeit*, calls down pure love. In the midst of difficulties and stresses, love grants us the vision for life as well as the strength to accomplish it. The consummate joy of life is being involved with the pressing issues of the day. When we proceed bravely into the issues of the day, pure love is already there, waiting for us.

And now I knew what pure love was. Alive, full of wonder, and yet always a mystery: Is it the sheer wonder of holding an infant, fresh from God and full of promise? Is it seeing the marvels of human existence—the beauty of a couple making vows at an altar to love and cherish? But the nagging realities of human society disturb our fantasies of pure love. And yet . . . pure love manifests itself in its glorious holiness at times of despair. Pure love is the encouragement we feel with a painful profundity when we know we are at our wit's end, when we feel despised and rejected by men and women—and then waves of compassion flow over us from the Source of all Being. The living water, pure love washes away our misfortune and we know our acceptance by the One, our despised and rejected God.

nineteen THE TRAGIC VOID

I saw your providence even in the smallest

matters, unceasingly spread itself over me.

—Jeanne Guyon, *Autobiography*

Sitting in the homeless shelter on Capitol Hill, I struggled to deal with everything that had happened. The homeless women and I shared stories, tears, and healing words of encouragement. Apple muffins, herbal tea, and donated sandwiches from Amtrak sustained us as we searched for fresh veins of hope in a troubled world.

I remembered my own sad introduction to suffering and death as a preteen in Alaska. My buddy Karen and I bicycled all over Eielson Air Force Base, racing, yelling, utterly confident in the power of life that resided within us. We swooped into existence, feeling as if we were baby eagles learning to fly. Yet unbeknownst to us, soon one of our own would be swallowed up, annihilated, and we would struggle to understand this, crying for healing, begging that this had not happened. But I get ahead of myself.

One summer our parents placed Karen and me on a bus headed towards summer camp in the hills outside Fairbanks. Karen and I surreptitiously loaded ourselves down with candy and cookies. We laughed and giggled, delighted to say good-bye to those all-powerful parents. They stood subdued, quiet, and authoritative, looking at our smiling faces in the blue Air Force bus window, our arms flamboyantly waving good-bye, while we shrieked fond farewells. Karen and I were a force to be reckoned with.

At the camp we threw ourselves into activities with sparkling joy. We made crafts and ran in the woods, we jumped into the freezing cold lake, and then charged back to the cafeteria, eating everything we could, but saving room for the omnipresent candy as we talked in the long, Alaskan evenings. Then I heard that at the end of the week the camp leader would crown a girl as Queen of the Summer Camp. She was to be the most talented and beautiful girl there. And lying in bed one night, I conceived an idea: Karen, my delightful comrade, was to be the queen. I was convinced of this.

Karen, lying in the next cot over, was informed of my decision. Immediately, she sat up in bed saying, "I could never win." And even I, her loving friend, knew she had a point. The twelve-year-old Karen was going through a gangly stage. Her braces glittered, her thin, bony body lacked curves, her naturally curly black hair stuck straight out around her ears. But, I thought, who has more spunk and joy and is nicer than Karen? Karen was meant to be queen.

So I started my campaign. I talked to all of the children, about one hundred of us, preteens and teenagers at the camp. "Karen for queen," I would assert, meeting with some skepticism. The reply would come back, "Why not Cathy?" who was a pretty fourteen-year-old. "No," I said firmly. "Karen." And the idea grew and became a force. Karen started walking differently. A presence enveloped her that made glittery braces and uncooperative hair trivial. Karen greeted her future subjects with dignity. And every night we discussed our day's progress in the campaign, as we relished yet another candy bar.

The night of the vote arrived. Karen walked into the hall, scrawny, little, yet radiant with splendor. Cathy walked in, abundantly pretty and self-confident. The secret ballot was taken; I had not a pang of doubt. Of course, Karen was to be queen, I believed.

The time came for the announcement. *And the winner for Queen of the Summer Camp is . . .* (long pause) *Karen!* I screamed with pleasure, Cathy appeared shocked, and the crowd went wild. The major in charge of the camp led Karen up to the podium, placed a crown on her head, which—quite frankly—only made her hair stick out at even more alarming, peculiar angles. But that didn't subdue the camp's high spirits. We stomped on the floor, we yelled, we danced around, chanting Karen's name over and over again. Karen, somewhat flushed and elated, waved elegantly at her wildly enthusiastic subjects.

I was now a faithful lady-in-waiting to Queen Karen. We returned home, quietly jubilant.

The mood at our home, though, was not always happy. The war in Vietnam was a conversation going on in my house; my father would talk of returning pilots telling of the difficult flying restrictions in Vietnam. During these stressful times, tensions flooded conversations like lightening flashing in a dark, midnight sky.

The next day Queen Karen and I walked across a field and she said sadly, "My mother is afraid my dad is going to Vietnam." References to Vietnam abounded in all our conversations. Death, body bags, troops headed to Vietnam, their planes refueling in our beloved Alaska. We knew some returned but many, sadly, did not.

But Queen Karen and I continued our frolicking, not fully understanding these references to death and war. We loved the intensity of our lives, while trying to comprehend the gruesome realities with which our parents struggled.

But the grim day arrived when I learned that hearts can be broken and sorrows abound. On this summer day Queen Karen and I were bicycling on the edge of Eielson Air Force base when we heard ambulances racing towards the reservoir, a large body of blue, sparkling water surrounded by green vegetation. We too headed towards this frigid lake. A helicopter flew directly over us towards the reservoir, frightening us with its ominous, thumping blades. We silently speeded up. We heard screaming ambulance sirens heading in our direction, with military police converging on the scene. When we arrived, we received stern orders to go home.

In our quiet, deserted house, I waited and prayed and read. Then my mother came in, weeping, telling me the news. My sweet brother Tim had been canoeing on the reservoir with two friends. The canoe tipped over, and they went down into the too cold Alaskan water. She quickly said, "Tim is okay; he and one friend came out, but Bill . . ." And my pretty mother sat and held her head and cried and cried. I sat quietly, a forlorn lump, remembering Bill, his quick smile, his close friendship with Tim, their laughter together.

My mother said quietly, "Tim is at the hospital. Your father is with him. After Tim calms down, Dad will bring him home."

Her bright, blue eyes filled once again as she wept both for the death of Bill and the pain of her son, Tim.

Then we heard the door open. My father walked in, looking as sad as a human being can. Tim, my sweet brother Tim, stood like a statue in the doorway looking shocked and wildeyed, not comprehending, not understanding. Every atom of his being seemed to cry out begging for relief from this ghastly reality. Death had grabbed his friend. His friend was *no more*.

Tears were the only relief and tears filled our lives for days. I sat in our darkened house, trying to help in whatever way I could. Somber adults visited us, but Tim remained tense, aching, distressed.

The day for the memorial service arrived. Bill's body was to be flown to the lower forty-eight for burial. But sorrow was still our only companion. Karen joined our family when we went to the church. We sat, Tim looking torn apart and grief stricken, remembering his friend's presence. There was no relief from this all powerful, ghastly reality of death. The base chapel was filled with mourners. All we longed for was Bill: come back to us, we cried, we need to see you and have you among us again. This teenager snatched from life—*we could not bear it.*

The memorial service dashed by, our hearts aching. Then a soloist from the choir was announced. The organ started.

Then in a shaking voice, she started singing, "In my Father's house are many mansions. If it were not so, I would not have told you so. I go to prepare a place for you, and I will come and take you to myself." The soprano sang this scripture over and over again. Her intensity and sincerity penetrated our grief. "In my Father's house—are *many*—mansions." She stood up straighter, her voice now strong and pure—and sang again, "In my Father's house are many mansions."

And I understood this beautiful, simple truth. Bill was in another part of my Father's house. He had changed rooms abruptly and too young, we humans say, leaving behind an immense hole. But Bill was not in a void—he was in our Mother's house. This gentle breath of relief, a truth comprehended, carried us thought the next hour, and then the next day, and then the next week. I had heard the musician's powerful whisper of hope.

But I had also sensed for the first time: death, the void, the nonbeing.

The same hope the soprano sang about so beautifully clung to me now. There are many mansions. The women and I walked out every morning in search of new lives for all of us.

twenty   PURE LOVE

Oh, how narrow is the gate which leads to

that life in God, and how necessary it is to be

small and stripped of all to pass through this

narrow door, which is nothing else than death

to ourselves, what largeness one finds!

—Jeanne Guyon, *Autobiography*

It happened. Life began anew and life was good. Like the cold Alaskan winter melting away, slowly the memories of the horrors of rural Virginia faded. In Alaska we endured the long advent prefacing spring. We straggled home through the snow and ice one day, and then the next day we wondered, will the season change, is the light shifting? What is that luscious scent in the air?

And the next day a new quality was there but we still waited, cautious not to get our hopes up that the new time of year (we didn't even dare to say the word spr___ng) was coming. But then suddenly, magnificently, miraculously, spring happened, spring sprung, spring shattered the cold, spring leapt into our lives. Snow melted and created rivers of purity; light streamed in the windows. The Earth stretched and yawned as if to say, "What a long, delicious sleep I have had!"

The Earth's fertility, the ravenously hungry bears after a long hibernation, the joy running extravagantly through our hearts, destroyed all memories of the dangerous winter. New life, sensuous hope, feverish ecstasy was all we knew.

In April, 1997, Norman Williams, a weekly columnist for the *Culpeper News* wrote a four-part series of articles in the

Culpeper News, telling the story of what happened in this rural area. The articles had a sobering beginning. "There was a time in Culpeper County when you could be hunted down and killed, like a wild animal, if you were a Native American (or 'savage Indian'). If you were of African descent, you could be bought and sold as though you were livestock (or 'chattel slave'). Neither Constitution nor local laws could save you. Since those terrible times, we have come a long way toward ensuring civil rights for all. Yet the sobering reality today is that in Culpeper County, if you are a woman priest, you can be denied equal protection of the law, and you have no recourse."[17]

Norman went on to tell the story of the terrorism and the justice that was denied by Sheriff Peters. He talked of the efforts of the two sheriff investigators. He wrote, "Thus the only two Culpeper County officers assigned to examine the criminal offenses against Rev. James and her defenders are on record as verifying those criminal offenses."[18] Williams went on to tell that the sheriff's investigator also began experiencing harassment when he started investigating these crimes. The investigator eventually resigned from the Sheriff's Department.

Williams courageously told that he and his wife experienced harassment after their public support of me. "In a small way, my wife and I also experienced the terror after we publicly supported Rev. James. For the first and only time in our years of living in Rapidan, our home was broken into. Nothing was stolen, but a glass of milk was left on the kitchen counter and our usually hidden emergency key was put outside under the faucet. Clearly, the intent was to frighten us."[19]

Williams chronicled the lengthy and detailed efforts to obtain justice from the Culpeper Sheriff's Department. Norm quoted both of the investigators at length. "Robert Dorsey, one of the Culpeper County sheriff's deputies who investigated these and other incidents, told my wife and me that whoever was carrying out this systemic intimidation was clearly intent on 'playing with Rev. James' mind' by instilling feelings of fear, anxiety and helplessness."[20]

Norman Williams wrote about our lengthy attempt to find help from Sheriff Peters. "Then-Sheriff Robert Peters and Commonwealth's Attorney Gary Close shut down Culpeper County's investigation of the terror campaign against Rev. James. They refused to transfer jurisdiction to the Virginia State Police (VSP), although two sheriff's deputies investigating the case have gone on record affirming that multiple criminal offenses had been committed against Rev. James."[21]

Norman Williams wrote, "Now there are several very troubling questions arising from this shameful story. Here's one: Is the Commonwealth's Attorney refusing to allow a meeting of the investigators and the State Police because it would too clearly reveal the identity of the criminals? Are the criminals who have been hounding Rev. James so influential that they can keep the Commonwealth's Attorney from discharging his sworn duty to enforce the law? . . . And so I would pose one more question: Do we wish to retain as our Commonwealth's Attorney a man with the peculiar view of justice that Gary Close has displayed in connection with the terror campaign directed against Rev. James and her supporters? I, for one, believe the answer is 'No.' In bringing this series of columns to an end, I want to apologize to Nancy James for the wretched treatment she has received from various citizens and from the law enforcement officials in our county. I know many people in Culpeper County share my admiration and respect for her, for the selfless work she has done here and elsewhere, and for the strength and dignity she has shown in the face of adversity.

We shall remember you and honor you, Nancy James! May your new endeavors bring you the fulfillment and happiness you so richly deserve!"[22]

In response to these articles a former parishioner wrote a supportive letter to the *Culpeper News* summing up what many people felt about this situation. She said, "There is no doubt in my mind that Nancy James was a victim of a campaign of terror that also included destruction of church property. . . . A campaign of this nature is done to elicit mistrust, suspicion, blame, anger, fear, hatred and helplessness, and with these come vicious rumors of false accusations. . . . What started out to be a church struggling with problems that other churches face turned into a nightmare for everyone with any connection with Ms. James or the churches she was associated with."[23]

I appreciated these thoughts in the local newspaper. Two local persons both took a courageous stand about this terrorist campaign. I felt like these people had shone a light. *This little light of mine, I'm going to let it shine,* I remembered from my installation service.

I mourned for the distress of the parishes and for the many hurt by this terror. I grieved that these crimes would never be dealt with by the courts and law enforcement agencies. I probably would never know the full story of how this harassment had been conceived and carried out.

Jeanne Guyon was sitting one day in the Bastille, when the door was opened. A guard walked in and announced to her surprise that she was to be released from the Bastille. Louis XIV had decided that she would never confess to anything, and now that she was elderly, she could go home. A great peace settled upon her.

The final days of Jeanne's life were spent writing and giving spiritual counsel to people from all over Europe. Jeanne spoke out of the abundance of her heart and her terrifying experiences, encouraging all to trust in her loving, dancing God.

A pure, new life had been granted to me. And I as started this life the bright whiteness of joy and peace enveloped me. This was like the whiteness of the Alaskan snow that intrigued me so deeply as a child. Glistening, blazing, flaming whiteness. And glancing at the whiteness I was surprised to see the colors, glowing reds, charming yellows, comforting blues mixing and blending and then once again only the Brilliant Silent White articulating endless words of wisdom.

I loved my life and work at the homeless shelter in Washington, D.C. The Rapidan church was underway with its renovation after the cataclysmic flood. Sheriff Peters had retired from his office, having never allowed even a single meeting with the Virginia State Police about the harassment. I was in the process of writing a dissertation on the theology of Madame Guyon at the University of Virginia. My unusual Culpeper journey was drawing to an end.

I led my last service at Emmanuel Episcopal Church, Rapidan, on June 6, 1997. The Rt. Rev. David Jones conducted the service. I baptized the second child of a couple I had married. I left the church with a poignant mixture of sorrowful and jubilant emotions.

I wondered, what would my future hold with the Episcopal Church? Would they support me in my work with the homeless? I had applied for a grant from a large, Washington, D.C., Episcopal Church. Would this be granted? I hoped and prayed that it would.

A week later I walked into the rector's office at St. John's Episcopal Church, Lafayette Square, for a meeting about this grant. I was apprehensive about meeting at this prominent church directly across from the White House and shy about the publicity I had received. The rector Luis León warmly welcomed me and we sat down. We talked briefly about Madame Guyon and he immediately understood the implications of her thought. Luis thoughtfully said, "We frequently misunderstand power. Madame Guyon understood that prayer is power. It sounds like Louis XIV knew how dangerous she was to his power." I told the rector what I had been doing for homeless women. Luis offered to help raise funds for the homeless women. What a healing this was for me! My beloved Episcopal Church would not desert the poor and homeless.

I felt ecstatic when I left his office, taking a long walk with my dogs that evening to look at the royal blue sky bright with shining stars. What had I learned during this long test? I had learned to stand firm in times of need and weakness. God acts and God cares and God watches over us.

How else, I wondered the next day, could I use my new understanding of justice? Then I thought, how else, but to write about the delightful, loving, dancing Jeanne? And after long preparation and many letters, I took a plane and landed in Rome, taking a taxi to the mysterious, beautiful Vatican. I met with Father Boyle, the director of the Vatican Library.

We sat in his dramatic office, full of glorious art, on thick, red carpet, amidst an atmosphere of mysterious power. I sat, realizing this was a fulfillment of my dreams.

"Madame Guyon was incarcerated for many years in the Bastille at the request of the Roman Catholic authorities," I started.

And the warm, loving Father Boyle looked at me saying, "Oh, yes. There was suspicion about her relationship with Archbishop Fénelon."

"I'm writing a dissertation about Madame Guyon and would like your permission to do research here using the papers surrounding the controversy."

He paused and then said kindly, "What an interesting subject!"

He went to his desk and called his secretary, saying, "Would you prepare a lifetime pass for Nancy James for the archives? She is working on Madame Guyon."

As I left Father Boyle's office, I saw a group of cardinals, dressed in their brilliant red, waiting to meet with him. I turned in amazement to see the powerful Father Boyle now waiting in great dignity as they respectfully entered his office.

I researched all day long and played all evening, going out to beautiful restaurants in Rome with intelligent Roman Catholic priests, talking at times about the innocent, suffering Jeanne and how justice was still denied her. And they listened, and after bottles of rich, red wine, we talked of Jeanne. One evening a priest leaned over to me and said, emphasizing each word, "Rome is a place for encounters. Encountering others and your own soul."

Indeed, he was right. I felt my soul growing in this magical, mysterious city, this place so beautifully blessed by God, Rome sanctified by the fresh blood of the martyrs. I felt my heart touched and warmed by the religious fervor, the intellectual stimulation, by the passion many felt for the Divine God. I found out in my research that Archbishop Fénelon and Jeanne Guyon wrote letters until the day he died. Later that evening at dinner, a theologian from the Pontifical University leaned over and said to me, "Now that was a love! That was an enduring love! Did they ever kiss? Who knows—they went to the grave with that secret." And I knew the love, their love, still lingers in this passionate air of the Vatican.

I walked slowly around Rome the day I left. I wept because I had found life again, had a renewed sense of the goodness of God, wept because I loved this place and I loved these priests, and I loved reading about the love between Francois and Jeanne. Yes, Jeanne had suffered, but she knew love, she had found a living soul that loved her, the beloved Archbishop.

I reflected on where my life was. Still the director of a homeless shelter, living alone with my dogs Pogo and Bear. But now I had hope. Where would life take me? I knew not. Would I suffer again? Probably. But now I knew the secret. Love in times of suffering, seek God, and answers come mightily.

Now, finally, I had insights about the priesthood. Being a priest is holding on to nothing, yet in the nothingness is Everything. The fullness of God's being descends, penetrating every pore, setting us ablaze, glorifying the Allness, the One, the completeness of her presence. Alaskan nature had helped teach me this with its magnificent beauty and divine playfulness and horrifying danger. The harassers had backed me into a corner and I had unlocked inward doors of truth and authenticity. I understood the priesthood of all believers.

And what about pure love, I wondered. What was this reality that Jeanne had written about? How do we understand this powerful reality? Then, I realized in a flash of insight, that pure love is like the midnight sun in Alaska when the sun glows nearly all night long. And I reflected again on the wondrous wisdom about love I learned so long ago in the land of the midnight sun, Alaska.

My brother Tim and I had reveled in our childhood life in Alaska. We created endless adventures for ourselves in this natural wonderland. But most from the lower forty-eight had a hard transition to this strange land. Adults sometimes became testy, irritated, sleepless at this weird phenomenon, the midnight sun. The base housing provided thick, heavy window shades to be pulled down in the evening so we could pretend it was dark. Of course, the shades didn't work well. But we knew enough to allow adults their nervous habits. Some adults feared that all these changes would make them unbalanced. But Tim and I and other children sensed, explored, frolicked in this sun that never went down.

Not that our transition to Alaska had been easy. The newfound amity between Tim and I surprised our parents. Previously, while residing in the lower forty-eight, my brother and I noticed each other infrequently. We argued about the last piece of fried chicken, sat together in the back seat of the car on our family vacations, and occasionally walked to the store together.

But almost from the moment of arrival at the Fairbanks Airport, we clung to one another, at first in fear. We arrived on a wet, gray, cool, summer day. Surrounding this town were giant mountains, snow-capped, distant, reaching heavenwards. What was this odd place to which we had come? The omnipresent power of nature, uncanny, unyielding, sheltered and shadowed us. We sensed the internal whispers of our mortality, the sublime fragility of human life. And Tim and I changed. Our differences seemed petty. We became friends, a brother and sister in a land turned upside down, a land where the greater light hung around for a much longer time than I had heard about in Sunday school in any routine place where we had previously lived. Life was new, weird, odd, brilliant; why not get along with this other person who also felt turned inside-out, upside-down?

Gradually, ever so gently, our fear turned into joy. My brother Tim and I accepted all the marvelous wonders this land offered to us. One day we would pan for gold in the fast-flowing rivers. We put our silver-colored, round pans in the water, scooping up rocks from the bottom of the river, shaking the pans gently, until only specks of gold remained in the pan. We knew then why the settlers had come to this foreign land, this strange land, the land of the midnight sun. Gold. Beautiful gold abided in the river, only waiting for us to come scoop it out.

And the blueberry picking! Our father would drive us out to the fields surrounding our military base and drop us off, telling us to stay away from the moose who also enjoyed blueberries. Carrying only our buckets we ran our fingers through the bushes, coming up with handfuls of sweet, large berries. Some went into the buckets and some into our mouths. We were never sure which tasted better—the juicy, sweet squirt of the berries in our mouths or the taste later of blueberry pies and pancakes. The pies overflowing with abundant fruit, running out with juice, eaten sometimes with our fingers, our clothing stained all summer with blues of various shades.

But especially in Alaska we frolicked on Midsummer Night's Day, the summer solstice, the longest day of the year. The old-timers, the sourdoughs, scheduled events in this all-night sun. Baseball games started at midnight and didn't need outdoor lighting. Adults who enjoyed drinking scheduled parties with ample liquid support for their happy moods. But others reveled in the natural wonder. We heard (was it apocryphal?) of people laughing and singing, swimming naturally in the Chena River devoid of clothing, leaving the trappings of civilization and social status and worries far behind. We knew primal joy in the presence of that magnificent sun, nature exploding in light, bathed in a golden glow, sparkling with fire.

For hard to imagine that greater light we read about in the Bible simply never left. That sun, no matter how some pleaded it to leave so they could feel normal and usual, like they had life under control, stayed glowing and bright. In the land of the midnight sun we prepared for Midsummer Night's Day. My brother and I played a big game of hide-and-seek. We decided to start the game at 10:00 P.M. We were to meet in the fields behind the houses. No adults were invited or even told. We knew this was the night the sun ruled the world with an authority that even our all-powerful parents couldn't question.

It was as if God laughed and said, *Let the festivities begin.* Adults drank, swam, and laughed while my brother and I and other children chased each other around in the midnight sun.

One time I was "It." My brother, older and stronger, was running for home and I followed as fast as I could on his heels. But Tim beat me, touching home. I fell down laughing and I yelled his name in disgust, *Tim!* And we looked at each other smiling. And I realized that the midnight sun had begotten another miracle. For I had the miracle of a brother who was my friend, who cared for me, who helped me through this strange transition to this foreign, alien place. The sun's vitality splashed freely and joyously on my brother and me that light-filled night, drawing us together, healing our differences, bringing us life. And in that magical hide-and-seek game, I found an authentic, inner home of beauteous love.

For my heart was now open to see that home was never a place or a building, but a blending and meeting of hearts. Truly I was home, even in this extraordinary Alaska, for my heart loved my brother Tim. I felt my heart reach out to him and experienced his kind response in return. For the first time, I knew life in the depths of my being, for I sensed the presence of pure love. The hide-and-seek game ended that magical night, with my heart created new and fresh and caring.

Yes, later life carried me away from the joy and the wonder of the physical Alaska, but now I knew an inward Alaska, sparkling with new life. This lesson of love stayed with me, so gently reminding me that in any place, teaching in the Lorton Reformatory prison school, hiding from harassers in my basement apartment, greeting poor women in the Washington, D.C., homeless shelter, I was at home, for our human hearts could love.

Just as the midnight sun guided me home in our childhood game of hide-and-seek, so Pure Love guides to a spiritual home all those who seek this powerful reality. Yes, those dull, dry days when Evil Incarnate confronts your very existence had actually been my blessing. *Eigentlichkeit*, authenticity, found me, answered my cries, graced my life with new direction.

And death, our ultimate foe—what is that like? Death, the large, hovering reality awaiting all of us. But still I pondered, is Pure Love stronger than death? Death, the ultimate separation, the cruel divider of hearts. Death had separated me from my father. Where had Pure Love been in that death?

Then suddenly I remembered my ecstatic yelling of my brother's name in that long ago hide-and-seek game. And I knew where my father was. He now lived in the land of the midnight sun. Only as he crept around the bush to run home, he yelled, Mom! And they ran towards each other, embracing, laughing, recognizing each other again. My father turned in time to see his older brother Bill race up to tag him. And the three rolled around, yelling each other's name, *Mom, Bill, it's me!* In the land of the midnight sun, the sun shone, never leaving.

The midnight sun dances on us all, calling us, creating new and beautiful designs.

The midnight sun, passionate in its purity, contemplates steadily, unblinking, challenging.

The midnight sun, mysteriously conscious, unites with us, primally, primevally One.

EPILOGUE

In the divine dance of innocent suffering

we discover our soul, who lives and yearns for

the grand reunion with the One Soul of God.

Magnificent gifts of love and understanding

rain upon us, and our dry souls open to

receive them. The vision dances round us,

offering us the only true home, the shelter

of pure love.

Grover Small, the retired judge who brought the homeless men
to Culpeper, died suddenly one afternoon in January, 1998,
after a short illness. The Honorable Grover Small was buried in
Arlington Cemetery. I thank Grover for his love and care for
the homeless during his later years.

Sheriff Peters retired from his position.

Michael Kaluta's career as an artist continues to thrive.

My dear brother Franklin died suddenly of a heart attack
on July 4, 2001. I believe that we will be united again one day
in the reality of Pure Love.

The Brandy Station Civil War battlefield avoided development when a Civil War preservationist group purchased the
entire battlefield.

I thank God that the Washington, D.C., prison, Lorton
Reformatory, was closed in 2001.

The Rt. Rev. Peter James Lee remains as the bishop of
Virginia. I thank him for his support during my dreadful ordeal.

I received a Ph.D. from the University of Virginia for writing a dissertation on Madame Guyon's theology. I had started
the task of thinking about Madame Guyon because of the ter-

rors of the harassment. In the dissertation I asserted that the church had made a mistake in incarcerating Madame Guyon. Her gifts and the gifts of her friend, Archbishop Fénelon, continue to dazzle us with their brilliance.

I experience the joy of a diverse community in teaching at American University in Washington, D.C. I remain active at St. John's Episcopal Church, Lafayette Square, in Washington, D.C.

And the homeless men and women who visited Rapidan? I frequently see them when I go places in Washington, D.C. Many of them now have jobs and families. Their faces still light up when we talk about those glorious, sun-filled picnics in Culpeper County. During those days we knew mystical flowers and treasures and overwhelming, ecstatic goodness.

ENDNOTES

1. Jeanne de la Motte Guyon, *Christ our Revelation* (Auburn, Me.: Christian Books Publishing House, 1985), 60.

2. Douglas W. Owsley, James K. Krakker, Milton Jacobs, Robert W. Mann, and Clark B. Hall, "Preface," *The History and Archaeology of St. James Episcopal Church, Brandy Station, Virginia* (self-published by Christ Church, Brandy Station, 1992), 11.

3. Jeanne de la Motte Guyon, *Autobiography of Madame Guyon*, vol. 1 (London: K. Paul, Trench, Trubner, & Co., Ltd., 1898), 116–23. (All of the detailed events from Madame Guyon's life are drawn from multiple sources. The primary source is listed in the note.)

4. *Episcopal Life* (September 1993), 28.

5. Guyon, *Autobiography*, vol. 2, 328.

6. Jeanne de la Motte Guyon, *A Short and Easy Method of Prayer*, (Philadelphia: Printed by Francis Bailey at Yorick's Head in Market Street, 1789), 10–14.

7. Ibid., 219.

8. Ibid., 235.

9. Catherine of Siena, *The Dialogue*, trans. Susan Noffke, O.P. (New York: Paulist Press, 1980), 59.

10. *Washington Post*, August 10, 1994, D1.

11. Ibid.

12. *Richmond Times-Dispatch*, September 25, 1994, G5.

13. Ibid, G1.

14. *Culpeper News*, December 22, 1994.

15. Jeanne de la Motte Guyon, *Poems*, trans. W. Cowper, Esq. Hamilton (London: Gall & Inglis, 1881), 410.

16. *Washington Post*, July 13, 1996, B6.

17. *Culpeper News*, April 3, 1997.

18. *Culpeper News*, April 17, 1997.

19. Ibid.

20. *Culpeper News*, April 10, 1997.

21. *Culpeper News*, April 24, 1997.

22. Ibid.

23. *Culpeper News*, May 8, 1997.

Book List

Following are the works of Madame Jeanne de la Motte Guyon referenced in this book.

Guyon, Jeanne de la Motte. *Autobiography of Madame Guyon.* Vols. 1 and 2. Trans. Thomas Taylor Allen. London: Kegan Paul, Trench, Trubner & Co., 1897.

Guyon, Jeanne de la Motte. *Christ our Revelation.* Auburn, Me.: Christian Books Publishing House, 1985.

Guyon, Jeanne de la Motte. *Poems,* trans. W. Cowper, Esq. Hamilton. London: Gall & Inglis, 1881.

Guyon, Jeanne de la Motte. *A Short and Easy Method of Prayer.* Philadelphia: Printed by Francis Bailey at Yorick's Head in Market Street, 1789.

Guyon, Jeanne de la Motte. *The Song of Songs of Solomon, with Explanations and Reflections having Reference to the Interior Life.* New York: A. W. Dennett, 1879.

Guyon, Jeanne de la Motte. *Spiritual Letters.* Auburn, Me.: Christian Books Publishing House, 1982.